M000199913

Thirukkural - Translation -Explanation:

Thirukkural - Translation -Explanation:
A Life Skills Coaching Approach

Prof. R. Venkatachalam, Ph.D.

PARTRIDGE
A Penguin Random House Company

\

Copyright © 2015 by Prof. R. Venkatachalam, Ph.D.

ISBN: Softcover   978-1-4828-4290-6
             eBook   978-1-4828-4289-0

Annotation Added

All rights reserved. No part of this book may be used or reproduced by any means, graphic, electronic, or mechanical, including photocopying, recording, taping or by any information storage retrieval system without the written permission of the publisher except in the case of brief quotations embodied in critical articles and reviews.

Because of the dynamic nature of the Internet, any web addresses or links contained in this book may have changed since publication and may no longer be valid. The views expressed in this work are solely those of the author and do not necessarily reflect the views of the publisher, and the publisher hereby disclaims any responsibility for them.

Print information available on the last page.

To order additional copies of this book, contact
Partridge India
000 800 10062 62
orders.india@partridgepublishing.com

www.partridgepublishing.com/india

Acknowledgements

My thanks to Dr.P.Desikan. He has gone through the manuscript of this book meticulously and made several corrections. It encouraged me a lot during the early days of writing this book. Dr. Desikan is a multifaceted person. After retiring from R&D Management in Petroleum and Organic Chemical industries he took to the study of classic Tamil and Sanskrit works. He has been doing serious translation works since 2003. He spends his spare time writing a column and sharing some editorial work for the online journal in English called the medha journal.

I have myself gone through his English blank verse translation of Ilango Adigal's epic Silappadikaaram. It is a delight to read. It is so lucid one forgets whether one reads in English or in Tamil while reading it.

My thanks to Prof. *Sirpi* Balasubramaniam, (former professor and Head Department of Tamil, Bharathiar University, Coimbatore, Tamil Nadu, himself a Thirukkural scholar and two time awardee and a former member of India's national academy of letters, called Sahitya Akademi,) who encouraged me to pursue my line of thinking by positively endorsing them in his tribute to my earlier book in Tamil which bears most of the concepts found in this book.

My thanks to Dr. Rajagopal, Parthasarathy Ph.D. Department of Mathematical Sciences, Kent University. He practices Thirukkural ever since his college days and has become a strong votary of application of Thirukkural in life. I remember gratefully the help rendered by him in spreading my previous books in Tamil namely Thirukkural puzzles and solutions – A psychological Perspective (2012) and Valluvam or Life is Worship (2013) among the Tamil diaspora at his place.

My Thanks to M/s C.V.Raju and Sanchu K Kesavamurthy of Mary Martin Software Services, www.marymartinsoftware.com They have designed the front cover page. They have developed a sketchy idea of mine into a pleasing image.

Introduction

Thirukkural is an epigrammatically written treatise on human life and its purpose. Its terseness is brought out by an anecdotal comment by an ancient Tamil poetess named Avvaiyaar[1] thus:

> Valluvar bores an atom, pours the seven seas into its cavity,
> and cutting the atom offers its cross-section to us in the shape
> of the *kural.*

Kural is the name of the poetic form which consists seven metres, four in the first line and three in the second. Its poetic form gave its name, '*kural*' and '*Thiru*,' an honorific was added later to denote its greatness making it Thirukkural. Similarly its author whose attributed name 'Valluvar' was also given the honorific making his name as Thiruvalluvar. The book, consisting three sub books, has 133 chapters with 10 couplets in each chapter. The three sub books are shortly called as *Aram,*[2] *Porul* and *Inbam.* The book of *Aram* espouses best soul-evolving practices in domestic and ascetic life. However, *aram* is the sine-qua-none of Thirukkural in the sense it runs as an undercurrent in the entire book of Thirukkural. Therefore if someone says Thirukkural is a treatise of *aram* he[3] is perfectly correct. *Porul* deals with

---

[1] Avvaiyaar is a woman poet belonging to the Sangam period spanning from 3rd century BC to 4th century AD. 55 such venba type poems on Thiruvalluvar and his work are available in works like that of K.Su.Pillai.

[2] Please read the legend appearing at the end of this section before reading further. I have used few Tamil words as they are because there are no equal English words for them. However the word 'virtue' comes very near to *aram.*

[3] 'he' is used throughout the book instead of he/she to avoid a minor impediment to readability. Thirukkural treats woman on par with man.

acquiring money and other assets and making use of them profitably in terms of common good and through it catering to the evolution of the soul. *Inbam* deals with love, which in addition to physical closeness deals with affinity between two souls.

Thiruvalluvar did not himself explained his couplets. Explanations of the couplets in the form of prose appeared almost after one thousand years. It appears ten prose explanations were written spread over several decades/ centuries and the last one was written by Parimelazhagar. It is also considered to be the best. The other noted explanations were written by Manakudavar, Kalingar and Parithiar. However, Thirukkural scholars in general are of the opinion that they do not differ much materially.

But I fear something else has happened!

In the absence of an explanation by Thiruvalluvar himself the terseness of his treatise made it open to interpretative explanations. I mean explanations based on external material were made creating a palimpsest. Out of the 1330 couplets I find explanation of around 267 couplets differ materially from the original and around 93 differ for various reasons like wrong emphasis, wrong understanding, lacking sophistication and clarity etc. I used inter-couplet consistency and overall homogeneity in a given chapter and the entire treatise to pass an explanation. Second, rationality and scope for application in day to day life were looked into while deciding the appropriate explanation for a given couplet.

Let me present few examples of explanations to establish my contention:

Before going further I would like to inform you that I underwent a difficulty which I did not envisage. Since this book is in English I used some of the best English translations of Parimelazhagar which are available as open documents in the web. But my publisher vetoed it on the valid ground that unless I have the written permission from the authors their translations cannot be used in view of the strict copyright laws. Left with no option I have translated the explanations given by Parimelazhagar for the sample given below into English. Since there are time and other constrains I could not provide translations for all the couplets. I request the readers to consult appropriate open sources for getting the translated version of Parimelazhagar. To indicate the couplet which gets a different explanation from me I have darkened the first letter of those couplets. Since the numbering is the same it is easy to locate the English translations of Parimelazhagar elsewhere.

Examples of couplets (in transliteration) dealt by Parimelazhagar:

IruLseer iruvin-aiyum seeraa iRaivan
PoruLseer pukazpurinthaar maattu.   5

Translation of Parimelazhagar's explanation by the present author:

God's glory is only the true glory. The effects of good as well as bad deed, which are basically illusory, would not stick to those who remain chanting God's glory

Discussion by the present author:

The explanation in short says, 'do away with action well done or ill done. Catch hold of God and remain in the praise of him'. Thiruvalluvar is a man of action and energy. You will find it yourself as you read later chapters. We have hundreds of couplets and several chapters allotted to how to carry out action. Therefore this interpretation and explanation cannot be accepted. Now read my translation and explanation.

Translation of the couplet by the present author:

In men who adopt essence of God and similarly exist
Two acts of darkness do not persist.   5

Explanation of the couplet by the present author:

One of the eight essential qualities of God is being compassionate[4] to all creatures. Those who adopt this attitude in them and put it into action would

---

4   Compassion = equity + love + action.

not commit the two mistakes of thinking evil and doing evil because they know this world and its products are not substantive or absolute, God alone is. This attitude will totally discourage them from thinking or doing evil.

SuvaiyoLi uuRoosai n-aaRRamenRu ainthin
Vakaitherivaan kattee ulagu   27

Translation of Parimelazhagar explanation by the present author:

According to Sankhya philosophy there are five divisions each containing five parts. Each of the five elements has a reason for their creation. Five elements namely earth, water, wind, fire and sky cater to the five sense organs namely body, eyes, mouth, nose and tongue. These have five senses. A person who is capable of comprehending this five divisions will be the master of the world.

Discussion by the present author:

The above explanation is a case of bringing in material from outside (Sankhya yoga) and superimposing it on what one has at his hand. The chapter is about paying respect to heroes of the past who lived a great life. They lived simple and pure life since they were aware that the life on earth is a prelude for a life at heavenly abode. Maturation of the soul is a lifelong process of prudent life. Therefore they were purposeful to the core in making use of the products of their senses.

Translation of the couplet by the present author:

A perspective deriver on the signals of senses five
To him the world remains alive.   27

Explanation of the couplet by the present author:

A person who discerns the lures of the five senses and derives soul evolving perspectives on their signals to live a purposeful life is profitably alive to the world and to its joys. (The five senses are instruments of a human. They have to be put to proper use so that they always remain tools in his hands, not his masters.)

aRaththaaRu ithuvena veenda sivikai
poRuththaanoo duurnthan idai   37

Translation of Parimelazhagar's explanation by the present author:

There is no need to read scriptures to understand the effects of dharma from scriptures. Just compare the palki bearer and the rider. It is the karma of the bearer he needs to do such a menial job.

Discussion by the present author:

According to a theory of dharma as found in scriptures one's action called karma has consequence. Good karma or virtue leads to punya (merit) and bad karma or sin leads to pap (demerit). A person's punya and pap from previous birth(s) have consequences in this birth. The above explanation incorporates this notion. But it is not appropriate because in the chapter itself there are two couplets which are a sort of definitions for *aram*[5] Couplet number 34 says keeping the mind free from poison, is all *aram* is about. Couplet 35 says jealousy, greed, rage and contemptuous tongue are the four poisons and *aram* is totally avoiding them. Therefore bringing in the deeds of previous birth doesn't incorporate Thiruvalluvar's thought. I rather consider Thiruvalluvar has written this couplet to negate the idea of pap and punya from previous birth into the scheme of *aram*.

Translation of the couplet by the present author:

Palki rider and its bearer differ glaringly
Don't say this is in tune with *aram*-ology.   37

---

[5]   The word *aram* doesn't have an equivalent word in English. The word dharma
       which is less equivalent to *aram* can be used with caution. Please read the meaning
       of this word and few others adopted from Tamil in the legend section before
       proceeding further.

Explanation of the couplet by the present author:

The difference between a rider and bearer of a palki is vast. While the rider enjoys a sedan the bearer has to suffer heavy weight and slippery path. But don't say this is a demonstration of how *aram* works. (Palki is a mode of transport and an able bodied man finds a job in it that is all. Nothing more nothing less.)

Ilvaazvaan enbaan iyalbudaiya muuvarkkum
n-allaaRRin n-inRa thunai   41

Translation of Parimelazhagar's explanation by the present author:

A house holder is duty bound to support the other three orders of life namely a brahmacharia, vanaprastha and ascetic.

Discussion by the present author:

This explanation is farfetched is inferable from the word *iyalpudaiya* which means order of life or activity of the same nature of a householder. Those orders are governance, education and commerce.

Translation of the couplet by the present author:

Householder is one, to the connected three
With practices best, lends support you see.   41

Explanation of the couplet by the present author:

The institution of home supports the other three institutions of the society namely governance, education and commerce.

Thenpulaththaar dheyyam virum-dhokkal thaanenRaanggu
Aimpulaththaa Roombal thalai   43

Translation of Parimelazhagar's explanation by the present author:

The principal duties of a household consists of taking care of the *pithir*[6], god, guests, relatives and members of the family.

Discussion by the present author:

The Tamil word *thenpulaththaar* found in the couplet refers to the persons who are dead and gone. (A comprehensive explanation is given as foot note to couplet 43.) It appears Parimelazhagar has superimposed a controversial theory of creation which says that Brahmin, the godly man, was created from the head of a primal and he uses the word *pithir* to refer to them. Thiruvalluvar has not referred to caste systems anywhere in his treatise. Therefore the notion that he supposes one caste as godly and the others as non-godly is an exercise of bringing an extraneous material into Thirukkural.

Translation of the couplet by the present author:

Ancestors, god, relatives and home
To their upkeep the home remains warm.   43

(Apart from the above three) institution of family also supports the religious rites to ancestors and gods and services to guests, relatives and its own members.

peRRaarR peRinpeRuvar perunjsiRappup
puththeeLir vaazum ulagu   58

Translation of Parimelazhagar's explanation by the present author:

If women worship their husbands they would attain great honour at heavenly abode.

Discussion by the present author:

---

6   *Pithir* is a Sanskrit word used by Parimelazhagar to denote a godly caste created by god at the time of creating life. The idea that god created castes and one of them is godly is contentious is obvious.

This explanation and that of the couplet 55 and in general the entire sixth chapter earned such an ignominy for Thiruvalluvar in the hands of women that it is rare to see a woman having respect for Thiruvalluvar. Unfortunately Thiruvalluvar is no way responsible for either the translation or interpretative explanation goes without saying.

Translation of the couplet by the present author:

If a woman gets a husband who is great
A place in heaven she gets.   58

Explanation of the couplet by the present author:

If a husband is a possessor of great homemaking qualities and swears that he would spare no effort in taking his family to newer and newer heights and acts resolutely (1021[7]) his wife will feel fully encouraged. As a result the best comes out of her too (56). Such interactional experience between two individuals involving a noble cause of home making and through it turning their children into best human resources is soul fulfilling and soul evolving. Therefore if a woman gets a great husband she would get a place in the divine[8] world which is greatest.

perumavaRRuL yaamaRiva thillai aRivaRintha
makkatpee Ralla piRa   61

Translation of Parimelazhagar's explanation by the present author:

Among blessings one may get, the best is begetting sons who are intelligent enough to know what is to be known and are keen to discharge their responsibilities. (Sons only are required because only sons can perform the last rites towards parents and thus saving them from falling into the hell called 'puth'.)

---

[7]   The number find here and elsewhere within brackets denotes the number of the couplet in the treatise of Thirukkural.

[8]   The word used by Thiruvalluvar is *puthezhir ulagm*. Perhaps we can translate it as 'heavenly abode'.

Discussion by the present author:

According to Parimelazhagar the word *makkatperu* i.e., gift of children refers to only sons. This is totally out of turn. Moreover the existence of hell doesn't find a support in Thirukkural. Wherever the word hell is used, it is used only as a metaphor. The notion of hell with dire conditions is familier one. Thiruvalluvar simply uses that notion as a metaphor in couplets numbered 255,835 and 919. Therefore to bring in the word hell, in the original sense of the word, into Thirukkural is an unnecessary act of bringing in extranious materil into Thirukkural.

Translation of the couplet by ther present author:

Offspring of high intellect are commendable
No other blessing is as creditable.   61

Explanation of the couplet by the present author:

The best outcome for a family is to grow its offspring in such a way that that he or she develops as an intellect good enough for a competitive and thriving society. There can be no better objective for a family.

thamporuL enpatham makkal avarporul
thantham vinaiyaan varum   63

Translation of Parimelazhagar's explanation by the present author:
The knowledgeable say the offspring is the property of their parents. What those offspring make would reach the parents according to their karma.

Discussion by the present author:

Again a full blown karma theory. "Whether you get good children or not or whether your children will support you during your later days or not depends upon your karma (fortune)" is not what is told in this couplet. The chapter is about parenting philosophy and techniques. The aim of the family should be to turn out the best human resources says the first couplet. Emotional maturity and intellectual maturity of children should be the goal of a family and dad and mum and other elders should do their best in this regard. This being so to hold Thiruvalluvar as saying, 'whether you will get good children or not depends upon your karma (fortune)' is untenable. In that case parent's hands are tied is it not?

Translation of the couplet by the present author:

Parent's offspring is their axe to grind,
Therefore what they aim and work will be found.   63

Explanation of the couplet by the present author:

The offspring of a household is at the custody of their parents. Whether the offspring would develop into useful human resource or not depends on how the parents parent them.

IinRa pozuthin peridhuvakkum thanmaganais
saaRoon enakkeetta thaay   69

Translation of Parimelazhagar's explanation by the present author:

The joy of a mother when she hears that his son is noble and learned excells the joy she had at the time of her son's birth. Further it is arrived from the words "when she hears", that due to her nature a woman by herself is not capable of perceiving the achievments of her son.

Discusssion by the present author:

To hold that women by themselves are incapable of evluaving their son's capablities is preposterous to say the least. Moreover the word *sandrone* is a technical word in Thirukkural which is given the go by, by Parimelazhagar. A person who is an embodiment of the five qualities namely love, humility, growth enabling, empathy and truth is refered as a *sandrone*.

Translation of the coupletby the present author:

"Your son is a sandrone"
Hearing this a mother's joy excels that when the son was born.   69

If a mother hears from disern-able persons that his son is a *sandrone* her joy exceeds that of the day on which he was born.

Magan thanthaikku aaRRum udhavi ivanthanthai
ennoooRRaan kollenum sol   70

Translation of Parimelazhagar's explanation by the present author:

A son's gratitude to his father is shown by earning this accolade: "What penance his dad would have done (in his previous birth) to get blessed with such a noble man as his son."

Discussion by the present author:

To say that a good and achieving offspring comes into the family by the penance dad did (in the previous birth) is not in line with the thinking of Thiruvalluvar. For Thiruvalluvar family is the training ground to turn out best human resources by hard work on the part of parents especially father. This couplet needs to be read along with the couplet numbered 67 which states that the duty of a dad is doing everything within his power to help his ward to reach the top echelons of the learned community. To such a dad the fittest gratitude his ward brings is blossoming into a fine human being emotionally and intellectually, thereby netting in an acclamatory appreciation for his dad from his fellow folk.

Translation of the couplet by the present author:

The gratitude a son owes his dad,
"What a hard work his dad has made!" is heard.   70

Explanation of the couplet by the present author:

The gratitude a son could return to his father is that he should excel both in his emotional maturity and academic maturity incurring this accolade: "Oh! How much 'penance like labour' his father would have rendered to develop such a fine human being?"

Anboo diyantha vazakkenba aaruyirkku
Enboo diyaintha thodarbu   73

Translation of Parimelazhagar's explanation by the present author:

For the soul the 'difficult to achieve' attachment with body materializes due to the principle that a body is needed for dispensing love.

Discussion by the present author:

To hold that soul embodies itself in order to enjoy love is a fine explanation. However, inasmuch as 'why the soul needs to enjoy love?' is not spelt out, it is an inadequate explanation.

Translation of the couplet by the present author:

Relationship of the soul with love
Operates through relationship with body.   73

Explanation of the couplet by the present author:

The soul needs to live in a body and attain maturity in order to reach heavenly abode. One of the aspects of maturity is the ability to dispense unconditional love. Since life on earth gives an opportunity to dispense love and thus enable maturity the soul reincarnates in a body again and again.

Seppam udaiyavan aakkanj sithaivinRi
essththiRku eemaap pudaiththu   112

Translation of Parimelazhagar's explanation by the present author:

The wealth of individuals, who dispenses strictly adhering to the principle of equity, will safely pass on to their progeny unlike the wealth of others.

Discussion by the present author:

The Tamil words *aakkam* and *echchathiRku* are taken to mean wealth and heir respectively whereas they can be taken to mean as outcome and remainder also. This difference not only makes the meaning of the couplet elegant it also make the couplet to fall in line with the thinking that runs throughout Thirukkural. Moreover to say that simply because a man is just throughout his life his assets will last for several generations of his heir is irrational is it not? Mind you, there are hardly any irrational notions in Thirukkural.

Translation of the couplet by the present author:

Men of equity evolve and that valance
Protects from lapse at the latter births in balance.   112

Explanation of the couplet by the present author:

If a man is nonpartisan in awarding equity to all the stake holders throughout his life his soul evolves. The soul thus evolved will put him on a protective mode for the remainder of his reincarnations i.e., the number of births needed further to attain a fully evolved soul to attain heavenly abode.

iyalbuLik koolloosssum mannavan naatta
peyalum viLaiyuLum thokku   545

Translation of Parimelazhagar's explanation by the present author:

In the country ruled by right sceptre i.e., following just rule, rain and yield will always occur.

Discussion by the present author:

A casual look at this explanation may make it to look harmless. But to say that the rains or crops will not fail in a country whose king is just involves a super ordination. Thiruvalluvar has not stated anywhere in Thirukkural that God will interfere positively (545) in some situations and negatively (559) in some other.

Translation of the couplet by the present author:

Aligning with the just law if a king rules
The country's yield corresponds to rains.   545

My explanation of the couplet:

If a country has a king who puts a proper system of rule in place men will earnestly and enthusiastically undertake agricultural activities and make use of the rains fully. As a result the yield of land and that of the rain would correspond most favourably. (Whereas if the king is a tyrant and unduly snatches the produce under the pretext of collecting tax the farmers will lose interest and will not undertake agricultural activities with the seriousness required, resulting in no solid relationship between yield of rain and yield of crop. 559)

So far we have seen examples involving God, pap and punya. Let us see some more Thirukkural couplets which are on mundane aspects of life.

piRanpazi kuuRuvaan thanpazi yuLLum
thiRantherinthu kuuRap padum   186

Translation of Parimelazhagar's explanation by the present author:

If a person slanders on another, then among his faults, those which are capable of creating maximum pain, will be chosen and hurled at him by his victims.

Discussion by the present author:

The above interpretative explanation might sound effective and as such a good caution for those who indulges in the act of slander. However, but for the, 'taken for granted manner' with which the Tamil word '*thiran*', found in the couplet is handled, this shallow explanation would not have resulted. An elegant and educative interpretation could be one which teaches a person to convert his slandering habit into a good critiquing habit. This interpretation also shows this couplet to be on a totally different but connected theme of constructive criticism.

Translation of the couplet by the present author:

If one is an able critique
His charges of blame on people do click.   186

Explanation of the couplet by the present author:

If someone makes a critical observation about another person his observation will be accepted as credible only when people hold him as a good critic after reviewing his ability for unbiased critiquing. (Probably Thiruvalluvar also means people use different yard sticks for critiquing their actions and those of others. This idea gets confirmed if this couplet is read together with the couplet 190.)

n-aththampool keedum uLathaagunj saakkaadum
viththagark kallaal arithu   235

Translation of Parimelazhagar's explanation by the present author:

Fame is the body nourished by the poverty to the physical body and by the time physical body disappears the body of fame attains eternity. Only wise realise this and achieve eternal fame.

Discussion by the present author:

The explanation holds as though achieving fame should be the main motto for human beings. But according to my understanding the chapter is about achieving name and fame from the beneficiaries of one's philanthropy and giving. Those acts are soul evolving acts. Getting the appreciation also from well informed world for their socially useful activities motivates them to move further and further in the direction.

The entire chapter has been wrongly understood or not profitably understood. This is because the Tamil words *eethal* and *isai* are treated as though they represent two different concepts. *Isai* means fame. *Eethal* means giving. Getting fame by giving is implied instead of one should give and independent of it get fame also thorough other activities. Because of this and also because all the remaining couplets speak only about fame the chapter is mistaken for emphasising fame.

Now coming to the couplet under discussion I think the couplet simply means a man whose soul is fully evolved and poised for salvation will see birth and death or prosperity and poverty as events which are unavoidable. They would rather catch an opportunity that comes in their way and push it to make life better for the poor people irrespective of the consequences to themselves. Because anything that is good for humanity becomes their duty and they will push it putting all their resources to use in spite of the uncertainties produced by death or loss. They are shrewd people because they are doing the right thing which will usher them into heavenly abode.

Translation of the couplet by the present author:

Prosperity and poverty (like birth[9]) and death are routine
Taking them on their side rare laurels only the soul-realized could obtain.   235

---

[9]   There are two bipolar constructs: prosperity and peril (1) and birth and death(2). The concept of birth is inbuilt when death is mentioned. Probably it could not be mentioned because of the restriction posed by the length of the poem being seven meters as a rule!

Explanation of the couplet by the present author:

Wealth and poverty occur in cycles. Similar is the case with birth and death. It is possible only for the wise (the growth enabler/soul realised) to convert the uncertainties into opportunities to contribute towards accomplishing socially useful products.

thannuyir thaanaRap peRRaanai eenaiya
mannuyirellaan - thozum   268

Translation of Parimelazhagar's explanation by the present author:

All those who live on the earth will worship him who has achieved the control of his soul by his penance.

Discussion by the present author:

If, ego is mellowed, soul becomes functional and through pursuing selfless service to humanity, it evolves. This is the purpose of life on earth. A man who achieves this is saluted by the world. It is not controlling one's five senses, it is rather regulating the five senses that matters and through it regulating the ego.

Translation of the couplet by the present author:

He who de-bloats his ego and gets at his soul
Humanity revers him in all.   268

Explanation of the couplet by the present author:

Through mellowing his ego a sage empowers his soul. This is a rare and much coveted feat. For this reason the folks of the land will show reverence to him.

aRivinaan aaguva thuNdoo piRithinn-ooy
than-n-ooypooR pooRRaak kadai   315

Translation of Parimelazhagar's explanation by the present author:

What use knowledge serves to an ascetic if he fails to feel the pains committed on the souls of others as his own?

Discussion by the present author:

The chapter is about 'not harming.' The poet calls 'the tendency to harm' as a disease. Then why imputing pain instead of taking it as it is? If we do it we get a much richer and educative interpretation. Human being has a tendency to hurt others. It is a disease in many. We keep it under check is another matter. However making use of this awareness when somebody hurts us we can overcome the urge to retaliate. That is what an intelligent move, from the perspective of soul-evolution, means.

Translation of the couplet by the present author:

What purpose intelligence serves if others affliction
One doesn't treat similar to his own?   315

Explanation of the couplet by the present author:

A person must be able to sense that the other person who hurts him is afflicted with a mind set to hurt others. After all he can make this out on the basis that he also suffers a similar affliction at times. Therefore, if he is not able to achieve this insight and act accordingly what is the use of his wisdom?

So far we have seen few discrepancies in the understanding of Thirukkural. I am of the opinion that the discrepancies and contradictions are due to the palimpsest interpretations given by the interpreters based on their orientation. Fortunately inasmuch as the original poetry is retained intact it is possible to attempt a soul evolving explanation to each and every one of the 1330 couplets.

But why this has happened?

I make a hunch. Thirukkural was written 2000 years ago. According to the noted Tamil scholar Dr.M. Rajamanickanar, Thiruvalluvar has lived sometime between the 3rd Century B.C. and 1st Century A.D., (vide his 'History of Tamil Language and Literature', page 123.). However, the reader may keep it in mind that fixing the period of Thiruvalluvar is an unsettled issue among scholars. Pushing his period up to second or third century is also seen.

During that period, Tamil land had three kingdoms called Chera, Chola and Pandya. Often these kingdoms were on war among themselves. However the land was very vibrant with lot of activities going on. Trade and commerce was booming with merchants and traders coming from Greece and Rome in the west, Burma, Malaysia and China in the east, Ceylon in the south and the Himalaya in the north. Philosophers and religious leaders also came along with traders. Soon Tamil land with its indigenous religions of Saivaism and Vaishnavaism and religions like Jainism, Buddhism and Vedic Brahmanism coming from outside became a melting pot. From this melting pot Thirukkural emerged!

(The philosophy of Thirukkural being a product of a melting pot is a unique one. It is a religion by itself essentially differing from all other religions but benefitting by the inputs drawn from every one of them. The presence of the four notions namely God, soul, reincarnation and the soul achieving the status of a *puthezhir* (attaining divine hood or reaching heavenly abode) makes it a religion. But there ends the similarity. To a great extent and in subtle ways Thirukkural differs from the conventional religions and with their contentious notions.)

Perhaps a preoccupied Tamil land would not lend a notable space for Thirukkural or there were enough reactionary views to silence a new narrative getting developed and propagated. Perhaps therefore no explanatory prose appeared either during Thiruvalluvar's life time or until several centuries later. There is some inferential evidence to this line of thinking in the fact that it took almost thousand years for the first explanatory prose to appear. Even then explanations based on material which falls outside Thiruvalluvarian thought only would be allowed! Or the interpretative explainers rather sincerely believed in what they wrote!

The central theme of Thirukkural is as follows:

The purpose of life on earth is achieving the evolution of the soul. The purpose of soul evolution is:

> Reaching the heavenly abode (*puthezhir ulagam*) ceasing further Reincarnations.

The approach for soul evolution is living a great life marked by the absence of:

> Jealousy
> Greed
> Rage and
> Harsh and pain inflicting words

And the presence of:

> Love
> Modesty
> *Oppuravu*[10]
> Empathy and
> Truth.

Similar to Herzberg's two factor theory of job satisfaction once the four pollutants subsides the maturation of soul begins by expression of love, modesty, oppuravu, empathy and truth.

A person who abides by *aram* would develop mental health (459) whose five indicating strengths are love, humility, benevolence, empathy and truth.

---

[10]   Means giving growth enabling help mostly material but also include giving one's time/energy and talent for educating, guiding and skilling others who need them. In short oppuravu means giving one's money, energy and time to another person or a cause. Oppuravu is translated as benevolence, philanthropy, social obligation, social entrepreneurship etc.

Thiruvalluvar calls the person who possess these five strengths as *sandrone*[11]. The strengths would expand as:

- Unconditional love;
- Never promoting oneself at the cost of others i.e. being modest;
- A heart and mind committed to enable the growth of the fellow citizens and other creatures;
- A strength to capture the inner sense of a fellow human in order to understand him as he understands himself and be of service to him;
- And abiding by truth at any cost.

Incidentally truth will decide the operations of the other four. A *sandrone* in whom all these virtuous strengths peeked highest would reach the heavenly abode. The couplet which says that the soul of a mentally healthy person reaches heavenly abode (*puthezhir ulagm*) goes like this:

> Mentally healthy achieves a place in heaven
> His clan has a role in it is a given.   459

While all the five strengths of a sandrone have the potential for soul evolution 'benevolence' is kept above all. A person who earns fame and name from the beneficiaries of his benevolence will attain heaven. Therefore there is no other act other than a benevolent act as beneficial to a human being. Look at the couplet which says so:

> Winning reputation out of altruistic action
> Soul (life) has no better compensation.   231

This is a startling statement: Life's purpose is soul evolution and evolution of soul is obtained through benevolent act in all walks of life. One should apply the sharpest intelligence and deepest love in his possession and act vigorously so that he would turn out enough to take care of himself and the needy. This

---

[11]   A *sandrone* is one whose personality is made up of the five strengths of love, sense of shame, benevolence   empathy and truth.

is in essence Thirukkural is about. Before concluding this section we will see a particular couplet which defines a good intellect:

> Intellect a mind restrainer
> Off from vices to good ways – a brain powerer.

Another for defining humanism:

> Loveless amass all for their share,
> Loving ones even their bones spare.   72

Another for defining spiritualism:

> Humility leads to heavenly life
> Self-aggrandizement leads to hellish strife.   121

Generally we treat emotion, intelligence and behaviour separately. For Thiruvalluvar they all unite. He cannot imagine an action without intelligence and benevolence. If intelligence is pursued without the concern for, 'good for all' that pursuance is a diseased one. Intelligence, emotion and action should be pressed into service for producing 'the good for all'. A life lived thus will enable the soul to evolve and fully evolved soul will reach the *'puthezhir ulagam'* (heavenly abode). With this when I approached Thirukkural I found couplet after couplet not given a 'soul evolving' meaning by early and current interpreters/translators. If we do not give the soul-evolving meaning to the couplets then lot of inconsistencies and improbable would appear and that is what has happened. In that case Thirukkural will not be more than a moral book meant for high school students where they are taught few catchy couplets mainly avoiding so called controversies. I say 'so called because there are no real controversies in Thirukkural whereas Thirukkural suffers the criticism of being a book lacking internal consistency with the presence of contradictions!

I claim my interpretation of Thirukkural has done justice to Thiruvalluvar because it has removed all the 'so called discrepancies, contradictions' and irrational and unacceptable notions claimed to be found in Thirukkural and made it to be 'THE' Treatise most importantly and urgently needed for humanity.

What is needed to be done immediately?

Efforts are on in India to make Thirukkural as the national literature. When the effort reaches the final stage a question of which version of Hindi and English translation to be authorised will arise. To meet that eventuality we should prepare ourselves right now. Central Government should form a 'Thirukkural Convention 'and give it the task of evolving a translated version of Thirukkural in English and Hindi which will be truthful to Thiruvalluvar. The convention should include members who have done real work in the field of Thirukkural. It should never be a political and or religion based decision.

To the best of my knowledge none of the popularly existing English translations of Thirukkural are truthful ones. They are biased. The bias is due to the bias that entered into the first crop of interpretations of Thirukkural in Tamil. Since they are several hundred years old and are astonishingly scholarly they are accepted with such reverence any voice to the contrary will be attacked. Pressures will build up. The Government should keep its head above and pursue the matter diligently and scientifically without yielding to pressure. Once it is made as the national literature of India it will attract the attention of the entire world. To that world a new bias free truthful translation of Thirukkural should be made available. Otherwise the world will quickly reject it as belonging to a particular religion.

Now coming to my book I have two objectives. One giving a truthful translation and explanation of Thirukkural and two making it applicable to life.

I have given below my e mail id, phone number for further consultation. Here after I will also try to write regularly in my blog on Thirukkural. Please follow them.[12]

---

[12]   91+ 9886406695 prof_venkat1947@yahoo.co.in
http://www.thirukkuralvenkat.com/

Since I could not find equivalent words in English for some of the Tamil I used few Tamil words without modification. I have given a legend consisting those words. Please read them and familiarise yourself with the Tamil words and their meaning.

Legend[13]

Aram:
Sometimes the word dharma is used as an equivalent translation of *aram*. I think it may not be hundred percent equivalent to the word *aram*. Whatever we find in Thirukkural by way of desirable action vis-à-vis soul evolution leading to *puthezhir ulagm* (heavenly abode) are acts of *aram*.

However, for the sake of giving a definition we can say *aram* means showing love to all living beings, taking care of guests, speaking truth, showing gratitude, maintaining equity in our dispensation, being humble, putting best practices in place of professional and social lives, never coveting another person's wife, displaying enormous forbearance, never feeling envy, never misappropriating what rightfully belongs to others, not slandering, not indulging in useless talk, being afraid of doing evil acts, involving in growth enabling activities towards fellow citizens, spending one's money in charity, being compassionate, not eating meat, not stealing, speaking truth under any circumstance, not developing rage, not hurting others, not killing etc., please do not take this list as exhaustive.

Arivudaimai:
Intellect +*Aram* (Intelligence + knowledge = intellect).

Aruludaimai:
This word roughly translates as compassion. But if you hold compassionate action as sympathy based then *aruludaimai* is not compassion. *Aruludaimai*

---

[13]   I have used few Tamil words as such to introduce them to English. I have to do so because there are no equal English words for them. One day English language may have to accept them into its fold like what it has done already in the case of a number of words from Tamil and Sanskrit. To indicate their origin I have put them in italics.

makes a person to act in support of another person to help him reap his equity. It is love plus action for achieving equity to a person or a living creature which by itself could not achieve it. It may or may not involve sacrifice on the part of the person who wants to be compassionate towards fellow beings. (You will be surprised to know Thiruvalluvar has no use for sympathy/grace etc.) However I have used the word compassion in place of *aruludaimai* because I thought it is a bothersome oriental word for an English reader. Therefore wherever you come across compassion understand it as *aruludaimai* not as grace or sympathy based.

Kamam:
A strong overwhelming wish/desire.

Oppuravu:
Means giving growth enabling help mostly material but also include giving one's time/energy and talent for educating, guiding and skilling others who need them. In short *oppuravu* means giving one's money, energy and time to another person or a cause. *Oppuravu is* translated as benevolence, philanthropy, social obligation, social preneurship etc.

Panbu:
It is a quality which combines love and a number of other qualities namely equity, a Sense of shame, following best practices in any situation, truthfulness, a sense of Humour, giving, using sweet words, not ridiculing others. In short we can say it is love coupled with dispensing equity.

Sandrone:
A *sandrone is* one whose personality has the strong base made up of love, sense of shame, *oppuravu*, empathy and truth.

Tapasya:
Is one who carries on penance (tapas) to realize God and obtain heavenly abode.

Few more words which I have coined in English are explained in the places where they are found.

A gist of what you have in this book:

Book on *Aram*

1. This chapter describes the qualities of God. At least three of the qualities can be picked up by you. The couplets in which the qualities found are: 4, 5 and 6.

2. This chapter is a eulogy on rain. You may leave this chapter with the thinking: I should do something to sustain rain to sustain myself.

3. This chapter is a tribute to all those great men of the past. It brings out their qualities which are reminiscent of what we read about God in the first chapter.

4. This chapter is a preamble for the entire treatise. It gives the definition of *Aram*. For Tiruvalluvar there is not a single walk of human life which we can exempt from the purview of *Aram*.

5. This chapter is about a home/household. A family or home/household is an institution with its vision and mission – is the message of this chapter.

6. Wife is the well spring of the family, a joint CEO of the institution and the bulwark of it, says this chapter.

7. This chapter gives few lessons on parenting.

8. This chapter says that if a human being totally cuts off from love he or she may not survive. There is an excellent example to explain this phenomenon in this chapter.

9. Taking care of guests to their heart's content is an important pass for your entry into haven, says this chapter.

10. One useful approach to make *Aram* to prevail around you is speaking sweet and kind words, says this chapter. Remember *Aram* is the master key for opening the doors of heaven.

11. 'Beware if you kill gratitude you will never reach heaven,' warns this chapter.

12. Oh! If only those CEO's and new crops in the line heeded to the advice found in this chapter they need not have been languishing/ waiting to languish in jail. This chapter speaks about equity and its fair distribution.

13. A close associate of equity is humility. This chapter is aptly placed next to the chapter on equity.

14. 'Best practices,' is not a new idea. This chapter is persuasive best on the need for putting best practices in place in all the activities of humanity.

15. Sleeping with the wife of another person/neighbour/friend measures the highest on the trespass of *Aram*. Never that person would pass the test of reaching the abode of God says this chapter.

16. This chapter says a forbearer by his act of forbearing raises far above than a saint who fasts and suffers to reach heaven.

17. 'Envy will push you into hellish life' is the central message of this chapter.

18. 'Let the swindlers beware that they will never be able to wriggle out of the mess they create for themselves leave alone reaching heaven,' says this chapter.

19. Do not slander on others. Beware your blame on others will be accepted only if you are good in estimating the blame in an unbiased manner, says this chapter.

20. "If you accept to give a lecture prepare well. Don't take the audience for a ride. It will remove the good will you might enjoy," cautions this chapter.

21. Fear hurting the interest of others. If you do not avoid hurting others it will soon become a habit with you. Then it will not be long before the god of *Aram* punishes you. You may recall that elsewhere I have told that God doesn't interfere. But here I say God of Aram will punish. Read the chapter and solve the problem.

22. A man of *oppuravu* (growth enabling philanthropy/ social engineering) will use his 'educated money' for growth enabling ventures. Even if you have no money to spare still you can be a man of *oppuravu*. Find out how from this chapter.

23. *Oppuravu* is like teaching a person to catch fish. But at times it may be required to give fish itself. Give to the needy says this chapter.

24. This chapter is about attaining fame. Fame is given to understand as the esteem you win in the hearts of others because of your giving and oppuravu.

25. Tiruvalluvar has never spoken about sympathy. He uses the concept *aruludaimai* instead. This is a very interesting chapter.

26. *Aruludaimai* and not eating meat are cohorts. Find out how from this chapter.

27. And 28. If you carefully read these two chapters you will find the differences between the true and pseudo tapasya.

29. Do you remember chapter 18? It speaks about scam. A strong sense of scale and prudence will prevent you from scam behaviour.

30. When will even a lie can be equal to a truth? The chapter is very famous because of its second couplet.

31. Do you easily get infuriated? Then this chapter is a must read for you.

32. This chapter says never harm others. You may ask what how this chapter differs from chapter 21. Chapter 21 says one should fear doing evil. This chapter says, as a policy one should avoid hurting others.

33. Senseless destruction of life of all forms has led to the need for maintaining bio diversity. This chapter has something to say on this topic.

34. Uncertainty is a certainty. This chapter advices us to accept this at the level of our feelings.

35. How about practicing renunciation even while living a full active joyful life? You will pick up that skill here.

36. God is the only Real stuff. All other things are superfluous or UN real. To know more read this chapter.

37. If things other than God are not real then not developing a deep desire towards them is in order says this chapter.

38. After studying this chapter I got the impression that the theory of fate as portrayed by Tiruvalluvar and the theory of Karma of Hindu religion are not one and the same. This is a very important chapter from the point of view of psychotherapy.

Book on Wealth

39. This chapter gives a list of desirable monarchical traits which interestingly are applicable for present day presidents/prime ministers/ CEOs.

40. The importance of education especially of mathematical and communication disciplines is not well understood in our society even today. But Tiruvalluvar has emphasised it some 2000 years ago. Find it out in this chapter.

41. Knowledge meagre is a coinage I have made to explain the theme of this chapter. What could it be? If you are curious go to this chapter immediately.

42. If you think you are not a good listener, then this chapter is for you.

43. Tiruvalluvar has used the Tamil word *arivudaimai* in this chapter it is intelligence + knowledge+ *Aram* or intellect +*aram*.

44. You can find a list of blames and the importance of removing them emphasized in this chapter.

45. If you don't have a mentor have one immediately says the chapter.

46. The company you keep maters. Know more about it here.

47. Are you planning for a project? You have a good road map here.

48. Do you over shoot? Better read this and get chastened by imbibing the sprit found in this chapter.

49. Opportune time/season is an important input for launching a fight. What is told for a king can be useful to you also – to fight your boss if you have one who needs to be given a fitting fight.

50. If you are about to become an expat, familiarize your self as much as you can about your host country and its culture so that you can easily acclimatize once you immigrate. This is the message I have derived from a study of this chapter.

51. Perhaps you are familiar with the big five personality factors in selection. Tiruvalluvar gives another ingenious list of five factors in this chapter.

52. Managerial skills are best if they sustain the productivity through their strategies. You have some interesting tips here.

53. Going to roots is suggested by Tiruvalluvar as a means of garnering strength for the king. We ordinary mortals can also find a lesson here.

54. Lack of focus can undercut your efforts tells this chapter.

55. Right sceptre indicates a system of just dispensation in place. We hardly find any government which works towards putting a system of just and fairness in the world today. Know Thiruvalluvar's notions on this subject.

56. What will happen in a rule by a tyrant? You have answers here.

57. If any tyrant king/president or prime minister thinks he can continue being so, he or she has something to listen to from this chapter before things go worst for him or her.

58. Empathy is what is needed not sympathy. Read more here.

59. Few lessons on espionage are found in this chapter.

60. This chapter contains some very famous couplets like: "Lotus's stalk grows to level with that of the water// A man of vision and effort raises his effort to reach the vision of his heart's quarter.

61. Laziness is a spoiler. How to manage it? This chapter tells you.

62. Tiruvalluvar also speaks about 'employee engagement.' Surprised? Read this chapter.

63. At every obstacle, who pushes ahead like a bull
    Has his visiting pain into trouble.
    Interesting? More of them in this chapter.

64. A secretary of state or a minister should be versatile. Find out how here.

65. If you want to be persuasive among your audience you have some tips here.

66. Ethics in business has become very popular after the scams in MNCs. But Tiruvalluvar has spoken about it even before 2000 years!

67. Achieving target on time is always a problem for the project leaders everywhere. The simple advice is: step up your effort whenever you think you may miss your date, says this chapter.

68. Strategizing is an important strategy, says this chapter.

69. The job description and job specification for the job of an ambassador is described by Tiruvalluvar in this chapter.

70. Is your boss a tyrant? Pick up few lessons from this chapter to manage him.

71. Learn the skill of reading body language, advises this chapter.

72. Do what you speak goes above the head of your audience? This chapter is a must read for you.

73. If you have stage fear this is a must read for you.

74. You may be aware of the fact that well being indices of countries are being estimated these days. Tiruvalluvar gives few standards in this chapter towards that end of making indices.

75. If you are an art director for a historical film you have some tips for designing your 'forts' in this chapter.

76. If you are an entrepreneur keeping working capital always ready cannot be more emphasised to you than by the example given in this chapter.

77. How to increase the military culture in an army is answered here.

78. This chapter discusses military prows.

79. To 83 these five chapters deal with all aspects of friendship. Chapter 82 has been differently interpreted by me

84. This chapter is about human folly.

85. Tiruvalluvar portrays a person called Knowledge-meagre-upstart. Know about him in this chapter.

86. This is an interesting chapter on other acceptance. A solution for secularism problems.

87. A commander-in-chief may think his army is the best. Nevertheless going to a war should be his last resort, says this chapter.

88. Break the enemy's overawe and leave him there; never go for a war says this chapter.

89. Be cautious of an enemy around you in the guise of a friend points out this chapter.

90. Don't rub a powerful person on a wrong side says this chapter.

91. This chapter is for henpecked husbands.

92. Embracing a prostitute is like embracing a corpse of a woman in a dark room. Disturbed to the core? Here Tiruvalluvar counsels persons who visit sex workers.

93. The difference between a drunkard and a poisoned is while the later dies instantly the former dies in due course of time. This chapter highlights the menace of alcohol and one who reads this might keep away from the slow killer of alcohol.

94. If you are a gambler and swear that you have a great skill in gambling your ruin is round the corner because there is nothing like great skills in gambling! Take the lesson from this chapter and benefit.

95. One's food is one's medicine. Some of the wisest advice is seen here.

96. Family as an institution is the training ground for inculcating *panbu*. A very inspiring chapter of hope for humanity.

97.   Self – respect is operationally defined in this chapter, making it easy to identify and maintain.

98.   This chapter explicates how esteem rests with energized and effortful mind.

99.   *Sandranmai* is a combination of five qualities: love, sense of shame, *oppuravu*, empathy and truthfulness. Like the famous Big Five personality attributes this is Thiruvalluvar's Big Five. Find out more about them in this chapter.

100. You might have noticed the Tamil word *panbu* used by me earlier. Like two or three other Tamil words notably *sandranmai panbu* has no equivalent word in English. Read to satisfy yourself about what I contend and also learn how *panbu* is nurtured in a home.

101. Wealth kept hoarded is equal to wealth not put to best use. This chapter deals with the malice.

102. Sense of shame is a very dear concept for Tiruvalluvar. He uses it liberally throughout his chapters. This chapter is an exclusive one on that topic.

103. Family through its management grows and benefits from panbu. This chapter is a must read for all.

104. Some agronomic practices to get the best out of agriculture are suggested by Tiruvalluvar here.

105. Thiruvalluvar's heart melts at the plight of persons suffering from poverty. This chapter is possibly an appeal to those who can eradicate poverty to do the needful.

106. Some cultures abhors seeking help like begging and consider it to be a national shame. But Tiruvalluvar has a different notion about the practice. In this chapter he encourages beggars to seek help from those who are capable of helping

107. Having said so in the previous chapter, in this chapter he discourages begging as much as possible. This chapter is another example attesting that one cannot find any contradiction in his concepts.

108. The last chapter in the book of wealth is about men without scruples. A very interesting chapter.

Book on Love

109. He is stunned at her beauty. While her ear ring is her plus his heart goes into nonplus.
110. He excels in reading her body language and finds a complying message in it.
111. They taste it for the first time.
112. Now he evaluates her beauty.
113. In separation they muse on the great qualities of each other.
114. He losses patience as well as his sense of shame. He decides to sit on a palmyra horse – a nonviolent demonstration – to impress upon her parents his ardent love for their daughter and give consent to their marriage!
115. Now the rumour in the village does the trick.
116. Now they are married but he is on a business trip and she suffers separation.
117. She pines and languishes.
118. She is in frustration. But says her eyes are responsible. Intriguing? Find the answer from this chapter.
119. You know one thing? Separation from her lover causes psychosomatic symptoms on her.
120. She suffers the anguish of loneliness.
121. This chapter describes her journey into memories.
122. She speaks of her dreams in this chapter.
123. Tide of time brings in painful evenings in the absence of her husband.
124. She becomes thin due to the separation.
125. She has a dialogue with her heart.
126. She breaks her self-restrain and empties her condition due to the feelings of lust to her friend setting aside the resistance and gets ready to seek him.
127. Perhaps something similar was happening with her lover too. Now both of them long for each other.
128. When they meet once again her modesty would not allow her. But her lover could read her body language. Embrace takes place. But she suspects something from his embrace. Perhaps he plans another trip?
129. She desires for embrace again.

130. The delay is killing. She chides her heart which goes after him creating the pain of love pang.

131. Her friend suggest to her to sulk. But she has some definite opinion about the mechanics of sulking.

132. Sulking is a fine art says this chapter.

133. She shares something with her friend about her experience with him.

The couplets whose first letter is in bold type are those I differ from others. The difference could be due to rewriting an unacceptable irrational interpretation given earlier or an improvement in the direction of a soul evolving meaning. I did not include the differences in the third book because the differences are very miner.

1

Praise of God

(This chapter insists on prayer in the form of surrendering.)

1. From 'aha,' alphabets across letters are born
    So also universe has *Adi Bhagavan*[14] for its origin.

    When we open our mouth the sound that emanates is 'aha'.
    From this sound of 'aha' other sounds of vowels and consonants
    are produced vocally. Alphabets of all languages symbolize these
    vocalized sounds. Universe with its living and non-living objects
    have similar relationship with God.[15]

2. What is the use of his learning if he doesn't?
    Worship the pure knower seeking to reach his feet.

    A purely learned person who, realizes that not this world and its objects
    are true; rather God and his world are, sets himself on the ways and
    means to reach him(356). Therefore what is the use of possessing
    knowledge if the possessor doesn't pray God surrendering at his feet?

---

[14] *Adi Bhagavan* are the Tamil words used by Tiruvalluvar to denote God meaning
      the original God.

[15] *'Adi'* in Tamil means first and foremost. Perhaps Tiruvalluvar wants to differentiate
      his notion of God from the number of other notional forms of Gods current at
      his time. The ideas and the attributes of God he has enumerated in the first eight
      couplets of this chapter suggest that he was not for the theology of various hues
      existed at his time

3.   He who surrenders to God who graced[16] flower-pure
      Would live a long soul fulfilling life.

      God goes, as evidenced early, to those hearts which are pure. Those
      who surrender at his feet while keeping their heart pure would live
      a great soul-fulfilling life on this earth.

4.   He neither prefers nor averts, on His feet,
      A surrendered man never meets pain.

      God doesn't have likes and dislikes. A person who surrenders at his
      feet will have no difficulties (because he will develop what is called
      detached attachment towards men and matter).

5.   Two acts of darkness[17] doesn't afflict him
      Who to reach God, the true object, serves the humanity and earns
      acclaim

      God is the only true object. The world and its products are the arena
      and objects of training for the evolvement of soul. Therefore in a man
      who endeavors to evolve his soul through the selfless service to the
      humanity, the two acts of darkness namely acting evil and thinking
      evil would not occur.

6.   God possess five regulated senses
      Genuine walkers of his path live long.

      All the five senses remain regulated in God. That is his nature.
      Those who learn the ability behind this blameless practice and put
      it to use in all the walks of their life will live long on this earth.
      (The ability consists of developing a healthy life promoting and

---

16   perhaps Thiruvalluvar is referring to someone who has realized God
17   Two acts of darkness' are thinking and acting evil.

soul-evolving perspective over the data brought in by the five senses and acting based on that perspective.)

7.   Spared are those at the feet of God the incomparable
     For others getting rid of worries is unachievable.

     There is none equal to God. Except for those who surrender at his feet it is impossible to come out of their worries.

8.   But for those who surrender at the feet of God – the ocean of compassion
     Others would never swim through the life's tribulation.

     God is a sea of compassion maintaining equity to all. Only those who surrender at His feet would be able to undergo the turmoil/tribulations of life.

9.   He has neither a goal nor intelligent
     If his head doesn't bow to the possessor of traits eight [18]

     The human who doesn't worship God, the possessor of Eight Propensities[19] is incapable of developing perspectives over the data his five senses bring to him (intellect) and has no use for the intelligence (aptitude) he is endowed with.

10. The ocean of births can be crossed by him
     Whose surrender at God's feet is firm.

---

[18]   I, the present translator presume the eight traits are mentioned through each of the previous eight *kurals*.

[19]   (1) He is the originator of everything living as well as non-living, (2) His knowing is complete and free from doubt. (3)He reaches the heart which long for him (4) He has no likes or hates. (5)He is the only true and essential Reality. (6)His five senses in their natural form remain regulated. (7) There is none other like Him. (8)He is an ocean of compassion (awarding equity to all creatures).

Those who surrender at His feet easily swim through the ocean of several births of domestic life and reach the abode of God. Others cannot. (Others cannot because they cling to worldly objects, instead of God, as though they are end unto themselves. The world and its objects are training ground and materials respectively. Those who forget this cling to them which makes life miserable because while amassing more and more of those so-called real objects, human beings violate several principles of 'aram'[20] which stunts the evolution of the soul. As a result they forego their opportunity (for want of an evolved soul) to attain the company of God and live in eternal piece.)

Skills to be learnt:

➤ Developing a mind-set of surrendering at the feet of God through an appropriate prayer.

Rationale:

➤ One thing we learn from this chapter and the entire book of Thirukkural is: God is the only Real Object and the rest – the material and non-material objects of the world – are not real objects. They are illusory. In other words what matters is God and nothing else. The life in this earth is like a training period. Successful completion of this training will usher us into God's company. The worldly objects, material as well as non-material are training materials and therefore are illusory, not real. Successful completion of the training denotes that the soul has evolved well enough to earn the company of God.

➤ The evolution is nothing but making *aram* as our true nature. In that sense the precincts of aram, which runs as the undercurrent of all the strengths found in the 133 chapters of Thirukkural need to be thoroughly understood and followed in all walks of our life. Anyone who masters these strengths and leads his life by strictly putting them into practice will have his soul fully evolved and would reach *puthezhir ulagam.*

---

[20]   Consult the legend for the meaning of the Tamil word *aram.*

> All the activities we carry out in life are nothing but prayers provided we carry them out remaining in our soul rather than in our ego. For example using a bath room becomes an act of prayer if one uses water restricting its use to a reasonable minimum so that someone somewhere is not left without that natural resource because he uses more than the share an equitable dispensation would allow. A person who thrives in his ego would see having the luxury of as much water as he would be pleased to, as the fruit of his hard work whereas a person living in his soul would see it as a matter of taking care of the need of other living beings while one is prudently taking care of his own need.

> Following the precincts of *aram* becomes easy to a person who surrenders at the feet of God. Surrendering means, like a refugee in a foreign country leaving his life at the care of the asylum giving country, the human being needs to leave his life in God's care.

> However, the asylum seeker is not absolved of his efforts to make his life comfortable. He achieves them by conducting himself very carefully following the rules and regulations of the host country.

> Likewise we have to do whatever we are capable of to live a professional as well as personal life fully following the precincts of *aram* and leave the rest to God. This is like a good student who studies well writes an exam and have patience and faith in the evaluators and the system. That is surrendering.

> To a person who surrenders to God his worth to earn the company of God comes from the effort he puts into his work following the precincts of *aram*. Every moment of work accentuates the maturation process. In whatever small manner if the soul is evolved it is welcome.

Coaching:

> At the start of the day in a prayer to experience surrender, we may say to God thus: "I know I have to complete the activities I have planned for the day following the precincts of *aram* in order to call it a day profitably completed in my path to reach you and remain in your company. Keeping this in mind I shall do whatever I want to do to the best of my ability, not sparing any effort, conforming to

the best practices which are harmless to me and to humanity and to all creatures and non creatures and leave the rest of my concerns to you. I request you to be by my side and pull me up whenever I deviate from the path of *aram* and guide me. I promise you that whenever you pull me up I will take every effort to rectify my mistakes. Thank you very much for giving me this opportunity."

➤ If one offers this prayer every day and imbibes the spirit, one may reach a stage wherein one doesn't even need to offer this prayer. Living a life of *aram* will become one's nature and life on this earth itself will feel like life in God's company.

2

The Greatness of Rain

(In praise of rain and insisting on its conservation)

11. **R**ain preserves universe through its shower,
    Hence, it is felt as the *amrita²¹*-power.

Rain is held as nectar of heaven because it sustains and rejuvenates life on earth. (The Tamil word used in the couplet is *amizhtham,²²* which means nectar from heaven believed to be capable of sustaining and rejuvenating life. It is the gift of God. Interestingly there may be some other truth in what he says, In the audio found in the blog given in the reference, a professor of Tamil Prof.T.Venugopal (Naganandi) has this to say: Water can be produced in a laboratory but plants would not grow in that water. However, as soon as few drops of rain water are added to it plants do grow. I am also aware that farmers claim that crops grow vigorously after rain because rain water enter into the plants through young leaves. If elixir like quality exists in rain water then there is lot of sense in Thiruvalluvar calling it as *amizhtham.²³*)

---

21 It is an elixir from the world of God which sustains life on earth.

22 Thiruvalluvar has used a few such mythological artefacts and mythological stories mainly for explaining his points to the people in whose culture such artefacts and stories exist.

23 http://voiceofthf.blogspot.com/2011/01/blog-post.html

12.   Rain makes every food,
      As water it is a food.

      Rain helps to build every food while it is a food in the form of
      drinking water.

13.   If rain fails the land despite its vast ocean mass
      Chronic hunger afflicts organisms en masse.

      Chronic hunger and afflictions will affect the earth if rain fails
      chronically, even though three-fourths of its surface is covered by
      water.

14.   Tillers would stop tilling the field
      With the prospect of a poor monsoon yield.

      If cloud, whose principal produce is rain, fails for long, agriculture
      will stop more or less completely and innumerable difficulties will
      set in.

15.   Lock stock barrel rain devastates,
      Then it is the ruined it reinstates.[24]

      Rain has a quality – it brings about the ruin of people as well as lifts
      them out of it.

16.   Unless clouds make their water shed
      Hardly sighted are green's head.

      Unless clouds release their yields regularly no green shoot will be
      seen on the earth.

---

[24]   'Then in support of the ruined it reinstates the ruined,' represent all the equivalent
       words of the couplet.

17. **If** sky with thick clouds fails to remiss
    Nectarines' of the vast oceans will be in amiss.

    The quality of the ocean will suffer if the rains are not sufficient. As a result, its ability to support the fish and other biotic progressively diminishes. (His observation gets our attention to the conditions prevailing at the oceans these days: Global warming due to depletion of ozone layer leading to erratic rains. In addition due to excess of CO_2 in the atmosphere it rains acids. We read the reports on how the protective shells of corals and other organisms are getting affected because of the increased level of acidity in the sea.)

18. When clouds become dry and offer no succor
    Worship of God with fervor would not occur.

    Worship of God by seers and all pompous religious celebrations and festivities will come to a standstill if rain fails.(Please note this concept is just opposite to the Hinduism concept that clouds are ordered to rain by divine beings who are pleased with the religious offerings.)

19. If heaven does not gift its clouds
    Philanthropy and penance would be in shreds.

    Charity and penance will come to a grinding halt if rains fails continuously.

20. **Life** is impossible without water
    So are best practices without rain's batter.

    Life in its variety of careers (other than the ones mentioned in couplets numbered 18 and 19) with their best practices is impossible if rain doesn't batter the earth regularly.

Skills to be learnt:

➢   To carry out professional, social and personal activities in such a way that one contributes to the maintenance of an environment conducive for proper rain fall – neither in excess nor in deficit during the course of one's life time

Rationale:

➢   This chapter insists we appreciate the importance and usefulness of rain. To sustain rain the environment needs to be protected.

➢   The best way to protect our environment, so that rains arrive only the way they are needed and do not cause pain by raining haphazardly or not raining al all, is by regulating human life as consumers.

➢   Nowadays it is common knowledge, thanks to the awareness created by various bodies, that erratic rains and hurricanes result from global warming (due to depletion of ozone layer which in turn is due to the emission of carbon dioxide by automobiles, diesel generators and cooling systems etc., in excess of what the photosynthetic activity of plant kingdom could absorb).

Deforestation, which is a symptom of human development has accentuated the problem.

➢   Further excessive release of carbon dioxide into the atmosphere turns the rains into acidic ones.

➢   This excessive production of carbon dioxide is directly linked to the extravagance in consumption indulged by humanity.

➢   In couplet 15 Tiruvalluvar says rain brings in destruction in two ways: by excessive rain and by no or very meagre rain. Next couplet says if there is no rain even a blade of grass will not show up.

➢   Whether one likes it or not everyone should do what one ought to do to address the problem. This is the fittest case of 'think globally and act locally.'

Coaching:

- ➢ You should be prudent in what you consume: food, water, energy and products of comfort produce lot of carbon footprint. I.e., your life style creates carbon emission which fills the atmosphere. There are methods to calculate carbon foot print one creates due to one's life style mainly eating, drinking and commuting. Assuming you calculate your carbon foot print and compare it with the recommended standard, if that foot print is more than the permissible limit then you should be honest enough to bring it down to the acceptable level.

- ➢ Consume vegetarian food as much as possible because it produces less carbon foot print than meat. A study has shown that it takes 16 pounds of grains to produce one pound of meat.

- ➢ While choosing a vegetarian food the notion of carbon foot print the food creates to reach one's dining table may be taken into account. Food from a long distance, needing cold storage and not available in a near by store, grown using fossil fuel based fertilizers are the considerations in this regard. Locally available food which does not need preservation may be chosen.

- ➢ Another idea is participating in carbon offset projects. You can participate in community projects in tree planting or afforestation.

- ➢ You can give preference to buy shares in companies whose Corporate Social Responsibility projects are in fact carbon offset projects.

- ➢ Deforestations are taking place indiscriminately due to the illegal activities by wood mafia. These people are supported by legislators. Legislators may be sensitized in this regard and may be watched by citizen group which will break the unholy nexus between the legislature and wood mafia. You may participate in such groups and give your contribution.

- ➢ A bare minimum use of water and commuting to the place of work and stores either by walk or by bike or public transport instead of big personal cars could be useful strategies.

- ➢ You may revisit the quantum of electricity you and your family consume. You may come forward to employ several consumption cutting methods. An interesting proposition may be setting the AC five degrees warmer than what is normally enjoyed. Similarly setting the fridge temperature a little high saves lot of energy. Turning off lights and computers when not in use, promptly using LED bulbs, using the washing machine and dishwasher in full capacity are some other methods to reduce the consumption of electricity.

➤   Cycling as much as possible will also help one to reduce one's carbon foot print. Cycling improves one's health immensely.

➤   Things of comfort need to be bought only when they are exhausted and not because you accost yourself for missing standards or feel poor and self-pitying in comparison to your over consuming neighbor.

➤   You may revisit standards excepting in the case of calories, nutrients and vitamins, strictly because most of them may have utopian elements in them. If you are extravagant remember you are stealing the equity of your poor brethren elsewhere. The Malthusian argument – you have talent, you work, therefore you can have as much as you want – has no place in a life where one's objective is to refine one's soul enough to reach God's world and live in eternal joy. The refinement mainly consists of taking care of the needs of one's brethren living elsewhere who are not as fortunate as one is. In practical terms one should honestly compare oneself with a much poorer person one knows regarding articles of comfort one stacks at one's home.

➤   Even if you do not believe or not interested to relocate to God's world still you have to prune your consumption if your present life style creates a carbon foot print several times more than that of the sustainable standard or that of the your poor brethren living in under developed or developing countries. Otherwise you may turn out to be a delinquent in as for as creating that carbon foot print in two ways: a poor fellow man while he is struggling to make both ends to meet, leave aside the fact that he doesn't enjoy the comforts you enjoy, suffers from the fury of cyclones and draught and so many other ills brought by erratic rainfalls and climate variation, second, he finds things he needs for living a decent life becoming dearer because you consume them more than your honest requirements resulting in short supply. You should remember your poor brethren will never be able to compete with you given their poor economic conditions. There is no level playing field in the world.

> ➢ As a family, members may collect data from studies on these and other relevant items and chart out the best practices and follow them strictly. It should be remembered that one's soul will evolve due to such activities. You will start enjoying it after the initial struggle.

Now we have the trend of e-publications and paper less offices. With cloud computing the trend is likely to be accelerated which is a welcome one in view of the fact that many forests will be saved due to reduced demand on wood for making paper. We can switch over to e-books more and more so that a lot of wood can be saved.

At the individual level we can exercise a strong preference to buy e publications instead of printed ones.

3

The Glory of the Great Men[25] of the Past

(In praise of those lived a soul full filling social life)

21. Writers looking for an outstanding theme
     Seek the practices of men of great fame.

     Authors who want to write treatises consisting of outstanding theme
     choose the life and best practices of great men who lived a soul full
     filling life in the yester years.

22. Enumerating[26] the greatness of the relinquished
     Is as difficult getting death figure furnished

     Enumerating the statistics of people who have passed away is a very
     difficult task. So is the enumeration of the rare attributes of the great
     men who lived a detached life.

---

[25] These men may be community leaders with one important identity that they
      have abandoned all their personal belongings and live like an ascetic. Men like
      Gandhi and Mother Theresa can be quoted as examples.

[26] Several examples in Thirukkural like the present one suffer from logical fallacy.
      But it may be remembered that it is a technique by which Thiruvalluvar tries to
      drive home a concept or idea. Such examples by creating an effective surprise
      installs an idea very strongly in the mind of the reader. All such examples in the
      treatise ar harmless.

23.   **D**iscerning life here and there[27] they live a life of *aram*
       Their esteem, million with great fanfare announce.

       The world's laurels are showered on those detached men who discern
       the purpose of the life on earth and the nature of life in the company
       of God and took to *aram* as their guide in all their activities in order
       to reach God's company.

24.   Firm control on his senses, like a mahout's hook, he[28] holds,
       Seed fit enough for heaven's fields.

       The mahout uses his hook to tame the elephant. Great men through
       their determination regulate their senses from indulging in sensations
       as they please. They are seeds fit enough to be sown in the fields of
       heaven.

25.   **F**or the power of the restrainer of five senses
       Lord Indira's[29] story offers witness.

       By the power of regulating one's five senses one can attain greater
       spiritual heights. One can even become the head of celestials as
       evidenced by the story of Lord Indira.

26.   Rare feats who accomplish are great men,
       Those who do not are small men.

       Those who are capable of achieving what most of the others do not
       achieve like some one's achievements are above the achievements
       of 99% of the persons in the field is called as great. (Remember
       this chapter is about remembering the life of great men on their

---

27   Here and there refers to life on earth and life at God's place or heaven.

28   He refers to an ascetic.

29   There are several stories around Indra the leader of the celestial world. Perhaps
       here a story that a great human being became the leader of the celestial world is
       alluded to by Thiruvalluvar.

anniversary day or birth day. They may also be ascetics or they might be some citizens in various fields. Poet hints at the possibility of dubious persons getting eulogised for ulterior reasons which should be avoided for the good of mankind. A society which respects ordinary people with great fanfare would vitiate the atmosphere of its ability to encourage great achievements.)

27. A perspective deriver on the signals of senses five
     To him the world remains alive.

     A person who discerns the lures of the five senses and derive soul evolving perspectives on their signals to live a purposeful life is profitably alive to the world and to its joys. (The five senses are instruments of a human. They have to be put to proper use so that they always remain tools in his hands not his masters.)

28. The worth and significance of men of codes,
     Perennial relevance of their thriving words vindicates.

     Great men's actions and message attain immortality because they are relevant for a long time to come.

29. **H**e who has matured into a hill of virtues,
     His anger doesn't stay even for few seconds.

     A great man's anger subsides quickly. (Because they are compassionate and tolerant at heart.)

30. Great man of aram are as much Brahmin
     Because they shows compassion to all men.

     Brahmin means men who show equity to all living creatures. For this reason they are worthy of tributes from the humanity.

Skills to be learnt:

> At the personal level living a life of Spartan.

Rationale:

> A great man who live for the sake of society is one who does not indulge in sensuous pleasures and lose sight of the purpose of this life on the earth. Instead, he controls and regulates his senses. He doesn't put himself at the receiving end of his senses, but remains a perspective builder on their signals. Such persons are great assets for a nation because they can guide people of the country to live a psychologically healthy and soul-fulfilling life. Thiruvalluvar gives a hint that all cannot raise to that level because it may need determination to abstain in the persona as a seed stock earned through previous births! What is the alternative for most of other people? In the present day world human being can practice abstention in a slightly different way. They can live a simple life and pass on the savings to dear and near ones who are not fortunate enough even to have the minimum.

Coaching:

> Men whose soul are well evolved will choose a Spartan life. They live for the sake of society and keep their personal belongings to the bare minimum. They may hold high offices. But on the evening of the day of their retirement they may be seen standing in the bus stand to catch a bus to go to an obscure place and their entire belongings will be hanging so lite on their shoulders in a shoulder bag!
> But a whole lot of humanity would keep them in high esteem because they have contributed significantly to the society through their office. These are the persons Thiruvalluvar refers here.
> What message a reader has from this chapter? How about restraining your needs as much as possible and pass on what is saved to one of your relatives who is not as fortunate as you are?
> How about keeping minimum belongings? If people do not buy again and again upgraded furniture and other household articles

companies will turn their attention to produce cheaper versions catering to the poor at prices they can afford. A sense of scale not grandeur should guide our perception.

➢ How about going to a social service center regularly and carry out some activity on a regular basis?

➢ How about making a solemn decision that you will not waste your office time? This is all the more important if you are in a government office.

➢ How about living in a moderate house, dressing moderately and driving a moderate vehicle? Only because people make an exhibition of their big cars and houses and other extravaganza and print and electronic media making a big business the aspirations of the society goes hey wire and all sorts of mistakes take place. A simple life lived by big personalities would go a long way to discipline the world.

➢ Couplet no. 26 gives a specific suggestion. Don't make all and sundry great by giving them undeserving recognition. This will vitiate the atmosphere for people who want to do great things for the society.

4

Emphasizing the Importance of *Aram*[30]

(Opening chapter for the rest in the book on *aram*.)

31. Social esteem[31] and wealth *aram* helps to gain
    What better life flourisher exists to attain?

    If a man follows the path of *aram* it is possible for him to attain social esteem and wealth also. Therefore is there anything better than *aram* for bringing betterment to human beings?

32. Adopt *aram,* no better way to flourishing,
    Worst ruin, none other than its vanishing.

    While there is no safer way than what is supported by *aram* to flourish in life non adaptation to *aram* is more ruinous to life than any other.

33. Invoking *aram,* needed acts, ceaselessly enact
    Have feasibility as a strategic tact.

---

[30] The Tamil word *aram* found in the couplets of the chapter has no equivalent in the language of   English. *Aram* is a common term standing for all the virtues finding a place either directly or by inference in all the 1330 couplets of Tirukkural. However, it can be defined as keeping the mind free from poisonous thinking avoiding debilitating envy, desire, rage and harsh words.

[31] Earning social esteem is soul evolving. A fully evolved soul reaches heaven.

Carry out activities that come in your way or you choose deliberately invoking *aram*. In all possible places and feasible ways act strictly following the precincts of *aram*. (The feasibility may involve redesigning a project depending upon the field conditions. That is done without defeating the sense of *aram*.)

34.   Poison less mind is what *aram* is all about,
       Rest, exercises in pompous reeled out.

Being pristinely pure at heart is what *Aram* is all about. (Envy, greed, rage and harsh words are the four poisons which would make the mind impure.) Anything pompous to brand the endeavor with the use of light and show, strictly speaking, is not an act of *aram*. (Thiruvalluvar has used the word *akula* to denote any activity sans a pure mind. If *akula* is equivalent to the Sanskrit word *viyakulam* then it can be construed that all other acts minus pure mind are manifestations of a diseased mind.)

35.   Envy, greed, rage and harsh words – practice none
       Then *aram* loads in.

Following the path of *aram* means not feeling envious towards others, not being greedy, not losing oneself in rage and not using harsh and unkind and useless words towards others.

36.   Follow *aram* in all your deeds don't defer,
       When you die it is your unfailing deliverer.[32]

As soon as you start your life start carrying out your activities in all walks of life following the precincts of *aram*. Don't think you can carry on with your life without bothering about *aram* and later when you are old you can switch over to aram. You should follow right now. Since it is a maturation process, your soul following it right now is necessary. At the time of decline or adverse situations your soul

[32]   The quality of *aram* ingrained in your soul facilitates you to get into heaven.

evolved through your *aramic* acts all along will guide you like a good companion as to how go about your life. One may postpone aram to a later date only if he holds it as a religious requirement.

37. **P**alki rider and its bearer differ glaringly
     Don't say this is in tune with *aram*-ology.

The difference between a rider and bearer of a palki is vast. While the rider enjoys a sedan the bearer has to suffer heavy weight and slippery path. But don't say this is a demonstration of *aram*-ology. (In those days palki bearing is a job. A man rides in a palki and another bears it that's all nothing more nothing less.)

(According to the theory of dharma one's action called karma has consequence. Good karma leads to *punya* (merit) and bad karma leads to *pap* (demerit). A person's *punya* and *pap* from previous birth(s) have consequences in this birth. From this point of view we can interpret this couplet as 'palki rider enjoys a sedan riding because of his *punya* and the bearer suffers because of his *pap*.' This understanding of this couplet is excellently brought out by Prof. P.S.Sundaram[33] in his translation which is reproduced below.

Why talk of virtue's way? Only behold
The palki-bearer and the one who rides.   37

I am of the view that while Thiruvalluvar agrees that karma does exist its ways as explained in Hinduism is not acceptable to him. He simply sees karma as a net result of what has been learnt in the previous births appearing as a character or nature in the present birth. This nature or character is carried from one birth to the next as imprints on the soul.

What has been learned can be unlearned. To put it differently a human being can work on his soul to change its nature or character.

---

[33] Prof. Sundram, P.S. (1989, 1990).TIRUVALLUVAR THE KURAL. New Delhi: Penguin.

38.   On all days doing acts of *aram* with no day left,
       A rampart blocking the path of rebirth kept.

       Good acts following *aram* done without any respite serves like a stone
       blocking the path of rebirths.

39.   *Aram* alone brings pure joy.
       The rest is spurious and fame denied.

       Joy got out of acts invoking *aram* is real joy. Others are spurious and
       do not get social esteem either.

40.   What is needed to be acted upon is *aram*.
       What is to be avoided is acts of blame.

       Acts fit enough to carry are the ones which are *aram* based. Acts
       inviting blame should be dropped at any cost.

Skills to be learnt:

Always applying the precincts of *aram* in personal, social and
professional life. Envy, greed, rage and inappropriate language are
the four poisons to be avoided in our thoughts and acts (35). Keeping
the mind free from poisonous thoughts is another requirement for
following the precincts of *aram* (34).

Rationale:

Following *aram* in all of human activities – personal, professional
and social – is the best bet for a human being. Sometimes the
economic success or professional growth may be less spectacular but
what is achieved following *aram* is stable (31). Therefore it is a good
policy to follow *aram* in your life.

Coaching:

- ➤ Normally you get into trouble or end up behaving in poisonous ways because you go after where your mind takes you. You justify your position seeing it from one side that is the side commended by your wish. You rationalize your actions to appease your conscience. In other words you heavily invest yourself in what you want and do, becoming insensitive to the sane voice present in you which is nothing but the voice of *aram* or conscience.

- ➤ The technique to remove the four poisons (envy, greed, rage and contemptuous tongue) from your mind is keeping a watch over your mind. Thiruvalluvar can be taken as your auditor of *Aram*[34] and you could position him inside your mind. Let him audit all your thoughts and behaviour with reference to the poisonous thoughts and acts.

- ➤ You may take stock of the day before going to bed by giving an appointment to your Auditor of *Aram* and find out from him how you have fared that day. Without agitating calmly hear him and acknowledge what he reports and make a resolution that you will avoid the poisons pointed out by your auditor and go to sleep (34).

- ➤ Don't feel intimidated or guilty. Any lapse on a day is ok provided you regret for what mistake your have done and re decide to avoid the same next day.

- ➤ If you practice this every day, you will find your poisonous thoughts and acts becoming fewer and fewer.

- ➤ Sometimes there may be some sort of going back or relapse.

- ➤ However, don't give up thinking that living a life following the precincts of *aram* is beyond your capacity.

- ➤ Start trying afresh. It is human to fail. Failure doesn't mean one should abandon effort.

- ➤ Check your intention to act. Are they born out of envy, greed, rage and a contemptuous mind? If they are beware you are faulting on *aram* (35).

---

[34] Consult the legend given in page no.8 for finding out what constitutes *aram* according to Tiruvalluvar.

➢ Remember if you avoid failing on *aram* your longevity will increase (38).

➢ Remember the pleasures achieved following the precincts of *aram* only are true pleasures others are not (39).

➢ Remember human being has a right to act according to the precincts of *aram*. He doesn't have any other right (40) in a civilized society.

5

The Institution of Home

(A soul fulfilling life in Home)

41. Householder is one, to the connected three[35]
    With practices best, lends support you see.

    The institution of Home supports the other three institutions of the
    society namely governance, education and commerce.

42. Recluse, hungry and diminished,
    Householder holds them cherished.

    The sages, the hungry people and persons who are on decline are the
    three sets of people the institution of family supports.

43. Ancestors[36],God, relatives and home
    To their upkeep the home remains warm.

---

[35] A house hold is an institution. It supports the other three institutions namely
education governance and trade.

[36] Carrying out anniversary oblations in memory of ancestors. The Tamil word used
in the place of ancestors is 'thenpulaththaar' i.e., persons living in the southern
land. Tamil scholars like Devaneya Pavanar are of the opinion that since the
sunken Lemuria continent ended the lives of millions the dead in general were
referred by the word 'thenpulaththaar' by the authors of those days.

Apart from the above three, institution of family also supports the religious rites to ancestors and Gods and services to guests, relatives and its own members.

44.   Fearing blame if sharing food is made as a heritage
      Life's journey never finds a shortage.

If the household makes it as a tradition to earn, fearing blameful remarks and criticisms and share the earnings with the needy it has no chance of going bankrupt.

45.   If love and *arm* are dispensed,
      Domestic institution's character and use are realized.

If love prevails in a family and it carries out its activities following the precincts of *aram* the purpose of home as an institution of love and character is well served.

46.   If virtuous path[37] guides life's purpose,
      What gain is achieved in other traverse?[38]

If a head of the institution of family conducts his business of running the household strictly holding to the precincts of *aram* that is enough. What additional benefits does he get in other walks of life? (Other walks refers to renunciation and tapas.)

47.   If a householder runs his home the way it should be
      He is supreme to other effort makers[39] that be.

---

[37]   Virtuous paths means carrying out the duties of a household following the path of *aram*.

[38]   Other traverses refer to other walks of life especially the career of a sage.

[39]   Effort makers refers to those sages who undertake severe penance or tapas to reach heaven.

If a householder runs his home following the two mottos of love and *aram* he is far ahead in his journey to reach heaven than those seers who make great efforts in penance to reach heaven.

48. **If** a home remains *aram* guided with best practices
It has the same penance qualities of tapas.

The effort of a householder who uses the best practices to put in place an *aram* based institution of family and the effort of a *Tapasya*[40] fall in the same level in the milieu of penance and its benefits.

49. *Aram* is the sine qua non of domestic life.
It is more welcome-sum if it doesn't earn other's[41] gripe

While *aram* is the central guide of a household's life it will be good if the household doesn't attract negative criticism from others for omissions and commissions. (The members of the household should act politically correct.)

50. Following *aram* if a great life is lived
Among the gods at sky the individual is held.

A great life is said to have been lived if a householder's life is conducted by the principles of *aram*, animated through best practices. The world will hold such people on par with gods at sky.

Skills to be learnt:

➢ Ability to live a householder's life based on love and precincts of *aram*.

---

[40] Tapasya is a Sanskrit word meaning a man practicing tapas or penance. The word tapas is already excepted into English.

[41] 'Others', refers to those who are competent to find fault.

Rationale:

- ➢ A home is the basic institution of humanity. Apart from its members it has services to offer to people who are their near and dear and it offers service to other institutions viz., governance, education and commerce. It also supports and upholds certain traditions like thanks-giving to ancestors and help people involved in religious services. It is as rigorous as the life of a man who undertakes penance. The basic principle which guides a household is compassionate love and following ways of *aram* in carrying out the daily chores and responsibilities of life. The householder should not be mistaken as living a selfish life. He supports several others thorough the Institution namely his family. It is as good a path as other paths for achieving the company of God. Therefore every effort should be made to run a household in the fittest manner.

Technique:

- ➢ The institution of family in Thiruvalluvar's days had duties for people belonging to other walks of life (41,42and43).
- ➢ Couplet number 44 gives the purposes of the institution of home or household: dispensing love and following *aram*.
- ➢ By providing succor to the dependents the family members express love and develop the ability to show the same to fellow human beings in all walks of life in a community.
- ➢ In the present day world especially with so much importance given to individualization and the onset of globalization hardly any community life exists. That means the ability to give love and live a life of aram is hardly learnt by the members of the family from the institution of family. (Is this a sweeping statement?)
- ➢ Out of ten couplets two couplets (44&45) say a family life lived through giving love and carrying out its business following *aram* will usher its members to God's land.
- ➢ Two more couplets (47&48) say a family life well lived is equivalent to living the life of an ascetic as far as accruing benefits are concerned. Remember an ascetics aim is to reach heaven.

- ➤ Since modern families are so preoccupied they can not receive the people who are in need of help like students, retired parents in law or support the activities of religion they can find out different ways to show love and carry out their activities following *aram*.

- ➤ A modern family can go out and give expression to its love and *aram*. For example a family and its members may make a policy decision that they will regularly visit a day care center and support inmates in various ways. Each member can adopt an inmate or few and take total care of them. This will give scope for expressing one's love and in due course of time each member will take care to infuse *aram* in what they do. In this context the relevant principles of *aram* may be equity and compassion.(33)

- ➤ Countries spend lot of money on treating depression. Depression is accentuated by loneliness very often leading to suicide. Supporting and creating a sense of belongingness and inspiring the youth who suffer from depression can avert many a suicide. A family can attach itself with agencies working with various groups and offer whatever help it can.

- ➤ The main idea is that the family should create a forum for its members to show love and receive love and carry out their activities in an honest and virtuous manner.

6

Goodness of Wife

(The good qualities of a good wife)

51. Possessing skills to brand a great home,
    Good wife lives within husband's income.

    A good wife possesses apt skills needed for running a great home.
    She upholds the brand of her home. Furthermore she has the ability
    to manage the home within the income of her husband/household.

52. In a wife if vision for great home is nil,
    Other glory, in spite life is null.

    A wife may possess other glorious attributes. But life in her household
    would be barren unless she possesses great vision-based home making
    strengths.

53. What does a household lack if wife is greatly skilled
    What riches stay if wife is unskilled?

    Will a home significantly lack anything if the wife possesses great
    home making skills in managing the nuances of a home? In the same
    vein can one say a home possesses as anything at all if the wife doesn't
    possess those skills? (Financial difficulties abounding, a family may
    not survive by strategic skills alone. But it is also true that great home
    managing skills can mitigate the financial troubles to a great extent.)

54.   What better pride than a woman to be found
       If in her fidelity she is hard wound?

       If the wife has the moral determination to be loyal to her husband
       there is no better reason for a home/husband to be proud of.

55.   Gets up meditating not on God[42] but on her husband
       Rain pours on her command.

       A plain word to word translation of the couplet would read like this:
       If a wife after getting up from bed offers prayers to her husband she
       gets enough power to command the clouds to pour rain.
       This couplet has created some stir in the mind of rationalists as well
       as feminists. Two questions arise: Has Tiruvalluvar kept the position
       of women one step below men and how can a human being make
       the clouds shed rain. The answer for both the questions lies in the
       word 'thozhuluthu' That word can be understood as meditating/
       concentrating instead of worshiping or praying only. Then it would
       mean as – instead of meditating/concentrating on god she meditates/
       concentrates on her husband. Why she should meditate or concentrate
       her thoughts on her husband? She should because it is a good way to
       renew her love and commitment to her partner. This devotion of her
       towards him would be reciprocated by her husband. It is not very
       difficult to imagine that anyone who has a supporter feels powerful
       and resourceful that the one who has none to fall upon. To give the
       reader an idea of how powerful one would feel perhaps Thiruvalluvar
       using a poetic surprise says the power is good enough to command the
       clouds to rain. Thiruvalluvar has used such poetic surprises throughout
       his treatise to drive home a point. By way of an example couplet
       number 484 can be cited. It means 'If a person acts in an opportune

---

42   The Tamil word 'thozhuthu' can be conceived (in addition to mean as prayer) as
      meditation or concentration. Perhaps the Kural tries to say that meditating or
      concentrating on her husband's love and support the wife feels powerful. And to
      impress on the reader about the power she feels the poet says it is good enough
      to bring rain.

time and place it is possible even if he wants to conquer the whole universe.' Here again it is a poetic surprise by way of emphasizing the use of opportune time and place for achieving a goal. There is also an evidence in the treatise itself about how Thiruvalluvar has conceived the word *thozhuthu*. Look at couplet number 1030.

56. Protects herself, nourishes the strengths of her husband,
     Upholds family's' worthy name, wife tirelessly makes it grand.

A good wife plays the roles of protector of herself regarding her wellbeing, a facilitator and supporter of her husband in all his activities nourishing his strengths and a protector of the name and fame of the family (She is the brand ambassador for the family.). In short she carries out the various chores of a family as an institution following the four precincts of *aram* and compassion and is tireless in these tasks.

57. What purpose gates and locks for woman precipitate?
     Self-restraint does capacitate.

Securing her behind iron doors will not serve the purpose of preventing her from losing self-restraint and crossing boundaries. Any amount of restrictions put on her will not work. However, her self-willed- restraint will take care of issues of chastity around her.

58. **If** a woman gets a husband who is great
     A place in heaven she gets.[43]

---

[43] A translation by P.S.Sundaram (referred elsewhere) according with that of Ellis is as follows: The woman who gets her husband's love // Gains the joys of heaven. The noted Tamil Interpreter Parimeelazhahar interprets it something like, 'If a woman shows reverence to her husband she will be honoured by at God's world.' These interpretations have earned a curse to Thiruvalluvar at the hands of feminists of course rightly. I feel these interpreters have done a great disservice to Thiruvalluvar. I expect after reading the new interpretation given her things will get settled.

If a husband possess great homemaking qualities and swears that he would spare no effort in taking his family to newer and newer heights and acts resolutely (1021) his wife feels fully encouraged. As a result the best comes out of her too (56). Such interactional experience between two individuals is soul evolving. Therefore a women who comes to possess a great husband would attain heavenly abode or heavenly honor.

59. If a wife hasn't earned social esteem
     Her husband's gait wouldn't have a bull like steam.

If a wife does not take care of the natural stakeholders of a home and earn their appreciation her husband would not be able to walk like a bull in the presence of his ridiculers.

60. Greatness is indicated by the household's health.
     Great offspring is another spring of that wealth.

A great home is evidenced by the presence of wellbeing. Its great offspring are the important symbols of the wellbeing of the family.

Skills to be learnt:

- ➢ Three skills (strengths) may be mentioned mainly based on the couplets numbering 51, 54 and 56. They are:
- ➢ installing in the wife the notion of playing the role of a joint CEO of a great home,
- ➢ wife and husband strictly avoiding extra marital relationship,
- ➢ wife having enough energy to play the roles expected of her in a family.

Rationale:

- ➢ Wife is an important asset for a family if she possesses the great qualities and skills to manage her household within the income of the husband/of the household. If those skills are absent the presence of other skills do not have much value.

➢ Second, it is very essential for the wife to remain faithful to her husband. This is possible if she develops right attitude towards spousal compatibility and willfully determined to remain loyal to her husband.

➢ Third, wife is responsible to maintain the brand image of the family among whom the family is connected.

➢ Fourth, wife should take enough care to maintain physical and mental health to run the household.

Coaching:

➢ A list prepared by husband and wife and parents-in-laws would inform what are the strengths already present in the wife and what are to be gathered. For example mothering the children need to be learnt because some dogmatic unhelpful beliefs may prevail in the family regarding child rearing. Thiruvalluvar has specifically insisted this skill in another place (69). The couplet concerned gives the goal post for a mother in a household in this regard.

➢ The mission statements for running the family may be made and followed. A periodical review and updating may be carried out.

➢ The problem of infidelity may be confronted by looking into the sex life of the couple.(54,57)

➢ Things become murky and later unmanageable only because of the approach of closing one's eyes and wishing away the various possibilities on the side of his or her spouse.

➢ Accepting the reality that unless one is extremely careful the chances to go wrong always exist and only protection from going astray is his or her spouse.

➢ Keeping this in mind a spouse should come forward to share. A spouse will do it if she or he is confident that no inescapable opinion will be formed based on the disclosure and a spouse can expect support from him or her to keep off from any wrong relationships.

➢ This is possible only when the couple accept that humans are essentially fallacious and the area of sex is no exception and the best way to come out of a mistake is to feel really sad about some wrong done or contemplated and deciding not to do it again keeping the spouse informed about it.

➢ Another cognate that confuses the mind which is set on infidelity is the thought that sex between consenting adults and remarriages in search of compatible spousal relationship including sexual compatibility is part of an evolving journey to find an ideal relationship. This is a myth. Rarely such things are achieved. Even if it is achieved the cost the society has to pay to support such idealism is beyond its means. If marriages break on account of incompatibility the worst sufferers are the children. Children raised by single parents, especially during the formative age are at a great disadvantage. Children in such broken homes live under permanent shock and develop behavioral disorder(s) in schools and later on develop into human beings not fully equipped to meet the needs of the society. Society is made to accept them and burden itself to make for the lacunae they create.

➢ Against the thought of better psychological and sexual compatibility a couple should erect the value of creating useful human resources. This value gives them a strong reason for holding together against any odds.

➢ There are two goal posts suggested by Thiruvalluvar to a father and a mother. For a father the goal post is: he should do everything in his capacity and command to see to that the offspring of the family is developed into a fine human resource fit enough to play an important role in the society.(67)

➢ For a mother the goal post is: develop her offspring as a *sandrone*. A *sandrone* is one who has the five important attributes of love, humility, benevolence (obligation to fellow citizens), empathy and truthfulness. (69)

➢ Sometimes a couple may feel discouraged to undertake such endeavor. They may say 'We don't have the parenting instinct.' They cannot escape saying so. After all, their life is made on the comforts provided by the human resources produced by parents who were very responsible. Therefore if some couple chooses not to procreate for whatever reason (other than serious medical reasons) they behave like someone who does not have a sense of gratitude. Yes! They enjoy the comforts of the society provided by the carefully created human resources whereas they care not to replenish the society with that kind of resources. They are ungrateful and irresponsible indeed! This thought is the best antidote for the debilitating thoughts around fidelity, not marrying at all or not having children. (62,63)

➤ Regarding maintaining a proper physical fitness to run the family a woman should take steps to have a high level of energy. Quality food, adequate rest with peace of mind and relaxation coupled with good work out and good techniques to de stress as and when needed are some of the prescriptions in this regard.(56)

➤ One main problem which saps all the energy and spoils moods and initiatives is the negative feedback a women gets from her dear and near. While it is good that she receives positive feedback it is not an absolute necessity that she always gets it. She can live amidst negative criticism if she refuses to take the criticism as an inescapable condition for her to remain happy. She can be happy irrespective of the negative criticism if she learns to separate out the criticisms into useful parts requiring some correctional acts on her part and useless parts which do not require any involvement at all.

➤ The contribution towards the maintenance of the house hold is the responsibility of both husband and wife especially when the wife also works. Cultures world over are male dominancy supporters. However, this cannot go for long. Many marriages break because the husband insists on a better status for him. Second the financial contribution is also uneven. Let wives be lenient towards husbands. Let husbands do 40% of physical work at home if wife also works or else 20% if wife is not an office-goer.

➤ Wife should focus her attention on her husband totally and permit herself to belong to him as she would do with God and enjoy the power of such belongingness (55).

➤ Wife has three duties: self-protection through good food and exercise, nursing her husband at times of need and doing everything to the best of her ability to protect the ethos of the institution of the family. She should be a person of impeccable integrity to uphold the brand name of the institution which solely falls on her shoulders (56).

➤ If a wife lives an illustrious life as envisaged so far, she will reach the abode of God (58).

➤ Remember if the wife faults on any of the above aspects and the institution of family earns disrepute because of it the members of the family especially the husband will lose his name and fame among members of the community he belongs to (59).

➤ Wife as a mother has to ensure that the offspring develops as a constructively contributing human resource for the society (60) and the husband is responsible for imparting skills to the offspring according to his/her potentials.

7
The Gift of Offspring

(The gift of offspring)

61.   Offspring of high intellect are commendable
      No other blessing is as creditable.

The best outcome for a family is to grow its offspring in such a way that that he or she develops as an intellect good enough for a competitive and thriving society. There can be no better objective for a family.

62.   For seven births evil doesn't afflict,
      For the household which brings blame-free offspring into effect.

Parenting offspring in such a way they grow into fine human resources free from blames is a two way process which brings benefits both to the children and to the parents. By their selfless service the soul of the parents mature so much that it can keep the man and woman away from blame-inviting activities for next seven reincarnations.

63.   Offspring are parent's axe to grind,
      Therefore what they aim and work will be found.

The offspring of a household is at the custody of their parents. Whether the offspring would develop into useful resource depends how the parents parent them.

64. The gruel stirred by offspring's little finger,
    Is sweeter than nectar.

    The gruel in which the little fingers of the offspring played is tastier than nectar for a parent who enjoys his/her child's company. (The emotional coaching of the offspring is a dual process in which the parents enjoy the company of their children while the children are also experiencing the same.)

65. Offspring's touch is body's pleasure;
    Babble, ear's sweet fare.

    Children with bare body[44] embracing their parents who are also bare gives lots of kinesthetic joy to parents. Similarly the babbling of children is a treat to the ears of the parents.

66. Flute and *yazh*[45] are sweet say some
    Baby's babble they did not consume[46]

    Some people claim that flute and '*yazh*' are very sweet to the ears. It is sure they are people, who have not heard the babbling of their children.

67. Best help a father extends to a son,
    Is making him best amongst the don(s)[47]

---

[44] The couplet says, '*mei theednal*' meaning touching the body which I have explained as 'embracing bare body' because only such an expression will bring in the kinaesthetic joy. However, with the scandals of child porno so rampant in the present day society I am afraid I may receive a negative criticism.

[45] Yazh is an ancient instrument similar to violin.

[46] 'Consume' is used in the sense that ears consume the baby talk.

[47] A don is a person playing an important role in a body of learned people.

The duty of a father is to help his son to be ahead of others in a forum of scholars.

68.   Offspring excelling parents
      Is good for all the earthly beings.

If offspring are better accomplished than parents it is good for the people of the mother land. (Tiruvalluvar perhaps hints at the possibility of some parents developing envy with their children when they excel them in their accomplishments. He counsels the parents that such thing is unwelcome because when every successive generation beats the previous one the land benefits by way of new innovations, methods and technologies and machineries.)

69.   "Your son is a *sandrone*"[48]
      Hearing this mother's joy excels that when the son was born.

If mother hears that his son is a *sandrone* her joy exceeds that of the day on which he was born.

70.   The return gift a son owes his dad,
      'What a hard work his dad has made!' is heard.

The gratitude a son could return to his father is that he should excel both in his emotional maturity and academic maturity incurring this accolade: "Oh! How much his father would have labored to develop such a fine human?"

Skills to be learnt:

➢   Parenting methods for fostering emotional maturity and academic excellence in the offspring.

---

[48]   A *sandrone* is one who has the five important qualities of love, humility, benevolence, empathy and truthfulness.

Rationale:

> Thiruvalluvar clearly says the responsibility of developing the offspring into excellent humans in terms of emotional maturity and academic excellence/skill impartment lie with the parents. Couplet number 63 brings this out. He also fixes the goal post for that in couplet number 67. He is quick to add that every generation should surpass the previous one in mental abilities and creativity and the parents should see it from the point of view of larger picture of the entire humanity benefiting from it rather than from the narrower perspective of what they will loose with their wards (68). Similarly the job of developing good values in the offspring is left to the mother. Mother is slated to make a sandrone of the offspring. (A *sandrone* is one who has the five important qualities of love, humility, benevolence (social entrepreneurship/social obligation), empathy and truthfulness embed in his personality.)

Coaching:

> Let the parents be very clear about one thing. Their children are their responsibility. Whether they would turn out into great human resources or useless problem-persons depends on how they parent them (63).

> To make the children to mature emotionally the parents should give them quality time by participating with them as if they are a little grown up children at the same time modeling the behavior they want their children to pick up (64, 65 and 66).

> By giving a quality time to your children you are demonstrating your love in words, feelings and action. This inculcates a sense of belongingness in the child which in turn fosters hope and trust in them towards the world. The child is now free to test its initiatives.

> Parenting is a well-researched topic with plenty of inputs available in documented form. If needed the parents may also undergo suitable training. The money and time is worth in view of great benefits the parents would be able to reap later in their life when they badly need support from their children.

- ➤ It is specifically the duty of the father to educate the son and daughter (67). He should have proper financial plans to achieve this.

- ➤ Let not the dad feel competitive with his wards. Instead let him enjoy the higher reaches they accomplish. After all they should know that the growth of the society depends upon such overreaching human resources of the world (68).

- ➤ It is mother who is more suitable to teach *sandranmai* (love + humility + benevolence + empathy + truth) to her wards (69). Gandhi has specifically stated in his autobiography that he decided not to tell lie after hearing his mother narrating the story of king Harischandra. Harischandra who was made to undergo unbearable sufferings starting with losing his kingdom refused to tell a lie in lieu of a paltry sum to pay for the cremation of his son i.e., even at the prospect of his son not getting a descent cremation the king refused to tell a lie!

- ➤ It is the duty of offspring to earn good name to their parents by what they accomplish (70).

8

Love

(A disposition of love towards family members and dear and near)

71. Is there a bolt to hide love's flow?
    Filmy tears and redden eyes of the affectionate show.

    Love cannot be hidden between those who are mutually interested. The eyes covering themselves in watery films glow when someone meets another in whom he or she is interested even if she or he doesn't want to show their love openly for some reason or the other.

72. Loveless amass all for their share,
    Loving ones even their bones spare.

    Loveless persons amass everything for themselves. On the other hand, people who have love at heart can lend even their lives to others.

73. Relationship of the soul with love
    Operates through relationship with body.

    The relationship between soul and love is similar to the relationship between body and soul. The soul needs a body to live. Similarly if there is no love in the person in whose body it lives the soul cannot express itself as a result of which the maturation of the soul would seriously get retarded.

74.   Love creates interest first,
        Interest creates spontaneous friendship next.

        Interest in a hither to unknown person arises out of pure love and
        matures into friendship even in the absence of deliberate plan.

75.   **T**he blissful acclaim to come next
        Is seeded through love at present.

        Those who dispense love in the present life will reap heavenly bliss
        in the afterlife.

76.   *Aram* alone, hold some, derives support from love,
        They know not, bravery too has a support in love.

        It is a mistaken notion that acts of *aram* alone are patronized by love.
        Heroic deeds of destroying evils also are born out of love.

77.   Sun scorches the boneless,
        Aram does the same to the loveless.

        The boneless organisms suffer at sun. Similarly the sense of *aram*,
        which lives in the heart of dear and near and those who matter in
        one's life and profession, will get activated and the man who commits
        loveless acts will be taken to task.

78.   **L**ove less life, a desert tree in wither
        Sending a shoot on a favorable weather.

        A person may live without showing and receiving love evidencing
        that life without love is possible. But that life is feeble and lifeless like
        a tree born on the humus in the cracks of a rock. Whenever there
        is a rain the tree may send a shoot only to wither soon. Obviously
        it cannot be said that the tree lives up to its engrained capacities or
        full potentials.

79. What purpose external organs serve?
    If in the soul love doesn't live.

    If love is absent in a man his soul would

80. Through love soul is expressed by humans
    Loveless are skin wrapped bones.

    The soul manifests through love. Therefore if love is absent in a human he or she is nothing but a bundle of skin wrapped bones.

Skills to be learnt:

➤ The ability to show love and receive love.

Rationale:

➤ Thiruvalluvar categorically declares that love is a fundamental requirement for the soul to evolve. Soul needs love as much as it needs body to exist. Therefore it is essential we learn to give and receive love. Thiruvalluvar makes the startling statement: soul's relationship with love is as integrated as its relationship with body.(73)

Coaching:

➤ To show love to your spouse the first requirement is getting rid of the resistance in you towards him or her. The resistance comes mostly because she/he fails your expectations. The moment a consumer raises an issue a good marketer tries to understand and meet her expectations within the elasticity her business provides. On the contrary if he should resist the consumer senses it without fail and the result is obvious. Same idea applies in relationship also. If your spouse is having bad feelings you must see it as a good opportunity to strengthen your love and affection to him or her by attending to it by giving him/her three important products of love: your time, energy and money.

- ➤ Yes giving love means giving your time, labor and money when needed by the other person and giving it whole heartedly – one of them, two of them or all of them.
- ➤ The other skills needed apart from willingly giving time, labor and money are unconditional acceptance, forgiving/seeking pardon, refined listening and sweet communication.
- ➤ All these skills are emphasized by Valluvar in different chapters which are being considered under appropriate chapters.
- ➤ Here he says, "Do not hide your love. Your body reacts before you. Watch it and act after sanitizing the love feelings of their self-serving agenda like self-pity or want to look good in the eyes of others or feel good or great or as a ploy (71).
- ➤ Remember love is something your offer to others without keeping anything exclusively for yourself (72). Differentiate this behavior from the gullibility of suffering for the sake of a person who might exploit you.
- ➤ Giving love and receiving love is rejuvenating and tremendously increasing the well being of the giver and receiver (78).
- ➤ If you declare any one is eligible for receiving your love you will find yourself developing interest on unexpected persons. They or those aspects of the world are the best choices to give your love (74).
- ➤ It is told that those who give unconditional love reach heaven (75).
- ➤ Love is guided by *aram*. Principally speaking, *aram* is upholding equity. It is for this reason an urge rises in you to act heroically. Do not douse it. Act on that. Know it as an act of *aram* (76).
- ➤ Without love your life is like that of a plant in a desert which cannot live up to its full potential. (You will be afflicted with a number of psychologically created but bodily based diseases. Diabetes, ulcer, migraine are some of the diseases you can expect to afflict you if you don't show love and affection to at least half-a-dozen people or to one or two social causes.) (78).

9

Hospitality

(Hospitality towards guests)

81. Family and its maintenance has one target,
     Hosting guests achieves it.

     The objective of maintaining a household is to carry out in a religious
     manner the objective of taking care of the visiting guests.

82. With the guest remaining in the outer court
     Consuming even an elixir is an undesirable act.

     Don't eat /drink even a potion rich enough to give eternal life without
     sharing it with your guest who is at your home at that time.

83. He who feeds the daily stream of guests
     Never suffers a scarcity of inputs.

     Never a household is depleted of its resources on account of feeding
     its guests. (This might sound unreasonable to you. It would reduce
     significantly if you consult couplets 84, 85 and 86.)

84. With smiles on his face he feeds his guest
     God of fortune adorns his house with full heart.

     Goddess of fortune whole heartedly adorns the house of the person
     who feeds his guests to their hearts' content by willingly and

religiously serving them. (For a full understanding please consult couplet 85.)

85.   **N**ourishes the guest and the remains he eats,
       Should he sow his fields?

First let us see the literal meaning of the couplet. It means that "Is it necessary that farmer, who derives contentment in eating what is remaining after feeding his guest Now please read the following to understand the riddle in this couplet and in 83, 84 and85. The word sow stands for all the agricultural activities to be carried out by a farmer in his field. In couplet number 1039 Thiruvalluvar has used a similar technique where he uses the Tamil word '*sellan.*' The word means 'the farmer who does not visit his land.' It is obvious that mere visiting would not do. One has to work. Therefore the word *sellan* stands for someone who doesn't work in his field.

In the present couplet the word sow means that a farmer who feeds his guests whole heartedly need not carry out all the agricultural activities himself. The men and women fed by him may come forward to work in his farm so that he need not carry out the agricultural activities by himself alone. In the light of this explanation the couplet could be translated as:

Nourishes the guest and the remains he eats

Will he by himself alone need to tend his fields?

I am emboldened to say so because in Coimbatore, Tamil Nadu, there was a practice among small farmers until as nearer as 60 to 70 years back to barter work. Farmers belonging to a locality would gather in farm 'A' on day number one and finish the needed work and then proceed to farm 'B' thus completing all the works of all the farms. In such a scenario treating the fellow farmers as guests and feeding them earnestly would result in their whole hearted cooperation. Is it not? In some parts of Tamil Nadu even today we have a tradition of people organizing feasts called *moichoru*. *Moichoru* is organized by families during times of dire need of financial help. Guests who enjoy a warm reception and treat would leave some money below the plantain leaves on which food is served. This is how goddess of fortune lives in the house of the person who is a great host.

86. Bids farewell to his departing guest,
    Waits on incoming, he is welcome at heaven's feast.

    He who continuously occupies himself in feeding guests is a welcome guest among divines.

87. No other investments has such returns here,
    Hosting guests is likened with sages' sphere.

    The bliss that must auger from such feeding is tantamount to great penance as for as heavenly dividends are concerned.

88. "Fed our guests wrecking ourselves but received no benefit,"
    Guys saying this didn't have religious commitment.

    Those who lost everything due to hosting guests are those who did it for a trade-off, (without the religiosity needed for such work,) the trade-off being good fortune visiting them as in the case of another genuine person who feeds his guests whole heartedly and with religious fervor.

89. Among the possessions if hospitality is not one it is stupidity of the first order.
    That was the case of stupidity kissed.

    If a person who has the means to feed his guests decline to do so it shows his culture of poverty. Some idiots do have such disposition.

90. When smelled *anicham*[49] loses its shape
    With a wry and cold look guest loses sprit.

---

[49] *Anicham* is a flower plant which has become extinct. It is a tender flower. Warm breath is said to whither it.

The guests are so vulnerable that they become thoroughly dispirited at the smallest indifference shown to them.

Skills to be learnt:

> To develop the attitude to willingly feed the guests who visit your home and enjoying doing so.

Rationale:

> Thiruvalluvar has allotted one full chapter for commending hospitality as an important part of a family life. Perhaps in those days in the absence of commercial eateries a social obligation for families existed to provide boarding and lodging to the travelers. Modern day equivalence for this may be the paid guest system. Apart from this there are a number of opportunities for families to take care of visitors/relatives. Therefore a conducive attitude to take care of guests need to be cultivated in every one. Taking care of guests whole heartedly earns a place in heaven.

Coaching:

The following advocacy is derived from the couplets:

> "Imbibe the spirit that feeding guests taking utmost care to make them enjoy their stay with you is not an option but an objective for the institution of family. (81//88/90)
> Never eat even an elixir yielding immortality without sharing it with a guest around. (82)
> Make note of this: life of the family as an institution which served well its guests will never suffer for want of resources. (83)
> Goddess of fortune would gladly come and live in such homes which show good hospitality. (84)
> If you are a good host several good things happen to you without much effort from your side (85)

- ➢ If rigorous hospitality is practiced it is equivalent to undertaking great tapas and hence earns heaven for the hosts concerned (87&86). (Tapas is a means to attain heaven.)
- ➢ Beware hoping for a place in heaven if you show hospitality in a sham manner you will only lose your wealth. (88)
- ➢ By nature if you are not inclined to entertain guests may be it reflects a culture of poverty running in you/your household. (89)
- ➢ Make note of this: guests are very sensitive to indifference." (90)

10

Speaking Sweet Words

(Speaking sweet words in a cool manner)

91. **S**weet words soaked in kindness and free from deceit,
     Men of true perspective[50] posit.

     Words which are kind and sweet and also free from deceit are used
     by those who have achieved the perspective that only God is real.
     This world and all of its objects are illusory.

92. An altruistic and hearty gift is bettered,
     By the sweet words across the board uttered.

     Speaking kind words across board is a better act than even giving
     whole heartedly. There can be dearth of resource making it impossible
     to give but for uttering sweet words no impediment exists. Therefore
     not speaking kind words doesn't have any excuse.

93. Sit across him and look sweetly at his eyes right?
     It is *aram* to speak sweet words from the heart next.

     Speaking sweet words from your heart sitting or standing before
     the person with whom you want to speak, looking sweetly at his or

---

[50] Tiruvalluvar uses the Tamil word *semporul* meaning true perspective. This word
      is used in couplet number 358 also. True awareness or perspective means this
      world and its materials are illusory objects. Only Real or True Object is God.

her eyes is the best practice with regard to, 'how to talk to another person.' Having no barrier in between and being fully present to the person is achieved by this practice.

94. Painful poverty reduces for those,
    Who for anyone, joyful words pose.

Pain inflicting poverty doesn't afflict you if you speak kind words to anyone and everyone. (This may sound impossible. Perhaps with such an approach you may enjoy the good will of your friends and others out of which help could come alleviating your difficulties to a great extent.)

95. For a humble person sweet words are jewels
    Other jewels on him are mere 'dwells'.

If you are a humble person it is an attractive addition for you to use sweet words. Other attributes which you may have are not in the same league.

96. Vice declines, new heights *aram* claims,
    If, goodness seeking, sweet word primes.

In search of wellness to all if humanity speaks goodness in one voice evil will decline to the ascendance of ethical goodness across humanity. The couplet can also mean the same at an individual level.

97. Goodness and civility are yielded
    When fruitful and courteous words are fielded.

If words which are useful to the listener are spoken in a courteous manner it not only inculcates similar manners in the listener but also creates a goodness around them.

98.   If sweet words bereft of meanness are spoken
       In the present and next birth good is given.

       Speaking words which are free from meanness yields good at the
       present reincarnation and in the next. How? Speaking words which
       are free from meanness lifelong helps the soul to evolve in the present
       life. An evolved soul takes the quality to the next birth and sports it
       bringing in several good outcomes.

99.   He witnesses kind words leads to good, yields
       Then what a person is he, harsh word molds?

       When a person observes that good things happen by speaking good
       words why at all does he choose to speak harsh words?

100.   Kind words not minded hard words mouthed,
       Likens leaving ripe fruits raw ones gulped.

       When you have an option to use kind and sweet words speaking hard
       words is like rushing to grab raw fruits when ripe ones are available
       in plenty.

Skills to be learnt:

➢   Ability to use sweet, genuine and goodness yielding useful words
      with anyone.

Rationale:

➢   Thiruvalluvar asks through couplet 99 that when a person observes
      day in and day out that speaking sweet words yields sweet outcomes
      why does it happen that he chooses to use harsh words. It is true,
      speaking sweet words has its own advantage in interpersonal
      relationship. Sweet words convey that you have no issue with your
      communicatee as a person but you may have some issue with his
      behavior (in case if you have one). This sets a good augury to the

conversation. Moreover couplet number ninety eight says words devoid of baseness would usher in heaven and life here on the earth also will be a happier one. Therefore it is a sill that must be learnt.

Coaching:

The technique is behavioral cum cognitive. The following advocacy is derived from the couplets.

"For speaking sweet words with a touch of coolness and without any deceitful motive the attitude needed is: even if you are not in a position to help someone, speak to him cordially (91&92).

> ➤ Sit across, look at the eyes of the other person and speak sweet words from your heart (93).
> ➤ Sit or stand before him or her at a reasonable distance and speak (93).
> ➤ Don't stare, gaze or look deep into the eyes as though trying to dig something or look beyond the eyes of the other person (93).
> ➤ A friendly and courteous look informing the other person, 'at this moment of time you are the only agenda I have,' would suffice (93).
> ➤ This physical closeness and a friendly look at the person at his or her eyes increases receptivity (93).
> ➤ Speaking from the heart need not always be totally revealing everything to the person with whom you are involved in a conversation. It simply means whatever you speak shall be authentic. Censoring something for some mutually useful reasons is ok and is not violative of authentic speak (93).
> ➤ Your words should reflect equity and they should not invite blame. They should deliver a good use for the listener (97).
> ➤ Take care to see that your words are not degrading the person even when you are to use words condemning his or her behavior (98).
> ➤ Remember this evidence always: Sweet words yield sweet outcome. Even in a trying situation they will reduce the heat to a great extent and because of that the opportunities for good things to happen increase (99).

> ➤ A feedback from someone who is genuinely interested in you on how you come when you speak and on what you speak as per the above guidelines, will be very helpful in honing this skill of, 'Sweet Speak'.

> ➤ Lastly but most importantly remember the fact using sweet words with a genuine concern for the listener is an exercise which evolves your soul (98)."

11

Gratitude

(Being grateful towards those who helped us)

101. A help with no obligation cannot be repaid
     Even if the earth and heaven are coupled.

     If someone helps us to whom we have not offered help earlier that
     help cannot be repaid with heaven and earth put together (because
     the repaying situation and the original situation in which the help
     received can never be made equal).

102. A timely help may be small but it's worth
     Is greater than the earth.

     A small help given in a most needed time is larger in its usefulness
     or value than giving the whole world (at another time with no such
     criticality/urgency/need).

103. A helper helps with no eye on return benefits
     Ocean is small if it is weighed for its goodness

     The worth of a clean help (with no aim of making a kill later) would
     make that of a sea smaller.

104. Help received may equal a minor millet,
     Appreciator equals it as a tree of palm got.

Help may be as tiny as a grain of millet. Those who are able to appreciate its contributory caliber in a process across the time will hold it as big as a palm tree (a tree belonging to palmyra family).

105. The size of a help is not decided physically
      Rather by the receiver psychologically.

How much gratitude a help would evoke depends not on the size of the help but on the help receiver's sense of gratitude and good nature.

106. Neither forget a pure friend,
      Nor the friend who from hardship did defend.

Do not forget a friendship of a person whose heart is pure. Similarly don't relinquish the friendship of someone who offered a timely help in the past.

107. In a clan he who wiped adversity,
      His friendship is remembered in all seven posterity.

Generations to come families will remember the help rendered by someone in the past in removing the adversity to one of its ancestors.

108. To forget good received is not good,
      But forgetting a hurt instantly is rather one should.

It is not desirable to forget a benefit received from someone. Whereas it is desirable to forgive someone instantly and forget the evil he or she has done.

109. The pain of a deadly hurt vanishes,
      When a good deed by him memory cherishes.

A person may inflict deadly hurt. The best way to forgive him and get rid of the painful memory is recalling with a sense of gratitude something good he has done to you on another occasion.

110. Killing any good can be redeemed
Reparation is impossible when gratitude is killed.

One can make amends for discarding a good thing that was in his possession. But nothing can be done in the case where the individual has forgotten the good thing someone has done to him due to his ingratitude.

Skills to be learnt:

> Two skills to be picked up in this chapter are: (1) be able to show the gratitude towards a help irrespective of its nature and size (2) be able to use the sense of gratitude to forgive people who hurt you.

Rationale:

> Giving and receiving help is learnt through socialization. It is a good strength for the humanity to possess for the obvious reasons humanity will become defunct without it. Therefore it is a welcome idea that one learns the nitty-gritty of gratitude which will help to sustain the helping tendency in a society.

Coaching:

The following advocacy is derived from the couplets.

> "You will be able to show a sense of gratitude if you develop the right *panbu* in your personality (105). *Panbu* simply means having a sense of equity and love towards fellow human beings.
> Sense of gratitude developed by your *panbu* will make you not to forget a help received from a friend that ended your adversity conditions (106).

> *Panbu* will make you to remember the help you received and remain grateful for it again and again as long as you live leaving an indelible impression on your progeny who will carry the memory as a historical event for generations to come (107).
> *Panbu* also will make you to forget a harm done by a person but not the help done by him (108).
> Do this exercise to learn that *panbu*. Take a sheet of paper and write down all the helps you have received – as many as possible. Make a categorization of them in terms of help that has come to you without any precedence on your part; a help that was timely; a help that was done not with an intention of creating leverage with you; a help small but very significant because of its criticality. Consider the list one by one and vividly recall in your mind the circumstance under which you received and feel grateful for it. You may imagine as if you are standing in front of the person and expressing thanks to him (101,102,103 and 104).
> You can use your sense of gratitude to forgive a person by recalling a help rendered by him. Anger towards a person over a hurt he has inflicted and a sense of gratitude towards the same person cannot coexist in your mind because they are incompatible. Therefore if you install panbu in your personality sense of gratitude will become activated in you which will take care of your anger towards another person.
> Beware without *panbu* you are likely to drop gratitude in preference to anger because anger is a powerful feeling compared to gratitude (109)"

12

Equity

(Remaining non-partisan)

111. Equity is just and fine when,
Stakeholder's interests are factored in.

A dispensation will be held as just and fair only when it provides the equity to all the stakeholders on a fair and just basis.

112. Men of equity evolve and that valance
Protects from lapse at the latter births in balance.

If a man has been non partisan in awarding equity to all the stake holders throughout his life his soul evolves. The soul thus evolved will put him on a protective mode for the remainder of his reincarnations i.e., the number of births needed to attain a fully evolved soul to attain heavenly abode.

113. In spite it yields good benefits throw it
If by erring on equity you got it.

No doubt one may have the prospects for good gains. In spite of that he should leave aside the accruals in full which are not his equity.

114. Someone been partisan or not,
Is revealed by the consequent.

The consequences created as an aftermath of one's actions will determine whether one has been fair and just in his dispensations. The consequences are nothing but the reactions of the stakeholders – if he has been just and fair the consequences will in the form of stake holders rallying around him if not it will be the stake holders opposing him tooth and nail.

115.   Decline and prosperity are life's hard reality,
       Not failing equity is *sandrones'* beauty.

Uncertainty born out of ups and downs is a harsh reality of the world. A *sandrone* is capable of fully appreciating this fact. Therefore he doesn't allow his heart to bypass equity and go after the uncertain things of the materialistic world. It is his beauty. (A sandrone under any circumstances will not fail in dispensing equity.)

116.   'He would be destroyed,' let him beware,
       Who transgress on fairness and acts bizarre.

Let all human beings be aware that once they transgresses the path of fairness they are bound to decline and get destroyed.

117.   The world will not look down
       On the fall of a just man.

The world will not consider the fall of a great man as lousy if he has rallied around justice and fairness and carried out good activities throughout his life.

118.   The hallmark of *sandranmai* is remaining neutral
       In this a *sandrone* is like a good balance.

The decoration of a man of equity is remaining nonpartisan like a high quality balance.

119. Not exhibiting bias in words indicates equity
If the heart has no biased and crooked kitty.

The practice of fairness in words indicates equity only when in the heart also bias is absent.

120. A trader's practice befits his profession
Other stakeholders interest if he treats as his own.

A trader's practice befits his profession only when he considers the interest of all the stakeholders connected to his trade on par with his interests.

Skills to be learnt:

➢ The ability to recognize the equity of all the stake holders and acting to give them their due, b) the ability to totally avoid manipulation of anyone in order to amass his or her equity.

Rationale:

➢ Every human being wants a fair share of what is his equity. Anyone who is a spoil sport of this earns the scorn and enmity of the affected person. Several such affected persons provide the breeding ground for a nemesis. Thiruvalluvar categorically says in couplet number 112 that practicing equity makes the soul to evolve. The evolved soul obviously puts a person on a strong phase of further evolution towards reaching the abode of God. In that sense an evolved soul protects future incarnations of the man. Further couplet 116 says that anyone who fails to act in a fair and just manner is bound to ruin himself sooner or later. Therefore it is necessary to maintain equity in our dispensations for achieving which one has to learn how to be equitable in our actions towards fellow human beings.

Coaching:

The following advocacy is derived from the couplets.

➤ "Learn to behave like an Indian scale. An Indian scale has two plates hung on two ends of a horizontal bar by means of chains. In the middle of the bar a needle is fixed which can move from a central position to either side of the bar along with the tilting of the bar due to unequal loads on the plates. If both the plates are loaded equally, the needle will be synchronizing with a standard indicating the middle position. You should behave like that scale with regard to taking care of equity of all the stakeholders on any issue including yours (118).

➤ Look at the example of a trader. A trader should do justice to all the stake holders of his trade. The stake holders may include him as an investor and worker in the trade, his customers, his employees, his suppliers, government, environmental considerations and a host of others. He should take care of the interest of all of the stake holders on par with how he would take care of his. In a bigger picture the earth and all its wealth belongs to all its living creatures. That means nobody has a right to grab the equity of others on any ground like someone being more educated, talented, innovative or what not. Anyone who wants to start an enterprise should immediately think of the equity of the person who will be affected by his action and take care of his equity (120).

➤ Sometimes a person may introduce a system of dispensation which is quite fair. But he may have a hidden agenda for it. Such an act fails on equity (119). Therefore keep a watch over your motive. If you have crooked motives, in the service of these you may seemingly behave just and fair in an incident that is not awarding equity.

A major hurdle to being fair is a sense of entitlement. One person in a relationship/ organization may feel that he or she is entitled for a better equity of any deliverables based on some ground. These entitlements will be accepted if they are honest ones. Several entitlements may be legally or by rules may sound correct but they may not be correct in the eyes of *aram*. In such conditions the stake holders who feel their equity has been siphoned off using, some obscure rules or conventions or precedence will rise against it (114).

➢ Therefore that this should be totally avoided goes without saying. The interpretation of any rule should be based on the precincts of *aram*. After all, the thought of rule of justice which forms the basis of aram has come first before any legislature on equity in this universe (543).

➢ You can immunize yourself against behaving in an unfair manner by picking the quality of a *sandrone*. You behave faulting on equity because of your genius of interpretation of rules and managing things in a world where a just order is yet to arrive. Therefore don't go by rule book alone. Use the qualities of not being envious, greedy, or scornful towards others who you think are standing between you and your so called equity. Don't forget the idea that you as a child of mother earth are a brother of all her children it is highly important for you to be benign, empathizing and truthful towards all her children (111)."

13

Humility[51]

(Standing grounded/humbleness)

121. Humility leads to heavenly life
Self-aggrandizement leads into hellish strife[52].

Humility leads to a heavenly afterlife. Whereas self-aggrandizement leads to
Hell like life here on the earth.

122. **A**dopt humility as a modus operandi
No other support of life (soul) is as handy.

If you practice humility your soul evolves. The purpose of reincarnation is to evolve at the level of the soul. Therefore there is no other attitude as useful as humbleness.

123. Acquire intellect and remain in the path learnt
Knowing your humility accolades are lent.

---

[51] The concept of humility arises from the root word humble. Humble means standing grounded. We are as earthly beings are on par with other fellow human beings. Our accomplishments are no cause do despise our fellow human beings.

[52] Strife means difficulty of any type.

A deep learning will lead you to a life of humbleness and studentship. Appreciating your humbleness along with what you have intellectually achieved people will shower their appreciation on you.

124. He remains humble but strong in his position,
That impression is greater than a mountain.

Someone who has actualized humility is as impressive as a mountain.

125. Humility is good for humanity,
For the rich it is an additional bounty.

Humility is good for everybody while it is added richness for the rich.

126. The one who tames his senses like a tortoise in birth one
Has the protection up to seven.

If a person tames his senses and makes use of them prudently and diligently his soul evolves in strength. A soul thus evolved can give protection for the individual from committing mistakes, for example on matters of dispensing equity for the following seven reincarnations.

127. Whoever let him be, let his tongue remain censored
Otherwise he lands in worry due to libel unconstrained.

It is important you restrain your tongue from being libelous. Otherwise you will get
caught in great worry.

128. One degrading word in a conversation is enough,
Its implication converts the good into a slough[53].

---

[53] Slough means a condition of degradation, despair or helplessness.

A single hurtful word by its implications can bring unwelcome repercussions and spoil your happiness.

129. Of scars of burns wounds are healed,
     Of scares of tongue wounds are concealed.

The wound caused by fire heals leaving a scar, whereas a wound by hurtful words doesn't heal. It may appear as though it has healed (person apparently may look like he has come to terms with his hurt) but it will be simmering inside and whenever the afflicted person recalls the incident of hurt it will pain him afresh.

130. On the one who mastered anger restraint
     A*ram* will wait on him to meet.

Humanity imbibed with the spirit of *aram*[54] will wait on that person who has mastered restraining of anger to shower its accolades.

Skills to be learnt:

➢   Ability to remain humble.

Rationale:

➢   Being humble means not attaching any importance to ourselves in comparison with others with whom we may be together at a given point of time. It is not low self esteem. Rather it is total absence of one-upmanship. It also helps to evolve your soul in your onward journey to God's world (126).

➢   This trait is useful for developing and maintaining healthy interpersonal relationship and also accomplishing more and more

---

[54]   Here and in chapter 21 Thiruvalluvar has pictured *aram* as a being. In fact he means *aram* as a phenomenon which by its presence in a set of persons in a society make them to unite as a single force to avenge an evil. Whereas most of the interpreters hold aram as a god whose job is to avenge the evil.

in all walks of life. This is possible because a humble person is open to new experiences and learning. He is more teachable than a person who is not humble.

> Lack of humbleness makes one to be stubborn which is anathema to learning because learning needs an open mind which believes that what it knows at best is tentative and requires updating. These two attributes are needed for trouble shooting and innovation also.

> If we are not humble invariably we exhibit one-upmanship, only to receive retaliatory responses from others or from a system which in turn hardens our personality towards aggressive behavior. The soul shrinks whenever we are aggressive or domineering. Whereas keeping on par with fellow human beings nourishes our soul. Therefore it is a welcome idea that we learn humility and practice it in our daily life.

> Remember remaining humble in one birth powers your soul enough to protect you from making excesses in seven births to follow. That means your journey to reach God's abode permanently is well served by being humble in the present birth (126).

> Another interesting fact is that if you have humbleness in your profile amply, people who are guided by a strong sense of *aram* would flock around you which in turn reinforces your humbleness (130).

Coaching:

The following advocacy is derived from the couplets.

> "Firstly, you have to separate your self-worth from what you do or do not do. For example, if you are lazy and also if you are humble you will say, "I am lazy these days. It is time for me now to become more active." If you are not humble you will not accept that you are lazy and try to explain it in n number of ways or say it with a sense of pride that others should appreciate that you are frank enough to accept that you are lazy!

➢ Humanity imbibed with the spirit of *aram*[55] will wait on that person who has mastered restraining of anger to shower its accolades.

➢ Secondly, when you feel superior to someone you can change that attitude by looking at the person as a resource. Surprised? Every human being is a unique phenomenon. His uniqueness may be due to his attitude, knowledge or experience or perspectives or his idiotic way of doing things. If you look up to him as he is freely available to you to pick up all those things to which you are exposed for the first time the exercise will make you more informed than before and sooner or later you will find some application for what you have picked from him. Always maintain the attitude of studentship to pick up things from all directions and all walks of life then you will automatically remain humble (130).

➢ Thiruvalluvar says humility can be learned. The best way is posting yourself with information about what is happening in your domain continuously and a bird's eye view about what are the advances achieved across disciplines. This will make you to get a mind set of a person who is standing before an ocean. Don't you feel humble when you stand at the sea shore looking at the roaring sea? (123).

➢ How about making humility as a guiding principle or philosophy of life? Thiruvalluvar says there is nothing better than that for the safety of your life (122).

➢ Never use words which are demeaning towards any one (127)."

---

[55] Here and in chapter 21 Thiruvalluvar has pictured *aram* as a being. In fact he means *aram* as a phenomenon which by its presence in a set of persons in a society make them to unite as a single force to avenge an evil. Whereas most of the interpreters hold aram as a god whose job is to avenge the evil.

14

Best Practices (Regularity)

(Following best practices in all walks of life)

131. Since best practices deliver excellence
They shall be preserved more than life.

Best practices in all walks of life based on good policies yield greatness
and success for life. Therefore they shall be preserved dearer than life.

132. **B**est practices as evidenced are the best bet
Therefore work as hard as needed to get them set.

In every field best practices need to be adhered to since by any
account they are found to be of constructive help.

133. **B**est practices make a standard family
Its absence makes a nondescript family.

Best practices need to be in place in a household otherwise the
household will slowly degrade and perish or become an unsavory
place to live and rear offspring.

134. **B**ad memory can be made up by revision,
Failing on best practices quells a Brahmin's[56] profession.

---

[56]   The present translator contends that the main debut of the chapter is stressing
the best practices to be adopted by humanity in all walks of life. *Kural* number

If a Brahmin (priest) forgets his scriptures and books they can be relearned but if he chooses not to follow the best practices meant for professional Brahminical (priest craft and rituals) life which equips him for his profession his career will come to an end.

135. **A** jealous person does not flourish,[57]
Without best practices growths diminish

A jealous person doesn't flourish. Similarly in the absence of best practices human beings do not attain great heights.

136. **H**ardy ones do not deviate from best practices,[58]
They are cognizant of the ruin causable by lapses.

Persons cognizant of the danger of losing the best part of their life for want of following best practices develop enough hardiness in their emotions, thinking and action, to install best practices in place without fail.

137. **B**est practices earns an exalted position
Failing on them brings disgrace out of proportion.

---

134 specifically talks about the practices meant for Brahmins. The Brahmins are expected to educate the society including teaching religious treatises and conduct religious services. In a way they are educators and moral teachers and custodians of moral wellness in the community. They follow the best practices by the way they lead their life which in fact is a career/profession to achieve these objectives. If they forget their texts they can relearn them. If they fault on the best practices which renders them as hazardous teachers then the society meets irrevocable loss

[57] Tiruvalluvar perhaps has few ideas more dearly to him than others. Such ideas he brings in along with a concept on hand. This strategy he has adapted in a number of places.

[58] Hardy persons are those who are steadfast in their policies, emotions, and behaviors.

Implementing best practices attracts great rewards. But if one declines in making use of best practices he would be blamed more than what he deserves.

138. **B**est practices are the seeds for eternal good
Foul practices seed eternal bad.

Whereas best practices net in benefits poor practices in any walk of life bring in chronic and paining botherations.

139. **M**en of best practices would find it hard
Even by a slip uttering a foul word.

Uttering bad and scornful words do not occur even by slip of tongue with men in whom best practices are deeply ingrained.

140. **I**n spite of vast learning they are illiterates
If they are insensitive to world's sensibilities.

One example for best practice is developing a keen sensitivity so that one doesn't offend the sensibilities of those one deals with. If he or she doesn't learn this best practice there is no use of his or her scholarship in various fields. (The best practice regarding how you treat the world around you is acting according to the now popular phrase 'politically correct'.)

(Unfortunately of late the concept of 'acting politically correct' is made use of to exploit the sensibilities by harping on a sensitive issue in myriad ways for gaining political advantages.)

Skills to be learnt:

> To ingrain the sense of 'best practices' very deeply in one's personality so that whenever one sets to act he or she should ask for the best practices for that act as vouchsafed by the past legitimate success.

Rationale:

> Every profession/walk of life has its own best practices. Best practices are in fact skill sets to be mastered by everyone in all their legitimate activities and adhered to. Tiruvalluvar gives this chapter like a preamble to the other chapters dealing with various life skills.

Coaching:

The following advocacy is derived from the couplets.

> "Whenever someone is set on a project say, parenting, he or she should consult the research literature and get to know the latest knowhow on child rearing and parenting (Chapter:7).

> In addition to a thorough learning of various aspects of child rearing and parenting the theory behind each of the practice also should be learned. If a theory is not learned then the best practice based on the theory will soon become corrupted.

> Tiruvalluvar insists following best practices in various professions, personal and social life. The chapter gives a few examples of where best practices need to be followed. They are the institution of family (133), in priesthood (134), in interpersonal relationship (139) and in social life (140).

> Apart from the above throughout the treatise best practices are described."

> The most important best practice is the ability to empathize with the sensibilities of people and not creating new sensibilities in them to cater to one's needs.

15

Not Coveting Another's Wife

(Being faithful to wife)

141. **S**leeping with another's wife is a folly
    Never exists in those insightful of *aram* surely.

    The purpose of life is to evolve at one's soul in order to attain heaven. Those who have this insight would never commit the mistake of sleeping with another's wife because it violates the principle of *aram* of equity; it goes against the institution of family; it lacks compassion for woman in view of the havoc it would create in her life.

142. Among the lowest with regard to *aram*
    None like the one who waits upon another's door

    There is none as low as one who waits upon another man to leave to enter into his house (with the aim of sleeping with his wife).

143. **H**e who sleeps with a non-doubting friend's wife
    Has status equaling a corpse.

    The soul of an adulterer takes a nose dive and reaches the lowest possible level. As such, it is as good as absent. In a dead person obviously the soul is absent. Therefore, there is no difference between a dead person and an adulterer. An adulterer has a very rudimentary soul or no soul for all practical purposes.

144. **A**ccomplished scholar, what use?
     Hanky-panky causes his greatness to diffuse.

     A person may have deep and varied scholarship in *aram* related
     literature but it is of no use if he enters another's house with the evil
     intention of sleeping with the householder's wife.

145. Holding it trifle sleeping with another's spouse,
     Is a guilt that causes eternal grouse.

     Holding it as a small matter if a person sleeps with another's wife he
     will be blamed for the remainder of his life.

146. Hatred, sin, fear and shame – these four
     With an adulterer hauntingly stay forever.

     A man is haunted by hatred, sin, fear and shame throughout his
     life if he indulges in illicit relationship transgressing the rights of a
     home. (This is the price he will be paying for a short term hedonistic
     pleasure he seeks by indulging in illicit sex with another's wife.)

147. 'He makes a home employing *aram* ', is a fait accompli
     Only when he shuns seeking another's wife firmly.

     A man can claim that he is a proud owner of a home which is run
     on the principles of *aram* only if he totally desists from infidelity.

148. A *sandrone*[59] doesn't covet another's wife
     For him it is the best practice and *aram* in life.

---

[59]   A *sandrone* is a gentle man whose is personality is seated upon the five pillars of
love, humility, social benevolence, empathy and truth.

For a *sandrone* not coveting another's wife is a best practice based on *aram*. Because he is truthful at his heart he will never fault on that practice.

149. In this sea grit world good belongs only to them, behold
Who never find themselves in another woman's fold.

If you ask who deserves good in life. The answer is he who never embraces a woman other than his wife.

150. Even if someone carries on a contemptuous sin,
Better if with another's wife he doesn't have fun.

Other contemptuous sins are to be avoided but sometimes can be forgiven. It will be good even such people do not indulge in illicit relations with others wives.

Skills to be learnt:

> Maintaining 100 percent loyalty to one's wife; not cheating her by developing illicit relationship with the wife of a friend/another person.

Rationale:

> Thiruvalluvar paints a horrible picture of a man who sleeps with another's wife. He is the filthiest person from the point of view of *aram* (consult the legend for the meaning).
> Whatever be his accomplishments they are of no use if he is not faithful to his wife. Such a person earns permanent blame, sin, fear and enmity. He can never escape from them.
> It is horribly painful to live under the shade of such accusations throughout one's life. Therefore the husband should find ways to stop this menacing tendency.

Coaching:

Thiruvalluvar uses the following admonishing technique to wean a man of his illicit relationship with his friend's or another person's wife:

- ➢ "You would not be indulging in this behavior if only you have thought about the consequences of what you do. I would rather call you a fool for that (141).
- ➢ You would not have done this had you been educated in *aram*. Never men of *aram* would degrade themselves like this (141).
- ➢ Even the most laggard on *aram* would not do a thing like what you have done (142).
- ➢ A corpse is dead and therefore has no soul. A man who sleeps with another unsuspecting man's wife is also soulless (143).
- ➢ You may have earned great esteem as a scholar on *aram*. But what use? After all you have entered into the home of a friend of you with evil intentions (144).
- ➢ You may think it is easy and not detectable. But beware you will not only get caught but also the blame on you will never end (145).
- ➢ Take it from me. You will never cease to be faced with enmity, sin, fear, and blame if you indulge in promiscuity transgressing the right of another person (146).
- ➢ I tell you, only a person who is not into infidelity at all, can claim that he is a family man (147).
- ➢ Not coveting the wife of another person is not only a virtue of *aram* but also a best practice to ensure the mental and physical health of the family (148).
- ➢ You can count on any of your blessings only if you totally desist from infidelity." (149).
- ➢ Even if you default on other virtues of *aram* it is good if you do not default on fidelity (150).

16
Forbearance

(Bearing others follies and excesses)

151. Earth bears those who dig it,
    As a best policy with your scorners you ape it.

    Earth bears those who dig it. On the issue of bearing those ridicule
    us we should behave like earth. It is the best policy vis-à-vis evolution
    of the soul is concerned.

152. Forbearance of transgression is always good,
    Forgetting is better, therefore one should.

    While bearing the transgression of others is good, forgetting is more
    desirable.

153. Inability to host a guest is poverty's worst,
    Of all strengths bearing brutish fools is the best.

    Of all the poverty having no means to feed a guest is most disturbing.
    Likewise if you consider various strengths the strength of bearing the
    activities of brutish fools tops them all.

154. If you want your greatness not to leave you
    Forbearance will achieve it, mind you.

Forbearance should be adopted as the best policy and best practice if some one desires to retain one's worthiness (in his quest for reaching the abode of God permanently).

155. Those reveled in punishing are slighted,
      Those forbear, are esteemed as gold.

Those who punish are not given any credit by the world. Whereas those who have demonstrated forbearance throughout their life are kept in high esteem on par with gold by the world.

156. Punishing yields a day's pleasure,
      Forgiving gets lifelong fame to treasure.

If you punish someone the joy lasts for a day or two. But forgiving nets in lifelong esteem.

157. Even when the other doesn't act appropriate
      Suffering a 'victim's,' pain don't act inappropriate.

Even when someone acts very inappropriately in the eyes of *aram* don't feel like a victim and retaliate in ways devoid of aram.

158. Making your forbearing his toast
      Win him who hurts out of boast.

In spite of being harassed by someone because of arrogance if you adhere to acts of *aram* (by bearing with him) then the other person will lose interest in harassing you. This is the best method to win him.

159. As pure as saints since they bear
      Painful words transgressors utter.

Ascetics are pure since the four pollutants namely envy, desire, rage and hurtful words are absent in them. They put up with limitless rage inducing utterances because of their personality. A person who is not an ascetic himself is held as pure as the ascetic when he puts up with limitless rage inducing utterances.

160. Men who fast are great,
Men who bear painful words are greatest.

Saints who fast as part of the procedure of penance are great. But they rank lower to human beings involved in worldly life putting up with the contemptuous words of others.

Skills to be learnt:

> Ability to forgive.

Rationale:

> Couplet number 154 says that if someone wants a sustained healthy character then he or she should be free from acting revengefully. You may ask why retaliatory acts should change our character. A revengeful retaliation is a groove. Once you are inside the groove it is very difficult to walk out of it later. Body, mind, emotions and behavior are all interrelated. One feeds on the other. Mind loses its freedom of option when some behavior is strengthened by some initial retaliatory success.

Coaching:

Three techniques discernable in this chapter are:

> Never accept a victim's position when someone hurts you (157).
> Hold that bearing with a ridicule is a noble policy and an effective strategy (158).
> Free yourself from getting into rage. Rather develop the habit of getting irritated
or annoyed (159).
> How to come out of 'victim' position?

The moment you act on your grievance your victimhood vanishes. The couplet doesn't ask you not to do anything rather it says do something within *aram*. Gandhi is made as a victim for no fault of his by the British. But he never accepted it. He acted against it. Whether one succeeds or not one should fight (157).

How to bear a ridicule?

> How about looking at ridicule as a feedback about you of course delivered in an unusual and unacceptable language? When you have this perceptive the next step is retaining those comments in a ridicule which you think is of use to you and treating the rest as trash or noise and dropping them away comes easily to you. You will become more convinced of this method if you also tell your ridiculer that you would analyze the feedback given by him and seeing him going flabbergasted! (157)

How to avoid becoming rage?

> You know the person who becomes terribly angry over ridicule is your ego. Ego becomes reddened on two occasions: (1) when it gets insulted or overpowered, (2) when it is made to feel guilty.

> If you address your ego thus: "Look, this person's actions and words are his products. I refuse to acknowledge them but for those which are valid. Since he behaves in this uncouth manner it shows he has not learned how to carry out a life of high quality. I retain my option to deny whatever he thinks of me and his subsequent action."

> Thus dissecting and owning some while disowning others relieves the ego of its rage and challenged feeling when it gets angry (158).

> More importantly you should call your soul to your help. Remember a person who is completely free from the four vices namely envy, desire, rage and hurtful words are is poised for a life in heaven (159).

17

Freedom from Jealousy

(Not envying other's prosperity)

161. Have this best practice at your heart,
     Expelling jealousy be that act.

     Entertaining no jealousy at heart is the best practice. (Remember in couplet number 154 the poet has stated that forbearance be enacted as the best practice.)

162. Jealousy free nature is the best of all treasures
     For attaining laurels none equally measures.

     Jealousy free nature is a resource in one's kitty. In getting an all-round appreciation there is no other quality equivalent to it.

163. Those who do not need good out of *aram*
     Growth of others, out of jealousy maim.

     Jealous people are not interested in the gains obtainable through the path of *aram*. Therefore instead of supporting others in their efforts to attain prosperity they will spoil their effort out of jealousy. (*Aram* here refers keeping free from jealousy. And living free from jealousy helps the soul to evolve.)

164. Out of jealous the wise do no wrongs
     Since they know their down fall such act brings.

     Some people are wise enough to realize that jealousy brings ruin.
     Therefore they do not act out of jealousy.

165. Ruining them, their enemy's may fail
     But their jealousy is of enough avail.

     Enemies may miss to hurt them. But for people who are jealousy
     their jealousy is enough cause for getting ruined.

166. He who by envy scuttles charity
     Perishes with his folk naked and hungry

     Some people, out of jealousy play spoil sport vis-à-vis others receiving
     help. Such people's dependent kith and kin sooner or later will be
     left with nothing to dress or dine (since jealousy economically ruins
     its holder in due course of time).

167. Resenting his jealousy the Goddess of Fortune
     Guide him to her sister Misfortune.

     Goddess of prosperity resents people who act jealously. She guides
     them to goddess of misfortune. (In the folk mythology of Hinduism
     a deity for prosperity and another for misfortune are in vogue. Since
     the belief must have been widely spread among his readers, may
     be Thiruvalluvar uses them to drive home his concept that those
     who suffer from jealousy are sure to loose their fortune and land in
     misfortune.)

168. Jealous the criminal[60] gets your fortune[61] ruined
And makes your life a hell blessed.

Jealousy, the criminal ruins the prosperity of its holder. Not only
has that it also pushes him into fire like hell. (Here 'hell' refers to
hell like life on the earth because of the misfortune that by and large
visits a person who is envious of others in a socially active and law
abiding society.)

169. Envious prospers and unenvious suffers
In discerning minds insight on these occurs.

Some jealous people do prosper. Similarly some people who are not
at all jealous do not prosper. Discerning minds may look for reasons
outside jealousy for this phenomenon. (I hold that this couplet needs
to be read along with the previous and the next. Please see what is
stated in the bracket in the commentary of the next couplet.)

170. The prosperity of an envious doesn't expand on and on
Unenvious is not fully exhausted on what he can.

There is no evidence to show that an envious person's prosperity
expands substantially while that of unenvious person's declines
completely. (This couplet along with the previous two couplets gives
the idea that though in general jealousy is ruinous sometimes factors
other than jealousy like a good and favourable season or place of
business may intervene to apply breaks on the overriding effect of
jealousy. Still at a basic level jealousy will at least stop growth which
is otherwise scaled to expand and lack of jealousy will help expansion
of wealth provided other factors do not intervene.)

---

60 Jealous is presented as an abstract noun.
61 The word fortune is not used here in the sense of karma.

Skill to be learnt:

➢ Achieving a jealousy free inner nature.

Rationale:

➢ The mental dynamics of jealousy is somewhat inferable from the couplet 163. The couplet says a jealous person is not enamored about the outcome of following *aram i.e.* not entertaining jealousy. Either he is ignorant or refuses the consequences of entertaining jealousy. Several couplets (162/64/65/66/67 and 68) speak about the impact of not following *aram* on the individual and on the outcome of their activities. In view of these couplets having no jealousy is a shrewd decision for protecting one's interest.

Coaching:

Read again and again the following and make them as your guiding commandments regarding harboring jealous in your heart:

➢ Catch hold of the best practice of: Never harbor jealousy in your heart. Work hard on that as long as needed to make being jealousy free as your nature. (161)

➢ Distancing from jealousy is the best maturity one can aim since there is none other so powerful in ushering you into the company of God in the afterlife. (162)

➢ Remember the best practice according to the principle of *aram* (here *aram* means not feeling jealous) is supporting the good efforts of others. Therefore out of jealousy never scuttle them. You are a fool for doing that because by doing that you deny for yourself the benefits of following *aram*.(163)

➢ Remember wise people know by evidence that acting out of jealousy is dangerous because such an act is against *aram*. Aren't you a wise person?

➢ Remember you don't need any other enemy to spoil your wellbeing. Your jealousy is enough. (165)

- ➢ Never out of envy, that the person you help will overtake you, refrain from helping others. If you do so you with your kith and kin will go with nothing to eat and wear. (166)
- ➢ Beware Goddess of fortune resents you if you entertain jealousy in your heart and act out of it. That makes her to shunt you to Goddess of misfortune. (167)
- ➢ Jealousy is a criminal. He will destroy your wealth and push you into the mire of hellish suffering in your earthly life. (168)
- ➢ You may have observed while some envious persons prosper non envious ones suffer loss. Don't jump to conclusions. If you watch closely you will find that the envious ones do not prosper steadily and non envious ones do not decline steadily. Some factor other than envy may intervene but that factor would never be able to make envy as irrelevant completely. (169 &170)

18

Not Coveting What Belongs to Others

(Not misappropriating what belongs to others)

171. Coveting, unmindful of equity, is a thought
     Decline of the family and error over error fraught.

     Coveting what is not ones is fraught with several consequences. The
     individual would move from error to error and his family would
     suffer an irreversible decline.

172. They who hold firm, 'inequity in lieu of a tradeoff is a shame,'
     From them comes no act of blame.

     Those who hold that acting in an unjust manner denying someone
     of his equity is a shameful act will not carry out a misappropriating
     act for achieving a gain.

173. For a transient pleasure they commit no ethical turpitude
     Because they are, keen on a blissful quietude.

     Those who are inclined to enjoy a life of blissful joy for ever will not be
     found erring on equity in search of transient (transient because they
     are sure to get caught and lose what they have amassed.) pleasures.

174. They would never covet what is not theirs because
     For the senses-won being a pauper is not enough cause.

Men who has won the lure of the five senses by developing a true vision on men and matter would never do the act of coveting what is not their due holding that their dire situation justifies it.

175. Deep and wide, let the knowledge be,
What use if from every source covets he?

A man may be a widely and deeply read person but there is no use of his accomplishments if he chooses to misappropriate from all the possible sources.

176. He covets compassion[62] and is on
Later covets wealth and schemes, his sense of equity is gone

A person may be compassionate and act accordingly. But the moment he covets wealth and put in place evil plans to acquire wealth he will start losing his compassionate inclinations and loose it once and for all very soon. He will move in that direction on and on only to get ruined completely later.

177. Misappropriating a property do not covet
Repercussions are too hard to prevent.
Do not aspire for wealth through misappropriation because the repercussions are too hard to manage.

178. Unshrunk Prosperity – what ensures?
Not misappropriating others' assures.

---

[62] The word compassion is used in lieu of the Tamil word 'aruludaimai 'used in the couplet. Compassion as it is generally understood meaning a kind heart and sympathetic action towards others. But aruludaimai is doing what is at one's command to wipe the sufferings of others concurring with the notion 'a life of quality' is the right of every one. Compassion or sympathy as it is known in English is not found in Thirukkural.

Do you know what protects your prosperity? It is not coveting the property of others.

(Perhaps this may happen at two levels. A person who indulges in misappropriation will become preoccupied with a number of issues increasing pressure and mental torture. This condition leads to himself not being able to concentrate on the nitty-gritty of his estate resulting in its loss gradually. Another possibility is those who are affected by his corruptive activities may join together and plan for his ruin in retaliation (204).)

179. Not coveting due to informed morals
      Fortune reaches such mortals.

Not coveting other's equity is *aram* and a wisdom. Fortune[63] joins the person with such wisdom and befitting action.

180. Thoughtless coveting delivers ruin
      The pride of a desireless-mind powers its ban.

Unmindful of consequences if someone covets others equity he meets ruin. A contended mind which is proud of its firm 'no greed stance' is the tool with which he/she can win the diseased mindset of coveting other's equity.

Skills to be learnt:

➢   A skill not to covet and misappropriate what belongs to others.

---

[63]   It is possible to hold fortune or wealth mentioned as '*Thiru*' in the couplet as an abstract noun. The message that someone is hundred percent honest may spread in the town attracting more and more financial transactions or other types of cooperation resulting in the accumulation of huge wealth.

Rationale:

> Coveting and usurping what belongs to others is attempted by many in the hope that they can carry on with it forever without any backlash. But this is not really so. Tiruvalluvar in couplet no.171 says that by misappropriating others equity an individual runs the risk of ruining his life and that of his family (for example recent history of corporate CEO's selling and buying shares using the inside information and making big money landed them in jail leaving their family in peril).

> He also says that the blame will continue to affect the prospects of the family for years to come. Maybe he means the story may be carried on for a long time to come around the family and prove to be a baggage, wriggling out of which the members of his family would find very difficult.

Coaching:

The following advocacy is derived from the couplets.

> "I want to warn you. Misappropriation will ultimately ruin you and your family (171). (Real life examples may be quoted to impress upon the person how it is a sure trap for ruin even though the going 'at present' may appear smooth.)

> If you have a sense of shame you would never covet losing yourself in the desire for what belongs to others (172).

> Whatever joy one has in misappropriating is mean. The great and true joy is one we get in the company of God. Can you aspire for such a joy if you are a swindler? (173).

> If only you realize that this life on the earth and its products are illusory the Real products and joy will be found only in God's world then you can come out of the self pitying symptom of 'poor me' and you will not clutter life with too many things (174/180).

> You may be highly educated and enjoy a status in the midst of all those who know you. But what use! Everything will be destroyed

and you will be hated by all those the moment they come to know about your frauds (175).

➢ I know you were a compassionate person early and enjoyed yourself for that. But look now ever since you started concentrating on money and choose misappropriation as a means to earn it your compassion has disappeared. It will take a very long time to get back your compassionate heart. But that could happen only when you take steps to stop misappropriation and start a new leaf of life (176).

➢ The income through fraud may appear to be plenty. But the repercussions are too many which you will never be able to manage (177).

➢ A sure method to secure what you have is stop coveting others (178).

➢ Only those who has the great intellect to realize that great virtue is not earning wealth through fraudulent means would attract wealth. (179). (Wealth would accrue because you would be doing things with a free mind which is no more occupied with jealousy.)

➢ It is a diseased mindset which covets the equity of others. Develop the antidote of a contended mind to fight that disease. If you remember that achieving a contented mind is a feat about which you can take pride once you achieve it, whereas amassing wealth through foul means is not a matter about which one can be genuinely be proud (180).

19

Not Slandering

(Making false and damaging statement about others in their absence)

181. 'Not knowledgeable in *aram* and hence acts wrongly'
Nice, if this is also told, 'But he doesn't slander willingly'.

Some people for want of knowledge in *aram* might indulge in inappropriate activities. Even for them a saving clause would be getting a word of praise that they wouldn't indulge in clandestine slandering.

182. Destroying *aram*? Acting inappropriately? Worst still
Smiling in person but slandering in absentia if you will.

Throwing a smile in person but slandering about someone in his absence is worse than doing other inappropriate activities deliberately destroying *aram* in the place of action.

183. Do you slander and lie as a means to live?
Instead die and prosper with what *aram* does give[64].

Do you slander and later deny for the sake of eking out a living? Instead of living like that if you die refusing to slander you will earn what a virtuous life upholding the principles of *aram* does give. Such a principled life helps the soul to evolve.

---

[64] The *aram* of not slandering at any cost will get the person into heaven.

184. Better indifferent words in his presence,
      Than words of dire consequence in his absence.

One may use inconsiderate or indifferent (due to lack of empathic understanding) words against another in his or her presence. But when the other person is absent he should not speak words that will bring in serious consequences. (Tiruvalluvar appears to mean that the slanderous comments uttered will be carried to the person concerned through grapevine and result in drastic consequence. As is the wont of grapevine, a communication through it will be distorted to a great extent from the original. It will be a tedious task to meet every one in a grape wine to clear yourself from a blame.)

185. Mean slanders he uses reveals
      What emptiness of *aram* his heart conceals.

A man may give a wonderful discourse on the subject matter of *aram*. But the slander he uses on another occasion reveals the real nature of his heart which is devoid of aram.

186. If you are an able critique
      Your charges of blame on people do click.

If someone makes a critical observation about another person his observation will be accepted as credible only when people hold him as a good critic. (Probably Thiruvalluvar means people use different yard sticks for critiquing their actions and those of others. This idea gets some confirmation if this couplet is read together with the couplet 190.)

187. With divisive analysis friendship they break,
      They are not skilled at friendly and humorous 'speak'.

Some people do not have the capacity to speak about others using warm and positive words and help friendship grow among them.

Rather they use divisive analysis to drive home their slandering and divide them.

188. About others what they will not vendor?
When even on close friends these tribes slander.

There are people who badmouth even about their close friends with other common friends or relatives. They are also vociferous making it to look like a celebration. With this background of theirs what they will do in the case of others who are not friends is a subject better left to one's imagination.

189. Is it for upholding *aram* their ilk bears them
Who catch an opportunity to speak ill of them?

Is it because the world wants to uphold aram of forbearance it bears the slander of some of its members?

190. If we could perceive ours as if we perceive other's misdeed,
Could there be any harm to the humanity indeed?

If human beings use the same standard to adjudge the mistakes of theirs and of others there will be no problem for humanity. (But according to Thiruvalluvar it is not the case. This Kural, the way it is worded reveals that the individuals use tough standards for others and not so tough for themselves.)

Skills to be leant:

➤ Doing away with slandering with: A) Developing good critiquing skills.

Rationale:

➤ It is unethical to slander someone in his absence but still it is a compulsion in some of us to slander others. The individual may think that he slanders only with his confidential friend about a third person. But grapevine will take it to the person concerned without fail leading to dangerous consequences like getting sued in a court of law. Therefore the habit should be stopped at any cost.

➢   We have a tendency to criticize others under some pretext or the other. This is also dangerous and may spoil our career. Therefore we should stop it. If it is needed only a feedback not a critical comment not involving a putdown may be given. For the feedback to be credible enough care should be taken to not only make it based on evidence but also provide the evidence to the person concerned. Filling up unknown areas with visualization and passing on impression as feedback should be avoided.

Coaching:

➢   Make a policy decision that you will never talk to your friend or an acquaintance about a third person except when you play an official role. But this is difficult because the need to say something about someone becomes like an agenda once it arises. This agenda needs to be gone through to discharge the energy it holds. Therefore the best way is to talk to the concerned person himself your feelings/ your compulsion to comment after taking an assurance from him that he will not get offended by what you say(184). (He will not if you strike a deal with him requesting for a similar service from him.)

➢   Sometimes the other person may not be interested to hear your feedback. It is also likely that he may even get offended at this offer itself. Such scenario you can avoid by modulating your voice in such a way that you don't come as offensive at all. But beware if you have a snobbish mentality of, 'I am holier than thou,' or any other grouse against him it will definitely come in the way you pronounce/intone or punctuate your dialogue even though you may carefully choose your words. In that case the best alternative is to work on your feelings. Couplets nos. 186 and 190 show some way.

➢   You should undergo some basic training on how to go about criticizing someone. In short you should be able to apportion the mistake or a lapse of another person equitably between the person and the situation. It is a fact that when it comes to others we attribute cause of mistake to something wrong with the person if we don't like him and to the situation in case we like the person. Whereas when it comes to criticizing us we always attribute the cause of the shortcoming to the situation unless we are trained in the art of criticizing. A person will accept our criticism only if he is satisfied with our approach to criticizing (186).

20

Avoiding a Talk not delivering Good

(A talk is for the (announced) good of audience not for showing the scholarship of the speaker.)

191. **S**peech delivering no good earns the disgust
Later from every corner disapproval greet

A speaker is supposed to speak to an audience to deliver a good to them. (It is not an opportunity to enjoy oneself.) Therefore if a speaker either speaks below the level of the audience or speaks irrelevant to the announced topic his talk will create a sour feeling in the audience and they will disapprove him without fail.

192. **T**alk yielding no good before several is bad,
Uncivil done to friends compared.

Speaking to audience not enabling them to learn something good and useful or what was slated for is worse than acting unsavorily to a best friend.

193. **H**is talk is elaborate but delivers no good
In fact shows he has nothing of that sort.

A useless talk with dubious elaboration undoubtedly show that he has no good stuff to deliver.

194. Speaking words not yielding good
     Robs the good several have towards him.

     Ideal talk lacking anything good to offer in front of the audience
     removes whatever good will the audience might have for the speaker.

195. Name and recognition would disappear
     If from a learned character words lacking good appear.

     A person might have won name and laurels in the past. But he
     will lose everything in no time if he slows down and fail to abreast
     himself of new material which are good for the listeners.

196. He talks and talks, an exercise in gratuitous speak,
     'He is not a man but chaff around,' goes the tweak.

     A man is described as chaff among the discerning population if he
     engages himself in long sessions of gratuitous talk which delivers no
     good at all.

197. If needed let sandrones use words which are not good[65]
     Provided they deliver useful words instead.

     At times *sandrones* may use words which are not pleasant or pleasing.
     It is alright as long as they also do not indulge in a purposeless talk.

198. Those who look for words with great use
     Never use words of not much use.

---

[65] Sandrones may use words which are not good deliberately in order to create an
atmosphere for delivering a useful talk. This couplet may be compared to the
famous couplet (292): Lie and truth are tallied together // If a lie clean good does
gather.

Men, who research to find suitable words to offer substantial good (pertaining to attaining salvation) to their listeners, do not use words which are pompous and hollow.

199. **M**en whose clarity is spotless
Do not utter words which are worthless.

Men who have no spots of doubt in the topic of discourse never use words which serve only as time fillers at the best.

200. **S**peak words meeting a purpose
Vain words never propose.

Always use words which serve the good purpose on hand. Don't prattle.

Skills to be leant:

➢   Ability to deliver a good to the listener through speech.

Rationale:

➢   Throughout the chapter Thiruvalluvar emphasizes that a speaker should deliver a 'good' to the listener through his speech. Remember the couplet 981 says *sandror* take them as their duty to do whatever good required to be done.

➢   The time of the listeners is very precious and they should be seen as people serious and eager enough to invest their time to learn some specific subject for which they have a good use. They are not to be taken for a ride by the speaker.

➢   Wasting the time of the listener is blemish. (Such a speaker's brand image will take a beating.)

Coaching:

- ➤ Thiruvalluvar outlines the technique to avoid prattling in couplets numbering 198, 193,199 and 200:
- ➤ One technique to avoid useless talk is developing an in-depth knowledge and a research approach towards any topic about which you want to speak (198,199 and 200).
- ➤ Second, don't use too much of explanation (193). (This may happen due to a need in some of us to explain as much as possible holding that the listeners need it.)
- ➤ Third, make a policy decision not to digress into something about which you may have deep knowledge but not relevant to the topic on hand and following it strictly (199). For example, if you are scheduled to talk to horticultural farmers on cultivating plantain if you elaborate on horticulture in general because you are enamored about the philosophy behind it you are not delivering a useful talk!
- ➤ Fourth, make enough effort to choose the appropriate words to articulate your ideas clearly (200). (Some of us have a tendency to use a word which is nearer to our thinking saving the labor of searching for an appropriate word.)

  Beware of the fact a word, concept or example not well instituted could very well constitute a prattle.
- ➤ You can take the help of your audience to find out the correct word which is in usage among them.(424)
- ➤ Similarly do not use bombastic words which will go above the head of the most of the audience.

21

Fear Evil Act

(Fearing to do harm others)

201. Evil actors fear not but seasoned men do
     Regarding the danger of evil bravado.

     People who are immersed in acts of hurt inflicted on others soon
     lose a sense of fear and continue their sinful activities with a sort of
     arrogance which blinds them from seeing the reality in terms of the
     precincts of *aram*. Whereas wise who take efforts to be free from
     sinful thoughts and schemes fear that arrogance and vanity.

202. Evil acts beget ruinous repercussions beyond cure
     Hence they are feared more than fire for sure.

     Since evil actors meet ruinous consequences which cannot be wiped
     out, any evil act should be feared as though it is a fire.

203. A leading wisdom is one:
     'Inflicting harm, even to enemies does shun.

     Of all the wisdoms the top one is the wisdom which forbids inflicting
     a hurt even to an enemy as a retaliatory measure.

204. Even by mistake do not plan for the ruin of others
     If you do so, aram will devise yours.

Even by mistake do not plan to ruin others. If you do so *aram* will plan your ruin[66].

205. Hiding behind poverty do not act ill
For, you will become poorer still.

Do not rationalize your evil act for example: 'Since I don't have I steal' and justify that you deserve it. If you do so you will economically decline further.

206. Never cause a hurt to others,
If you want no painful afflictions yours'

If you are interested to lead a life free from painful afflictions do not hurt others.

207. From a most dreaded enemy one can escape
Escaping one's nemesis has no similar scope.

Dreaded enmities, we can possibly escape but not the effect of nemesis.

208. A sinner's[67] ruin is as certain
As his shadow to him pertain.

It is certain a shadow remains with its object. It is similarly certain that a sinner will be ruined.

209. "I love me most," if this is your case
Even a bit of evil you shall not cause.

---

66 The concept of *aram* is a abstract noun. Please consult the rationale section of this chapter to get an idea of what Thiruvalluvar says about *aram*.

67 The word 'sinner' has no connotation to divine law. It means 'a guilty person.'

If it is true that your wellbeing is your primary concern then never entertain any evil thought.

210. Ruins, he is secured from, let him know
If he doesn't harm others by his evil rooted actions.

One can fully secure himself against ruin if he totally keeps himself away from evil actions which are dangerous.

Skill to be learnt:

> Remaining completely free from evil acts.

Rationale:

> Thiruvalluvar says an evil doer is sure to get punished. He posits the idea of *aram* which will see to that every evil doer is punished. Therefore there is no wisdom in doing an evil act holding a position that getting caught and punished is not imminent.

> Thiruvalluvar has not used a concept of God of *Aram* as claimed by many interpreters. Perhaps he has observed the wrong doers who escape for some time ultimately get caught and take the punishment. The whole thing happens in a sequence as if some one is orchestrating it. This phenomenon he calls as an entity by name (God of)*Aram*.

> My understanding of the concept of 'God of *aram*' goes like this: Thiruvalluvar has identified three qualities present in human beings. They are: a need to uphold equity (chapter 12), a need to empathize with fellow human beings (chapter, 58), a need to take compassionate action to alleviate the sufferings of fellow human beings (chapter, 25). These qualities are distributed across the society.

> Any evil act like someone committing a rape of a teenage girl gets the attention of these people quickly because they keep open their eyes and ears (empathy) and their sense of equity and compassion makes them to act to fix the offender and get justice to the victim. These activists quickly hover over the offender through networking. This virtual structure serves like an atmosphere. We can call it as '*aram*

sphere.' This aram sphere which is invisible but which never fails to act makes it as though God acts on the evil doers. (Please remember I have mentioned elsewhere that according to Thiruvalluvar God does not interfere in human life according to my understanding of Thiruvalluvar.)

> Recently when a not widely known Gandhian Anna Hazare started a hunger dharna in New Delhi a large section of the population got electrified in hours. Literally the middle class who joined him could do so because they used twitter and face book extensively. All of them had a shared concern in it. The concern being they wanted a law which has been pending for a very long time for creating a position of Ombudsman for enquiring into the corruption charges at all levels including prime minister and president and bureaucrats and prosecuting the guilty. An *aram* sphere once created gains autonomy. Some may go out and some may come in but the sphere will stay. This idea can be used to discourage people who hurt the interest of others for personal gains.

Coaching:

> The technique is derived from couplet 204. Whenever you are inclined to a thought of doing something hurtful to others or a sin against God or humanity towards which your conscience says, 'Don't do', 'stop it,' you can do so if you have the practice of imagining that you are under a network called Aram sphere. Aram sphere is receiving constant field report about you and will punish you in an appropriate manner in an appropriate time.

> If another thought comes to you that you know several people who have made similar mistakes but nothing untoward happened to them remember that *aram* sphere takes its own time to build but once built it is very difficult to escape punishment. It allows you enough time to realize your mistakes and mend your ways. But once it is activated it is very difficult to escape. Also remember an *aram* sphere is specifically built for you whose only occupation is fixing you!

> The Hindu dated 10.11. 2014 has published an interview it had with Deb Roy the founder of Laboratory for Social Machines at

the Massachusetts Institute of Technology (MIT) which studies human interaction online to create more responsive governments and systems. The title of the interview is 'Imagine a future where everyone could express himself. . .' According to Roy the voice share and its foot share on the ground doesn't match. The institute will be working on this issue. With the advance of such technology democracies would get great opportunities to transform the voices of their populace into actions. This is how God of *Aram* would work in the future.

➤ Another pitfall is a false entitlement one entertains. Sometimes thieves too entertain a notion that since they don't have and their victims have there is nothing wrong in stealing from them. This is totally wrong. Never allow your condition as an excuse to commit evil acts like amassing wealth from others. Whenever you feel you are entitled on any ground to receive some thing or act in a particular way become cautious. Invariably you will find your entitlements would be ultra vires as for as equity is concerned. Guided by that fake sense in all likelihood you will end up in swindling which you cannot stop after a certain stage (205)

22

Enabling Growth

(Philanthropy, Social Responsibility)
(Social obligation)

211. **R**ain rains out of duty not for a tradeoff
     Even otherwise what the universe could return in lieu of?

     Rain takes it as its duty to rain. It doesn't expect anything in return
     and continue to rain. Even otherwise what return gift is the universe
     capable of returning as an expression of gratitude? (Similarly a
     socialpreneur does not expect anything in return to his help. Since
     help comes from him under no obligation such help cannot returned.)

212. **W**ealth earned employing body, mind and soul
     Is meant for growth enabling goal.

     Goods that are earned through hard and engaged enterprise
     are meant for reinvesting into growth enabling ventures (social
     entrepreneurship) at the individual level to deserving individuals.

     (However, the recipient should deserve such a help. Whether he
     deserves or not is decidable on his ability to make use of the help in
     such a manner that he reaches a stage of not only not needing help
     any further but also being able to help other needy and deserving
     individual. This concept has some similarity to the concept of
     Corporate Social Responsibility. But the idea of Thiruvalluvar unlike
     in the context of CSR is not an act of gratis. He means whoever has

developed enough should enable the growth of another needy person in some way like giving him time, labor or money. Secondly, the exercise is not a free bonanza rather a fiduciary one. This is a happy marriage of capitalism with communism.)

The concept of 'generativity' enunciated by Psychoanalyst and developmental psychologist Eric Erikson comes close to this: Both *oppuravu* and 'generativity' are carried out by persons who are mentally healthy because they were fully benefitted by their immediate family and society during developmental stages.
To recall Thiruvalluvar's concept namely *'sandranmai'* which embodies mental health in its florescence in this context will not be out of place because *oppuravu* is one of the five components of *sandranmai* (983).

213. **E**ither in heaven or on earth no activity found
     Better than growth-enabling kind.

No other act that is carried out on the earth or at heaven can be more apt than the one contributing ones share to social responsibility or *oppuravu*.

214. **B**eing sensible shows someone as alive[68]
     Not being sensible qualifies to be among not alive.

One who could sense the conditions of fellow human beings and has the motivation to do something to lift their conditions to meet certain standards alone is said to be living (anyone who lives in his soul alone is said to be living). Those who are not capable of this sensibility are as good as dead (they are soul less).

---

[68] The Tamil phrase 'uyir vaazhvan' may mean that a person who is empathic to the need of another person lives in his soul not in his ego.

215. Like a public tank whose water brims
     Growth enabler's wealth society's growth primes.

A common tank in the midst of a town is meant for everybody who needs water. Similarly the wealth of someone who is a *perarivalan* (a person who is enlightened enough to decide that the best use of money is to keep it under the disposal of needy persons who can benefit from it) is meant for the use of the society.

(The tank through its bunds keeps the water safe so that everyone who needs it can benefit and wait for the next fill. It should also be remembered that the users arrange to maintain the tank so that it is replenished every time there is a rain. Similarly a *perarivalan* will maintain his wealth in such a way it is protected from depletion by carefully deploying it to needy persons and reequipping it by the proceeds from them. Number of other words are used in different couplets in the chapter to mean the same entity namely *perarivalan*. To reflect them in translation I have used words like 'enlightened' and 'seasoned' etc in line with different Tamil words used by the poet to denote the same concept.)

216. Wealth at the disposal of a seasoned
     Are the edible fruits on a public tree.

Wealth of a seasoned person is like the ripe fruits on a tree in the center of the town open to all.

217. Every part of a medicinal tree yields medicine
     In philanthropy each of his penny the wise puts in.

All the parts of a medicinal tree are useful to whoever knows how to use it. Similarly an enlightened man does not spare anything. His wealth is useful to all those who can benefit from it.

218. **M**en who are conscious of their duty to the society
     Will not back out even when they attain poverty

     Those who think they are always obliged to the society will never
     stop their help even when they are economically run down. They will
     switch over to other modes like offering labor/time and knowledge
     to the needy persons and help them to grow. This is like being on
     the call of duty always.

219. **S**easoned men feel poor not because their wealth is dimed
     But because their capability to give is mimed.

     Seasoned people at times of economic downturn in their lives will
     not feel poor. But they will, if their capacity to help the needy in
     other ways also gets annulled.

220. **I**f accrued poverty prevents continuing a help
     It deserves to be made good by selling oneself.

     Thiruvalluvar declares that if ruin is to result on account of acting
     in a socially responsible way one should sell himself and complete
     the task. (Perhaps Tiruvalluvar tries to say that since one is sure
     to reach God's land if he is so adamant in his socially responsible
     activities nothing wrong if he has to sell himself for the sake of it
     after all it will be his last birth here. It would be very apt to quote
     an interesting historical piece here. Colonel John Pennycuick who
     built the Mullaperiar Dam at South India underwent extraordinary,
     extraordinary difficulties financially, professionally, physically,
     domestically and most importantly army-service relatedly to
     complete the construction of the dam during British rule after
     getting dismissed from the service. He has written something like
     this in his diary: 'My visit to this universe is only once. My coming
     here would not happen again. Therefore I should do something
     good. There is no room to drop this or postpone this. Because I am
     not going to come here again.'

Skills to be learned:

> Ability to imbibe the spirit of *oppuravu* (social entrepreneurship/ growth enabling/ social obligation/ philanthropy)

Rationale:

> World's resources belong to the human and other creatures of the world. The purpose of wealth - the monetized form of world resource - is to re plough it into growth promoting ventures at the individual level so that national product will increase catering to the increase of the holding of every stake holder i.e., every citizen of the land and other creatures.

> Second *oppuravu* always need not be providing hedge money or venture capital or other forms of economic support towards promoting growth. At the individual level it can be any act towards sustaining and increasing national product. For example, if a person decides to use a public transport sacrificing personal comfort for commuting to his office it is an act of *oppuravu* because he is doing it as part of his decision to contribute to the reduction of carbon foot print.

> Skill imparting/ guiding and counselling also will come under *oppuravu*

> Tiruvalluvar present a happy picture of marrying the individual effort and common good in his concept of *oppuravu*.

Coaching:

The following counselling material is culled out from the couplets of the chapter.

> Thiruvalluvar strongly suggests that wealth earned through hard labor and fully engaged effort should be re ploughed into the society for promoting growth at the individual level. Of course taking care of one's needs reasonably well goes without saying.

> ➢ The individuals should behave like clouds in this respect. Clouds do not expect anything in return for the help they render to the world (212&211).

> ➢ Growth promotion involves activities in the areas of education, health, nutrition and individual entrepreneurship without expecting anything in return like the cloud which rains without expecting anything in return.

> ➢ The inputs for bringing in the needed change of attitude in the individual can be garnered from couplets: 213, 214, 215,216,217,218, 219 and 220.

> ➢ The individual should be impressed that no act by him either in this world or in the heaven can be held as highly desirable or important than involving himself in the schemes of *oppuravu*/social entrepreneurship/responsibility (213).

> ➢ The individual can claim that he is living in flesh and blood only if he has a powerful sensibility to understand the conditions of fellow human beings against some standard or against what he possesses. Otherwise he is equal to the dead. Something worth mentioning in the context of acquiring sensibility is: it will grow in leaps and bounds once an individual allows himself to be impacted by the conditions of people who live below standard conditions. (214).

> ➢ The individual should be impressed with the fact that an enlightened wealthy person will consider his wealth as a common facility like the water tank in the middle of the town or a fruit tree accessible to everyone or a medicinal plant whose parts from top to bottom can be used as medicine (215/16/17).

> ➢ The individual should be impressed that it is not always giving his money; even if he lacks money he can give his time/labor and knowledge towards social responsibility/entrepreneurship or *oppuravu*. In the realm of friendship if a person is trying to find out ways and means to cooperate with his friend and adapt to his needs to an excellent degree he is said to show oppuravu. Similarly, in the field of work whether a person is evasive or rigorous keeping an eye on the social usefulness on what he does matters. In the field of love a socially useful and quality accomplishment could be doing a sacrifice of your time, money and labor for the sake of your loved ones. Mind

you this is not a prescription to lose. You will reap ample rewards for what you do. If you reflect, you will realize that an individualist's agenda is well served in this approach on a sustainable basis. (218).

➤ The individual should be impressed that he can consider himself as poor only when he is not able to use his other resources (other than money) also (219).

➤ The individual should be impressed that if he were to become poor due to his socially responsible activities he should sell himself and complete the task. Such a move is worth taking because the act has the potential to usher him into heaven (220).

23

Charity[69]

(Giving to poor without saying 'no')

221. Giving to the poor is alone charity
Other gifts indicate a hand-loan[70] strategy.

Gifting a poor and needy person is alone charity. Giving to other persons who are not poor are like hand loans. (Hand loans are repayable without interest.) (This couplet gives a definition for charity or helping a needy person. A help mostly financial, is given to a person who badly needs it without expecting anything in return. Any financial help to other persons who are not poor and desperate would not be considered as charitable.

---

[69] This chapter and the previous one may appear to be similar raising the question whether there is any redundancy here. Charity is gifting something to a person who needs it badly. Whereas *oppuravu is* a long term planed activity of nation building working at the level of the individual. To give an example: charity is like first aide and *oppuravu* is a planed treatment.

[70] Hand-loan is the translation for the Tamil word *kuriethirppu*. This refers to the practice existing even today of taking a loan from a friend or relative for a very short period. Normally no interest is levied.

114

222. Receiving a help as a policy is ok but not desirable;
     Even if heaven is forbidden[71] charity is commendable.

     Even though as a temporary measure it is ok to receive a help it is a
     harmful practice on the part of the receiver if he continues to exploit
     that space. In the case of someone who is capable of giving he shall
     continue it even if he was to lose the opportunity to reach heaven.
     (Thiruvalluvar's egalitarian stance is strewn throughout the treatise
     of Thirukkural making it hard to miss. But at the same time he is
     very clear that human beings should move past of the dependency
     they unfortunately found themselves in. In this couplet you can see
     his thinking coming out clearly. There is also a counter to the notion
     held in some quarters (is it from scriptures?) that beggar suffers his
     karma and therefore interfering in the scheme of karma tantamount
     to obstructing the path of karma and such an adventurism would
     make one to lose his opportunity to reach heaven even though he is
     otherwise qualified.)

223. "I don't have," creates pain to the receiver
     Not saying so is a great family heritage given.

     Saying bluntly "I don't have," acts like an overdose and creates a
     disproportionate pain in the person who seeks help. The seeker
     might collapse for several seconds. Therefore a man hailing from a
     family of great helping tradition will never say so.

224. Remaining in pitying mode, but not helping, lasts,
     Until seeker psyching it, with his smile indicates.

     A person may act as if he or she is pained for not being able to help.
     This feigned pain lasts only as long as seeing smile on the help seeker
     who (either got helped in real time by another person or psyched the

---

[71] Thiruvalluvar has a dig at the notion that poverty is one's karma which one
     should undergo to finish it. Therefore helping a sufferer being an anathema
     should be avoided. He takes this argument by its horn and pooh-pooh it.

denier's mind) and showed an understanding smile as a response. (Perhaps this person belongs to a family of rank misers, but pretender of great tradition!)

225. **F**eeding the hungry is able
Enabling beating the hunger is ablest.

Of all the strengths the best is one which relieves hunger. But the strategy to help him to move into a position of needing no further help is a much better strength. (You may notice while the first act is the central theme of this chapter the second act forms the theme for the previous chapter. Do you remember "Instead of gifting fish teach fishing"?)

226. Quelling the horrendous hunger is an act
For investing one's wealth a mankind has got.

The best proposal to invest money is spending the same to eradicate poverty. (The goodwill created among the members of community and the beneficiaries is saved for a possible future help, the helper may need. This idea is inbuilt in the next couplet.)

227. His resources who shares with others
To him the prospect of hunger never occurs.

Anyone who shares his food and other resources with the poor will never be afflicted by the fire like condition of hunger later.

228. The hard at heart, as time tides, lose what they hoard
Perhaps does not know the joy of gifting, behold.

People with stony heart hoard and lose it in due course of time. Perhaps they don't know the joy of giving.

229. That which is hoarded – all alone eating
Is painful than begging.

If a person reflects he would find that hoarding and eating what is hoarded all alone is more painful than begging. (Any miser who lives in the midst of great givers sooner or later gets sensitized is obvious. The new sense creates a sting of conscience in them when they continue their miserliness.)

230. Dying is most painful. It too is sweeter
When, due to poverty, gifting does shatter.

Even dying, the most painful experience, becomes enjoyable when one escapes through death the pain of not being able to help others.

Skills to be learnt:

➤ Ability and attitude to give to someone in need.

Rationale:

➤ Thiruvalluvar says donating or giving is a joy (228). When you give and when the receiver says, "thank you," you feel good about yourself. That is the reason for your joy. Two competing thoughts which stand against reaping this joy are "my money is my equity earned through my hard labor and it is up to others to create similar equity for them" and "if I give they will lose interest to create their own equity." Both ideas are based on the premise that earning equity is open on a level playing field for every one which may not be the case.

➤ Read what Warren Buffett has to say on this: "A market economy creates some lopsided payoffs to participants. The right endowment of vocal chords, anatomical structure, physical strength, or mental powers can produce enormous piles of claim checks (stocks, bonds, and other forms of capital) on future national output. Proper selection of ancestors similarly can result in lifetime supplies of such tickets upon birth. If zero real investments returns diverted a bit greater portion of the national output from such stockholders to equally worthy and hardworking citizens lacking jackpot producing talents, it would seem unlikely to pose such an insult to an equitable world as to risk Divine intervention."

➤ For want of a level playing field some unfortunate people are always at a disadvantage position and they require to be helped. Another point is that they contribute in their own limited way to the national output which caters to the equity of any rich person. Therefore a rich person who has more than what he can consume has an obligation to part with a portion of his wealth to the poor otherwise as Buffet has suggested Divine intervention may take place. The chapter is named as giving that would have meant giving to a beggar. In today's world we may have to change the begging context to helping context.

Coaching:

➤ The skill to donate others can be developed provided we develop a suitable value and a decision based on that value. The incentives for developing the value are given in couplets 223,225,226,227 and 228.

➤ Your claim for a noble family lineage can be substantiated only if you exhibit the signature quality of a noble family. That quality is: members of a noble family would never say the painful words "I don't have" (223).

➤ If you want to claim that you are a man of great strengths make your claim after gifting substantially to the needy since that is THE Strength (225). (Of course that strength is ranked below the strength of social engineering or *oppuravu* which lifts a person from his position of aid seeker to that of aid giver)

➤ Mentally accept the fact that the best investment you can make of your money is investing it to wipe out the hunger of a destitute (226).

➤ Develop a strong belief that if an individual shares what he has with others he will never have the fate of going without food (227).

➤ You should gift as often as possible and feel the joy and esteem you feel when the recipients of your help thank you profusely (228).

24

Fame[72]

(Esteem from the public or from the beneficiaries of one's growth enabling or philanthropic actions)

231. **W**inning reputation out of altruistic action
Soul[73] has no better compensation.

For the soul the best compensation for living a life of ups and down and uncertainty on the earth is getting evolved well enough to reach the abode of God. Giving is an exercise of the soul. Such selfless exercise is soul-fulfilling leading to the evolution of the soul. A fully evolved soul reaches heaven. (A soul which embodies itself to be

---

[72] This chapter is very famous because of the couplet number 236. The couplet is translated by Reverent GU Pope as, "If, man you walk the stage, appear adorned with glory's grace; // Save glorious you can shine, t' were better hide your face." I am of the opinion that this chapter is about earning reputation from the beneficiaries or others for acts of philanthropy or growth enabling activities. It doesn't talk of other achievements and fame obtained on account of them. Tiruvalluvar has extensively written on the topic of helping the poor and needy. While chapter 23 talks of simple first aide like help of benevolence, chapter 22 speaks about growth enabling help. Chapter 25 talks about compassionate action i.e., struggling for getting justice to the weak. This chapter (24) is a finishing chapter on the topic.

[73] The Tamil word used is *ouir* (life) Normally it means life but in several places Thiruvalluvar uses it in lieu of soul. This is one such place.

born on the earth may take several births to fully evolve to reach
the abode of God.)

232. **G**iving by altruists in regard to requesters
Make the substantial theme for men of letters.

The themes of all the best treatises happen to be about the
philanthropic acts of persons who have helped others.

233. **O**ther than the episodes of altruistic acts
None the world keeps in its tracks,

This world remembers only those altruistic contributions of people
which stand apart from activities of all and sundry.

234. **I**f a fame of horizontal proportion is earned
The divinity will extol them not men of letters, behold!

If some one's contribution towards growth enabling ventures are so
good that the fame it netted withstands the tide of time, God's world
would appreciate him or her not men of thriving literature.

235. **P**rosperity and poverty like birth and death are routine
Taking them on their side rare laurels only the soul-realized could
obtain[74]

Wealth and poverty might occur in cycles. Similar is the case with
birth and death. It is possible only for the wise (the growth enabler) to
convert these uncertainties into opportunities to contribute towards
accomplishing socially useful products.

---

[74] A line by line translation of this couplet will read like this: Like wealth and
poverty death also // but for the men of wisdom this rare is impossible. There
are few couplets for understanding which a holistic reading of the chapter is
necessary. This is one of them.

236. **S**how your face if you plan to deliver a fame earning act
Otherwise never go before sufferers since it lacks tact.

If someone wants to arrive on a scene where people look at him for help let him do so provided he has the mind, determination and means to take actions to alleviate their sufferings. Otherwise let him not show his face at all among them.

237. **I**f someone chooses not to act earning fame
Why the hell his retributer he blames?

If someone has carried out a shabby job of social usefulness or shirked from it he should curse himself for that. Instead, why should he find fault with those who retribute him for his actions?

238. **I**t is a blame for men of the world
If they do not leave esteem behind, it is told

It is a blemish for humanity to live a life without making a contribution towards alleviating the suffering of fellow brethren and earning their esteem.

239. Of blame free yields land remains poor in several fields
If lives, devoid of acts earning reputation, it holds.

The world needs *oppuravu* (philanthropy) for converting its potentials into blameless national products which will help the nation to prosper. Therefore if a land happen to bear persons who are not interested in earning public esteem through philanthropic acts the lands productivity and national productivity would suffer.

240. Life of men with no baggage of blame is well done
Life of men with no client-esteem is ill done.

A person is said to have lived a worthy life if he has alleviated the sufferings of fellow humans. Similarly a life is worth lived if the person concerned did not earn the blame from fellow humans.

Skills to be learnt:

> Carrying out philanthropic activities by investing one's money, time, skill and energy.

Rationale:

> The need to pick up this skill is clearly stated in the first couplet. The couplet says soul has only one object to be embodied here. The object is to achieve enough maturity for itself to reach the abode of God.
> The news appearing in Hindu dated 5.1.11 had these observations by the Nobel laureate Venkataraman Ramakrishnan: He has asked the Indians not to confuse scientists with movie and cricket stars. According to him when he escorted Nobel laureate Thomas Seitz – who arrived on his invitation to the 'Pride of India Exhibition' at the Science Congress – they were mobbed by the public and students and that the tour could last only for 15 minutes. He could not explain to the visiting laureate the advances in Indian science. What Venkataraman Ramakrishnan wanted to show was the work of Indian scientists. Scientists are not cricket stars to be surrounded. Thiruvalluvar, as per my understanding has written about such work only, not about achieving stardom/popularity or fame.

Coaching:

The following advocacy is culled from the couplets:

> Ingrain this idea clearly in your mind and power it with your heart: the fee a human being get for spending his time on this earth is getting number of opportunities to evolve at the level of his soul. The evolution of the soul is achieved by involving oneself in giving

whatever one has at his disposal – money, labor, time, education and skilling etc., (231).

➤ Remember the substantial theory writers revolved around the fame of great givers only (232).

➤ Don't forget that this earth remembers none other than the altruistic act of its sons (233).

➤ Know it, people at God's world would appreciate you, not writers of great treatises, if you muster a long lasting fame by your growth enabling acts, (234).

➤ It is true good times and bad, life and death alternate and nothing is permanent in this world. This creates lot of pressure on ordinary men who might lose interest in carrying out the socially useful activities. But soul realized men take the pressure on them positively and endure to carry out to fruition whatever socially useful project they started. You should aim for such laurels (235).

➤ Appear before sufferers who need help in all forms if you intend to offer any one of them in accordance with your capacity. Otherwise do not go there as a spectator (236).

➤ Especially if you go to a place where people who need help are waiting and you are a person who has never helped any of them despite you have the means to do so the situation will turn awkward and you will be decried. In that case you must realize that you must curse yourself for what has happened rather than finding fault with those who decry you (237)

➤ Remember it is despicable for anybody to remain without earning the esteem. Are you one? If you are, then when people retribute you for it do not blame them (238).

➤ The world has people with full of potentials. Those potentials can be converted into assets only when they receive the help needed to educate or train themselves or start a venture. Therefore if a country has people who are capable of launching philanthropic activities to help the community choose not to do so they are like dead weight for mother earth. Do you want to be a dead weight? (239).

➤ Imagine that you are on your last day on this earth. If you take stock of what you have achieved in terms of socially useful contributions how will you rate yourself. If you rate yourself as not up to the mark, take it, you are not living a life as intended to human by God. Therefore start doing things afresh following what you have been told so far(240)

> Remember extending help to promote growth in any form like giving money, knowledge, skill time and energy is welcome. All of them are soul evolving activities only if properly approached.

25

Compassion[75]

(Love+equity+action)

241. A compassionate heart is the treasure of all
Material treasures, even with lowly fall.

Of all the treasures a human being can be proud of, the possession of
a compassionate heart is the best. Material treasures do not qualify
to be called as treasures as they are available with lesser beings (mean
people in whom compassion is absent).

242. Strategically and ethically dispense grace[76]
Other avenues reviewed, advocates its embrace.

---

[75] The chapter is named as *aruludaimai* in Tamil. The word has no single equivalent
word in English. Aruludaimai = love+equity+action. A genuine activist who
struggles to win the equity of a victim is motivated by this streak in her or his
personality. For example fighting for the cause of tigers is an act of aruludaimai.
Please keep this in mind whenever you come across the words compassion or
grace in this chapter I used them in lieu of *aruludaimai*. Otherwise concepts
of compassion or grace or sympathy as they mean in English are not found in
Thirukkural. The German word Gemeinschaftsgefuhl has maximum similarity
with *aruludaimai*.

[76] The word grace also comes very near in some sense but very different from
aruludaimai.

Find out strategic but faultless means and carry out kindly acts to
fellow humans. A study of all the other approaches shows that it is
the only worthy guide for living. (Compassion is the scaffolding
which will take us to heaven. This is inferable from the next couplet.
Tiruvalluvar uses two couplets in many places to do a full justification
to a concept.)

243. In their hearts those who compassion hold
      Don't have to reincarnate into this painful world.

Men who cherish compassion in their heart and keep themselves at
its service will attain the company of God after their natural death.
They would not be required to reincarnate in this painful world.

244. Men set to set equity can never keep mum
      Therefore no action is life threatening to them.

A person who is genuinely compassionate and take care of others life
will not desist from any act towards the goal in view of the risk it has
for the security of his life.

245. Men of compassion refuse to suffer
      Wind grit universe has evidences to offer.

As evidences found in the history of this world swept by wild winds
show, compassionate persons refuse to suffering as acknowledged by
M.K.Gandhi's life.

246. Those who have lost the purpose of life are insensitive
      Therefore in unkindly act they remain active.

People carry out a graceless unkind life because they are devoid of
the purpose of life on the earth. The purpose being evolving oneself
at the level of his soul to become eligible for a life at heaven.

247. To wealth less this universe deny life's shine;
Uncompassionates are denied the world of divine.

Anyone who is poor will find no means to enjoy this world and hence this world is as good as lost to them. Similarly definite is the fact that humans with no compassionate heart and action do not have a place in heaven.

248. Paupers may flourish one day
Failures of compassion never make it on a later day.

A person who has lost his wealth may become wealthy again. In the case of people who lose their compassion their loss is beyond redemption.

249. A man with no compassion discharging an act of aram
Is similar to a knowledge less grasping absolute truth.

A person who is not compassionate trying to follow *aram* in his day to day activities is like a person low in knowledge going after the task of finding the absolute truth.

250. When you take on a person weaker than you
Think of you when a stronger comes against you.

If you mentally capture your position and feel the agony when a person stronger than you takes it on you, then you will avoid going against a person weaker than you.

Skill to be learnt:

➢ Ability to show compassion to fellow human beings. Compassionate behavior means doing everything in ones command to uphold the right/equity of fellow organisms human as well as animals.

Rationale:

➤ So many wrongs are taking place every second in this world. The right of humans and animals and the Mother Nature is crushed by persons and systems which are not compassionate at heart. There are also wonderful people who take it up on them to fight and get some relief to the sufferers. Without sacrificing much each one of us can do our bit to help people to enjoy their right.

Coaching:

The following counseling material is culled from the couplets.

➤ Introspect within yourself. Are you a compassionate person? Don't worry if you get a negative answer. This is true of several people. It doesn't say anything specifically bad about you. It only says that there is scope and need to pick up the skill.

➤ Have you ever been aggressed by a person more powerful than you? If you have an experience then try to remember that experience and the feelings you had at that time as vividly as possible and note them down in a sheet of paper (250).

➤ Did your list have any of the following:

➤ I felt humiliated. 2. I felt like weeping. 3. I wanted to take the help of my parents/friends/relatives/police to punish him. 4. He has no business to hurt me

➤ You will find your feelings were all built on the injustice done to you. Is it not so?

➤ Given an opportunity and the needed support you would like to take it on him and punish him for all the injustice he has done to you. Is it not so?

➤ If you do so you have been very compassionate to yourself. All you need to do is to extend the same to others also. That is what makes you as a compassionate man/woman. How you contribute towards is the ingenuity left to you.

➤ When a person involves himself in a compassionate act there is no doubt that he acts from his soul. It is a two way process. While you are acting compassionately it not only benefits the person for whom your actions are meant it also benefits you in the sense your soul evolves. An evolved soul is a guarantor for further evolvement graduating itself towards reaching heaven (243).

➤ If you are a compassionate person you will never mind any suffering due to your compassionate act (245).

➤ But remember in the today's unprincipled mafia ridden world it is very dangerous to act compassionately. The case of so many whistle blowers meeting death in India is frightening. (We have all sorts of mafia. The recent one is in vegetable sales.) Therefore the whistle blowers should be careful enough not to push their agenda too far. They should wait for the time to do its bit of work while preserving all the evidences without attracting the attention of the evil doers. (488)

➤ You may donate your wealth. But you may not reap any benefit out of it if you don't donate out of compassion. Therefore when you donate do not have any ulterior motive.

➤ Believe really that fellow human beings have a right for a trouble free life and it is your duty to help them to achieve that because of your enhanced position in the society.

26

Denying Meat

(Vegetarianism)

251. **H**e who eats animal fat to fatten himself
How would discharge compassion to lives beyond self?

    How will meat eaters, who in order to enhance their tissues eat other
    animal's flesh, be able to show compassion? (Showing compassion
    means upholding the right of fellow human beings and other creatures
    to live a happy life and doing whatever is within one's power to actualize
    that right. Therefore his contention that people who kill animals to
    fatten themselves cannot practice compassion sounds logically correct.)

252. With a non-prudent wealth doesn't thrive
With a meat eater compassion doesn't survive.

    For want of prudence and a sense of scale on the part of its possessor
    wealth doesn't flourish. Similarly with meat eaters compassion
    doesn't stay (because of the inconsistency in both the cases.)

253. Like an armed man's heart
On good, a meat eater cannot set his heart.

    Weapon possessors have the tendency to use their weapon for non-
    good purposes. Similarly minds of people who enjoy eating meat
    motivate them to go in the wrong path.

254. **k**illing the act of killing is compassion[77]
Eating killed meat shows meaningless passion.

If you ask what is not being compassionate, it is killing not-killing. If you ask which act of human being is hollowed the answer is: I eat meat but don't blame me for breach of *aram* because I did not kill but only eat what has been killed by some one.' (The hollowness referred here is clearly brought out in couplet number 256.)

255. **S**oul is active in a non-eater of meat
The habit is a hell which never lets it out.

Soul's evolving process hinges on not eating meat. Meat eating habit is a hell which never opens its mouth to let out its captors. That means for want of an active soul meat eaters cannot be compassionate.

256. If the meat eating world does not kill to eat
None would come forward to sell meat.

Eaters of meat cannot blame the killers accusing them of intimidation. After all if the meat eating world does not indulge in eating meat nobody will kill for the sake of trade in meat. In as much as the meat eating world induces killing the blame of killing falls on them not on the butcher. To say 'we eat only because someone kills,' is a rationalization to circumvent the breach of *aram*.

257. "I can empathize the pain of a deadly wound,"
If true, desisting from eating meat, he must be found.

If someone claims they can certainly empathize with the pain of death they should substantiate their claim by abstaining from eating meat.

---

[77] The poet actually states something like this: what is not compassion is killing non-killing // What is meaningless is eating that meat. Since the double negative is little confusing (at least for me) I avoided it in my translation.

258. Men whose brains of criminal thoughts divested
     Consume no life on which death was willfully inflicted.

     Men whose mind is free from criminal thought will never eat another
     life on which death has been forced.

259. Not killing for meat yields good
     Its goodness is better than mantra and sacrificial fire.

     Chanting mantras and pouring ghee in religious oblations to appease
     gods can be less useful to obtain the blessings of heavenly beings than
     simply abstaining from killing for the sake of eating.

260. Them who desisted killing or eating meat
     All living beings with folded palms and reverence greet.

     Persons who do not consume meat and persons who do not kill to
     produce meat will be revered by all with folded palms. (Thiruvalluvar
     who tries to differentiate between the trader and the eater of meat
     by taking a tough stand on the eater(256) and somewhat excusive
     of the trader earlier in this chapter even them in this couplet saying
     that those who do not kill (trader of meat) and those who do not eat
     will be equally revered by all.)

Skills to be learnt:

➢   Becoming a pure vegetarian out of a compassionate position of
    upholding the right of the animals to live.

Rationale:

➢   Acting out of compassion according to Tiruvalluvar is doing what
    you can to uphold the equity of every living organism – human as
    well as other non-human creatures. Therefore he says if people want
    to be compassionate they should relinquish the habit of eating meat.

Coaching:

The following counseling material is culled from the couplets.

- ➢ The first step is getting the notion of compassion very strong in your mind (251 and 252).
- ➢ For achieving this join a vegetarians club and give/organize seminars on the concept of compassion (254,257).
- ➢ At the end of such exercises you should have developed a mindset where you will find it impossible to eat meet (258).
- ➢ In the initial stage one thing that will discourage and kill the effort to become a pure vegetarian is the enormous self-pity that we may develop. Since meaty proteins are tastier than vegetarian proteins anyone who is a meat eater will find it very difficult to forgo meat (253). (Interestingly it appears scientists are nearing a solution for this. Advances in stem cell research will soon make it possible to produce meat in laboratory where the killing of an animal is not involved.)
- ➢ Self-pity can be fought with a strategy of looking at the meat of an animal as a wound with blood and other waste. If you can visualize this picture as strongly as possible it is possible for you to slowly come out of the habit of meat eating. (258)
- ➢ Join the biodiversity movement in your area. The fundamental idea in biodiversity is that every living organism has a right to live under the sun so humanity should do everything within their power to conserve them. The idea that human is more privileged than others and all other organisms and resources of the world are meant to serve humans is an erroneous notion. This will be learnt in such groups (Refer the chapter number 33 for knowing Thiruvalluvar's ideas regarding biodiversity).
- ➢ Once you have the notions of compassion with regard to meat eating and biodiversity idea suggesting the right and place of each creatures as God's children to exist here you can take the next step:
- ➢ Erect two images in your mind. 1. I am a meat eater.2. I want to be compassionate and I want to support bio diversity. Make these images as strongly as possible in your mind. The stronger they

become the more the need you have to come out of the conflict between these two.

➢ It is at this juncture your joining the vegetarian club on a trial basis will work in favor of deciding against meat eating. Like AA groups the experience and support of those who relinquished meat eating will help you also to relinquish eating meat.

➢ Once you become a strong vegetarian and a supporter of biodiversity the idea of not killing any animal becomes so strong in your mind then you will find it difficult even to pinch a green twig from a tree!

27

Penance

(The essential meaning of penance)

261. Enduring pain and never hurting any life
With these penance is rife.

Thiruvalluvar is of the opinion that carrying out penance is a career like the career of running the institution of home. One should engage himself fully in the chores of an ascetic career which involves undergoing physical miseries. He should also see to that any of his ascetic activity doesn't harm any life.

262. Penance is meant for those whose nature is so
It is wasteful that others make it as their go.

Only those, for whom penance is an endowed urge[78] should adopt it as a career. It is futile if others who are not so endowed undertake it.

263. Is it to cater to those in penance,
Others do not take to penance?

Men in household involve themselves in taking care of ascetics. Perhaps for this purpose they remain as householders. (In couplet 41 it was shown that among the several duties of a householder

---

[78] Perhaps a soul which was engaged in tapas/a great life following the precincts of aram in the previous birth now wants to continue it as a means of realizing self.

taking care of ascetics was one. After categorically declaring only people whose mind is naturally attracted towards penance should chose to become ascetics, Thiruvalluvar tries to take care of the rest saying that they can also participate in the great human endeavor of realizing God by feeding and taking care of the ascetics with a spirit of devotion. It is stated severally in devotional literature of Tamil that one can attain God by serving great ascetics with utmost devotion.)

264. Winning the hearts of enemies and making a stranger as affectionate
In an ascetic such abilities are innate.

Ascetics by their pure disposition do sanitize men of their enmity and make strangers as affectionate.

265. Tapas gives what they wish as they wish
Hence effort is invested here on this crush

Ascetics achieve their objective through tapas. Lured by this several people try to undertake tapas. Perhaps an ascetic may achieve a connection with his soul and live a totally unencumbered bliss. No doubt this is quite attractive to everyone.

266. Those who are involved in tapas has chosen it as their career[79]/[80]
Others who enter it due to other attractions harm the career.

It is by their aptitude ascetics are in the career of tapas. Others for whom it is not so may develop some fantasies towards an ascetic life and chose it. Since there is a serious mismatch they will not succeed in their endeavor. In a way they may harm the career.

---

[79] Couplet 262 and 266 read more or less same. But there is a shuttle difference. While the former deals with those who were in tapas in their previous birth the later deals with new entrants.

[80] This couplet and the last one of the chapter provide a prelude to the next chapter which is about pseudo ascetics.

267. Fire refines the gold
Physical miseries do the same to an ascetic.

The more the gold is heated the more it becomes pure. Similarly the more a saint endures the sufferings of an ascetic life the more pure becomes his soul.

268. He who de-bloats his ego and gets his soul
Humanity worships him in all.

An ascetic through subjugating his ego empowers his soul. This is a rare and much coveted feat. For this reason the folks of the land worship him.

269. Escaping reincarnation and thus escaping death one will pass
If he is hell bent on harvesting the fruits of tapas.

The question of death arises only for a mortal. One can escape from it if he attains heaven. If a person engages himself fully in rigorous penance it is possible for him to reach heaven and thus escape the Lord of Death on the earth.

270. There are not many ascetics because few do mediate
Whereas many only imitate.[81]

Genuine saints are rare to see. This is because very few carry out real penance. Several others, who are sham, pretend to do so. (This couplet seems to be a prelude to the next chapter.)

---

[81] The couplet only says there are not many who are involved in the career of sainthood because undertaking tapas is very difficult and hence all and sundry could not undertake it. But many seem to be faking. Therefore apparently it may look that many are involved whereas genuine ascetics are few.

Skills to be learnt:

> ➢ The notion of penance which is an act of rigorous adherence to certain practices can be extrapolated to a civilian life. Carrying out ones activities professional, household and societal with devotion i.e., involving mind, body and soul and being compassionate to fellow human beings is equivalent to offering penance (261).
> ➢ The modern day concept of engaged employee or the concept of karma yogi share the basic philosophy of penance.

Rationale:

> ➢ Main objective of penance is concentrating on God. The body and its activities are hindrances to this. Therefore, an ascetic undergoes severe austerities like totally cutting him off from any comfort with no need to mention abstinence from sexual pleasure. He may starve, subject himself to hot sun or with help of asana and through total vegetarianism etc., he may purify his soul. But for people who are in families and in careers this is not possible. So what use has this skill for them?
> ➢ The notion of devotion can be adapted by a householder cum career maker. In the domestic sphere we have seen family man and woman have several obligations like showing love to all the family members and others connected to the family(8), taking care of guests(9),maintaining equity(12) charity(23) and compassion(25). All these activities need to be carried out with devotion. Similarly activities of the profession need to be carried out with full application of mind and energy. Tiruvalluvar says such householders would get whatever a saint gets (46. 47 and 48). Read those couplets given below:

> If virtuous path[82] guides life's purpose,
> What gain is achieved in other traverse?   46

---

[82] Virtuous path is carrying out the duties of a household following the path of *aram*.

If domestic life is practiced as a natural career
It is supreme to any other career.   47

As a natural career if family life remains *aram* guided,
It has the benefits of tapas accrued.   48

Coaching:

The following counseling material is culled from the couplets.

- ➢ Carryout domestic and career related work in a religious manner. Being religious means working as seriously as possible sparing no efforts and longing for reaching God (261)
- ➢ Even while you are thoroughly involved in domestic/societal/ professional activities practice detached attachment. Keep God as your permanent witness and work fearing him. (266)
- ➢ Swami Vivekananda the great saint of modern times calls this approach as *karma yoga*. Through this path also human being can attain heaven or soul realization.

28

Imposture[83]

(Impure life)

271. **A** hypocrite's foul conduct reveals,
Elements smile within on what it conceals.

A fake saint may hide his foul conduct. (An example for foul conduct may be secretly breaking celibacy.) But the five elements know what he conceals. They will smile on his foolishness. (Through grape wine the news would spread to all who know the fake saint and they

---

83   This chapter is about people who are fake saints. Chapter 3 is something like a preamble which describes the qualities of people who relinquishes their householder life and other profession they are in at a given point in their life and move into a renouncing mode. Some of them (Chap:35) may choose to live away from home developing a sense of total detachment and start concentrating on god. Another set of people(chap: 27) who graduate further take to tapas where they completely cut themselves off from any bond with their kith and kin and start the tapas with the aim of knowing the absolute truth and seek the merger with god so that they cease to have any more birth. In the modern times there may not be many who are finding themselves in these two stages.

The modern versions of these people may be like Dalai Lama and several Hindu saints who lived recently and may be living currently and a few Christian religious celebrities. Since saints command immense respect from fellow human beings it has given rise to numerous fake individuals who find spirituality a good business ploy and exploit their innocent subscribers. This chapter is about them.

would laugh within themselves without taking it up with him for reasons of decency.)

(The question whether Thiruvalluvar has used the concept of five elements in a mystic sense can be answered thus: Thiruvalluvar has made use of the cultural belief regarding five elements that they become cognizant of what happens everywhere to every living creature to create a surprise to derive home his point.)

272. His tower like posture shines,
     What use? His heart knowing it, he sins.

A man may have a very impressive saintly look but it is of no use if he commits a sin with full awareness.

273. Like what a grazing cow sporting a tiger's skin makes
     He has no strength of mind but has impressive looks.

A cow because it is veiled by a tiger's skin can never become one. Similarly a man because of his respectable ascetic look cannot really become an ascetic (unless he is a man of conviction and determination).

274. Feigning sainthood a fake hoodwinks his followers unawares
     Like a man hiding behind a bush catching the fowls.

A fake saint's act of feigning sainthood and hood winking his unsuspecting followers is like a hunter catching the unsuspecting birds by hiding himself behind a bush.

275. Claiming detachment the sins they spring
     Haunting sorrows bring.

Fake saints claim they are detached. But they commit sins which make them exclaim in pain, "Alas! What did I do" later.

276. Deceitful and hardened criminal, none as worst found
     Than, those greed at heart but pose detachment profound.

     Some people do not develop detachment at the level of heart. But
     they fake as though they are. They betray and exploit others who
     flock to them. There are no greater hard-core criminals than these.

277. Abrus berry has a red shine and darkish nose
     Fake ascetic while dark at heart remain lustrously poise.

     An abrus berry with shinning red color body has a black tip. Similarly
     a monk with impressive outward looks has a dark inner life.

278. Mind being poisonous they partake in auspicious baths
     Behavior conceits! Many are such loathes.

     There are many fake monks who carry out annual rituals like holy
     dip in remembrance of their gurus.

279. Bow[84] and *yazh*[85] are bent alike but what they deliver are unlike
     Good and bad among men be treated alike.

     A musical instrument called *yazh* and a bow are similarly curved.
     But the purposes their curve serve are different. Similarly though a
     fake ascetic and a genuine look similar they differ in their objectives.
     Therefore men should be careful in dealing with fake ascetics.

280. Sporting beard and long hair are not required
     If what the wise world despises are not acquired.

---

[84] In the couplet the word *kanai* meaning arrow is used. But by implication it means
      only a bow.

[85] *Yazh* is an ancient instrument similar to violin in its mechanism.

External appearances like growing long hair or tonsuring is not needed if you do away with what is prohibited by your folk in ascetic-hood.

Skills to be learnt:

> Ability to shed the clandestine wish to fake ascetic-hood with an aim to enjoy the comforts and respect offered by the society.

Rationale:

> To thine own self be true, and it must follow, as the night the day, thou
> Cans't not be false to any man – said Shakespeare
> This chapter is about persons who are not authentic ascetics. They are pseudo ascetics. Pseudo ascetics in due course of time commit such horrendous mistakes which haunts them throughout their lives. The lesson for others who are not in the career of ascetic-hood is: totally avoid hypocrisy.

Coaching:

The following counseling material is culled from the couplets.

> The first couplet in the previous chapter defines what ascetic-hood is. It says enduring the difficulties in carrying out the task of penance and fully immersing oneself with a single minded devotion in what he chooses as his career and not hurting anyone in the process is what asceticism is all about.
> Fully immersing oneself involves identifying 'who one is' first and genuinely choosing a task which provides full scope for immersing that 'who one is'.
> How to identify who you are? If you find out what are your skills, abilities, experiences and beliefs and aspirations you get a good picture of yourself.

➢   Next ask the question: Am I carrying out a life fully utilizing me in terms of my skills, abilities, experiences, aspirations and beliefs? Identify all those activities you do which do not fall under what you have identified earlier.

➢   If there are too many things which fall outside then you are not living an authentic life. Beware! Your laziness, not having proper work habits and other problems may intervene to confuse your assessment. For example, you may have good potential for doing a teaching job but still you may not be happy about your job because your laziness prevents you to put in the needed hard work for preparing for the classes netting in poor peer and student evaluation. You may think you are not cut for teaching. It is not really so.

➢   Secondly, accept your limitations. Most of us do not have extraordinary potentials for anything and therefore even with their best realization still we may be thoroughly unsatisfied with ourselves and start imagining we are in a wrong place! Simply ask the question: Am I enjoying what I do? If your answer is "Yes" then you are fine. What is needed is doing something to which we have a natural inclination and not sparing any efforts, nothing more nothing less.

29

Not Swindling

(Cheating others of their wealth)

281. Protect your heart from thoughts to steal
     If protecting yourself from ridicule is your goal

     Anyone who seriously wishes not to receive condemning ridicule from fellow humans should protect his heart from thoughts of stealing.

282. "Let me cheat others and swindle,"
     This is hazardous, never give it a handle.

     One may think that a thought to steal what belongs to others crossing his mind is not a great issue. It is not really so. It is a serious issue therefore by all means remove that idea from your mind.

283. Wealth amassable by fraud appears limitless,
     But soon disappears traceless.

     When we cheat others we may think that the outcome is enormous and quick to come. But it will also disappear in the same speed.

284. Love of fraud fully ripened
     Consequential pains never end.

If someone is in deep love with fraudulent means of earning he will end up in dire consequences, wriggling out of which is impossible.

285. Developing compassion they never boot
      After all they wait on others in order to loot.

Empathizing fellow human beings and working for their cause, because their compassionate mind feels obliged to do so, is absent in those who wait for the moment on which others lose their vigil in order to swindle them.

286. **If someone is in deep love to steal**
      He is incapable of acting on a sense of scale.

A person who deeply loves swindling has no sense of scale. Rather he is incapable of it.

287. **S**ense of scale developed as a strong skill
      Delivers on the intention to swindle a kill.

If someone has developed a strong sense of scale then living a life with reasonable level of facilities becomes his nature. He will never indulge in swindling.

288. **W**ith a sense of scale what is born is *aram*
      With a fraudulent mind it is deceitful venom.

Aram naturally dwells in the mind of people who has a strong sense of scale. Similarly in the minds of fraudulent people what resides is plans to deceive.

289. **M**en who masters only fraudulent means
      Would fall since with no sense of scale they transgress.

If a person knows only fraud and has no sense of scale he falls because he cross all limits.

290. **A** fraud's soul keeps off from him
Heaven welcomes an upright person.

The soul of a fraudulent person distances itself from him. Whereas heaven welcomes an upright person.

Skills to be learnt:

➢ Ability to use the sense of scale to steer away from fraudulent way of making money by cheating or exploiting others.

Rationale:

➢ Squandering another person's wealth is dangerous. A sense of measure or scale guides him to live an optimal life. A deeply ingrained sense of measure or scale protects a person from shamelessly pursuing accumulation of wealth through perpetuating frauds on others. It is not possible for a person to appreciate the gravity of an issue if he doesn't have a sense of measure. Therefore one should develop a strong sense of measure or scale which will guard him from going astray.

Coaching:

Cautioning the individual about the dangers of swindling and instilling a strong sense of measure or scale in him are suggested:

➢ In general people who indulge in fraudulent activities strongly believe that their methods or modus operandi are fool proof and they would never get got. Thiruvalluvar says if someone wants to avoid a ridicule later he should keep off from fraud in the first place (281, 283&284). That is by implication he says no one can escape from the outcome of a fraudulent act. Any person who accepts this proposition would keep himself away to a very large extent.

➤ If we are compassionate towards less fortunate poor population of the world we would not push our needs unilaterally making it difficult for the poor and downtrodden to escape a raw deal (285).

➤ A strong sense of conservation and prudency would help a person to satisfy himself with a reasonable level of facilities. Such a life hardly wants a person to commit frauds (286, 287, 288&289)

➤ Will you not enamored to follow a life guided by a sense of scale if you know that a prudently frugal life is soul evolving because of the component of compassion present in it and a fully evolved soul is welcome at heaven? (290)

30

Truth

(Always speaking truth)

291. What is truth if you ask, it is
     What is told harm to none has.

     Speaking without leading to any harm to others is what is called
     truth. Apart from telling something not contradicting what you
     know in your heart of heart you should also speak which in no way
     leads to any harm to anybody (save deposing before an authority).
     (That means there will be plenty of occasions in which you will
     choose not to reveal your heart.)

292. Lie and truth are tallied together,
     If a lie clean good does gather.[86]

     (To remove any confusion on account the first couplet Thiruvalluvar
     adds a very powerful rider to the standard on speaking truth in this
     couplet. He gives a stunning statement on truth.) In fact a lie should
     enjoy the same status as that of a truth if it brings in unblemished
     good.

---

[86] If lies bring in blameless good they are considered as good as truth. For example
      many lives of Jews were saved during Hitler's time by the lies told by non Jews.

293. Don't lie on what your heart does know
     If you do so your heart will burn you, you know.

     Never tell something which your heart knows as false. If you do so
     later you will find your heart burning you.

294. **N**ot lying if one adopts as the best practice
     He occupies the hearts of the populace.

     If a person pursues the best practice of never telling a lie he wins a
     special place in the hearts of all who knows him or her. (If a person
     finds it difficult to abstain from telling lies let him remember what
     would be his condition when he loses his credibility and good will
     amongst his peers and well-wishers.)

295. Taking the heart along, if the mouth speaks truth
     Tapas and philanthropy together remain beneath.

     If the mouth always speaks the truth from the heart such a person is
     far above to a *Tapasya*[87] and a philanthropist put together.

296. **N**othing is as estimable as not telling a falsehood
     With no effort it nets in all other *arams*.

     There is no strength more estimable (earning fame) than speaking
     truth always. This one habit earns the benefits one might get by
     living his life following every other *aram*.

297. If not lying is adhered without a let up
     It is well even if no other act of *aram* is taken up.

     Even if a person doesn't practice any other *aram* it is alright so long
     as he speaks truth without any let up.

---

[87] *Tapasya* is one who carries on tapas (penance) to realize God and obtain salvation.

298. Water cleans the body and makes it smart
 Absence of lies does the same to the heart.

 Body is cleanable with the use of water; heart through keeping it off from lies.

299. **O**ther lights a *sandrone*[88] doesn't choose for guidance
 For him truth alone could give credence.

 A *Sandrone* guides himself with the doctrines of love, humility, growth enabling sprit, empathy, and truthfulness. Whenever he is confronted with a 'difficult to solve' problem he chooses truth as his guide in preference to the other four.

300. Among the many things we have truly seen
 None other than truth remains stable and clean.

 Thiruvalluvar says among several virtues he has closely looked into for their solemnness nothing is as solid as truth in prevailing over an issue. (This is one of the three couplets in which he refers himself as 'We'.)

Skills to be learnt:

> An ability to speak truth without any let up.

Rationale:

> The answer to the question why we should speak truth lies in the last couplet of the chapter (300). The rule of truth is stable and unassailable and in this universe nothing else prevails like it.

---

[88] Sandrone is a Tamil word for which there is no equivalent word in English. A *sandrone* has the virtues of love, humility, growth enabling sprit, empathy and truthfulness or genuineness.

Coaching:

The following counseling material is culled out from the couplets.

➤ Speaking truth is the safest path. Speaking truth is given a new standard by Tiruvalluvar. He says if what you speak is not harming any one it is ok even if it is a lie. It is a deliberate decision based lie like what several Germans spoke to save the lives of Jews during holocaust (291/92).

➤ Don't tell a lie when you know it for sure it is a lie. If you do so, be informed, your conscience will burn you like a torch of fire (leading to several psychosomatic problems) (293).

➤ Will you not be interested in winning the esteem of your colleagues and other fellow beings by speaking truth? (294) (Truth wins the hearts of fellow humans because every one long for it because of the security offered by it.) Any one not credible will not be successful in the long run.

➤ Doing penance and thriving in philanthropy are activities which pave the way for reaching the kingdom of God. But even both of them put together are far inferior than speaking truth without a let up in winning the kingdom of God. Will you not be interested in reaching heaven? (295) (The purpose of penance is to reach heaven. Since Thiruvalluvar says the status of a truth speaker is higher than him I have concluded a truth speaker would attain heaven.)

➤ Do you know speaking truth without a let up is the best device to earn esteem and it also earns the benefit of every other aram without doing anything in that regard ?(296/27).

➤ Do you know the best way to keep your heart pure is to desist from speaking untruth? (298).

➤ Make note of this: A *sandrone* holds speaking truth as the most relevant among his qualities to express himself. (299) (His other qualities are love, humility, *oppuravu* (growth enabling spirit) and empathy. If a person starts speaking only truth other things will come on their own.

➤ Learn this from Thiruvalluvar. He says: "Among all of my experiences with men and matter nothing I have found as established as truth. Also no other *aram* is more venerable as truth." (300)

31

Managing Anger

(A justified cause not withstanding not getting anger)

301. Anger controller is one who controls where it works
    Where it doesn't how does it matter whether or not he shirks?

    There are places where an individual's anger works. I will call him
    a controller of anger if he controls his anger in such places. There
    are places where his anger will not work. If he chooses to get angry
    in such places too, saying anything about his behavior becomes
    posthumous therefore not necessary!

302. Where it doesn't work anger is harmful
    Even where it works none worse still.

    Showing anger where it is not effective or showing it where it works
    are equally fraught with ill outcomes. In the first instance it may
    invite retaliation and in the second it is harmful to the process of
    soul evolution

303. Since always evil is brought about by anger
    Not showing it with any one[89] shall linger.

---

[89]   Either a powerful or a powerless.

Since anger is certain to bring untoward losses it is better to avoid it with anyone.

304. The destroyer of laughter and joy
Is there a worse foe than anger? O Boy![90]

Anger destroys joy and smile. Therefore anger is the worst of all enemies.

305. Concerned with your safety? Control your anger,
Behold uncontrolled anger is your destroyer.

Since uncontrolled anger destroys you, control it. If keeping yourself safe is your aim.

306. Anger destroys its holder
And, his boat his kith and kin shoulder.

Anger held for long by a person against others destroys him or her. Similarly an incessantly angry man is deserted by his kith and kin who could not put up with his anger. As a result he loses the protection he can count upon at times of need from his kith and kin. The kith and kin are like live boats.

307. Employing anger as a means brings ruin for sure
As sure as an earth slamming palm pain acquire.

For someone, who holds anger as a strategic means to further his interest, suffering a
ruinous outcome is as sure as a palm suffering pain if it chooses to slam the floor.

---

[90] O! Boy is added for the sake of providing rhyme.

308. **A** person may harm you as painful as a flame of fire
     Still if he nears you it is good if you show no ire.

Sometimes people who have hurt you as bad as burning your skin with a torch of fire may change their mind and position himself around you. In such situation it is desirable that you desist from showing anger. (Mind you! His style of seeking apology/rapprochement may be being around you without saying anything. You should have the empathic skill of understanding his inner mind and desist from showing anger.)

309. The man attains what his heart has endeared
     If he keeps his heart rage cleared.

It is possible to attain what you want in life provided you don't have the habit of getting angry.

310. **Limitless angerers**[91] are as good as dead[92]
     With no rage men are on par those in sainthood.

Persons who crosses the golden line of acceptable and useful anger are as good as dead because their anger makes them totally out of touch with their souls which is the condition with a dead person as well. Whereas if they forgo anger they are on par with saints.

Skills to be learnt:

> ➤ Managing anger effectively

---

[91] Angerers is the term I have coined to denote persons who hold anger.
[92] Dead in the sense they are totally out of touch with their soul presenting a picture of human being without a soul.

Rationale:

> The chapter uses the Tamil words *veguli* and *sinam*. Both mean rage. Irritation or annoyance is not considered here. Serious uncontrolled rage should be totally avoided. Several couplets in the chapter emphasize it. We also see in everyday life how rage is destructive. Even countries and their governments fall prey for it and create decades of untold suffering for its people.

Coaching:

> Couplet number 307 provides the insight to control anger. It says the strategy of employing anger as a means to achieve some end is not only futile but also self-destructive. How sure the destruction is? As sure as the ground slamming palm hurting itself!

> Further couplets 303, 305,309 specifically say to stop anger. What remains if anger is stopped? A lingering feeling of an unfinished agenda results. That feeling should keep us on the toe to work to finish the agenda. It is anger or rage related feeling but not rage or anger itself. It is called annoyance or irritation.

> Annoyance and irritation will help us to achieve what we want to achieve. Because an annoyed person will take a suitable action like suing someone in the court of law or arguing his case coherently or by organizing a mass movement or taking it up in the appropriate forum which is powerful enough to provide the remedy(309).

> What should you do to a person who presently keeps himself around you after harming you as badly as burning your skin with a torch of fire? The answer is: "You should accept him." Sometimes people may not openly express 'sorry' but may show it through their body language. Such signals should be watched and acknowledged in a similar vein. This requires you to forgive him. Don't you find this is wonderful alternative to finish the agenda of unfinished feelings? (308).

➢ How to get into the mood of annoyance or irritation instead of rage? Whenever you are into rage check within yourself for the following:

1. Do you think that by angrily acting and retaliating, your opponent can be taught a lesson effectively and once and for all so that he will not repeat the mistake and repent for it?

2. Somehow do you hold somewhere in you that your anger is a good strategy?

3. Do you feel very powerful when you are in rage?

4. Do you feel very confident that you are making much progress while in anger?

5. Do you think showing anger only is manliness and not showing is gullibility and self-deceiving?

An answer in the affirmative to any of the above questions is unhelpful. Instead of them catch hold of the following:

➢ I should control my anger even in places where I can win because a defeated person or hurt person is like a wounded tiger. He may be suppressed for the time being. But on a later day I will be put to trouble by him.(301/02)

➢ Pushing anger to higher levels is counterproductive after a point. I may win. But it is sure I lose my peace of mind and joy. More over future repercussions cannot be ruled out. (303/04)

➢ If I should get what I want to get my mind should be free from any other preoccupation. If I hurt someone out of anger then I would be forced to concentrate on him. This preoccupation would undermine my ability to carry on the essential activities in order to get what I want to get (309) I know the undermining of my ability takes place because of the debilitating thoughts that crowd my mind as aftermath of my anger. An angry person who has hurt another is always on his toes. (305)

An exercise: (798)

➤ A simple exercise is to put down on a piece of paper the thoughts that go in our mind before, during and after the rage and evaluate them for their usefulness.

➤ You will find most of them are not helpful.

➤ Discard which are not helpful and write another set of thoughts which will be helpful and put them strongly in your mind.

➤ These thoughts are like the software in your brain to act in situations of anger which should be activated as many times as possible leading to the erasing of the other set of debilitating software we have within us.

Another exercise: (476)

➤ Remember when you are in anger the situation is that you have started climbing a tree. There is a limit up to which you can climb after which the branch becomes tender enough to give in leading to a fall. This thought would censor your anger appropriately. You would start using measured words and actions. Similarly if you think you are invincible you are sadly mistaken.

➤ Practice what is called a self-observer while you are in anger. The moment anger builds up become aware of it and moderate it in such a manner that it is effective to get your grievance addressed. Two persons must come into your existence: the one who is angry and the other who observes the level of anger and take care to see that the anger doesn't go beyond its useful level. This comes by practice. Never give into the feeling that, 'I should stay in my anger and step it up if necessary.'

➤ By practice you will be able to become aware when you're crossing the limits.

32

Not Harming

(Not harming others in retaliation)

311. 'Never harm others' is a policy held by a pure[93] person
Even if he is to miss big money and subsequent position.

Harming the interest of others or the country sometimes may yield
wealth which thereupon would also bring to the person concerned
fame and recognition among the country men. But those who keep
their heart spotlessly pure make it as a policy not to tread that path.

312. Even when others hurt out of fuming mind
Pure men have the policy of not retaliating in kind.

A person may get angry and hurt. But not hurting him back is the
policy decision of people who are blame less and pure at heart.

313. **W**hile you have not hurt him he hurts you.
Still retaliation ushers in irretrievable low (of soul), mind you.

Sometimes someone may hurt you even when you have not in any
way caused his or her wrath. But a hurt in retaliation by you is not
desirable because the defacing effect which it will cast on your soul
cannot be wiped within the present birth

---

[93] Purity is being free from the blames of envy, greed, and rage and throwing hurtful
words at others (35).

314. His sensitivity is raised if a good is delivered.
      An effective punishment to a hurter thus rendered.

      An effective punishment – discouraging the person who wronged
      you from doing it again – is achieved by raising his sensitivity to
      find out by himself to what level he has descended by his hurtful
      behavior. This is achieved by doing something good and memorable
      to him totally contrasting to what he has done to you. (Not hurting
      him back is also equivalent to doing him good!)

315. What purpose intelligence serves if other's affliction
      One doesn't treat similar to one's own ?

      A person must be able to sense that the other person who hurts him
      is afflicted with a mind set to hurt others. After all he can make this
      out on the basis of a similar affliction he suffers at times. Therefore,
      if he is not able to achieve this insight what is the use of his wisdom?
      (Remember Thiruvalluvar is of the opinion that human beings are
      prone to make mistakes like hurting others. A man said to be an intellect
      should know it. And this awareness will go a long way in helping him
      drawing appropriate strategies in dealing with a person who hurts him.)

316. To others let him not do what he has learnt as harmful
      Regarding this, let him be truthful.

      A person may find a number of things as hurtful to himself. Let him
      not do the same to others.

317. To any one, any day, any level of harm
      Even at the mind not doing is great and warm.

      To anyone under any circumstance, even at the level of thinking, do
      not inflict even a small harm.

318. What is harm to himself he who realizes
      How on earth, harm to another, materializes?

It is surprising how a person having known something is hurtful to him as a human being without doubt does it to another person.

319. Harm done to others in the forenoon
Attracts harm to you in the afternoon.

Anyone who hurts another in the forenoon is sure to receive it back in the afternoon.

320. Evils boomerang on the inflictors of evil
They don't inflict them who want no such peril.

Those who are aware that evils done to others would boomerang, never hurt others since they do not wish such outcome for themselves.

Skills to be learnt:

➢ Not entertaining the thought of hurting others at the mind. Totally avoiding hurting others.

Rationale:

➢ Hurting a person starts a chain reaction. It hardly ends. Since we lose our time and energy in the process we slowdown in our career and other life related objectives. Hurting also puts us on par with the other person regarding acting senselessly. For this reason our image amidst our well-wishers takes a beating. On account of these reasons and others one should totally keep himself from hurting others not only physically but also mentally (311/12/16/17/20).

Coaching:

A few situations can be thought of on why we hurt others:

1. We don't want to be seen as week by a person who has hurt us and therefore we resort to retaliation.

2.   We may hurt others to achieve something for ourselves.
3.   We may hurt someone due to a mistake that we make in attribution.
4.   We want to uphold certain values around us.

The first situation involves a mindset wherein you feel some one has put the ball in your court and now it is your turn to play. How about saying "I am not game" (312&314)?

1.   Saying so and remaining in the mindset for a while changes your position from being a part of the problem to that of a solution giver. You can just tell the person who has hurt you, "Look it appears you feel hurt. Your tempers are high and they are bound to be so. Even if I am in your place may be I will also behave in the same way. However, I will take some time and get back to you and we shall discuss it."

2.   Two things happen here. One, your ego agrees for this proposal because you have given it a hope that it's hurt will be taken care of if not immediately at least later. Second, your hurter starts moving in the direction of reflection rather than jubilating in his success of hurting you! Before going to the second meet you must introspect and find out what is your contribution to the tussle (315).

3.   Rarely tussles are unilateral. Precisely finding out where you went wrong and creating the mind set to make the amends prepares you for the best negotiating position (315). At the meet apologizing for what was wrong on your part at the outset creates a congenial atmosphere. Both of you can discuss and at a suitable time you can demand an apology from him which in the case of most of the people will result in one.

The second situation of hurting another person to win some gain is born out of the thought that opportunities are limited and there is no other way other than snatching others.

1.   This mindset is born out of what is called culture of poverty. Couplet number 1040 brings this out clearly. Each human being has a space for himself provided he equips himself or herself to reach there.

Therefore what is needed is to find out what it takes to create a niche for you and start doing it.

2. It is unwise to hurt others to achieve something we want for the simple reason the moment you hurt another person in order to further your interest you are on a new mission which in due course of time will take all your time and energy and ultimately finish you. Recall the example of adding links to the chain. You must make a suitable policy and adhere to it very strictly (311&312).

The third situation has to do with our ability to apportion the sin to the right source. All of us are 'sinners.'

1. On an intellectual understanding of this concept we all do wonderfully well. But when it comes to action we are not. When some one hurts us if we realize, "the tendency to hurt others for various reason is prevalent among all of us. What we see in the other person is the same as what we have," it will take us in a trajectory totally different from that of retaliating. Thiruvalluvar pointedly asks if in our wisdom we are unable to make this out what use we have for our wisdom (315).

The fourth situation arises because of the mindset all of us suffer: what I hold as appropriate should be accepted and followed by all others at any cost.

1. We don't realize that this position is untenable because each one holds a similar personal position and swear on it; at best it is a clash of personal rules!

2. Therefore when you persist on something and demand the other person should agree with it, look for the possibility of a personal rule ruling the roost. Read couplet 855 and its explanation for finding out what Thiruvalluvar recommends for you.

33

Non-Killing

(Maintaining Biodiversity)

321. If you ask what is *aram* it is killing the killing.
      Since all other evils are netted in due to its fuelling.

      The best policy from the point of view or *aram* in respect of
      conservation is abstaining from killing animals in the universe. If
      animals are killed for the sake of commerce the act necessitates the
      person to pursue a number of other evils leading to his destruction.

322. **N**ourishing all lives by facilitating their shares
      Tops the themes of all creeds say the scholars.

      Consuming the resources of the universe in such way that one's
      consumption doesn't endanger the existence of other forms of life
      is the most important doctrine of all those of great thinkers and
      writers.

323. What is uniquely good is non-killing
      What closely follows it is not-lying.

      Non killing is the utmost behavior of *aram* for the humanity to
      follow. Not lying ranks next if the question whether not killing or
      non-lying arises.

324. Which is the best practice? It is, non-killing
     Built into any code under the humanity's mulling.

If you ask which is the best practice for personal and public life
the answer should be, 'any strategy which houses non killing
(maintaining bio-diversity) as an essential ingredient.'

325. Fearing it as a crime, killing, men shun
     They are ahead of family-life-fearing renounced men.[94]

Killing for any reason is a crime. Men who fear committing such
crime desist doing so at any cost. Such men should be esteemed
higher than those who renounce worldly life fearing the difficulties a
house holder's life poses. (Perhaps Thiruvalluvar wants to involve the
emotion of the reader by digging at those who choose monkhood as
an escape from the dire conditions of a family life so that the concept
under consideration will be etched in him strongly or it may be a
sarcastic and contrasting reference to the deceptive monks to serve
the purpose on hand.)

326. If non-killing is practiced by one as a matter of best practice
     He is spared of rebirth and hence lord of death has no chance.

If a person religiously practices non killing of animals for food or for
sacrifice and make every effort throughout his life to save them from
getting killed his soul evolves and he ceases to reincarnate therefore
Lord of Death would not be able to visit him.

327. Even if you should lose your life
     Never wipe out another life.

Even if your life is to be ended never kill another living organism.

---

[94] Thiruvalluvar says people who forbid themselves from killing are superior to
saints.

328. Flourishing through right means a *sandrone*[95] relishes
      But obtaining it through killing he despises.

      There is no doubt a *sandrone* likes great outcomes for his effort. But
      he despises those obtainable through foul means like killing other
      forms of life.

329. For those capable of assessing meanness
      Killers are on par with butchers in brazenness.

      Butchers are brazen and are indifferent to the animals they knife.
      Killer (exterminators of animals for trade) are also held alike by those
      who are capable of measuring meanness in all its shades.

330. Men who earlier killed now suffer
      Adversity and disease as life's offer.

      Men and women who suffer severe afflictions, poverty and other
      calamities at present must have been those who devastated life on
      this earth during their hay days and lived a reckless life with their
      ill-gotten wealth. (These people may live a long life but with Lord
      of Death perennially haunting them. If the reader considers along
      with the couplet 326 the meaning of that couplet would become
      very clear.)

Skills to be learnt:

➢   Keeping a watch on your consumption and tailoring it in such a way
       that the same level is sustainable on worldwide basis without unduly
       destroying other forms of life.
➢   The ability to differentiate between wants and needs.

---

[95]   A *sandrone* is one whose character stands on the five pillars of love, humility,
       oppuravu, empathy and truth. Oppuravu is Thiruvalluvar's word for social
       engineering/social responsibility/ social entrepreneurship /philanthropy etc.

> Strictly avoiding products got out of indiscriminate killing and destruction of nature.

Rationale:

> World is not a place of infinite supply. In no way God has designed the world exclusively to cater to the needs of humanity. The universe is not anthropometric.
It is biosphereometric. Each form of life has a purpose and exists on this earth on its own right. Human being should live a highly synchronized life with all other organisms and nature. This is the essence of this chapter.

Coaching:

> Couplet 322 makes an interesting reading. It refers to a sort of knowledge that must have existed at the times of Thiruvalluvar. The knowledge or consciousness was: share the resources with all the organisms of the earth or biosphere.

> This is in direct opposition to unlimited consumption by human being which is accepted today and mostly the world seeing no great harm in it.

> Adam smith's idea is still very much alive.

> One hope is human beings ability to empathize. Thiruvalluvar has beautifully stated, "This world exists because of empathy" (at least with few) (571).

> With renewable energy research at its all time best, laboratory based production of animal protein and fat being a possibility in the near future, rapidly increasing net work connectivity will make the world to boldly allow its empathic antenna to get beneath the skin of all the organisms living here not only human.

> Thiruvalluvar tells you to strictly follow the idea of sustaining biosphere by erecting *aram* in you in the form of the policy: I myself will never kill or be a party to it in order to consume the flesh of an animal or enjoy any of its products like skin or fur.

➢ In today's world this may be a tall order. We can rather modify the policy thus: "I will progressively reduce meat eating and other forms of consumption which require enormous killing of various animals and destruction of nature" (324).

➢ Thiruvalluvar says you are far, far better than those who take to penance fearing worldly chores (325).

34

Impermanence

331. Holding impermanent as permanent is a folly
Of all it is lowly.

   Men of shallow knowledge and poor understanding of the reality
hold things which are mortal as immortal. This ignorance ranks at
the top of all ignorance.

332. In a theater crowd gathers and melts
From its owner wealth similarly fleets.

   Wealth is fleeting in nature. When it leaves you it does so in a swift.
This is similar to the audience in a theater who are slow to fill the
theater but quick to leave once the play is over.

333. With you your wealth is mortal
Therefore when you have it, create institutions immortal.

   Before it disappears from you invest your wealth on socially useful
and personally satisfying projects so that the wealth which was
mortal with you become immortal in the form of some facility
serving the cause of humanity.

334. Each day appears as if it is another eventless day
For men of perspectives it is a knife slicing life every day.

A day is a like a knife which slices life bit by bit. Men of perspectives are aware of this. Others may consider passing of a day as if it is of no significance.

335. Before tongue gets sucked and breath doesn't exhale
Go after good deeds and doing them excel.

Don't wait or postpone worthy projects. Death may come at any time. Therefore rush to do useful things and excel in them.

336. He was here yesterday today he is gone
This is universe's pride, don't bemoan.[96]

A saga of achievement for nature is bestowing uncertainty on life!

337. No one can assure that they will live for a whole day
Still men aspire, not one several millions, every day.

Men do not realize that they cannot guarantee life to exist for that full day under consideration. But still they aspire for so many different things. (Thiruvalluvar seems to suggest men would do well if they are cognizant of the transient nature of life while they are pursuing their ambitions. Such a mindset will usher in a sort of acceptance of impermanence in the mind which is appropriate for pursuing great tasks.)

338. Chick as it emerges deserts its shell
This portrays soul's relationship with the body well.

A chic discards its shell when the time comes. Soul leaves a body in a similar fashion (to be embodied in another body).

---

[96] The words 'don't bemoan' are added for the sake of rhyme. They also go with the meaning of the couplet.

339. Waking and sleeping with no gap alternate
Birth after death are similarly proximate.

Birth and death are very close like waking and sleeping. (It appears Thiruvalluvar suggests that life and death are the two sides of the same coin. Men may know it intellectually but they don't get the mind set for it. He insists on the acceptance of it.)

340. Is it soul (life), a sharer of place in several bodies
Still to reach the home where with God it resides?

(To drive home his point of impermanence of life because it only has a mission to reach God, Thiruvalluvar exclaims), 'Is it because life (soul) doesn't have its own abode it lives here and there in the corners of the bodies until it evolves enough to reach the company of God?"

Skills to be learnt:

➤ Accepting the uncertainty of, what at times seems a randomly cruel universe where probability and chance exist and absolute certainties never will.
➤ A non-utopian view that refuses to believe in a life either full of unrelenting happiness or a place doomed for pain and anxiety.

Rationale:

➤ The world is like a river. If you stand on the bank of a river you will watch the river is not the same even for a second but at the same time the river is permanent. The moment you are born your journey towards death starts. The journey may stop abruptly or it may take a full hundred or more number of years to end. What can be said about longevity with certainty is that every one of us have only a fair chance of living a full life.
➤ Accepting this uncertainty at the level of feelings and at the same time doing everything to live a productive life contributing to the

happiness of ourselves and of fellow living organisms indicate a healthy state of mind. Such a life is soul fulfilling.

Coaching:

- ➤ The impermanence can be broken by leaving a trace of ourselves which will stay longer than ourselves.
- ➤ Establishing a philanthropic institution or participating in its establishment in some way for helping the poor children to gain education is a way by which you will live after your death.
- ➤ Passing on your special skills to a set of youngsters, who could be living in all probability after you, is a philanthropic act and you will live through them after you die.
- ➤ Or you can give your labor and time to some good cause. You may recall the story of an old man who was found planting the saplings of fruit trees which normally take several years to bear fruits. When asked was it not unwise for him to do so, he replied, "Well I am enjoying the fruits of the trees planted by my grandparents and I hope my grandchildren will have the same privilege!"(333)
- ➤ Keep it in mind these things cannot be prioritized for the later part of your life. We may die at any time. Therefore we have to plan our time in such a way that apart from the interest of the career, interest of fellow humans should be also our concern. There are several careers which have scope to incorporate social wellbeing into the work. If your job is one such consider yourself lucky. Otherwise you may invest your spare time for a social cause (335).
- ➤ Don't aspire for too many things as though you will be living indefinitely (337). This is an exertion which leaves very little time for you to enjoy life. After all you have to be kind to yourself.
- ➤ In summary a reasonable list of what you want to enjoy and what you want to accomplish should be pursued so that you will not feel that your life has been a waste later when you take stock of your life. Feeling of dejection is the result of a soul unfulfilling life. This is certain to happen when we sit at home after retirement and take stock of our life and find ours was a waste. If we have done something worth remembering and proud of having done that we have a sense

of satisfaction otherwise a sense of dejection. At that stage it would be too late to do anything worthy. We will die in dejection!

➤ Be careful of not clutter your life with too many projects and ultimately achieving too little only to feel dejected during the last days.

35

Renunciation

(Setting aside the attachment to men and matter of the world)

341. He who has detached from x... y... z
Is free from pains they individually afflict.

Whatever from which we are detached loses its power to inflict worry on us. (Detachment is understood as not investing ourselves on an object as though we are authored by that object.)

342. When a pinning attachment develops detach
That yields several catch.

The moment a desire develops drop it. A mind freed thus is capable of earning several joys. (A mind which is not attached enjoys the freedom needed for several innovative ideas to solve life's problems.)

343. Discipline your senses
And achieve a detached longing for their products.

The five senses are the gate ways for several products paving the ways for attachments. Therefore detached attachment should be developed towards realms even while enjoying some of them. Therefore when they are lost no pain would be experienced.

344. **P**ossessing nothing is the essence of renunciation
Possession of even one gets him back to the day of initiation

Having no possession at all fully qualifies detachment. Keeping even few things is bewitching which will get one back to the stage of highly attached! (There is an Indian story about a saint who had nothing but a pair of loin cloths. His loin cloths were often bitten by rats. He brought a cat to take care of the menace of rats. To feed the cat he brought a cow and ultimately he had to bring a woman to tend the cow!)

345. **W**ho is he considering a 'minimum possession'?
For intenders of no rebirth even body is an extraneous addition.

For a person who wants to cease reincarnation even his body is an extraneous addition. That being so where is the scope for talking about some possessions or minimum possessions which are enjoyable only through his body?

346. **"I"** and "Mine" is the vein glory of human beings
The destroyer of them reaches beyond divine beings.

A person who has relinquished his pride born out of "I am somebody," "I possess these," reaches the God's world which is beyond the world of heavenly beings. (In the parlance of psychology 'I am somebody because these are mine' refers to one's ego. Therefore what is commended by Thiruvalluvar in this couplet is one should move beyond ego and live under the guidance of the soul.)

347. **A**dversities do not afflict those
Who do not keep possessions as their base.

Those who do not base their life and its joy on the material possession they might possess are not afflicted when they lose them.

348. **T**hose who are bent to make it, renounce all
     Those who fancy it are into the fall.

     Renouncing as means of reaching God is very difficult path since it
     calls for the total renunciation of all worldly objects. Those who are
     bent upon achieving it do so with ease. But those who fancy reaching
     God but are not mentally prepared to relinquish gets into trouble
     when they attempt to live like a saint.

349. **A** fully relinquished reaches the desireless stage
     Seeing impermanence is the next phase.

     A fully relinquished individual would cease to be born again. Thus
     he or she would be able to perceive and realize transient nature of life.

350. **I**ncorporate the nature of God – The Desireless[97]
     For achieving the state of desire less.[98]

     God is best example for modelling detachment. Learn that attitude
     and incorporate in your personality in order to become desire-less.

Skills to be learnt:

> Ability to live the life by a series of considered decisions to renounce.

Rationale:

> You may ask what use I have for the concept of renunciation or
> relinquishing. After all I am not interested to renounce you may say.
> You can use the concept little differently. See below:

---

[97] Desireless is the noun coined by me covering the meaning of God as enunciated
in the particular couplet.

[98]

Coaching:

> Two things are possible: 1) You can convert your demand for things into one of strong preferences. 2) You can shift your attachment around things to live effectively in any situation.

> It was 5a.m. in the morning when I was writing this. It was time for my morning cup of coffee. I went into the kitchen and found coffee powder exhausted. I enjoy coffee so much the scenario of not having want I needed so badly made me go mad. But wait a moment. Why not tea at least for a change? I coolly prepared tea and I found it was equally enjoyable. The secret was without agitating further after the initial struggle within me I accepted tea as an alternative. Accepting alternatives without much agitation is the secret of happiness. So the technique is, don't swear on anything as an absolute need for you. While it will be great if you have something you need never to get stuck with something and waste your life if you don't get it, is the mantra. There are other things which even if not to our full liking could still be good enough. Strongly prefer but never demand (341).

> The secret is practicing to detach from something the moment the desire is born. No doubt it is very difficult and distressing. This thinking you will find valid as long as you have not detached from anything so far. But try it now. You will find the detachment is not that distressing. You will find later the mind landing on alternative sources of joy. Look at my detachment towards coffee above.(343)

> Treat your five senses as gateways to allow the world into you. Controlling them, we think is impossible because we are guided by them instead of our guiding them. For a few days, say for a week practice this: Don't see your favorite video, don't eat your favorite food, and don't wear your favorite dress.

> I know after that week you have developed a sort of craze for whatever you have missed. But now under each item you say to yourself that you will allow only one or two things. Practice this for 14 days. You will find this time it is relatively easier for you to detach from excluded items.

- ➤ Then in the final round differentiate between essential and non-essential items and strictly choose essential items and start enjoying them whole heartedly.

- ➤ If you take this exercise seriously you will end up with few essential and quality items to support your life.

- ➤ The thought of feeling poor of oneself for not having something is the culprit. This thought makes us to remember the things we miss and makes us feel bad and we believe that we are not able to detach with something. To do away with this tell yourself that you will not even think about something which you have detached for few days. Whenever the thought comes say no to it. You can loudly say no so that the thought stops. (344/45/46)

- ➤ Let the thought that your troubles are due to your attachments be very clear to you. If you have any doubt in that work on that. (347)

- ➤ Never give in to the illusion of standard of life and start allowing few non essential things in your life. That is the starting point which will make once again clutter yourself with all things not very much essential (348).

- ➤ Remember life on this earth is only a probation for the life with the company of God. If you strongly believe the real and beautiful life is awaiting you and to reach there you have to evolve here then detaching is possible. (350)

- ➤ If you want to live in God's company you should possess God's qualities. (4,5,6,8)

36

Awareness of Truth

(Looking for the soul-evolving meaning in anything)

351. Contending worldly materials as 'REAL' is due to delusion
The wretchedness of life are due to that confusion.

God is only absolute, essential and 'REAL' material. Therefore holding
the non-real materials of the world (they are not real in the sense that
they are only training material to evolve one's soul) as profoundly
essential is the ignorance which is the cause for living a distressing life.

352. Confusion will go and happiness will be born
If with delusion gone pure perspectives are on.

If the delusion is replaced with an accurate perception that God
alone is Real, the person concerned will come out of the confusion
of holding world and its material life as real. Then he will find
happiness.

353. Clarity in mind leads to delusion's death
For them the sky[99] is felt right on the earth.

Humans, who are free from the delusion of holding this earthly
produces as real and worthy to cling will find this earthly world
transforming into a world of God and yield pure joy.

---

[99] Perhaps by the sky Tiruvalluvar means the world of God.

354. **F**ive senses bring data but no purpose is served
     If delusion free perspectives are not carved.

     The data of the five senses are of no use if what is received through
     them is not processed and right perspectives are not developed about
     the nature of worldly things and the joy they bring in and the nature
     of God and the joy in his kingdom.

355. **W**hatever be the object and whatever be its nature
     Wisdom is distilling the fact constituting its signature.

     Any worldly object need to be understood in terms of its true and
     characteristic meaning.

356. **L**earned and realized Real, these men
     Tread the path of no return here again.

     Those who has learned and found the truth about the Real (God
     and His world) start living a life following the precincts of *aram* in
     order to avoid coming to the earth again.

357. **I**f men reflect and realize the tilt their mind suffer
     They would never another life prefer.

     If the mind realizes that it is biased/tilted towards worldly objects
     then it will renounce this life which is one sided and biased towards
     the world and it's so called comforts.

358. **I**ntellect is seeking the great Truth[100]
     In order to get rid of the folly of rebirth.

---

[100] The great truth is God is absolute and life in his company is the only worthy thing
to be pursued. This world and its materials are nothing but ways and means to
evolve our soul to make ourselves fit enough to achieve God's company.

The intellect consists of visualizing in the mind's eye that God is only Real not this world and its materials. If that is achieved then reincarnation will stop.

359. **R**ealizing the effect of tilt and crushing it
Has the disease quit.

If we realize that we have made our joy dependent on a number of worldly things and start acting independent of them then the disease of dependency will die.

360. **I**f and when Desire, Rage and Illusion are culled.
The disease of tilt is cured.

The dependency is removed paving the path to realize God when we remove the compulsion in our craving which is the cause for desire, rage and the ignorance (the world is real). (Craving for worldly substances and getting into rage when frustrated happen because we also ignorantly hold worldly substances as absolute and nonnegotiable instead of holding them as strongly preferred items. We all know nothing is indispensable excepting air, food and water. But still because of our ignorance we hold worldly substances as essential whereas God is the only real, true substance.)

Skills to be learnt:

➢ 1. To imbibe the notion that the worldly materials are not the real ones and God is only Real.

➢ 2. To develop the idea that life on the earth is an opportunity to prepare ourselves to reach God. The preparation consists of dealing with worldly material in a detached manner since they are not real whereas God is only Real. This universe and its products are training materials which one should use to evolve himself to reach God.

Rationale:

> Since we hold non-essential or unreal things of the world as essential or real we are going after them in head breaking speed with strong passion. The reason why we hold non-essential or non-real as essential and real is because we suffer from something similar to what psychologists refer as cognitive bias. The bias leads a tilt towards world objects as real whereas God is only Real.

Coaching:

> The technique for shedding our cognitive bias lies in the couplets 359 and 350.

> We express ourselves as our ego not as our soul. Ego simply means what we possess. The more the possessions the more the ego is bloated. Therefore we are happy, (in the ordinary way we understand the word,) only when we possess a variety of things. In other words we are dependent on what we possess in order to feel happy.

> Is it possible to remove what we possess and still be happy? It may be possible for few people like some of our saints or ascetics. But for ordinary mortals it is not possible. Moreover if life is a training to evolve the soul and materials of the world are only training materials then how to get rid of training materials?

> How about converting your deep desire into strong preference? How about converting your rage into simple irritation? How about changing your perception that this world and its materials are only preparatory whereas man's abode is with God?

> How to shed craving desire is explained in chapter number 37.

> How to convert the rage into anger or annoyance or irritation has been described in chapter number 31.

> How to change our perspective regarding the meaning of life on earth the entire treatise of Thirukkural is about it.

37

Banishing Desire

(Setting aside desire on anything which may arise due to habit)

361. Reincarnating again and again, a condition
Living being's compelling desire causes this rendition.

Developing a craving desire for earthly possessions is the root cause
for continuous rebirth for all the living things. Strong preference
is ok but not nonnegotiable desire. Such desire seeds continuous
reincarnations.

362. Reincarnation should end when you wish so
Desiring desirelessness makes the go.

A thing at the top of your wish list can be only deliverance from
rebirths. This is achievable provided you desire desirelessness.

363. Being desire divested is the best asset
As a heaven ushering asset nothing betters it.

A man's best asset is a mind which is desireless. Because either at
the present or in the future no other asset can be better than that in
achieving heavenly abode.

364. Absence of desire indicates purity of mind
It comes if on realness of world truth is found.

Craving (desire) is one of the four pollutants of mind (34&35). The mind can walk out of this pollution if it realizes the truth that the world and its objects are not real god alone is real. The world and its material are training ground and training material respectively.

365. Detached is one who has yarns none
     Others detachment not at all won.

Some people may be frugal to a very great extent and may abstain from many physical comforts of life. Still they cannot be held as totally desire less if they have one or two pet desires.

366. Crooked understanding of *aram* should be feared
     'Desire betrays its holder,' shall be remembered.

Man needs to develop a cautious fear regarding crooked interpretation of what *aram* is in any context. In this regard he should safeguard himself from the desire which will betray him and make him to interpret *aram* in a crooked angle. (This couplet and the previous one are closely related. A man may have relinquished everything excepting few objects. For retaining them he may give an interpretation taking recourse to *aram*. Thiruvalluvar cautions him that his desire is responsible for that crooked interpretation and walk out of it.)

367. If desire is thoroughly done away
     Good acts come in the manner you say.

If by practice desire is totally shunned then good behaviors preventing you from going astray will start coming in.

368. Men with nil craving (desire) have no pains
     If they have, pain one after the other trains.

If 'no desire' is achieved 'no pain' results. If, there is desire pain after pain results.

369. Happiness pours nonstop if desire
The pain of all pains does disappear.

Continuous joy comes in if desire the creator of pain of all pains is killed. (It may appear this couplet and the previous one are similar. In my opinion they are different. The previous couplet shows way for avoiding a trail of hardships. The present couplet shows way for continuous joy. Since absence of pain is not joy automatically, there is a need for the present couplet.)

370. Unquenchable desire is checked out
A state of eternal bliss is checked in.

If unquenchable desire is removed lock stock and barrel a life in eternal bliss at heaven is obtained.

Skills to be learnt:

> Converting our compelling desires into a simple wish list.

Rationale:

> Becoming totally desire less may be too difficult to achieve and may become counterproductive for the welfare of humanity for the reason a nation's output depends upon consumption of people. Any nation whose output is low cannot keep its population in healthy and happy state. What is possible and desirable is converting our compelling desire into simple wishes. The Wish lists don't have two things. There is no mad compulsion and there is no time frame within which the list should be serviced. While every effort will be made to fulfill the wishes heaven will not come down if they are not met. And always one can rewrite the wish list subjecting it to a study of feasibility. Regarding time frame the whole life can be year

marked for realizing a wish. In India many mothers save money little by little to buy a small jewel to gift their daughters at the time of their marriage. The happiness and satisfaction when they realize their wish is something that cannot be stated in words! It may take literally years for them to complete the project!

Coaching:

- ➤ Couplet number 364 gives the technique. The couplet says examine the truth of your desire.
- ➤ For example, one issue which middle class people are seized up with is maintaining a standard of living.
- ➤ This desire can never be quenched. Newer or greater desires line up as soon as we satisfy a desire in this regard since we raise the bar on standard even without our awareness.
- ➤ In arranging to satisfy these desires we often run into improper means like utilizing credit cards which is a trap to live beyond our means or motivate our self enough to indulge in frauds.
- ➤ Living beyond our means brings in lasting pain and suffering. This is one perspective of truth.
- ➤ Another perspective of truth can be built around the question, "Do we really need a thing or do we in order to justify our desire convert a want into a need"? This question makes us to revisit our so called standard of living. You will find many of our standard of living concepts are created to satisfy our megalomania rather based on true needs.
- ➤ These two truths will convert our desires as motivators at our service not as an inescapable force to which we should stand catering to.
- ➤ A second idea derivable from this couplet in the context of the general message of the chapter is: the only real object is God. Therefore, if at all humanity develops any desire it should be the desire to reach God. Since a life on the earth is the means through which we can reach God we cannot avoid living. What is possible is to live like a lotus leaf. The leaf is practically sitting on the water but doesn't allow water to stick to it. Similarly we shall live with worldly objects day in day out but not holding them to profile us.

> Couplet 370 gives yet another solution for converting our compelling desires into a simple wish list. It says stop desiring a thing which you find impossible to stop desiring. For example if you are a person going after new models of cars any number of times you have a nice platform to operate. Remember it is your ego which produces this demand. As long as you reside within your ego you will feel its demand to be reasonable. Now seat your ego before you on a chair (imagine your ego has come out of you and is sitting before you) and ask 'him' to give at least five valid reasons for going in for a new car. You will find that most of the reasons given by the ego border on cosmetic reasons and nothing real. The so called driving pleasure exists in the mind rather than in reality.

> To conclude it can be said that a worldly life which is marked by contentment with whatever essential commodities one needs is a well lived life evolving itself to reach God. Remember Thiruvalluvar considers the life on the earth as a training period to be successfully completed to be confirmed for a permanent life in heaven.

38

Destiny[101]

(Fate)

371. **If** productiveness is destined industry sets in
     If sloth is destined inertia is the given.

     A favorable situation for working hard and making great strides
     materializes in this birth if hard working nature is ingrained in the
     individual's soul by the productive life the individual lived in his
     previous birth(s). In case the individual has lived a lazy life in the
     previous birth(s) he or she would continue to do so in this birth also
     (Perhaps developing an insight into his nature if the individual puts
     his body, mind and soul into hard work deliberately and consciously
     then the condition will change. 620.)

372. **With** sloth as destiny folly results
     With productiveness as destiny knowledge widens

     Sloth or laziness (non-productiveness) inherited as ones karma makes
     him poor in knowledge acquisition. Whereas if being productive
     is destined as his nature(karma) knowledge acquisition would be
     robust, wide and deep.

---

[101] Thiruvalluvar uses the word *oozh*. While destiny is understood as unchangeable
       in some quarters Thiruvalluvar sees it differently which is very encouraging.
       Please look for it in this chapter in chapter number 62.

373. One may learn books of several spheres
     What show up are what he prior bears.

     One may study several highly specialized books in several disciplines.
     But he can excel only in those knowledge domains for which he is
     destined the most of all due to his studies in the previous births.

374. Nature of world's affairs are of two different models,
     Earning wealth and learning knowledge are not parallels.

     Regarding amassing wealth and acquiring knowledge and scholarship
     the model differs as evidenced in the world. In the case of acquiring
     knowledge two things are needed: one should specialize in the
     domain where best achievements are destined for him and he should
     have inherited a hardworking nature (productiveness) as his fate. In
     the case of acquiring wealth other factors prevalent in the world also
     matters. An atmosphere poised for growth and an atmosphere not
     congenial for growth vary in their effect on the economic adventure
     of the individual. Similarly the place of the economic activity and
     season of a particular commodity in terms of favorableness also
     matters.

375. (If economic surge is absent) good into bad morph
     (If present,) bad strategy turns good enough.

     If the atmosphere is undergoing an economic surge (as an effect of
     plan and strategy) even worst proposals may net in wealth. If not
     even best proposals will go awry. This applies to the place of the
     enterprise also.

376. If (shrewdness is) not destined, what you own will leave you
     If (shrewdness is destined) no force can divest what is owned by you.

     Being shrewd is karma given and shrewdness alone retains the right
     to own. Others for want of shrewdness will let go what they possess
     by inheritance or otherwise.

(Shrewdness is part of productiveness is obvious the opposite may be carelessness or laissez-faire.)

377. **R**ule Giver's system works on the choice in dispensation
Enjoying the millions is not at the earner's discretion.

Productiveness karma may or may not league with stinginess. If too much stinginess instead of prudence is inherited as ones karma he or she would hoard a lot and fail to enjoy.

378. **W**ill men if destined to receive a steady food supply
To take to renunciation, their mind apply?

Thiruvalluvar seems to suggest that sometimes men may hurry to take to penance because they are destined to remain without any means to maintain themselves due to laziness or lack of productiveness/ shrewdness karma. (Once someone takes to renunciation it is likely householders take the responsibility to feed him. I do not know whether Thiruvalluvar digs at those persons who have renounced with a hidden agenda! I develop this doubt because he expresses a similar opinion in couplet number: 325.)

379. **G**ood things, arrive he rejoices,
How he grieves when bad things are destiny's next choices?

Good and bad fortunes (opportunities) come cyclically. Therefore one who enjoys a good cycle should not curse a bad cycle. He should accept it as a hard reality.

380. **W**hat is more powerful than fate's preference?
Your proposal is superseded by its interference.

Fate is very powerful. Man may propose but it is destiny which puts the manner of disposal in place. (Unless you become conscious of the nature of your fate and work very hard on it to change it, it would remain very powerful.)

Skills to be learnt:

> Accepting the nature of fate and learning to cope with it.

Rationale:

> The unhelpful effects of one's fate need to be tackled if an individual wants to live a happy life in his home as well as profession

Coaching:

> Introspect yourself. Do you have a natural tendency to sabotage your effort? Like you work in fits and starts. You change your interest frequently. You excuse yourself frequently and for no valid reasons from your task on hand. You choose an area for your work out of fancy rather than it is a call of your soul. You may have other idiosyncrasies as well. But the main ingredient of all of them is self-sabotage
>
> If your answer is 'yes' for any of the above then you have the fate of low productiveness. This is a real stumbling block. But don't lose heart. There are two couplets (619&620) which give the relief you need. Couplet 619 says: Excelling in a field, fate (God) may not favor// But additional hard work nets in equal to the labor. The word *daivam* in general means god but in the particular couplet it means fate. This claim is supported by couplet 620 which says fate can be won through engaged labor. Read the couplet: Even the fate is won // By an aptly engaged effortful man. The Tamil word Thiruvalluvar used for 'engaged labor' is *thalanmai*. It means engaging oneself on a task by mind, body and soul. Yes fate limits but hard work through one's body, mind and soul could loosen the limits and rewrite the contour. Hard and engaged work is a habit which one can pick up.
>
> In the case of education or acquiring knowledge it seems human beings are differently positioned with regard to their potentials (373). Modern science agrees with it and we have Differential Aptitude Test(s) to guide the individuals in the selection of a domain (favored by his destiny). Now this concept has taken a different shape: we

have Strength Finders in addition to DAT. No one can find fault with you for not having the aptitude in a given field. But you will be blamed if you do not chose the field in which you are destined the best and pursue a carrier in that (618)

➢ Spells of advantageous period and disadvantageous periods and usefulness of a place are noticed. Earning money is easy and even mistakes in strategies are made up by an advantageous period and place. Waiting for an opportune time like markets maturing for a certain industry or enterprise and places in which they would do well need to be taken into consideration (374 & 375).

➢ Shrewdness confers the right to own. In case you are not a shrewd person catch hold of a person who is shrewd and ask him to monitor your activities and advice you suitably. Abide by what he says. You can also take the help of professional counselors (376).

➢ You may also have a fate, let us name it hording. You may earn a lot but because of hording fate you may fail to enjoy (1001). Look into yourself if you are miserly act on that tendency.

➢ In general, save authentic renouncers, persons who by their fate end up penniless take to penitence. Therefore keeping in mind such dire consequences one should fight his fate which are disadvantageous and create good karma in one's life time (378).

➢ Don't lose heart when something goes wrong wait for good times (379).

➢ Watch your activities and any time you think you ought not to have done something perhaps it is your karma which has led you to do that. The antidote is keeping a watch on you round the clock and steer away from any unproductive act (380).

The Book of Wealth
and Wellbeing

39

The King

(Monarchical Traits)

381. Troops, people, wealth, ministers, allies and forts
A king who excels in these is a lion among the less endowed.

A ruler who has well trained troops, highly resourceful people, able administrators/ministers, forts and friendly kings in the neighboring countries is a lion among kings. (A lion ranks far above all the other animals in a forest.)

382. Courage, generosity, wisdom and perseverance are the four bars
Not falling short in them constitutes a king's caliber.

A king's caliber consists of being fearless, generous towards his citizens, being well informed about the various constituents of a country like people, economy, military, security of the country, ministerial colleagues, and friendly countries, and full of perseverance and enthusiasm. (Even today these constituents have the same importance for the rulers like president of a country. Most of the attributes may be applicable to a CEO of a multinational corporation also.)

383. Promptness, education, daredevilry – these three
Shall never depart a king destined to rule.

A king should be prompt, scholarly and daring. In these traits he should remain strong. (You will find these qualities are very much needed to today's president of a country or CEOs of a corporation. With promptness new initiatives can be started and achieved on time. With learning and wisdom starting and executing projects could be strategized. With daredevilry (risk taking) projects can be fearlessly but carefully carried out.)

384. Not faulting on *aram*, remaining blame free and valor benign,
     These hall marks make a king sovereign.

     A king's acts should never fail on the test of *aram*; should be above blame and valorous enough to benefit his citizens.

385. Inputs, earnings, preservation and an efficient distribution in place,
     A kingdom is worthy of its salt if it achieves an excellence in these.

     Timely inputs, voluminous produce, preserving the same and distributing to the citizens – achieving an excellence in this makes a kingdom a worthy one. (These are very much applicable to a well-run government or a CEO even today. Excellent CEO maximizes revenue by harnessing the full potentials of the inputs and equitably sharing it with all the stakeholders based on an ethically sound basis.)

386. Grants easy access, hard words does not use
     If a king remains so, his land will give him high praise.

     A king should give audience to his citizens easily. He should avoid hard words with them. If he remains like that his people will praise him and his country, as excelling other countries.

387. Speaking sweetly if a king liberally gives
     His people remain as he pleases.

     Kings citizens behave pleasingly with a king provided he uses sweet words and apt dispensations. (Generally demand and supply and grievance redress mechanism of an establishment, be it a kingdom or a modern day organism is easily described in writing than achieved in the field. Therefore if a king, (a president or a CEO) is able to accomplish it people are very receptive to them to do their bit to achieve the goals of their leader.)

388. With a system of impartial justice if a King protects his citizen
He is held in God's position.

If a king is equally just towards all his citizens his people keep him equal to God. (According to the theory of equity in the field of motivation people lose interest in their work if they observe that the organization doesn't have an equitable distribution of equity. Therefore if a king (a president or a CEO) is able to accomplish it people are very receptive to him to do their bit to achieve the goals of their leader.)

389. A king who bears words, bitter enough, his ears detest
People stay under the shade of such a seasoned king's estate.

If a king has enough patience to put up with words which even his ears dislikes to hear, people like him and continue to stay in his country. (He does this because he wants to know the side of the complainant which comes to him amidst harsh accusation.)

390. Liberality, compassion, right scepter and people's care
He is a lion among the kings who possesses these.

A king should be liberal in taking care of his citizens. Moreover he should be compassionate enough to see that justice is rendered in his dispensation. Such a king would be held as the best among the kings.

Skills to be learnt:

> The traits that a president of a country/a CEO or an individual (an individual is a CEO of I Inc.) can pick up from the list meant for

a king given by the poet are: 1) fearlessness, 2) philanthropy(social responsibility, 3) domain knowledge and bird's eye view of other fields, 4) vital energy, 5) promptness, 6) daredevilry, 7) *aram* based behavior, 8) robust benign dispensations towards stakeholders, 9) resource management yielding maximum ROI, 10) granting easy access to genuine visitors, 11) speaking sweet and kind words and last but not least 12) rendering distributive justice to all the stakeholders.

Rationale:

> You will find the list meant for a king prescribed by Thiruvalluvar before more than 2000 years ago very much applicable to a present day president/prime minister of a country, CEO of a corporation or even to an individual who views himself as the CEO of 'I Inc.'

Coaching:

> Some attributes recommended for a king appear to be applicable for all the human beings. They are: lack of fear and anxiety, generosity, intellect, risk taking ability, agility, education, boldness, never faulting on the precincts of *aram*, removing hazardous activities and materials, never aggressing on others, strategizing to ensure productivity and preserving them, being easy to approach, never using harsh words, speaking sweet words while helping, offering a just dispensation, putting up with angry and foul worded feedback, philanthropy, and taking care of the citizens.

> John Steinbeck said, "It has always seemed strange to me … the things we admire in men, kindness and generosity, openness, honesty, understanding and feeling, are the concomitants of failure in our system. And those traits we detest, sharpness, greed, acquisitiveness, meanness, egotism and self-interest, are the traits of success. And while men admire the quality of the first they love the produce of the second."

This quote reflects the difficulty anyone who is in governance in any position has to face if he or she wants to destabilize this association so that the inequity prevalent everywhere in the world can be removed at least in one place – the place which he commands.

➢ A CEO needs the system to support him. Unfortunately the system is crooked by the presidents, prime ministers and political bosses which percolates to the chief administrative personnel like commissioned officers and to every level reaching the bottom.

➢ When one after the other slowly but steadily the officers of the government start accepting the wrong association mentioned by John Steinbeck the whole country is lost and becomes the subject of study for those who spend time on reading statistics on corruption index and articles and debates why India is the most corrupt country.

➢ But it is high time the rulers wake up. Otherwise an *aram* sphere will be formed by those people who somehow manage to keep their head above all these murky things and the fall of the sitting government and the ruling class will become a reality.

40

Education

(Learning what is needed for a life of aram)

391. Learn until things are crystal clear
Then live by what is learnt, ever.

Learning should be thorough: it should involve interpretations
of what is learnt and relating the same to life's experience. (In
modern parlance a strong cognitive network must be formed on
each concept learned connecting the same with relevant issues
seen in the world.) Once having learnt like that it is important to
practice what is learnt. Learning through refreshing as and when
it is needed is also required. (The purpose of education is applying
it to solve day to day problems of the individual as well as of the
country.)

392. **N**umerals and letters are the two eyes,
Through them the world perceives.

Mathematics and language abilities are important subjects of
education. A meaningful perception of world and its happenings is
possible only for those who possess enough skills in both the realms,
Therefore only when someone possess these skills they can claim that
they have vision. (Mathematics especially is a fundamental ability.
Countries whose citizens are poor in mathematics will trail behind
other countries whose people are good in mathematics.)

393. Only learned have eyes
     Others two sores.

The best use for which eyes can be put to is using them to get educated. Therefore only an educated can claim that he has got a pair of eyes. Those who are not educated are as good as having two wounds on their face not eyes.

394. They meet and put their heads together happily
     Later part company memorably.

Professional scholars find their fraternity very much invigorating. They meet discuss and with the memories and sweet toasts of recognitions and the 'aha' experiences they part. Nothing more nothing less!

395. If like a poor before rich an unlearned becomes conscious
     And learns he is great otherwise not.

A poor person becomes conscious of his condition when he stands before a rich person. (It normally motivates him to do the needful to become rich.) Similarly if an unlearned on becoming conscious of his condition in comparison to a learned takes steps and becomes a learned he is held as high. Whereas the one who is not motivated and remains unlearned is held as low.

396. Sand yields water in proportion to digging
     Human learns in proportion to striving.

The more you dig a sand bed the more water it yields. Like that the more a student plunges into his subject the more scholarly he becomes.

397. With no much difficulty any town is theirs
     Why then some never makes education theirs?

Thiruvalluvar wonders why some choose not to get educated when with education they can move anywhere and make a living.

398. Education obtained in birth one
      Offers support up to birth seven.

A sound education obtained by a person in one birth can help his soul evolve so much that it can keep the person away from blameful activities up to seven reincarnations.

(Keeping the notion that all human endeavor are potentially soul evolving or fulfilling Thiruvalluvar says that a well-educated man's soul evolves enough to protect him from defaulting on *aram* for seven subsequent reincarnations. It also goes without saying that harmless learning should be pursued. Otherwise the soul will suffer to come out of which it may need several reincarnations!)

399. His learning makes him and others happy
      On seeing their happiness he is more incentivized.

A learner enjoys his subject and therefore his exposition. Others who catch up with him express joy out of their experience. That experience of others motivates him to go deeper into his studies and reach new heights.

400. Harmless education is a soul evolving asset
      Other assets do not belong to the same set.

Education harboring no ruin is a soul evolving asset. Other assets do not fall under the same class.

Skills to be learnt:

➢   1. Ability to overcome mathematics phobia, 2.Ability to enjoy comprehensive reading of long passages, 3.Ability to appreciate the need for higher education at least to the level of post-graduation in today's world, 4.The ability to appreciate what one has learnt by practicing it.

Rationale:

- ➤ Thiruvalluvar commends a broad based education by mentioning that numbers and letters are as important as eyes for a human being. Numbers refer to mathematics and science subjects and letters to the rest of the subjects which are learnt through written words. Language with reasonable grammar ability, science, history and a host of other subjects make all the difference among the societies who are good at them and those societies which are not.

- ➤ Especially a society whose members are not good in mathematics and science cannot escape poverty and all other ills issuing out of chronic poverty and serious disparity.

- ➤ Through the couplet number 396 he says lack of progress in studies only indicates lack of burning mid night oil. A sand bed yields water commiserating with the depth it is dug. Similarly learning increases the more one is at it. Therefore more and more drill is needed in case of a poor learner.

- ➤ For Thiruvalluvar whether it is running the family or running the country or working in a science laboratory *aram* is very important. Therefore principles of *aram* should be guiding our educational endeavors. What to expose one with is a serious question for which a thoughtful and considered opinion needs to be built.

Coaching:

- ➤ Mathematics phobia is a common phenomenon. There is no doubt a strong mathematics affinity is genetically given. But it has nothing to do with learning mathematics as much as needed for our day to day life and career. The phobia is due to the confusion people have over what constitutes mathematics meant for day to life and career needs and mathematics of higher order like learning calculus, higher algebra and trigonometry or arithmetic involving long divisions needed for a career in mathematics.

➢ What we need for daily life and mathematics-non-intensive careers are addition, subtraction, multiplication and division (392).

➢ The phobia we develop over the advanced mathematics we allow towards these four functions and say we cannot manage this.

➢ Separate these two. Burn some mid night oil (396) and thoroughly learn these four functions and avoid the danger of being a mathematics-phobic parent and successfully avoid passing it on to your children!

➢ Learn the basics in calculus algebra and trigonometry so that you can use them in whatever career you are. The fear is because of the unfamiliar language of notations.

➢ Do not fear notations. If you take several days to learn their symbolic meaning you will find them intelligible like any word in the language whose meaning you know (395).

➢ Learning concepts through long sentences and passages is nightmare for several students. The do very well in reading short passages and comprehending but are allergic when it comes to reading and comprehending long passages.

➢ One simple reason is students do not have the patience. They want to pick up things very quickly. In practice this leads to picking up something as quickly as possible or what is called skimming. This is ok in short passages where you are able to skim substantially. But in long passages it is not possible. In modern days most of us are required to read long passages and understand the critical meaning of what is written to take appropriate action.

➢ The secret is we always want to spare labor. Biologically people are inert and unfortunately we can not afford it in modern days! What is the way out? You can trick the brain. Tell the brain I want to understand what is said in this first sentence instead of fixing the whole page as the target. You will find it cooperates with you. Then go to the second sentence. Now by sentence by sentence if you progress soon you will have comprehended enough and feel good about the exercise because of the mastery you have gained (396). This mastery is quite reinforcing and slowly you will find it is not that difficult to read long passages.

➤ Thiruvalluvar asks a pertinent question in couplet number 397. The question is: "When people can relocate anywhere in the world if only they have proper education and live a happy career ridden life, why are they not pursuing education? In our times we can change the question a little. Why do people settle down to work with a high school level education? / Why do they stop with first degree? / Whey do they stop only with a post graduate degree? /Why do they do not pursue education up to Ph.D.?

➤ The cognitive structures in the brain which are against a serious pursuit of education by a high school or college student are in the form of crowd beliefs or philosophies towards life and education. Broadly speaking they may fall under any of the following or a combination of two or more of them.

➤ At this age of mine I have a right to enjoy life with its myriad offerings. If I do not I am a fool. What I wear, what I drink and where and with whom I party, show who I am. Let me take all the trouble to make it great now. If I don't do them now I will be never be able to later.

➤ Picking up a girl and seeing life is very important for me. Any way what is needed is hands on experience not an abbreviation after my name. I know I can come up like anything. Those brats from the college are mere book worms. I don't want to waste my youth for the sake of those abbreviations!

➤ I know I need a good education for making a great career. But I can always catch up. Let me prioritize it. Moreover I find none of the subjects here interesting. I know I will crack something suitable to me soon.

➤ My teacher says I should push much hard with my writing skills. But she doesn't know that in these days of doing, writing doesn't make much sense as a skill for a fruitful employment.

➤ Let my people who break their heads over me know that I am very clear about what I should be doing later. Therefore let them leave me otherwise I don't care for them.

➤ Above beliefs and a number of their variations create emotions and emotions motivate behavior and a behavior is invariably reinforced by the gang life or the college environment produced by similarly placed friends or gangs ultimately strengthening the cognitive structures even stronger. You can see how one feeds on the other.

➤ This cycle needs to be broken. The best way for doing it is to attack the beliefs. Your belief is what a strategy for a business or for a military commander in a war field. Business model or military strategy is based on research inputs not on whims and fancies of the personnel concerned. Do a quick research.

➤ Make a mental list of all those whom you know reasonably well who are comparable to you in socio economic background, parentage and location of living and mark those who have made it better compared to you right now and those who are lagging along with you. What are the differences among them?

➤ Analyze them in terms of beliefs they hold towards education. You will find those who made it and those who do not differ in their belief system in the line mentioned above.

➤ My experience has shown that a sort of self-pity-induced thought is the fundamental reason for the inability to deliberately shed the joys preferring hard work. We feel justified in our thought: "I feel bad for not catching up with an opportunity to enjoy life." Since our cognitive structure supports it strongly we also think we are reasonable and we are not at fault after all it is what, 'my brain tells me and I am helpless.' You forget one thing it is you who created that thought and put it in the brain in the first place. At the time of creating the thought you were its master and soon became the servant for it.

➤ If you develop the idea that your self-pitying thought is your creation then you will find it loses its power to milk your sympathy in support of it.

➤ There is an important person who is always with you. He is called soul or conscience. His other name is God. Request him to review your thought and approve it. If he approves it jolly well go ahead enjoy don't worry about education!

➤ You can use the two chair technique for this exercise. Sit in one chair as you and ask the question and move to the other chair and sit on it as your soul and answer.

41

Unlettered

(Not learning what is needed to be learnt)

401. An unlettered addressing lettered is odd
Like playing dice without a board.

An unlettered person trying to lecture a learned audience is similar to playing a game of draught without a draught board[102].

402. The clamor for oration of an unlettered man
Equals a breast-absent child fancying as a woman.

An unlearned man's clamorous effort to give a scholarly address before a learned audience is like a small female child (as indicated by "breasts-absent child") fancying herself as an adult.

403. It is fine with unlettered
If they keep quite before lettered.

---

[102] The example given by Thiruvalluvar refers to a game in vogue in villages even today. Lines are drawn on the ground demarking boxes in a row one above the other. The player standing before the first box throws an angular stone after calling out a number indicating the box. A score is earned if the stone lands at the box called out. Since the English reader may not be aware of this game the game of darts which has lot of similarity to the game mentioned in the original is used.

There is no issue with ignorant persons as long as they do not open
their mouth before learned scholars.

404. **An** unlettered may deliver a piece of knowledge in his talk
The learned would not tap it since they know it is just a spark

Sometimes an unlearned can be impressive to some length. But
scholars who could sense his lack of depth will not show interest to
avoid a disappointment later.

405. **T**he mastery of an unlettered turns poor
When before the scholars they pour.

With laymen unlearned can be very impressive. But their shallowness
reveals itself quickly when they take a lead and interact with scholars.

406. The unlettered among the audience are nominal
Because contribution wise they equal brackish soil.

The unlearned may serve the purpose of achieving a packed house.
Other than that they are as useless as a brackish soil.

407. An illiterate man's handsome looks is hollow
Like the beauty of a clay doll is just a show.

At the surface level a girl clay toy may look pleasing. Beyond that
it serves no purpose. Similarly the handsomeness of an unlettered
person serves no purpose because he is insignificant among scholars.

408. The wealth at the disposal of an illiterate person
Causes more pain than the poverty of a good man.

The wealth in the hands of an ignorant person is more harmful than
the poverty of a good learned man to the society.

409. Though born lower, the learned
 Is beyond comparison with the high-born but unlearned.

A learned scholar may belong to a lower social stratum. But he will be held higher than a person who belong to a higher social stratum but not learned.

410. The comparisons of an unlearned with a highly read
 Resemble those between a human and animal yield.

An ignorant person varies from a learned person as much as a human varies from an animal.

Skills to be learnt:

➢ Developing an awareness regarding one's level of competence in his domain of knowledge and conducting oneself appropriately.

Rationale:

➢ If a person who is not well read doesn't have the awareness of his level of knowledge it will have negative consequences for him. Therefore he should become aware of it so that he can do the needful to improve his competence or manage his situations effectively (401).

➢ Therefore he should become aware of his level of knowledge so that he can do the needful to improve his competence or manage his situation effectively (402, 404).

Coaching:

➢ A client who wants to participate in scholarly discussion would do well if he develops a content page of his field by taking all its contours from sources concerned and tick off those areas where he is not at all competent, mark those areas where he is somewhat competent and areas where he is fully competent(405).

➢ This feedback will help him in which group he can participate and in which he should not (410).

➢ This meticulous understanding gives him a fair account of his position and if he wants he can take steps to improve (396).

➢ This is also useful in today's world where getting fired from the job one holds is common place.

➢ Some people think that if only they get a nice job they can learn the skills needed once they are on the job. Holding this as a strategy they try to pose in their interview as though they are such a stuff whom the company which interviews them could ill afford to miss! Most of the times they also get selected only to be exposed sooner or later and getting relieved. Now to find a job becomes very difficult for them because the new recruiter will always find out the reason for their previous exit!

➢ Some of us entertain a thought that once born in a well to do family our high status is a given one and pay little attention to educate ourselves enough. We do not realize that our high status would not pass in the present day world. Unwanted issues would crop up if a person not well educated or qualified otherwise gets jobs meant for well learned in a democracy. This should be avoided to safeguard oneself from ignominy (409,410).

42

Listening

(Knowledge through listening)

411. Knowledge acquired through listening is a wealth
     It is supreme to every other worth.

     Listening to scholars and to those who are capable of delivering a
     wealth of information and perspectives is the best strategy to acquire
     knowledge in an easy way. Since knowledge is power and a well-
     informed person could convert his knowledge into wealth it is more
     worthy than other material wealth.

412. When ears are at a pass with nothing to heed
     Let us also bestow stomach with a frugal feed.

     Eating becomes a secondary activity when we are in the midst of a
     listening session. Perhaps the stomach may be fed frugally in between
     the sessions.

413. Those well fed in ear's food on earth
     Are on par to Gods in heaven[103] in worth.

     Men who accumulate knowledge through listening are equal to
     heavenly beings who are worshiped through chanting mantra and
     oblations. (Men who enhance their knowledge through listening

---

[103] Consult couplet no.346.

thereby evolving their soul well enough reach realms beyond heaven where the Godly beings live. Therefore they are equal to them.)

414. Maybe he hasn't read deep but let him listen
During his days of low spirit it is his lean on.

A person may not have the habit of reading from the original source and also to a desirable level of depth. But still let him listen to scholarly discourses. When he is in a low spirit he can draw insights on his situation based on the knowledge he has gained through listening.

415. A hand-staff on a slippery path gives support
Similarly words of men of best practices sport.

A stick in hand offers the best support on a slippery land. The counseling given by a man who adheres to best practices serves a similar purpose. It helps the counselee to act appropriately in a tricky situation.

416. Listen at least to a few good things
To that extent it helps to win acclaims.

Someone may not be interested in vast listening. But let him listen as little as possible. Listening helps an individual to take appropriate actions leading to achieve great laurels.

417. Those who listened and analyzed much
Even by wrong understanding do not speak foolish.

A person who has listened a lot of knowledgeable discourses and achieved a minute understanding will never speak nonsense on a particular issue in spite of the fact that his prior understanding of the issue is wrong.

418. His ears hear therefore not impaired
Still a deaf, after all knowledge they never heard.

A person may have sound hearing efficiency. But his ears are as good as deaf if he has not subjected them to intense listening of scholarly material.

419. If lessening to deep scholarship is absent
Humility in their exposition would not be present.

Learning by hearing scholarly exposition makes one to become research minded. Humility is the hallmark of such person. With others humility will be naturally absent.

420. They know the taste of tongue not ears
Whether they are alive or dead how it matters?

Some people know the pleasure of eating only, not listening at all. Who cares whether such people are alive or dead?

Skills to be learnt:

➤ Developing the habit of listening to lectures or discourses of scholars whose depth of knowledge is more than what one has.

Rationale:

➤ Listening to the speeches of great men in your disciplines increases the bandwidth of your intellect.

➤ Seminars (now webinars added) and lectures and conference papers especially TED talks presented by a scholarly person in that discipline before the material takes the shape of a book is an opportunity to learn. Perhaps in Tiruvalluvar days it must have been the principal method of dissemination of knowledge.

➤ With the present day possibility of webinars it is a good idea to keep informed of the latest in the subject through listening

➢   One specific advantage in this method is when we listen to others we can enter into discussions. The learner who prefers listening is also interested to note the tone of voice, speed and intonations and pitch of the voice of the speaker which gives the shade of meaning which he alone understands, not a person who reads. Moreover listening to discourses may suit the learning mode of some people. Further what he has already learned through a written material gets clarified when he hears from a person in a different form, sometimes from the same person who has written it.

Coaching:

➢   Learners differ in their learning styles. Some prefer reading. Some prefer listening and some prefer hands on experiences. You decide what your learning style is.

➢   The listener's attitude should be that of an obedient student at the time of listening. He should suspend his ideas and opinions and biases until the end. He should give a full supporting environment to the speaker then only the best will come from him (414).

➢   Second the listener should not allow his mind to jump to conclusions in the middle and switch off assuming that he or she has understood the speaker. Then he is likely to ask questions bewildering the speaker (417).

➢   Third, a good listening also requires an attitude of respecting a fellow human being. When you are set to listen to someone you accept that you have wholeheartedly allotted that time to the speaker. That time is no more yours. You should happen to the speaker throughout the appointed time. This type of engrossed audience while bringing the best from the speaker also gives the listener an in depth knowledge (419).

➢   Fourth, a speaker is a presenter not a narrator. That means there is always scope for novelty and creativity. You should carefully look for those. That is possible only if you stick to him earnestly (418).

➢   You should not be indifferent to a material under the notion that something was not important. The best way to get rid of this mentality is taking notes using your own words and understanding which can be used by you during the question hour (419).

43

Intellect

(Rational intelligence)

421. Intellect is a fortress that guards one from ruins.
And beyond the destructing ability of enemies it remains

Intellect is a device which protects a man from a ruinous onslaught.
With him this is an inbuilt protective fort formidable even for enemies.

422. Intellect restrains mind;
Weans it from evil and leads to good.

Intellect prevents the mind going after things of its liking or of
aimless wondering. It also makes the mind to take to blameless and
appropriate paths.

423. Grasping the truth is a function of intellect,
Whoever have or whatever has given the vent.

Finding out the fact of a matter is the function of intellect with no
undue regard for the source or circumstance of the information. (In
other words it appears Thiruvalluvar says no knowledge can be built
based on an authority. Going beyond any connotation and sometime
using a connotation for the purpose of understanding is emphasized.
Interestingly he suggests a person in search of truth should get out
of his past wisdom in order to build new perspectives.)

424. With simple terms moving the hearts to receive
     Intellect gauges what his listeners conceive.

A man of intellect explains using simple terms making the listener to open up and understand what you say. Similarly he also comprehends the meaning of what the listener says examining it at its factorial level. To put it in another way the couplet says speak in simple language so that others clearly understand you at the same time try to capture the space of the person who responds to what you say.

425. **U**nlike the lily which opens and closes.
     Wise men constantly align with their fellow citizens.

A wise man has a natural affinity to the masses of the world. His mind has the equipoise (unlike a water lily which opens and shuts) which sustains his affinity.

426. **A**ligning with the way the knowledge world[104] trends
     Intellect, new ones comprehends.[105]

Updating ones knowledge is a continuous activity with the wise persons. They post themselves with the latest in the field from the peers.

427. Intellects knows what is in store and its consequences
     Others are incapable of such sequences.

---

[104] 'World' here refers to the other intellects or knowledgeable persons of the world. Remember in couplet 140 'world' refers to the population which one deals with in his social entrepreneurship endeavour.

[105] A simple word to word translation reads thus: Intellect is carrying on with life as the world does. The present translator has adopted a stance which he has used in translating a similarly sounding couplet in chapter 14 under the number 140. It is not very difficult to find that the word to word translation does not go along with the other couplets in this chapter.

The intellectual person knows what waits in store. Others are incapable of it

428. Dismissing a fearful danger is foolhardy
Intellect fears what could cause jeopardy.

What is to be apprehended as dangerous the intellect never fails to do so. This ability is absent in others who are not intellectual.

429. They who in anticipation protects themselves
Them never a disease destabilizes.

Intellects are proactive enough to prevent upcoming onslaughts of adversity. Therefore they do meet an adversity which destabilizes them.

430. An intellect, on account of it, possess every worthy thing
Whatever a non-intellect may possess he has nothing.

A highly intellectual man is resourceful in the true sense of the word. Whereas a person who is not intellectual may possess several things, still he is not resourceful.

Skills to be learnt:

> To develop intellect.

Rationale:

> Intellect is a comprehensive strength embracing inborn intelligence, education and knowledge by the application of what is learnt and vetting the whole thing in *aram*.
> The resultant abilities are: 1) protecting oneself from ruin, 2) steering away from foul acts, 3) an inquisitive brain, 4) concern to reach to others and learn from them, 5) unfailing love for fellow citizens, 6) Orienting oneself with the considered opinion of the intellectuals

of a given field, 7)being apprehensive of impending events and 8) knowing what is to be feared and what not to be feared, 9) futuristically proactive, 10) feeling powerful.

> These capabilities are must have commodities for the humanity goes without saying.

Coaching:

> Ten traits of an intellect is lined up for you below to check within yourself how much you measure on each of the trait. Remember all the above traits are learnable. Therefore if some of them are not present in you or their presence is meager start acquiring them.
Let us start one by one.

1. Do you feel insecure in your professional and personal life? If so, can you trace your anxiety to something absent in you? If your answer is in the affirmative start working towards it. Please remember a feedback from relevant persons on your assets is more useful unless you have the talent of introspection to a considerable extent.

2. Do you really believe whatever one does should be a good one to the doer and to the society at present and in the future? If needed change your activities suitably. Doing good is soul evolving and in that respect there is no activity in life which doesn't lends itself to soul evolving.

3. Are you a person so disciplined that you accept what authorities in knowledge says as a disciplined soldier? Thiruvalluvar says one should satisfy himself rather than going by authority. The later doesn't help the soul to evolve.

4. Do you have the ability to explain in simple terms making hearing you a joy to your listeners and obtain the same by listening to what they had to say? Remember the joy present on both sides is mutual in evolving the soul.

5. Do you have considerate disposition towards humanity around you? Remember a mentally healthy intellect has a natural affinity towards mass because of his equanimity of mind.

6. Are you up-to-date in your field? If not you have to and earn the esteem of your colleagues and family members. An esteem earned as a result of a good work is soul evolving!

7. Are you futuristically proactive? If not soul killing situations would line up for you.

8. Are you insensitive to the consequences of what you do? Acting unethically ignoring consequences will bring in formidable difficulties and life will become a hell leave alone evolving soul.

9. Can we say you are a futuristically proactive person? Remember a stich in time saves the dress.

10. Do you feel powerful enough to meet the challenges of your life? If not it may be due to the fact that you are not well equipped on a number of parameters both at your profession and in your personal life. An examination of the issues which confront you currently and finding out whether you have matching solutions would clarify the situation. If not you may start acting on them.

44

Avoiding Faults

(Removing the six faults)

431. Haughtiness, wrath and meanness bereft
     Public esteem on their laurels are apt.

     If a person is totally free from the shortcomings of haughtiness,
     snobbish arrogance and meanness in thinking and action and attains
     prosperity then he deserves social esteem.

432. Miserliness, mean pride, useless joy
     Are faults in a king O! Boy![106]

     A sick attachment towards wealth, feeling superior to all and indulging
     in incessant useless merriment are faults in a king. (These are all
     addictions. The caution found in this couplet may be applicable to
     anyone in modern days.)

433. For the one ashamed of blame, a millet[107]
     Assumes the size of a palm fruit.

---

[106] 'O! Boy,' is added for the sake of rhyme

[107] The millet mentioned in the couplet is called as thenai in Tamil. It was under
substantial cultivation until a few decades ago. Luckily an effort to revive such
yester year's grain are on in Tamil Nadu now.

Those who have a keen sense of shame will hold a mistake in size as small as a millet grain equivalent to that of a palm tree.

434. Keep yourself off from making an offence
Because it is a substantial foe against your defense.

Not committing blameworthy mistakes should be kept close to heart as a substantial policy and agenda and followed at any cost. Because a mistake is an enemy capable of delivering one's ruin.

435. The one who does not avoid faults in the first place
His life gets destroyed like straw in a fire place.

One who doesn't proactively act and prevent a blameful mistake is bound to get ruined like a straw before a fire.

436. In the light of his, the king considers others' fault
Could this king be faulted for default?

When charging the citizens on their faults if a king takes into account his mistakes of similar nature will there be any grouse for his citizens?

(His mistakes need not be current they can be from the past. He would have taken punishment for that or as a King he may be immune to the punishment. These are not the issues here. The issue is the moderating effect on the scale of punishment the King would award if he has the habit of viewing the faults of citizens from such an angle. There is also another perspective. Since the faults of the citizens and that of the king are talked about we can surmise human beings irrespective of their status are basically fallacious. You will agree this approach is good for all who make accusation on others in the sense they will not resort to very harsh punishment which by the by will be counterproductive.)

437. Not put to productive use, miser's guarded wealth
      Loses its purpose[108] and perishes in stealth.

The wealth of a miser who feverishly guards his wealth loses its
purpose and gets lost and therefore according to Thiruvalluvar it
is a mistake to be miserly. (Wealth's purpose is served well when it
is productively re ploughed into the society wherefrom it has been
earned creating lively hood to fellow human beings. In that angle
wealth is capable of delivering freedom from rebirth.)

438. The trait of a stingy heart
      Incomparable, stands apart.

There is no other human mistake which can be classified along with
a human mind's mistake of not helping the needy because of his
attachment to wealth.

439. Self-eulogizing do not indulge ever,
      Doing useless things covet never.

Don't wonder at yourself. Do not carry out useless things in order to
satisfy your ego which indulges in self-eulogizing. (A king (any officer
capable of impacting others life or career) should not concentrate on
himself by eulogizing himself or have others to do it to him. This
takes away his precious time needed to analyze his environment.
Second if he takes undue pride in himself he may land in a mindset
that whatever he does must be correct and inadvertently commit
mistakes.)

440. Your love on anything shall not manifest as an open rave
      Then enemies up to destroy you will have nothing to drive.

---

[108] The purpose of wealth is to provide livelihood for as many as possible. A wealth
in the hands of a miser who does not employ it for the purpose for which it is
meant will allow it to be squandered after his death.

If you pursue your interests in a moderate fashion without escalating them to the level of blind love, making it like a fanfare, then your enemies would have no chance to exploit your weakness and destroy you.

Skills to be learnt:

➢ Avoiding the mistakes of haughtiness, snobbish rage, meanness in thinking and action, and addictions like addiction for wealth, self-aggrandizement and indulgent pleasures like alcohol, game etc.

Rationale:

➢ It is obvious that totally avoiding the mistakes mentioned above are very pertinent for the wellbeing of human beings. Remember a psychologically healthy human is poised for no reincarnation stage.

Coaching:

➢ Thiruvalluvar has used a technique of showing the consequence of one's mistakes vividly and discouraging him from pursuing it madly in this chapter. This technique is discernable by his example. The person who has a strong sense of shame will consider a mistake as small as minor millet as, as big as a palm fruit (433). A vivid picture of a mistake can be achieved by blowing it to its full ramification and understanding its repercussions. Therefore the skill is: always ramify your mistake to its logical end and see for yourself what results before acting on your whims. Then check within yourself whether you want to proceed still!

➢ There is another skill needed as a prerequisite for the above skill. That skill is given in couplet 434. Mistakes should be viewed as substantial and should not be viewed casually. A mistake is a poison however small it is. You, as 'I. Inc.' should be alert enough to observe any mistake you do, take it seriously and subject it to the exercise of ramification. This comes by practice.

➢ You will agree this ramification technique is applicable for all the mistakes mentioned under the heading of skills to be learnt.

45

Getting Mentored by Great Man

(Seeking the counsel of great man who is capable of guiding one into right path)

441. Asses for *aram* talent and maturity
     Obtain his counsel and remain in amity.

     Cultivate men who carry out their professions following the principles
     of *aram*, matured in intellect and with the required talents as your
     advisors. (As an I.Inc. chose a great professional of your domain as
     your mentor and cultivate association with him.)

442. Cultivate him who can cure the present ill
     And those proactively well.

     Men who could offer remedy to your present difficulties and steer
     you away from future ones are the ones you should associate with
     without fail.

443. Developing a great man as ones own
     Is rare amongst rare ever done.

     Developing relationship with great men and maintaining it is very
     rare to occur.

444. If you can make the great to relate to you
     The accruing strength tops any other mind you.

If by his conduct one gets great men as his men that strength is the best he can aspire.

445. **S**ince counsels are the eyes of the king
He shall surround himself with men who know the in thing.

The king's ministers (secretary of states in a presidential system) are the information gatherers and solution providers. Therefore he should have men who possess capabilities in both the strengths as his ministers or associates.

446. If by what he does the fittest take him as their peer
His enemies would have nothing left to maneuver.

His enemies would have no options left if the person conducts himself in such a way that the best and fittest experts accept him as their peer.

447. If a person seeks and benefits from a reproving associate
His ruin none can create.

Our worst critics are our best friends. Therefore it is necessary to retain them on our side. In that case no one will be able to ruin us.

448. With none to reprove him – an unsecured king
Gets ruined even with nobody available to pull the string [109]

A king is safe if he has ministers (chief executives) who reproach him if they think such acts are essential. Therefore if a king chooses not to have the company of such ministers then he will get ruined even without anybody doing a thing or two towards that end.

---

[109] The idiom, 'no body needing to full the string,' is brought in truthfully reflecting the meaning of 'no one need to do a thing,' constituting the last portion of the second sentence in the couplet.

449. Man who doesn't invest has no profitability
      Without pillar like associates one doesn't have stability.

      Those who do not invest do not reap profits. Likewise those who do
      not have pillar like support of associates will never be able to enjoy
      stability. (Your associates are part of your investments.)

450. Severing the union with good mentors
      Is ten squared ruinous than several enemies

      Losing the association of good men is ten times squared harmful
      than having enemies.

Skills to be learnt:

> ➤ Cultivating association with a person who is knowledgeable in one's
>   own profession and periodically consulting him on significant issues
>   in one's professional and personal life.

Rationale:

> ➤ A mentor shares his wisdom with his 'mentee'. It is easy to learn
>   from a mentor instead of oneself learning it the hard way wasting
>   much energy and time often due to a strategically wrong move.
>   Mentoring is skill specific counseling received from a competent
>   person. Therefore it is a must.

Coaching:

> ➤ A middle aged competent person normally is inclined to offer
>   consultation to a younger person provided he develops a sort of filial
>   feeling towards the young person. Choose a mentor who is upright
>   in *aram* based best practices, matured intellect in general and in
>   particular in his and your profession (441).
> ➤ Take this very seriously because this is as important as any other
>   important assets you may think of. It is a master strength. (443/44)

> ➤ See to it that your man is research and application oriented person. (445)

> ➤ You should take care to see that through your authentic interaction with him he should think that you belong to him. (446)

> ➤ Rejoice when he indicts you for something. It is indicative of the fact that he is doing a proper job of mentoring. (447)

> ➤ The whole idea is not a fancy or fad. The pillar like support of your mentor is essential for your growth. (449)

> ➤ Under any circumstance do not severe your connections with a good qualified mentor. (450)

46

Avoiding Mean[110] Company

(Not maintaining company with low people)

451. **E**steemed men fear low men
But low embrace as kith and kin.

Men esteemed for their accomplishments (fearing degeneration in their acclaimed endeavor) avoid low people. Whereas low people encircle their likes as though they were their kith and kin. (And they are aversive to esteemed men.)

452. The soil builds the taste of the water,
Men's' thinking their 'Alma mater'[111].

Rain water is pure and tasteless. When it falls on the earth the salts present in the site dissolve in the water and the water spring from that site tastes accordingly. Similarly men's thinking, knowledge and perceptions are influenced heavily by their counterparts present in the men with whom they keep company.

453. **O**ne's nature is born in his mind
But his character is shaped by his kind.

---

[110] Men who are low in achievement/ (character) / knowledge/intelligence.

[111] The word alma mater is used to bring out the idea that a group cultivates its member like the atmosphere in a college cultivates a student.

It is true that man's nature is inborn. But his character is shaped by the pressures he is subjected to by his peers and elders in the group to which he belongs.

454. It appears knowledge comes from one's mind,
In reality it is from the people of one's kind.

What happens to the initial intelligence is orchestrated by the ingenuity and initiative of the group or society to which he belongs to. It is like, 'a man is an enterprise of his society'.

455. Purity in mind and action comes
From the frame of reference one avows.

Purity in thinking and action (following the doctrines of *aram* in thinking and action) are attainable provided the group to which one belongs to or what is called as his reference group is pure (aram-led) in thought and action.

456. Good outcomes emanate from hearts pure
Ignoble act never comes from him whose group is not impure.

If one's heart is pure its outcome (action out of its thinking) will be blame free. If the community to which one belongs to is pure no useless or hazardous act will come from him or her.

457. That mental health is an asset for men is a fact;
Community health grows man's fame worthy act.

A healthy mind is an asset for human being. If a community to which he or she belongs is also mentally healthy it will help the person to grow in such a way that he enacts several fame worthy acts.

458. A *sandrone's* mental health is of sizable measure,
A healthy companionship protects even him from any pressure.

Even in the case of a *sandrone*[112] for whom a healthy mind is a given thing a healthy kinship provides a good support enabling him to continue to maintain it.

459. Healthy mind achieves its owner a place in heaven
Even that has the protection of the community is a given.

A person with a healthy mind will attain divinity and would stop reincarnating. However the health of the mind is better protected by the health of the mind of the community which one keeps as his company. (Therefore, if you want to attain divinity see to that you do not belong to a bad company. You may have noticed the implied theory of social conditioning. Also remember even for a *sandrone* a good company gives the added protection to protect his five qualities (458).)

460. No better facility than a good companionship,
No worse harrow than by a bad kinship.

A good companionship is a support. It is better than any other support. Similarly nothing is more pain yielding than bad company.

Skills to be learnt:

➢ The skill to avoid the company of people who are low in mental health and low caliber.

Rationale:

➢ The chapter speaks about the impact a group which is low in mental health, intelligence and accomplishment could create on a person who is a clean slate with potential for high achievement in his profession.

---

[112] A sandrone is one whose personality is made up of love, humility, growth enabling, empathy and truth or genuineness.

> A well accomplished and well-disciplined person might lose his credence in due course of time if he associates with a group low in accomplishments and mental health. Therefore he or she should avoid the company of low people.

Coaching:

> The first step is to convince yourself with what is stated in the couplets regarding the nature of people who have no accomplishments to their credit and also poor in mental health. You must also accept the impact of the company one keeps with such low people. This is essential because you may fall prey for the thought that as a human being it is your bounden duty to help people to come out of their low level of mental health and accomplishments. Second, you may also think you are capable of keeping yourself not affected by them while helping them to improve. Both of them may happen in exceptional cases. But the contrarian is true most of the times (452, 454).

> Identify people or a group who go after winning high esteem through their accomplishers and join their fraternity. Sometimes these places may not have the popularity or other opportunities. Never mind them. Look only for the level of performance for example if it is a university department how many publications have come out of it in a given period of time would be the question you would do well to ask.

> Moreover your accomplishments would reach newer and newer heights provided you keep persons who are similar to you or better as your peers. (457)

> Thiruvalluvar gives two goals for human beings: they should not only accomplish but also do it following *aram* (455).

> Since a man with a perfect mental health like in the case of a *sandrone* too would be benefitted by the company he keeps it is essential you keep the company of people who are mentally healthy (458).

> Check within yourself where you stand on a ten point scale on the five traits of a *sandrone*. Make a bar diagram and find out where you are too poor and plan how you can improve.

> ➢ Last, there is a bonanza. Thiruvalluvar says high level of mental health would usher one into heaven. And high level of performance is supported by the group which is mentally healthy. This is the most important reason for avoiding the company of people who are not esteemed (459).

47

Acting with Deliberate Analysis

(Research based action)

461. Consider investment, income and accrual
    And initiate an action after thorough perusal

    Thoroughly study the quantum of investment, income and accruals
    and satisfy yourself about the viability of the venture before initiating
    action.

462. Researching and deliberating with expert peers
    Later hard decision by the actor hardly fails.

    Three things should happen here: First, one should study and
    understand enough about the venture. Second, he should collect
    the opinion of a panel of experts who are smart, well read and have
    hands on experience. Third, taking into consideration all the inputs
    he (Prince/CEO) should think within himself and arrive at a decision
    before deciding to act. With such an effort unachievable is rare.

463. Capital itself is at risk leave alone profit:
    The wise would not initiate such ventures at any cost.

    Certain ventures are inherently risky. One may lose capital itself
    leave alone income loss. Wise people are careful enough to avoid
    such ventures.

464. Men who fear mistakes leading to a precipice[113]
     Never would initiate an unclear enterprise.

Men who fear degradation (It can come through the loss of money, status, loss of face and good will etc., with fellow human beings earning their ridicule.) will never attempt a venture which has grey areas.

465. **W**ithout a challenge-wise strategy attacking an enemy for his head
     Strengthens him like a nursery plant transplanted on a bed.

Taking on the enemy should be done carefully. Planning, taking into consideration
various dimensions of warfare, is needed. An ill planed attack will result in enemy
emerging stronger like a transplanted plant on a ridged bed receiving nutrition and
water.
(The above explanation results from the direct translation of the couplet. But there is
an issue here. The chapter is on venture management. Where is the need to talk about war here unless we presume that war is also seen as a project by Thiruvalluvar!) But a different interpretation will show this couplet is very much on the theme of venture management as given below:
A venture will have several pitfalls. The pitfalls are its enemies. A nursery plant becomes strong and gains strength day by day once transplanted and cultivated. Similarly the absence of proactive action to avoid pitfalls of the project (enemies of the project) will make them more detrimental and the project will suffer.

---

[113] Precipice means dangerous situation.

466. Priority and necessity should help the decision to act
Inappropriate choice in either is how ruin is brought[114]

Not skipping an inappropriate action or skipping an appropriate action both pave the way for ruin. Another possible interpretation is: prioritizing appropriately is necessary for avoiding ruin.

467. Plan and carry out action
'Let us plan along the way,' is a mistake ridden notion.

A well deliberated and detailed plan is necessary before launching an action. A sort of heuristic action plan will bring ruin.

468. If efforts are spared when project is planned
A venture will fail though severally manned.

If efforts with full energy and expertise to carve efficient planning are not carried out before starting a venture it will eventually fail. Any number of men with concerted effort will fail to turn the tide later.

469. Awarding good[115] to men may go wrong
If a mismatch between the offer and their skills sprang [116]

Even helping a man may go wrong if the beneficiary's character and strengths are not factored in.

---

[114] This couplet is so worded that another interpretation – prioritizing and avoiding inappropriate actions can also be given. The translation includes both.

[115] Good may mean position or hike in benefits etc.

[116] This couplet is translated in line with the meaning of the other couplets in the chapter concerned. A different translation like, 'good deeds may also go wrong if they are enacted without taking into account of the character of the recipient' is possible.

470. The world doesn't accommodate what it doesn't prescribe
     Hence reflect and enact what it doesn't proscribe.

     An executive has to be culturally sensitive while planning his venture.
     The world will be indifferent to things which are alien to it. (Perhaps
     the modern ideas of sensitizing expats to the culture of the country
     where they works and cultural marketing may be remembered here.)

Skills to be learnt:

➢ Skills and strategies relating to starting and running a project

Rationale:

➢ There was an estimate that out of 200 business ventures started only
  40 survive. Sometimes the banks way of financing and managing
  the scene contribute to a large extent to this condition. (The present
  translator gets this idea after discussing the same with few bankers)
  Some bankers work a lot on the paper to make a proposal viable and
  the entrepreneur also writes and rewrites his proposal accordingly.
  But the entrepreneur's level of preparation, skill set and planning are
  not taken into consideration as an important input by the banker.
  Ultimately the project fails. The entrepreneur's life becomes more
  miserable than before starting the project. This chapter shows the
  way for a prospective entrepreneur what to look for and what to avoid
  to avoid a painful failure.

Coaching:

➢ It is OK if you don't start a new venture. Sky will not descend on
  you. But if you fail the sky will really descend on you (468)!
➢ Check whether what you invest brings back a profit in a sustainable
  way (461).
➢ Consult persons who know the inside story of the trade or business
  venture as and when needed during the planning stage. (462) (Never
  consult an arm chair expert.)

➤ Don't be attracted by great possibilities and go on head braking speed resulting in: 1) not only you haven't earned anything; 2) you have also lost what you had on hand.(463)

➤ Don't start any venture unless you are crystal clear on everything if you are a person who really worries about risking your skin (464).

➤ The enemies of a project are its pulling factors. Absence of sector wise planning based on real research input strengthens such factors. Totally avoid such pitfalls (465)

➤ Prioritize and avoid unnecessary expenditures during the earlier stages (like elaborate landscaping of the premises even before the product rolls out) (466).

➤ Don't leave planning aspects to be attended during the course of the project. Such an approach will result in a situation wherein any number of experts will not be able to bail out the project (467).

➤ Be culturally sensitive and act politically correctly with all the stake holders and factor them in at every stage (469).

48

Ability to Estimate one's Strength

(Estimating the four strengths needed for the success of an operation)

471. The force needed and one's stock of it; the opponent's might
    And force to accrue from support groups – weigh these and act.

    If one wants to beat his enemy in a war first he must estimate how
    powerful his opponent is and the force needed for taking it on him.
    Second, he should check how much force can come from his own
    sources and how much from his friends. After weighing all these four
    he must act only if balance of force is in his favor. (This first couplet
    of the chapter obviously speaks about a war strategy. But the rest of
    the couplets of the chapter confines themselves about estimating
    ones abilities and resources accurately before launching a project.
    It appears the first couplet is an example for what is stated in the
    remaining nine couplets.)

472. What is feasible, not what is probable,[117] one who remains with it,
    Stabilizes, proceeds to the next, has nothing that he can't achieve.

    Assess what is feasible and act; consolidate yourself in the resultant
    position and proceed to the next. If you do so there is nothing that
    you cannot achieve.

---

[117] 'Not what is probable,' is added for the sake of bringing in the emphasis found
in the couple by the way the words are worded.

(Remember the observation: "Think Big Start Small Scale Fast.")

473. Strength of self, not evaluated, propelled by a spirit of adventurous enterprise
Many get broken much before they could make a rise.

Many people are ignorant of the level of their strength. Spirited by a sense of adventurist enterprise they step up beyond what they could sustain and get broken.

474. Would not abide by what he has and the limits of his givens,
But takes pride in them – he meets his ruins.

Some persons over shoot without feeling contented with what they have. This they do because they disproportionately eulogize themselves. Such people meet their ruin quickly.

475. Cart, overloaded with peacock feathers breaks at its axle
Feathers, light they may be, are sure to beat the tensile.

Peacock's feather is very light. But a cart overloaded with the feather will break at its axle when its tensile limit is crossed. This means one should not up the ante beyond a point.

476. A climber of a branch will meet his end if he breaches
The high but safe reaches.

If a person climbs a tree he should take care to see that he doesn't go beyond a certain height. If he reaches the highest tip where the wood will be tender and weak he is bound to fall to death as the tip will break. (One can take risk that is adventurous, exhilarating, and exciting, but should gauge well so as not to become foolhardy in the process.)

477. Consider your income consider what you give
      A healthy proportion is what it should be.

      One should not dispense an undue share of his wealth in philanthropy.
      That is the best strategy to manage his wealth.

478. Let the incoming channel be narrow no harm should come,
      Until you grant a broad outgoing channel that makes you succumb.

      Income may be small. It is harmless as long as the outgoing sum is
      not broader.

479. The one who lives with no measured prudence,
      His life gets destroyed in the promise of a fake abundance

      A person's financial activities may depict a picture of abundance. But
      if he spends beyond his means he will meet his ruin all of a sudden,
      as though the misery has come from blue.

480. Philanthropy that is not feasible,
      Will ruin wealth which makes it possible.

      Philanthropy is a by- product of an economic enterprise. Therefore
      it should not eat into the capital by diverting funds into acts which
      are not yielding returns or building assets. If this is forgotten and
      philanthropy is recklessly pursued (like the enormous well fare
      measures of some democratically elected governments) then the
      wealth will get reduced quickly resulting in a grinding halt to all
      philanthropic activities. (Some of us suffer from an unnatural 'other
      pity'. Too much of pitying of others like too much of self-pity is a
      disease. One must check within himself for the presence of this trait
      and do the needful to remove it if it is present.)

Skills to be learnt:

➤ A skill to deploy an action in tune with ones strength. A strong sense of measure or metrics.

Rationale:

➤ One of the reasons given for the collapse of leading world economies is governments and societies spent beyond their means. This chapter looks at the absence of this sense from various angles. It is needless to say that developing a sense of measure it essential for a happy life.

Coaching:

➤ If a king/president wants to go on a war he should take into account the force needed to win the war. How much strength from his forces and from the forces of allies could be gathered is the next question to be found with an accurate answer. Third step is finding out whose side the balance favors.(471) (Treat this as an example to the remaining of this section)

➤ In the case of an entrepreneur he should start a venture according to his capacity keeping a saving margin of capacity. Once he achieves a target he should stay their and stabilize. Then he can think of making the next move. If he acts like this there is nothing that he cannot achieve. (472)

➤ Don't take risks out of an adventurous spirit. (473)

➤ Overestimating your situations and your power do not overshoot. (475)

➤ Don't be foolhardy and pursue unachievable goals. Beware, while climbing a tree if a boy goes beyond a point the branch will snap leading to his death.(476)

➤ Don't spend a portion of your wealth disproportionate to your income on philanthropy. (477)

➤ Don't spend beyond your means. Post yourself with feed backs on daily basis and carry out the course corrections (478)

➢ Beware of a fake abundance like borrowed richness and spend leading to the closure of the shop all of a sudden. (Especially avoid spending through credit cards.) (479)

➢ Philanthropy is a bye product of an enterprise. If this perspective is missed and philanthropy is pushed beyond the limit it will ruin the enterprise.(480)

49

Opportune Time

(The strength of appropriate time in an action plan)

481. A crow defeats a more powerful owl in daylight
To win his enemy, taking the clue, a king shall wait.

    Compared to crow an owl is a stronger animal. But due to its day time blindness it gets killed by the crow during day time. Similarly if a king wants to destroy his enemy he should look for an opportune time.

482. Acting in tandem with seasons, take my word
Is your fortune binding cord.

    Utilizing the opportunities a season offers is a wizard-cord which binds you with an unending flow of fortune.

483. Is there anything too hard to achieve
If with proper scheme timely action you give?

    With timely action and appropriate scheme/strategy there is nothing that one can not achieve.

484. A target as large as the universe is attainable
If in an opportune time and place action is doable.

If a person acts in an opportune time and place it is possible to achieve the whole universe if he aspires so. (It should be remembered Thiruvalluvar is only emphasizing the importance of time and place for a fruitful action. May be one should not take it literally in modern times.)

485. The whole world, those who want to get
     For an opportune time resiliently wait.

     People who are after goals as large as the universe remain steadfast without panicking for an opportune time.

486. A motivated person's apparent inaction
     Is like a charged ram's backward traction.

     A ram may appear as backing out when it tracks backward a little before charging on its enemy. Similarly a person who is highly motivated may remain action less waiting for an opportune time.

487. Men of clear intellect do not instantly fling
     They preserve their anger alive for a timely bang.

     Men brilliant in strategizing do not show anger instantaneously. They keep it alive until an opportune time arrives and release it as bang.

488. If you meet a formidable foe wait
     When his time is up his head will be found lying east. [118] [119]

---

[118] It appears Tiruvalluvar conveys 'the death of the foe' by saying that the head will lie eastwards. The tradition of laying a dead person with his head on the direction of east prevails even today.

[119] It appears Tiruvalluvar has conceived the possibility of formidable enemies in which case the best action is waiting for the enemy's natural decimation.

Some enemy's are formidable. In that case the best option is to wait for the natural decimation of the power of the enemy. (This shows how Tiruvalluvar is practical in his approach to issues in life.)

489. If impossible to happen happens
Do the 'difficult to do' before the time toughens.

Purely due to circumstances a formidable target may become achievable. If that happens act immediately and achieve what you otherwise would not be able to achieve in normal times. Mind you! You have to act fast since the situation will revert back in no time.

490. Model stork's arduous waiting for the fish
And later it's piercing strike on an opportune finish.

A stark for hours together stands on a single leg for a hefty fish to arrive. Once a fish of the size it is satisfied with, appears it swiftly pierces the fish with its beak.

Skills to be learnt:

➤ Ability to make use of right time as an important edge in the plans of going for a war.

Rationale:

➤ This chapter is written to highlight the use of time/season as a window of opportunity for waging a war/launching a project etc.

Coaching:

➤ Be informed that a crow which is not a match in body power to an owl will kill it during day time due to owl's poor day vision (481)
➤ Be informed making money is facilitated by seasonal opportunities. In that respect a best season is a guaranteed money spinner. (482)

> Time is an important input. Added to it are the tools and strategies to achieve the unachievable like wining a large land by a king or a business enterprise by an entrepreneur. Veterans who know this keep cool waiting for their innings. (483/84/85)

> Let us say you are insulted by a colleague in the office in the presence of other colleagues. What will you do? Will you instantly retaliate or wait for your day to deliver what he deserves?

> Generally most of the people will lock their horns instantly and take the fight to its logical conclusion.

> Some brilliant people will take it cool.

> It doesn't mean they have forgiven the offender nor that they are shy/afraid of taking action to defend their self-respect.

> If they love themselves and also hold it very important to help the society to grow the same quality they have to act. They know it.

> Apart from that they also know everything has a time and place and there will come an opportunity in which they will be able to take care of their grievance!

> They are like that ram which reclines on his hind legs only to deliver a powerful punch on the enemy (486).

> Therefore do not mistake waiting for the opportune time as a symptom of cowardice or weakness on your part. It is a strategy born out of your brilliance. (487)

> Inordinate waiting is possible if you are clear and confident that your wait will pay. See the tactics in this regard a stork employs. It stands and stands motionless on a single leg letting all the small fish to go until a fish of its liking comes. (490)

> Another type of waiting involves allowing nature to solve the problem. We may have a formidable enemy in whose case the appropriate move is to wait for his natural decimation or death.(480)

50

Knowing the Place

(The Criticality of Place of Action)

491. Despising your enemy or starting the war shelve
     Until a critical front is found after careful delve.

     A critical front from where a successful war can be fought need to be
     identified as a strategy. Until such time no war efforts, not excluding
     provocation through ridicule or throwing challenges be carried out.

492. Being conflictingly powerful powers great fights
     Still attacking from one's fort offers several benefits.

     A king may have military prowess to strike first and win. Even for
     such a king winning the war is easy if he fights remaining in his fort.

493. Even the weak will win by choosing a critical vantage
     Against those who doesn't care for such an advantage.

     Even an army which is incapable of throwing a strong fight can win
     provided it pays attention to the place of fight and chooses a critical
     vantage front to fight with an enemy who doesn't pay attention to
     the same.

494. The foes who intended to fight will abandon the thought
     If the host stays in the apt place and does fight.

If a king stays in his vantage front and gives a fight the enemy who comes all along for a spirited fight will abandon his plan.

495. In deep waters a crocodile is a sure predator
     On the land any beast is its eliminator.

A strong crocodile in deep water kills even a mammoth animal like an elephant! Nevertheless a small beast can do the same to it when it is on the land. Likewise a king in his place will be formidable compared to another place which is not his.

496. The majestic car with mighty wheel does not navigate on sea
     Similarly a sea boat does not run on road you see.[120]

A temple car (made of wood and steel having massive size wheels) will not be able to navigate on the surface of water. Similarly a boat will not travel on road. (It appears Thiruvalluvar underscores the adaptive advantages of a place in this and previous (495) couplets.)

497. After due critical selection of a vantage place
     Courage only is needed with skill and supplies in place.

If a king has selected the fittest front to station his army and has men and material arranged the next thing his army needs is courage and nothing else.

498. His force may be small but arrayed in an adaptive place
     A vast army on arrival loses its nerve and face.

An army may be small but if it chooses a front where it can bring out all its might (like a crocodile is adaptive in deep water) then the upcoming enemy studying the situation will lose his confidence and leave.

---

[120] The words 'you see' are added for the sake of providing the rhyme effect.

499. Though strong fort and other fortifications enemy may lack
For want of acclimatization the prospects for an attacker is bleak.

An enemy who goes on a war at the place of a host is in a disadvantage
position for want of acclimatization with the place.

500. An elephant with no fearing eyes[121] gores a spear wielding man
A jackal wins such a beastly animal stuck in a marshy plain.

An elephant is a heavy animal with wide and lengthy legs. Once it is
stuck in a marshy land it proves to be a formidable trap for it because
the more it tries to come out the more it will immerse in the mud.
An elephant trapped likewise is an easy target for a score of jackals.

Skills to be learnt:

➤   Ability to acclimatize to new places.

Rationale:

➤   The skill advocated in the chapter is very appropriate to armies and
the lesson is meant for army generals. We gather from media that
the wars in Afghanistan and earlier in Vietnam or Iraq have put
American forces in great disadvantage because the army personnel
were finding it very difficult to acclimatize to war fronts.

➤   At the level of an individual, the decision to relocate for taking up
jobs and shifting the families etc., to a foreign land like in the case
of expats working in MNCs and their family may have a lesson or
two in this chapter.

---

[121]   Studies have shown that it is very difficult to observe or record the blinking of the
eyes of an elephant. Since Its hearing efficiency is very high it takes on a person
within seconds on his coming with it face to face. Tiruvalluvar's observation may
be understood in the light of this information.

Coaching:

> The idea which runs as undercurrent in this chapter is: the place of action is a critical input. How to make use of this idea if you are not in an advantageous place? The answer is acclimatize with the place as quickly as possible.(499)

> Getting acclimatized to the place where a migrant works can be made easy by understanding about the place of work and the country where it is located:

> The bureaucracy approach to outsiders varies a lot from country to country

> The administrative vocabulary though English in many countries there is variation the way it is used.

> The embassies of the parent countries are found to be most unhelpful in many cases.

> Trying to bypass certain rules will land one insurmountable trouble.

> In some areas in several adjacent countries the procedures are very stringent. Once we get got into some trouble it is the end of it for years together.

> Cultural issues especially following one's religion in a new country should not be carried out in such a manner that it becomes an eye sore for people in the host country.

> Generally there will be more number of barriers than facilities in many countries and life is difficult. Therefore learning as much as possible and acclimatizing to the new environment as soon as possible is needed.

51

Considered Selection

(Choosing suitable personnel)

501. *Aram*, wealth, pleasures and dangers of life,
Skills on these shall selection criterion be.

While selecting an executive like a minister or an officer the king
need to evaluate him on how he fares on the four qualities namely
1) *Aram,* 2) Wealth, 3) Sensual pleasures 4) How he will act with
regard to state secrets in the face of threat for his life.

502. Of good family, free of faults and fearful of shame,
The selection of one who possesses these worth's the game.

A good family among other things fosters two important humane
qualities in its offspring: Being just and fair and being afraid of
blame. A candidate apart from descending from a good family
should also have no criminal record about him and be mortally
afraid of shameful blame.

503. Deeply learned and blame free men are in existence
Still it is rare to find them totally free of ignorance.

Even though the candidate may be highly learned and is free of
shortcomings, still it will be very difficult to find one without a trace

of ignorance. (Therefore in practice some tolerance level may be fixed as far as education is concerned to pass a candidate.)

504. Check strengths and shortcomings
      Which are on the higher side shall guide the postings.

      Take into account the strengths and shortcomings in the candidate's knowledge and skills. If good strengths are preponderant over shortcomings then he or she can be selected.

505. For the greatness and the lowliness a proof is shown:
      His past actions offer a touchstone.

      One's past performance or a demonstration of performance at the time of (like the modern day, In-basket selection procedure) selection can prove to be a touch stone for his ability to perform.

506. Choose not men with no close knit kinship for a game[122]
      With no group to belong they wouldn't be ashamed of blame.

      Do not select a person who has no strong reference group in the form of closely knitted relatives. When issues arise regarding his performance it is not possible to pull him up using the services of his relatives and members of other reference groups. With no one to whom he belongs, therefore no fear of scorn, he would have no motivation to perform to the best of his abilities.

507. With a vested interest choosing a not well learnt
      Brings in folly's full brunt.

      If a person who is not well learned is selected due to vested interests such an act will bring along with it a volley of difficulties later.

---

[122] The word game stands for any opportunity for which a person is chosen

508. A selected outsider turning out to be an incapable,
Such a testing procedure brings pain unstoppable.

Selecting an outsider without screening him properly brings in unstoppable difficulties.

509. Do not pass any one without scrutiny
In case you have, find out how best you could use his capability.

Never select any one without a close scrutiny. Due to some circumstances if you have done so find out what best use he can be put to.

510. Trusting without testing and mistrusting the trusted
Means endless troubles caused.

Both putting trust on someone whom you have not properly verified and suspecting someone whom you have inducted after a full verification will bring in insurmountable pains.

Skills to be learnt:

> What to look for in a man while selecting him and how to assess him?

Rationale:

> Thiruvalluvar insists on personality educational and skill variables in selection process. He has devoted few couplets for each of the two.

Coaching:

Consider personality variable first:

> How he handles issues relating to *aram*, money matters, sensual pleasures and dare devilry (having no fear for life in carrying out his duties) (501).

- ➤ Is he from a family known for its great qualities (502)?
- ➤ Is he having a professional zeal to excel in his profession?(506)
- ➤ Is he free from criminal mentality and does he has a sense of shame which would prevent him from committing blemish acts (502).

Consider education and skills next:

- ➤ How about his education? Weighing with inadequacies what is preponderant, inadequacies or adequacies (504)?
- ➤ What about his actual performance (505)?

Check his reference:

- ➤ Does he have good references who can be contacted in case he errs to get their help to mend him (506)?

Never select based on vested interest:

- ➤ Are you selecting someone based on vested interest (507)?

No arbitrariness in selection:

- ➤ Never select someone without thoroughly collecting data and researching them (508).

Create a pool:

- ➤ Due to some reasons if you selected someone, find out for which job his profile suits and appoint him for that (509).

One word of caution:

- ➤ Selecting someone without following all the procedures suggested so far or suspecting someone after selecting him following all the procedures will bring in insurmountable difficulties (510).

52

Evaluating and Employing

(Deploying the personnel suitably)

511. Losses and gains shall be assessed
Best practices which yielded gains shall be accessed.

An executive should look for best practices and adopt them. Selection of best practices is done by screening the practices for their benefits and hazardous side effects based on past evidence and deciding on the balance.

512. Maximizing yield and sustaining it with suitable strategy,
A 'capable means finder' shall act to make the synergy.

Maximizing the output and doing what is needed to sustain the maximized output are the two criteria for adjudging a practice as the best one. The one capable of doing research to establish such best practices and achieve sustained productivity shall hold the helm of affairs.

513. Love, intelligence, intellect and absence of greed
Screening for the presence of these a selection shall be made.

As far as personality and other attributes of such an executive are concerned the four most important ones are: 1) capacity to dispense love, 2) intelligence, 3) intellect and 4) absence of greed.

A selection shall be made ensuring the presence of these in the candidate.

514. Even after following several best practices of selection
      Candidates could vary in the process[123] of execution.

The person assigned with a responsibility may have the best job skills. But any job is a continuous process, maintaining the flow of which requires additional process skills. Therefore going by job skills alone is wrong. Process skills also need to be looked into when assigning a job.

515. If feedback based course correction skill is absent
      For his 'domain expertise,' alone employ him not.

During the process effecting the necessary changes is part of the process itself. If this flexibility and presence is lacking one should not be delegated simply because he or she is an expert in the subject.

516. Deciding the actor, target and its completion date
      Acting at their behest is the best mandate.

The target and date of achieving it need to be fixed and communicated clearly to the doer. (This is the best strategy for motivating an executive).

517. This is the task, this is the person, and this is the method,
      Deciding so unconditional delegation is made.

---

[123] The modern concept of executive presence is inferable in this and the following couplet(515) because after delineating the best practices concept (511), philosophy for resource management (512) and traits for the chief executive (513) the couplets 514 and 515 are positioned and they speak about something beyond the above but similar to the modern concept of executive presence.

After clearly defining the task and deciding the methods of carrying it out leaving it to the responsibility of someone well selected is a must.

518. **If** someone stakes a claim for a job on valid grounds
Leave the job within his bounds.

(This couplet is very interesting. It says if someone comes forward to undertake a work and satisfy all the conditions so far discussed then it is good to offer him the job.) If a person possessing all the criteria comes forward award the responsibility to him. This couplet has an important lesson for modern day HR practitioners. Instead of going by bell curve and axe the underperformers they can redeploy them for a job where they will be better suited after little training besides the naturally occurring transfer of experience. Such a practice will improve the overall morale and attract the talented ones to the organization.

519. **A** wizard at work employs friendship and cordiality
If a mischief is apprehended wealth becomes a casualty.

A delegated person's 'on the job moves' should not be suspected. If he is suspected the task assigner will lose his fortune. (A person may exhibit a process skill like developing a level of interpersonal relationship with his workers and associates. This should not be mistaken for planning a coup against the establishment. If an executive is mistaken like that and relieved of his work or punished then the king will lose his enterprise.)

520. King shall feel his men every day
Since aping the righteous officers the people stay.

A king should watch his men without their knowledge. If they are on the right path the citizens also will be on the right path. Because they are the role models for people.

Skills need to be learnt:

➢   The ability to delegate responsibility and treating the delegatee as
       an intrapreneur. [124]

Rationale:

➢   The nuances of task management revolve around what is called
       clarity at all levels of action. The intrapreneur is one who has fire in
       his belly. He knows the in and out of a task. He also knows what is
       to be done and what is being done, what is the gap in size and kind
       lie between the two. In short he is the solution provider. Therefore
       it is rational to select such a person and delegate the task to him.

Coaching:

➢   Choose the person who is capable of implementing a policy after
       collecting enough data on the plus and minus points by doing
       research (511).
➢   This is possible for a person having a high level of intellect. (513).
➢   In addition the candidate should have the attitude and ability to
       do research and find out methods to sustain the productivity (512).
➢   He must have the task skill and process skill (514).
➢   He must have the soft skills of love and creating a sense of
       belongingness among work force (513).
➢   Fix the target date (516).
➢   Delegate the task treating him as an intrapreneur (517).
➢   Sometimes if you find someone who claim that he has all the
       qualities you are looking for you may assign the task to him after
       going through the selection process as described above. (518).

---

[124] In a faithful delegation the delegator delegates i.e., totally leaves the task to
       somebody, hoping that somebody is equivalent to him in every respect. Instead
       of him he is there, otherwise there is no difference. For that reason the 'delegatee'
       is referred as intrapreneur i.e., works-spot level or action-level entrepreneur.

> Never suspect the on the field/floor activities of an intrapreneur for a coup (519).

> Keep a watch on your officers and chief of services because they provide the model for all around them and through them to the people at large (520).

53

Taking Care of Relatives

(Taking care of relatives especially of the yester years)

521. Presently out of relationship but old life is merrily eulogized
Only among old relatives and associates this is practiced.

Individuals who were associated early as a family or close knit unit
are capable of nostalgia because of which they can revive relationship
in spite of having been cutoff for a long time happily remembering
and discussing old memories.

522. If relatives with unsevering affection are aligned
One after another benefits are gained.

Several assets and strengths will accrue, non stopping, if we cultivate
relatives whose affection is stable.

523. Without the strength of an affectionate socializing
Life, like a bund less pond, goes diminishing.

If one doesn't maintain an affectionate interaction with close
associates who are nearer (and through networking with whom who
are farther) his life will be like a pond remaining baron for want
of proper bunds. (There is a beauty in this couplet. A habitant not
surrounded by affectionate kith and kin and friends and a pond not
surrounded by a bund are compared.)

524. The benefit of one's wealth
Is getting surrounded oneself with kith.

A rich man reaps benefits from his wealth by surrounding himself
with kith and kin and former cohabitants and live like a single unit.
It is worthy benefit.

525. Gifting and speaking sweet words if enacted
The actor lives with piles of relatives surrounded.

Kith and kin and former associates with whom one had lost touch
will come to live surrounding him if he speaks sweetly to them and
help them.

526. He rolls out large gifts, never catches fiery rage
Him, in the vast land, none beats in kinship size.

If a person disperses large funds in help to his relatives and do not
get into terrible anger then no one can beat him in the size of his
relatives and associates.

527. Crow never hides its find. It invites its flock through crowing
Assets accrue to men with a similar showing.[125]

When a food is found a crow crows to invite other crows to share
the food. It is the nature of crows. Great things happen to people of
such nature.

---

[125] Tiruvalluvar says this quality of inviting fellow beings to share what one has is an
asset building exercise in the sense that such contact can be profitably used by the
person for his asset building exercise. (For crows this may prove to be a survival
value like when they are preying on their meal in large numbers any predator
cannot cause extensive damage.)

528. **If** a king doesn't hold them as general public
But as relatives their surrounding him would click.

Old relatives and associates have special attachment. Recognizing that if a king treats them, especially with his private wealth, they will surround him reviving the old relationship. Rather they will be with him for the sake of old relationship.

529. The relation who left returns
When the reason for leaving leaves.

Sometimes someone close to the king may leave him for some reason. He may also return to the king once that reason disappears. (Thiruvalluvar suggests that in such situations the king (the CEO) should take him back provided there are no other issues.)

530. One who left for no known reason may try to relocate
King shall deliberate and accommodate.

Sometimes a person who has left earlier (for some selfish reason) may come back because things have terribly gone wrong for him. King should not say no to him rather accommodate him after studying his intentions thoroughly.

Skills to be learnt:

➢   The ability to revive an old but dormant relationship and association when an opportunity arrives.

Rationale:

➢   Old relationship is easily revivable because of the nostalgia. It has mutual economic advantages (521/22).

➢   Second it nourishes one's soul because all the bad feelings and old issues are easily revisited and solved because of the involvement of soul and nostalgic feelings ego taking the back seat.

Coaching:

- ➢ The idea of going to the roots, limited to one's childhood relatives and friends, can be attempted. Being selective in landing on a very few manageable contacts and reestablishing relationship may produce gratifying experience (522).

- ➢ A life without at least a few solid relatives with whom we interact is like a pond without bunds. The life will be as barren as that so called pond. Therefore to get some life into your life catch hold of some of your old relations whom you like and start interacting with them (523).

- ➢ Your hard earned money has the best use delivered when with diligently using it you get your relatives around you (524).

- ➢ Gifting to the relatives who are in need and speaking sweet words without rage gets you surrounded by your relatives (525/26).

- ➢ If you carefully choose some old associates based on their honesty and hardworking nature and involve them in your economic activity they would prove very useful in building asset (527).

- ➢ Treating old associates specially as differentiated by how you treat your present associates creates a special bond with them (528).

- ➢ Some old relatives/associates would have left you for some reason and may return now because that reason doesn't exist anymore. Take them without any question (529).

  Some old relatives may have some selfish reason for coming back. They may be also taken back but after checking him thoroughly (530).

54

Lack of Vigilance

(No letup in a chosen work)

531. Loosing vigilance in the midst of great glory
Is worse than unlimited anger display.

Anger crossing its useful limit is destructive to the person who displays it. Lack of vigilance or consciousness in the midst of happiness due to great victory is detrimental. (For example, for want of vigilance one may forget to take some strategic action before a specified period following a successful accomplishment of a project.)

532. Chronic poverty blunts intelligence;
Lack of vigilance kills fame's[126] deliverance.

Growth of intelligence depends upon intake of nutritious food and intellectually stimulating environment present in a family during the developmental periods. What is missed in one developmental period cannot be made good later. Similarly lack of continuous vigilance on a task will lead to failures leading to nil or ill deliverance of public-esteemed acts which cannot be reversed.

---

[126] The word fame stands for the acts carried out winning the appreciation/positive feed back from the competent persons of the society or the beneficiaries.

533. **A**bsent of vigilance spoils achieving public-esteem in full,"
World writers of all hues make this forceful.

Those who lack vigilance can never achieve fame (positive feedback and appreciation from the general public or from the beneficiaries because they will invariably fail in their promises or their lethargy would make them to miss a target in time). This is the considered opinion of world scholars across the board/denominations.

534. **C**owards have no security
Relaxed life has no prosperity.

A person who suffers from phobia will feel insecure in spite of the very high security given to him. Similarly forgetters of task on hand can never attain prosperity.

535. **H**e who fails to act in advance due to lack of focus,
Suffers from the ensuing and regrets.

Obstacles and downturn will result if proactive actions are not taken on the appropriate time due to lack of a focused monitoring of one's affairs

536. **N**ever forgetting one's duty to any one
Is better than any other done

Never forgetting one's responsibilities to others is a great quality. No other quality equals it.

537. **N**othing unachievable exists, provided
The tool of vigilant effort is applied.

Nothing is unachievable provided the tool of being constantly focused on the task is made use of.

538. **A**ppreciate and carry out an esteemed act
     Disparager has his soul for seven births at naught.

     Appreciate the need, and focus and carry out acts which are socially
     beneficial. Those who do not do so and set aside such acts with
     contempt will suffer due to a crooked soul for seven births. (In other
     words the soul would require seven births to ward off the ill effects
     mustered in one birth.)

539. **T**hink of those who got wrecked due to their disregard[127]
     When you are dogged in pleasure and go out of guard.

     When you gloat in joy and lose your vigilance or focused attention
     remember those, who in similar situation overlooked their schedule
     only to get wreck.

540. **A**chieving what you intend is easier provided
     Your focus on it is deep rooted.

     If your focus about achieving something is not subjected to laziness,
     wavering and forgetting, it is easy to achieve what you want to
     achieve.

Skills to be learnt:

➢   Ability to keep a stable focus on the target and activities planned to
     reach it. (This includes a vigilant awareness of one's mindset also.)

Rationale:

➢   Thiruvalluvar says in couplet number 533 that the considered
     conclusions of the scholars who has researched and written on the
     topic of vigilance was: lack of focus would kill the mind set to
     excel in their work leading to negative feedback from those who are

---

[127] 'Disregard' stands for disregarding the targets which won acclaim.

competent enough to give the feedback. It is also common knowledge that any act which suffers from a lax mentality on the part of the doer, suffers. Some of the behavioral problems the lax can lead to are: obesity, excessive smoking, inappropriate work relationships, addiction to internet, gossiping etc.

Coaching:

➤ Two techniques could be picked up from this chapter for learning the skill of keeping a constant vigil on the activities leading to obtainment of the target:

1. pick up the best practices of the competent people which received positive feedback from the colleagues and other players in reaching a target(538),
2. When you are in a relaxed mood enjoying your time losing focus, remember those who got ruined because they did the same (539).

➤ The first technique may need a bit of research by you. If you are in a field consider the best person in the field and find out his daily routines and evaluate each of them to find out which one will suit you and which one you have to change a little to suit your situation and adapt them.

➤ The second technique also can benefit from real life examples of how someone kissed ground from his or her high world of fame and name and trace the fall to his or her losing focus at the height of happiness. You may recall similar experiences from your own life and take a decision that you will watch yourself closely and make it a habit to recall the fall of people or yourself in the past whenever you tend to lose control over you. The recall would become automatic after practice and will stand you in good stead.

55

Right Scepter

(The unswerving scepter)

541. **N**ever cherry picks to empathize, discharges equitable rule
That is how a right scepter prevail.

A king should not selectively empathize. Second, whomsoever it may be, a king should apply standard codes and discerning as his tools to dispense royal justice.

542. The world looks up to rains for surviving
Kings right scepter is citizen's purveying.

Every living creature of the universe look upon rains for surviving. Kings right scepter (dispensation through just and standard rule) in the same breadth is looked upon by citizens as safeguarding their existence.

543. **T**he scriptures of sages on *aram* rose
In response to what earlier scepters' had to pose. [128]

The experience of successes and failures of earlier scepters of kings had provided the input for sages to develop the *aram* based later codes.

---

[128] The rule earlier kings provided.

544. To the king who rules in line with the feedback[129] of the citizens
The citizens orient without any aversions.

If a king takes into account the feedback of the citizens and incorporate them appropriately in his rule his citizens will follow his footsteps without any reservation.

545. Aligning with the just law if a king rules
The country's yield and rain corresponds.

If a country has a king who puts a proper system of rule in place men will earnestly undertake agricultural activities and make use of the rains fully. As a result the yield potential of the land would be fully realized.

546. Might of the armor[130] doesn't win success
It is the scruples which his scepter access.

A king is able to establish a successful rule not by terrorizing the people with his military power rather by putting in place a system of governance guided by scruples of justice.

547. The king protects the land and its people
His protection his crook-free system ensures to be stable.

A king protects his world of citizens. He is protected by the system he has put in place powered by the right scepter.

548. Hard of access and unjust dispensation
If a king is so, his fall is a self-propelled mission.

---

[129] Since the King has power as well as responsibility to the welfare of people he cannot be unilaterally acting. He has to take his citizens along with him. This was like an unwritten law.

[130] The armor specifically mentioned in the couplet is spear.

The king should grant easy access to his citizens and keep neutral/impartial in his ruling. Otherwise he will fall by his own misdemeanors.

549. Guarding from external attack and quelling internal offence[131]
       Is the job of a King, not a malice.

Protecting each citizen from the attack of fellow citizen and outsiders and punishing the offending citizens is part of king's duty and therefore not blameful.

550. King ending the lives of wicked through execution
       Is on par with a farmer weeding the crop for its protection.

Execution of a criminal by the king is like removing the weeds for the sake of crops. (This idea of Tiruvalluvar may not appear to be modern. It is not really so. I will explain how: If the main crop needs to be protected weeding is absolutely necessary. Similarly for upholding the safety and security of innocent victims and large population the criminals who are hard core and beyond correctional/interventional efforts need to be executed. This will be a deterrent for future offenders and to that extent good for the citizens.

But for execution to become an effective deterrent the time gap between the date of crime and date of execution should be very short. In India the criminal suffers for decades in jail before execution takes place conferring additional punishment not intended under the relevant rule of law. Second in a corrupt environment crimes go unestablished in the courts due to spoiling the case at every level by influential politicians and officials abetted by them. Moreover the trials also may take years, even decades to come to an end due to maneuvers. In that case the fear component becomes absent in the minds of evil people. These are all extraneous to Thiruvalluvar's

---

[131] In the next couplet executing a cruel person is mentioned. Therefore it is inferable Tiruvalluvar's time practiced differential jurisprudence.

prescription and not to be incorporated in evaluating Thiruvalluvar on this subject.)

Skills to be learnt:

> The ability to maintain neutrality between contending parties by understanding both of them with the same level of empathy i.e., avoiding selective empathy. Carrying out what is needed to be done after the understanding and acting transparently.

Rationale:

> This chapter apparently has been written for the use of a king. However, any one in a leadership position would find critical use for this skill or strength.

> Interpersonal relations suffer due to cliques that form even at the level of a family and close relations. This is true of an office setting also.

> A leader needs to spend enough time for each party/group to understand them empathically. After understanding the contending parties care need to be taken to do justice for both the parries.

> Initially one may be unpopular with both the parties. But in due course of time they will find him harmless and will come around him. Using the newly built influence one can lead the group.

Coaching:

> Empathic understanding means borrowing the internal frame of reference of a person and looking at how a person subjectively perceives an issue. To use an American phrase it is "to walk in his moccasins." You assume as if you are he or she when you try to understand him or her.(541)

> One simple technique to acquire the skill is retelling what you have heard from the other person using another set of phrases other than what the other person has used. In this exercise if the other

person agrees with what you say it shows you have understood him. Practicing this technique for some time gets you the skill.

➢ The second step in impartial empathic understanding is maintaining neutrality in giving the benefit of empathic understanding to all the parties concerned (541).

➢ Normally most of us achieve empathic understanding with few people because we are terribly interested in them. With others we do not do the same. This has to be avoided.

➢ For example, a husband who exhibits a perfect empathic understanding of his parents does not reach the same level of empathic understanding with his wife!

➢ Similarly a wife who has a perfect empathic understanding of her parents fails to understand her parent in-laws.

➢ Orienting ourselves to the needs of others and doing everything in our power without affecting our interest wins the heart of others. (544)

➢ If we take sides in our dispensation we will get terribly affected because of the tardy interpersonal relations we would set in motion. (548)

➢ Following certain rules which is clear to everyone and never allowing it to be corrupted by vested interest will stop the formation of clique. (546)

56

The Cruel Sceptre

(Misrule)

551. A king who unleashes a trail of pain on the people
     Is crueler than the killer who kills for money.

     A tyrannical king who inflicts a wave of pain on the people is worse
     than a professional killer.

552. A tyrant king requesting the citizens to pay is similar
     To "Stop and deliver" shouted by a spear toting dacoit at a traveler.

     A tyrant king requesting the citizens to pay tax is equivalent to a
     dacoit commanding a traveler to drop his possessions into his bag.
     (A king, who is a tyrant, creates a fear psychosis. As a result of which
     even when he notifies as mildly as requesting to pay tax citizens
     develop fear and anxiety. Citizens know, like the traveler knows,
     that there is no escape.)

553. A king who does not govern by just rule every day
     His country will become unruly and chaotic day by day.

     Every day, every issue, if a king doesn't study and apply distributive
     justice and rule, then every day in every way the country will become
     unruly and will move towards chaos.

554. If a king abuses his scepter and acts not on a researched base
His wealth and his subjects together he will lose.

A king needs to do research to find out the appropriate action in
every case taking into account the rule of the land and the situation.
Contrary to this if a king disregards the rule and resort to motivated
dispensation then he will lose his wealth and citizens.

555. It is the tears of the harassed citizens: Is it not
The destroyer of the wealth[132] of its powerful clout?

The phrase 'tears of citizens' stand for the distress of citizens and
the word 'wealth' stands for the kingdom. If citizens are distressed
by the crooked scepter of the king to such an extent that it breaches
their tolerance level then they will revolt resulting in the ouster of
the king (like what has happened in French Revolution and recently
in Middle East countries).

556. A king's permanent companion is a right scepter
If it is absent king's fame will be a non-sticker.

A king's life companion is right scepter. If he lacks it his rule may
continue but will lack the sheen.

557. As the world under the condition of no rains attain
So the lives under a king with no compassion remain.

If a king lacks compassion his people will suffer. Their condition
will be similar to the untold misery and pain when the rains fail
long enough.

---

[132] Holding the Tamil word *selvam* in this couplet and in couplet 566 as country and
rule is more apt than holding as wealth. In Tamil words often take contextual
meaning is a well-known fact.

558. Property yields more pain than poverty
If people live under a king whose rule lacks propriety.

The life of rich becomes more miserable than the poor if the king
is motivated to steal from his citizens under the guise of a scepter
(cruel scepter). (Many businessmen lost their property during the
dictator's rule in Africa.)

559. If a king rules through a crooked rule
People go action less and uses of rains fail.

In a country under just rule the king and citizens influence each other
mutually. In a country ruled by a tyrant king this instrumentality
is absent and the people feel powerless as a result of which they lose
interest in agricultural operations in spite of copious rains. This
results in agricultural yields which are heavily short of the yield of
the rains.[133]

560. Cows go dry men of six duties[134] forget their scripture,
If the protector, protection of people, doesn't care.

If the King whose duty is to protect his people fails in his duty the
wealth of cattle especially that of cows will decline. Brahmins who
have six fold activities towards the society would forget their books
and would behave haphazardly. (There is also another interpretation
which says the people in various avocations, a six of them very basic,
would forget their scriptures regarding their vocations. The vocations
are plough, weaving, ministering, ruling trading and teaching. But
this interpretation may be little farfetched.)

---

[133] Here and in couplet number 545 interpreters in general (save non-believers of
god) take a position that nature will behave differently in countries ruled by just
and unjust kings. Thirukkural doesn't contain such irrational notions.

[134] This has reference to Brahmins who has six duties to perform. They are: learning
Vedas, teaching Vedas, carrying out prayers, and making others to perform the
same and giving gifts and receiving gifts.

Skills to be learnt:

➢ Avoiding tyranny or being too hard on people around you like life partner, children, parents, friends, colleagues and your employees.

Rationale:

➢ Even though this chapter is meant for a king the notion of being tyrannical in modern days is found among people like tyrant bosses. Tyranny is also discernable in relations like husband and wife, student and teacher, leader and follower, manager and staff or supervisor and worker. Therefore this chapter has some lesson for all of us who might share this attribute a little or more.

Coaching:

➢ Playing one-upmanship is born out of a feeling of insecurity. To come out of this feeling human being indulges in keeping others always suppressed (551). They always compete in order to suppress not out of a sport man's spirit but by excelling they can maintain superiority which gives them comfort. Where they are not able to compete they ignore what others have achieved or they will belittle what others do as of no consequence or of no relevance. We need two techniques: one for how to come out of one-upmanship and another for how to handle a person who plays one-upmanship.

How to come out of one-upmanship mentality?

➢ Picking the skill of self-awareness is the answer. Watch yourself for one thing. With any one do you feel a neat, "I am better than thou"?
➢ Even with persons known for very high caliber than you do you feel competitive?
➢ If you lose out in competition do you come with explanations like, "I could not believe this"
➢ If your answer is "yes" for all the three questions then you are most likely a one-upmanship candidate.

- ➤ To relieve yourself of this one-upmanship mentality you have to achieve an accurate understanding of your strengths and weaknesses and try to work in the areas of your strength.
- ➤ But even in the area of your strength if your aptitude is not very high it becomes almost impossible for you to crack great achievements.
- ➤ Accept that without any agitation with this thinking: "If I am a mediocre so be it, I am one. That is fine. There are a number of areas where a lot of work needs to be done. I will excel in volume rather than innovation or creativity. After all, the world needs a lot of mediocre but hardworking, fun loving compassionate workers like me. There are/were a number of mediocre workers in the world who live in the heart of people because they have shown exemplary human qualities and achievements!"
- ➤ Similarly if you have a strength which is more than most of the people still you need not feel one-upmanship because what you have is mostly due to a genetical accident. It is a 'genetical accident' is borne by the fact that what you accomplish is disproportionate to the labor you put. There is also a possibility that some one better than you may be around the corner!

How to handle a person who is a stubborn one-upmanship man?

- ➤ Since one-upmanship is born out of insecurity feelings it is very difficult to change this position by confronting the person who has it.
- ➤ Such persons can be handled differently. Couplet 158 says when some one does you a harm out of a mentality of superiority you can mend him using your solemn character.
- ➤ Since a person with one-upmanship mentality has the knack of provoking you into a competitive argument and put you down the best option is being alert and refusing to be drawn into the game. If you do it deliberately every time he provokes you then he will lose interest.

➢   Remember that behavior which is not regarded or not disregarded will lose force and will die a natural death.

➢   The technique given under the chapter "Forbearance" (Chapter: 16) can be successfully employed to put up with a person without provoking him and creating an urge in him not to play the game of one-upmanship.

57

Not Acting Terroristic

(Measured Punishment)

561. What constitutes a king's skill in crime management?
It is analyzing and awarding a deterrent punishment.

A king should be skillful in analyzing and awarding punishment which discourages the offender from repeating it and others taking guidance from it. That means punishment should be harsh but not too harsh inviting retaliation and revolt at least psychologically if not immediately physically in which case the punished will commit more mistakes in the future guided by a sense of vengeance.

562. If you desire a long and prospering ministry
Charge the accused sternly but punish modestly.

While making the charge sheet the king can be very extensive but while punishing he should mellow them to the extent that the punishment becomes a good deterrent.

563. If a king inducts dread and rules crooked
His fall, sure to happen, stands marked.

If a king's acts are fear inducing in the minds of his citizens and added to it if he also crooks the rule then for sure he will get ruined quickly.

564. 'Our king is a tyrant' – if the citizens have this to speak
His end comes quicker than bespoke.[135]

If people exchange the note whenever they meet that their king was a tyrant the end of his rule arrives more quicker than what is evidenced from outside.

565. Hard audience and hard looks: his vast wealth
No better than that of an ugly demon's.

If a king doesn't give audience easily and when he does if he is very rude with his visiting citizens his wealth is as good as possessed by a demon. (People will be thoroughly discouraged to seek his audience for the purpose of requesting him for help. Wealth possessed by a demon is of no use for others is obvious.)

566. His words are harsh, he lacks empathy
Long inherited rule doesn't stay due to his antipathy.

If a king uses harsh words and he also fails to look into the concerns of his citizens from their point of view, due to his negative attitude born from his deep seated aversion towards his citizens, the long rule he has inherited would end.

567. Tyrant words and normless punishment
A file hard enough to shred king's winning might.

A king may be as strong as iron vis-à-vis his power to fight and destroy his enemies but it will be eroded bit by bit if he uses tyrant words at his citizens and awards disproportionate punishment to them.

---

[135] Bespoke = indicated

568. A king who doesn't consult his minister[136]before acting
And rebukes when he volunteers has his wealth[137] diminishing.

A minister is a co-professional as far as administration is concerned. Therefore a king benefits most by consulting him. But if a king not only not consults his minister but also rebukes him when he appropriately intervenes will soon find his diminishing in area.

569. **A** king who doesn't arrest his egotism[138]
Slips into arrogance, soon falls his kingdom.

Egotism or arrogance getting activated out of the feeling that he has got slighted/trespassed or overruled etc. by his ministers and other advisers is detrimental to a king. The king should arrest that egotistic thought whenever it occurs otherwise the extent of his kingdom would reduce in size. (For example, if he insults his minister who tries to give him a sane advise he might join an enemy king and work against him resulting a portion of his kingdom slipping out of his hands.)

---

[136] Minister is a co professional to a king. This idea is brought out by Tiruvalluvar nicely by referring the minister with the Tamil word *inam* meaning one's own tribe.

[137] Wealth means country.

[138] The Tamil word *seru* appearing in the couplet means enemy. With that meaning the couplet has been translated by the pioneer Rev. Dr.G.U.Pope as: Who builds no fort whence he may foe defy // In time of war shall fear and swiftly die. The chapter counsels against tyrannous nature a king might have. Therefore to hold one of the couplets (569) as speaking about an enemy advancing with his army sounds odd. The oddness disappears if the enemy referred to by the poet here is: செருக்கு (*serukku*) appearing shorty as செரு (*seru*). செருக்கு means arrogance; head weight in lay man's language. An arrogant king because of his bloated ego would heavily put down anyone including his minister who advises him contrary to what he wants to hear.

570. A tyrant king attracts unlettered counsel
The earth has no bigger burdening ill.

Generally a tyrant king attracts counsels not well educated in
political as well as ethical sciences. There is no worst burden to a
king if he surrounds himself with a score of such advisors. (Birds of
the same feather flock together.)

Skills to be learnt:

➢ An ability not to breach the fine line of being just and fair in dealing
with a person who has offended you/committed a mistake.
➢ An ability to act soft in interpersonal interaction.

Rationale:

➢ We act tyrannical because we disregard the right of a fellow human
being for an equitable treatment from us. Acting equitably even with
a person who is guilty of a crime is a must. This chapter emphasizes
this.

Coaching:

➢ It is possible for us to dispense equity in interpersonal relations if we
first accept that as children of mother earth we are all on par as far
as our status as human being is concerned. If anyone has an issue it
can be only with the behavior and not with one's status as human
being. The second notion is in order to guarantee equity to ourselves
and to the fellow humans we have to strive hard to put in place a
system which awards it. The policy which forms the under grid for
such a system is: "Act compassionately with all living and non-living
beings of the planet."
➢ In the chapter 'Compassion' couplet 250 says "If we can mentally
capture our position when a person stronger than us takes it on us
and feel the agony then we will avoid going on a person weaker
than us."

> The couplet number 566 in the present chapter says "if a king uses harsh words and he also fails to look into the concerns of his citizens from their point of view, due to his negative attitude, born from his deep seated aversion towards his citizens, his huge wealth (kingdom) will vanish." Clubbing these two couplets we get the reason why some of us act tyrant and how we can come out of it.

> We act tyrant because we fail to see how it hurts others. Sometimes we think some one deserve such tyrant action. But is it really so? This question can be answered if we empathize with others. Most of the issues will be solved if we develop an empathic understanding of the other person. Once we understand some one empathically he comes forward to open up and we are in a negotiation which can take both of us solving the problem in any other way rather than being tyrant against each other.

> The word compassion has a profound meaning in Thirukkural. It is not a sympathy driven behavior. It is rights a driven behavior. Acting compassionate means readily coming forward to give the equity to him or her. In the case of persons not powerful enough to assert themselves to achieve their equity compassionate action is standing by their side and fighting for it. (The notion about compassionate behavior is discernable if all the *kurals* where the word compassion appears in Tirukkural and the chapter titled Equity (Chap: 12) are studied together. The couplets where the concept is found are: 176,241,242 to 248 and 251, 252,254,285,755,757,914 and 938.

> One thought that would demolish compassion is: some of us think that we are entitled to certain things because we have earned it through our labor or other means. This sense of special entitlements which we in due course of time push to the level of inalienable right creates the problem. Remember any one who has more than what he reasonably needs is a thief opined Gandhi. Using his intelligence, loop holes of the law or other illegitimate means like muscle power if a person amasses wealth more than what he needs he is a thief because to that extent he has robbed others.

➤   If we remember by being compassionate (doing our bit in upholding the equity of fellow humans) we evolve at the level of our soul which would one day usher into God's world we will be motivated to act compassionately with everyone around us.

58

Empathy

(Acting empathically)

571. Empathic skill – an immense joy yielding beauty
Is a fait accompli – this universe thrives by her bounty

Empathizing[139] is a beautiful skill. It is a fact that many people possess it. It is only because of that quality happiness exists in this world.

572. With empathy remains the socialness[140] of the world
Who lacks empathic skills hence is world's load.

Because of the presence of empathy socialness of the world thrives. Therefore those who lack this skill are burden to this earth.

573. What use is a tune if with no song it does consonant?
What use are eyes not catching up with the opponent?

---

[139] Empathizing means understanding a person using that persons' frame of reference. In other words understanding him as he understands him; walking in his shoes. Thiruvalluvar has personified the concept as a great lady being the fountain head of joy.

[140] Socialness is a word coined by me to mean the give and take in every sense among the members of the world.

A tune is meant to go along with a song. Otherwise no purpose is served by it. Similarly if a person is not able to see eye to eye (reading from the same page/empathizing) with another person in order to understand his perspective there is no use for his eyes.[141]

574. **W**hat use eyes are on the face?
If they are unable to measure other's sense.

If person X is unable to empathize and make out person Y's subjective feelings and thoughts what use have his eyes?

575. **E**mpathy spilling out of the eyes is their adornment
Hence eyes with no empathy are held as wounds.

Eyes are decorated by their skill of empathy. Therefore if someone's eyes are not capable of such a skill then they are as good as a pair of wounds. (The eyes of a person who is capable of empathic understanding will show a friendly/warm/ understanding acceptance of the opponent making them shine like a jewel.)

576. **H**e who cannot see along the angle of others
Is as insensitive as the trees.

A tree is insensitive. Similarly a man who is incapable of aligning with the angle of others in order to understand them is as insensitive as the tree. (It appears that there is another deep sense in this concept. Perhaps Thiruvalluvar says that a tree doesn't have soul therefore it cannot empathize. The same applies to a man who is incapable of empathy. Absence of soul means presence of ego in full measure.

---

[141] Eyes are capable of reading the signs. A sign of happiness/anger/disgust/ disapproval etc., appears in the eyes of the person who feels so. Later in consonance with words and body positions and through probe one can get at the inside of a person to a very large extent. Perhaps because eyes initially paves the way for further enquiry and his helpful throughout the skill is given a name involving them.

Ego is incapable of putting itself in another person's place in order to understand his side of the story.)

577. Since empathy in looks defines bona fide eyes
Eyes with empathy are real eyes. Others are lookalikes [142]

The eyes are defined as organs capable of understanding the other person from his angle. They do so by capturing the mind as reflected in the signs of the eyes and body of the opponent. Therefore if someone's eyes lack this ability they are only lookalikes of eyes not real ones.

578. Empathy shown to associates not affecting the target,
Earns you a right on what from the world you could get.

A superior should have an empathic understanding of the need of his subordinates. And he should also do the needful without fail. But there is a limit. He can go up to an extent that going any further will adversely affect the task allotted to them. If the superior is capable of such discerning then he naturally earns the right over world. Right over the world in the present context consists of a right over time, labor and money of his employees.

579. Empathizing with those who hurt us
Leads to forbearance and in it its greatness rests.

Empathizing with someone who hurts and bearing with him is a supreme quality of an empathizing heart. (Perhaps the person bears with his attacker because through his empathic hearing he understands that there was some provocation from his side.)

---

[142] A word by word translation of this couplet bringing in the poetic beauty is very difficult to achieve for the present translator. Therefore a translation bringing out the import as much as possible is attempted.

580. **P**oison poured, he sees but drinks and remains quiet
Since, by empathy he finds reasons to quit.

It is possible for someone who is very high in empathic understanding
to drink poison offered by another person because through empathic
understanding he finds a justification for that. His decision is guided
by his sense of equity and sense of shame.

(The story of the ancient king of Pandya dynasty illustrates this
extremely laudable quality. The king called Nedunchelian by mistake
gave order for the execution of an innocent. When the wife of the
deceased came to his court and proved that the king was wrong in
his ruling he readily agreed with her and swore that his life should
immediately end. After saying so he died instantly. (Perhaps the
sudden awareness that he has done something terribly wrong was
so shocking for him he died out of it. That he had a strong sense
of shame and sense of justice and ability to empathize could be
garnered by reading the entire scene of the trail at his court which
he conducted.)

Skills to be learnt:

> Ability to perceive an issue from the point of view of the causer of
  the issue.
> Ability to rise to the occasion after an empathic understanding
  and doing the needful. (After an understanding the other persons
  point of view it need not always doing something favorable to that
  person. It can be even negating or punishing him for something. An
  empathizer is like a judge who tries to find out the side of the accused
  keeping himself independent of the pleader and defense lawyer.)

Rationale:

> Thiruvalluvar says ability to understand the view point of others as
  they understand is a strength, needed for the successful functioning
  of the world. Without that the world will be very dry and no evolution

of the society would have been possible. Therefore it is necessary to learn the skill.

➢ Anyone who is good at empathic skill will be good at interpersonal relations also.

➢ Psychologists call this skill as empathy. I am of the opinion that the Tamil word *kannottam* which is the title of this chapter is the Technical word in Tamil standing for the English word empathy.

Coaching:

➢ How to empathize is learnable from the couplet number 576. The couplet says the people who are incapable of aligning their eyes with those of others (that is borrowing the understanding of the other person temporarily to understand him from his angle) will be as insensitive as a tree.

➢ One simple way to empathically understand another person is checking with him whether what you have understood of what he has stated has been accurate or not. Rephrase what you have heard using a different set of phrases other than what he has used and ask him whether they represented what he said earlier. He might agree totally or partially. Ask him to correct. The resultant material represents his position.

➢ No doubt this is a bit laborious. But the benefit is enormous. Aligning your vintage with that of his you can see exactly what he sees!(579)

➢ This ability is inborn and some of us are very good at it. For others it comes with little training. But for people with psychological difficulties this is not easy to achieve.

➢ If you have too many interpersonal problems or you have very few friends or people try to avoid you, your problem may be lacking empathizing skill. Do the needful to pick it up.

59

Espionage

(Spying)

581. Two things should exist with a king
A fleet of spies and great political treatises.

A king should have these two: enough number of spies and a collection of great political treatises capable of shedding unforeseen light on statecraft.

582. What others talk, do and intend, a real time update
On these should be the king's mandate[143].

A king should track and update himself what others talk, do and intend. This is part of a king's profession.

583. What one spy brings verify with another
A king who doesn't do this has no future.

An information brought by one spy should be verified by comparing it with what is brought by another spy on the subject. If a king does not do this his kingdom would not lost long.

---

[143] Mandate = bidding

584. His personnel, relatives and enemies – spying them
Must also occupy the spying realm.

The terms of reference for spying consist of king's officials, princes, relatives and enemies.

585. Of unsuspected mien and keeping a constant alert,
Leaving no clues as to what he is at, is how a spy does act.

A spy should bear such postures keeping him out of doubt i.e. he should be able to put on different disguises without evoking any suspicion. He should not allow himself to be disturbed by a suspecting or scrutinizing eye of an officer serving the enemy king. He should never let out what he has under any condition however torturing it may be.

586. Robed as a monk a spy accesses a number of places
Further, he doesn't give up under duress.

His hosts never suspect an efficient spy because he dresses and posses in such a manner leaving no room for doubt at all. He may use the garbs of a saint and other respectable persons for winning the confidence of the enemy. Further, he never lets out his identity due to torture.

587. Whom he spies hides but the spy accesses,
Further through an insider he verifies.

A spy's host may carefully hide. But a spy manages to smell. Next he somehow verifies what he has picked up through an insider once again without letting him know of it.

588. Get the material got through one spy
Verified through another guy.

A king practices a cross check. He collects material from one spy and checks it against what he got from another spy.

589. A spy doesn't recognize a second spy, managing that
Accept their story verified by what a third spy does get.

He manages the business of espionage in such a manner that one spy doesn't know that there is another spy around. Managing like that the king next compares what he has got from the first two with what he gets from a third one.

590. Don't honor a spy in the open on any pretext
If you do, you are letting known your text.

A king should never honor a spy in the open. He may do it hiding under some pretext. But still it will be sensed and king's effort thus far will take a beating.

Skills to be learnt:

> The lessons on spying found in this chapter may look redundant in the context of elaborate knowledge that must be available at present in this domain especially from the experience of cold war.

> The translator has no knowledge and claims no comparison while he explains the skills found in this chapter. The skills can be divided into two parts. One set of skills are meant for the king (the present day president or prime minister or a CEO). Another set is meant for the spy himself.

> A king has to thoroughly master himself the text on spying and the operations and be able to guide the personnel involved in espionage. He should not exclude anyone on any consideration from the list of people to be spied. He should also have espionage at multiple levels and use them to cross check the information.

> The skill set relating to a spy consists of skills in remaining incognito, winning the confidence of insiders and collecting information and

meticulously and secretly checking the same from a different source. All these are done without creating any suspicion.

Rationale:

- ➢ Even in today's world espionage is needed mainly because the world has not come out of the mindset that there is no enough space for all the countries to materialize their developmental goals.
- ➢ They believe that only those countries which are most competitive can grow. They also believe that the best way to do it is to undercut another country.
- ➢ Though it might sound awkward to spy other countries especially their policies it is a necessity in the present day world.

Coaching:

- ➢ Each of the five couplets numbering 585,586,587,588 and 589 provide techniques for spying.
- ➢ Couplet 585 gives the list of skills for a spy: remaining incognito, managing the eye not showing fear and not spelling the beans under torture. If someone develops suspicion and starts accosting the spy he should not show fear in his eyes. If he shows it will increase his accosting person's suspicion. Spy training world over cover these aspects. In general training for avoiding fear consists of shifting our mind from fear mode to fight mode. Fear mode is useless in that situation. Whereas fight mode can result in success. If a spy is previously trained to always get into a fight or attack mode rather than a fear mode he can get rid of fear in his eyes. Remember the couplet: 585.
- ➢ Couplet 586 apparently show no much difference from 585 but it is not so. It includes one possibility for remaining incognito: wearing the posture of an ascetic and having the body and muscular system to bear body torture. The spy training procedures adopted by nations include specific muscle toning exercises to withstand torture. Spy professionals also enter into a nation as an expat worker and spy for their nation.

➢   Couplet 587 says a spy should stay around a place and smell events.
He should psyche out details from someone talking about general
matters; creatively psyche out
details from a casual conversation which he has with some and cross
check it with another material got from a second person again in a
casual conversation. The idea is any talk he has should be designed
as a racket. This is possible if the spy posts himself with as much
information as possible about the country so that he has a feel of the
country in which he spies.

➢   Couplet 588 and 589 is meant for the authorities who are to use
the information. They should arrange for several sources to collect
information and pass an information for action only after cross
checking it based on the inputs from various sources.

60

Vigorous Mind

(Vigorous action powered by self-efficacy)

591. Resource worth the name is will and effort
Who doesn't have it, has what else of similar import?

A man may be very resourceful like possessing education wealth
etc. Of all of them the signature possession is his willingness to act
vigorously to achieve what he aims. This willingness arises only when
he feels that he is capable. NO other resource of a human is equal
to it. Therefore one cannot claim that he is resourceful unless and
otherwise he possess the habit of vigorously working on a task on
which he sets his will.

592. A vigorous mind is indeed what asset could be,
Monetary wealth dwindles or vanishes as the case may be.

An asset is the asset of a resolute mind. After all material assets will
fleet and therefore are not dependable.

593. "Oh! We have lost our wealth," – they do not regret
Since their vigorous mind will keep them aloft.

Those who possess vigorous mind never loose heart when they lose
their wealth.

594. Fortune storms in on its own accord
      To reach him, a man of vigorous action.

      Any wealth or object of your liking will reach you as if it seeks you on
      its own provided you put in unwavering effort towards realizing it.

595. The height of lotus stem equals that of water
      The growth of man equals his vigorous labor.

      A water plant grows to the extent needed to stay atop water level.
      Similarly if a man wants to accomplish great things in life he should
      step up his efforts suitably.

596. If you envision a goal, make a great one
      Even if it is to fail it has elements of the win.[144]

      Any aim worth the name must be big and great. Sometimes one may
      not succeed in achieving such tall aim. Still he must have gained
      substantial experience out of his effort which he can make use of
      in his next effort. Therefore a vigorous effort cannot be dubbed as
      a failure.

597. Fortunes may decline but resolute men do not relent
      Like an elephant pierced with spears advances, they are gallant.

      An elephant in the battle field is unstoppable in spite of getting
      severally wounded by enemy's spears. It advances. Like that a man
      of vigorous effort is not cowed down by failures, obstacles, causing
      physical as well as financial and mental pains.

598. He who doesn't have vision and effort in heart
      Never achieve the status of, "Benefactor of the world."

---

[144] Won stands for those visions of him or others which ended in successful fruition.

Some men rise to the level of providing succor to others. They are looked upon by others for what they dispense. This is a great status and joy which is attainable to only those whose minds and hearts are galvanized with visionary energy and unwavering effort.

599. An elephant possess stout body and sharp tusks
Still in fear it groans when a tiger attacks.

An elephant possesses large body and sharp tusks. It is formidable indeed. But when a tiger attacks it groans in fear. (In couplet number 597 Thiruvalluvar refers to elephant in a different light. Perhaps elephant is vulnerable to the strategy of a tiger which bounces on the elephant from behind and strikes powerfully on its head and start eating it even while the elephant is alive. Elephant could not tackle this attack due to its body structure. By this example Thiruvalluvar indirectly suggests that vigorous effort with strategy is more powerful in brining desired results than by vigorous effort and alone.)

600. A vigorous vision at the heart is the real strength
With its absence he and a log are on the same breadth.

A real strength for human being is his ability to have a vision and acting vigorously to achieve it. Such visions are positioned in one's soul. Therefore if it is absent he is as good as soulless. In that respect he is equal to a tree.

Skills to be learnt:

➤ Vigorously working towards achieving a willed and visionary target.

Rationale:

➤ With suitable strategy committing everything one is capable of towards achieving what one willfully wants is the best approach to realize what one wants.

Coaching:

> Internalize these notions: Real asset or possession is your vigorous action which you are capable of actualizing towards a vision which you may cherish. Other material possessions sometimes may leave you. When material possessions are lost men of vigorous action will not lose heart and succumb to it. Others will. (591/92/93)

> You know one thing? Anything you wish to obtain reaches you on its own provided you invest your energy in an unwavering manner and work towards obtaining it
> That object or thought should be of great appeal to you so that it commands all the psychic energy in your possession towards releasing the physical energy. If you hold a vision due to some fancy you will lose interest in no time or it will not be stead past. How to know what is dear to your heart? If too many objects attract you do a thorough study and find out which ones are fancies and which are serious and prioritize them (594).

> Remember a lotus plant grows its stalk enough so that its flower stays above the level of water. Like that a man of vigorous action also increase as much effort as needed to achieve a target (595)

> Aim high and strive hard. Sometimes you may miss your goal. But it is not a waste of time because you are rich by the possession of several inputs accumulated through your experience. Those inputs you can invest in your renewed effort or sometimes in the next project (596).

> Men of vigorous action are also resilient and would not easily give up like an elephant in a battle field advancing on a target in spite of fierced by a number of arrows by the enemy (597)

> Remember men of vigorous action only can attain the great status of 'benefactor of the poor and needy.' Being a benefactor is soulful filling. (598)

> Strategize your efforts so that efficient use of vigorous energy is ensured (599). (The example of tiger and elephant refers to the strategy of tiger attacking the elephant from behind by climbing on it using its tail as a rope and slamming the elephant powerfully on the head and start eating it even while the elephant is alive. Contrast this with another example involving elephant in couplet number

597. There the elephant is not a victim of strategy because the lancer throwing soldier can be chased by the elephant which is not possible in the case of a tiger which attacks the elephant from behind.)

➢ Never forget this: With no energized vision oriented effort you are like a log of wood which is quoted as the standard example for soullessness by Thiruvalluvar (600). Only when your soul is also involved in your effort your effort will be in its peak level.

61

Absence of Laziness

(Lack of sloth)

601. The family, a gem in perpetual shine[145]
Polluted by laziness loses its sheen.

A family flourishes in perpetuity like a gem which emits light continuously. The gem needs dusting now and again in order to facilitate a continuous glow. In the case of a family the dust which blinds the shine is laziness.

602. If you want your family to become an ideal one
Let restricting rest not to court laziness be won.

If you want your family to flourish, have laziness short enough so that it merits to be called as rest. Have the courageous discipline of calling laziness as laziness. Don't call laziness as rest when it is not. (Thiruvalluvar's notion of laziness is very clear. He says a rest taken more than what is needed is laziness.)

603. The fool enjoys laziness as a pleasurable pursuit
His family collapses even before he plummets.

---

[145] Since Tiruvalluvar uses the Tamil word *kundra* which means never ending may be he refers to self illuminating stones used in temples to light during night. It appears these stones need to be dusted to maintain the illumination.

He is a fool who enjoys laziness as a normal phenomenon for which he or she is entitled and there is no need for concern. His family will suffer a system collapse before he himself collapses.

604. **W**hen the sloth-loving house holder banish efforts
The family as a system decays and crimes flourish.

If a family man sloths and fails to accomplish the upkeep of the family firmly the family as a system will collapse and the estranged members of the family will indulge in crimes with no one to supervise or control.

605. Procrastination, forgetting, Laziness and doze
These make the boat, ruin prone passionately choose.

Postponing things as different from prioritizing, forgetting, laziness and dozing for example, during day time for long hours or simply lying and daydreaming constitute the small festive boat which people, bent upon to get themselves ruined, will clamor to sail.

606. The lazy man may have a land lord as his patron
Still great benefits fail to happen.

A lazy man is incapable of cashing in on an opportunity. He may enjoy the affection of a landlord/king. But still for want of making active contact he will fail to grab great benefit from that source.

607. Those sloth and fail to accomplish great deeds
Are slated for thunderous reproof in insulting words.

Due to laziness if an individual fails to accomplish he will be subjected to loud and clear admonition.

608. Laziness residing in a family
Enslaves it to its enemy.

Laziness once interred into a family stays in it and makes the family to stoop before its enemy and family becomes a slave to its enemy.

609.   The mistake that crept into a family's governance
       Dies as and when sloth management is changed.

If the way with which laziness is managed in a family is changed for good the family will free itself of the ills of maladministration.

610.   A king in whom sloth is totally absent attains
       What bestrode by Lord pertains.[146]

A king who overcomes sloth can bring vast territory of land under his rule.

Skills to be learnt:

➢   To come out of the habit of procrastination.
➢   To stay focused on what we want to accomplish.
➢   To reduce laziness and sleep to the level of proper rest.

Rationale:

➢   Laziness and its accompaniments are dangerous says the canto. Laziness seriously and negatively interferes in the management of a family leading to its ruin slowly but steadily. Therefore the family should get rid of laziness using suitable management techniques.

Coaching:

➢   The chapter offers the following intervention in the form of an advisory to manage laziness among the members of the family:

---

[146] Lord Vishnu, in his Trivikrama avatar, as mythology would hold, measured the whole universe by just one step of His foot.

➢ Let the members be seriously informed that the family's capacity will be substantially reduced like a self illuminating gem whose yield of light reduces due to a coating of dust. (601)

➢ Make your laziness short enough so that it qualifies itself to be called as rest (602).

➢ Any member of the family who grants a permission for himself to be lazy (i.e., who is taking rest more than what is needed) is a fool. Let him be aware that his family will go to dogs even before him (603).

➢ Beware a family gets ruined and find itself committing one crime after another if its members are lazy. (604)

➢ Those who walk on the path of ruin have four companions for their journey. They are: procrastination, forgetting, laziness and sleeping. Therefore when you find any of this with you for long know it that you are on your path of ruin!(605)

➢ The ruin due to laziness may visit you in three ways: you may not be able to utilize the opportunities that come on your way (606), people who were otherwise willing to support you will ridicule you seeing your laziness and abandon you (607), by flex of time you will find yourselves to be subservient to your enemies (608).

How to manage laziness?

➢ A technique can be developed by bringing couplets 602 and 609 together.

➢ Couplet 602 says a person should take care to see that the rest he takes doesn't extend more than what is required in which case it is called laziness.

➢ Couplet 609 says the difficulties a family may suffer due to maladministration will disappear if the ways and methods with which laziness is managed in the family is suitably altered.

➢ Clubbing them together the family members can make a policy. An example of a policy can be like this: Family members shall be aware that rest is a break from work to refresh and rejuvenate. Therefore no one shall take rest or involve in entertainment more than what is needed. Second, anyone who is taking more time to finish a work than what is needed should know he or she is lazing and should avoid it.

➤ While individual members can be encouraged to strictly implement the above policy a system of periodically pulling up the errant put in place will go a long way to remove laziness from the family.

➤ A method of confrontation allowing every member to confront the other who remains lazy can work well. But the members should be thoroughly oriented for the method otherwise it will lead to petty quarrels and the family may even break.

62

Engaged (Strenuous) Effort

(Manliness)

611. "This is an impossible task," saying so never give up
    Think of the ensuing esteem then eengaged effort springs up.

    Giving up, thinking that you are not a match for a task even before
    you attempt it, is not desirable. Avoid it at any cost. Keep before
    your mind's eye the public esteem your effort would bring then you
    will become fully engaged with that task! (One good thing about
    life is that one would reap joy equivalent to the difficulty of what
    one accomplishes.)

612. Never slow engaged work which is on its go
    World turns away from men of such show.

    World sidelights those who leave a work unfinished or poorly finished.
    Therefore never resist and spare effort. (It seems Thiruvalluvar
    suggests inertness being a part of human nature people resisting
    hiding behind some excuse or the other is a fact. Therefore you
    should be cautious to look for such resistance in you and come out
    of it remembering the pride and other benefits you are likely to get
    once success arrives.)

613. Effortful engagement at a work is a great quality
    On it depends the pride of playing philanthropy

Engaged effort is an asset and a great human attribute. Your pride that you provide to enable growth amongst the members of the community depends on how far you are effort fully engaged in your work. (After all only when you produce you can cater. Is it not?)

614. **P**hilanthropic act by a man who doesn't work hard
Like a coward's sword goes bad.

If a person who is not an industrious worker wants to play the role of patron it will not be effective for want of sufficient resources. It will be as good as a coward trying his hand in a duel of sword.

615. **H**e has passion for work not for pleasures
He is a pillar to his kith in their adversities.

A man who does not aspire for pleasures but always aspires for work is the under grid for the safety and security of his kith and kin.

616. **E**ffortful engagement in work makes one wealthy
Its absence ushers in poverty.

Engaged efforts bring in wealth and other resources. Lack of engaged effort nets in poverty.

617. **O**n a lazy lap dwells the Goddess (*Maamugadi*) misfortune[147]
At the foot of perseverance the Goddess (of lotus) fortune. [148]

Goddess of misfortune comes and stays with him who lacks the habit of working perseveringly and purposefully and Goddess of fortune stays with him who works fully engaged in what he does.

---

[147] In Hindu mythology a Goddess is adopted as a source of misfortune

[148] According to Hindu Mythology Goddess of fortune is said to sit on a lotus flower. In the couplet lady of fortune is mentioned as lady sitting on lotus.

618. Not born with a particular aptitude is not blameful
Not engaging oneself in what one is endowed is shameful.

A person may not have been blessed with an endowment of a particular aptitude/intelligence or not amply. He should never be blamed for it. But if he doesn't find what his real aptitudes are irrespective of the fact whether they are ample or not and put in an engaged effort in those given strength(s) then he should take the blame.

619. (Excelling in a field) God doesn't favor
But hard work nets in equal to the labor.

God doesn't interfere in support of you in your endeavor. But you will reap as much as you labor.

620. Even the fate is won
By an aptly engaged effortful man. [149]

By engaged labor what is not endowed is made good. (It will not be out of context to recall the story of Chinese professor of law Prof. Amy Chua at Yale and her daughters. A saga of hard and continuous work producing wonders with the daughters is a mind boggling story to read and enjoy rather than what could be briefly explained here!)

A perspective over the notion of Fate:

Thiruvalluvar's treatment of the subject of fate is fairly elaborate. He has allotted one full chapter (38) for the topic and three couplets in this chapter. A very interesting point in chapter 38 is fate operates differently with regard to acquiring knowledge and acquiring wealth (374). In the case of acquisition of knowledge, productive fate will help the individual expand his knowledge by increasing his inquisitiveness whereas a nonproductive fate will usher foolishness (372). The second

---

[149] A fate of inadequacy can be made good by a fully engaged effort.

idea is in spite of wide studies mastery is achievable only in those domains which fate has endowed (aptitude) him and also to the level of the endowment (373). With regard to earning wealth right time/season and right place play an overwhelming effect irrespective of the fact whether on has a productive fate or not. Next whether one will be able to enjoy what he has earned or not depends whether the person is fated for shrewdness or not. Shrewdness obviously is part of productiveness. If some one's fated to be not shrewd he would become a pauper and might take to renunciation. (Don't generalize this to all renouncers.)

This is a gloomy picture indeed but for the couplets 618,619 and 620) found in this chapter.

These couplets give the remedy for one's shortcomings regarding his fate! More under 'coaching' section.

Skills to be learnt:

> Transforming oneself into an engaged worker i.e., involving oneself in industrious/vigorous effort in a domain always keeping the purpose in sight.

Rationale:

> An engaged worker is one who creates wonders in his discipline either in academics or in industry/business. He is the one who sweats, innovates and sustains a business. The industries look for candidates who have a strong base in domain knowledge complemented by flexibility enabling oneself to provide a good response in a real time to a problem in industry. This challenge is successfully met by an engaged employee. Because of him his domain sees growth every day. It is because of the growth of the domain more and more employees get opportunities in his domain and thus he literally provides the succor for others. Providing succor to others is divine and therefore helps the soul to evolve. A fully evolved soul would reach the world of God making his life well lived.

Coaching:

> Don't get disinterested in carrying out a task holding it to be too difficult. If you start doing it you will find soon it is not as difficult as you thought. (611)

> Don't do during your working hours any work not related to your domain. If you keep your purpose always before you such drifting will not take place. For example, a professor of psychology sitting at his desk can read a book on psychology. Such a work will be an engaged work. But if he is found reading a history book for the simple reason that he has some interest in the subject that professor's engagement with his job or purpose takes a beating! (612)

> Imagine with your engaged work habit you turnout a very innovative product and earn great financial rewards. Now you are in a position to donate some money to the public school, whose student you were, to improve its facilities at theatrics. Think of the pride you will be accorded by the local community when you visit the school on the day of inauguration of the new facility. You will become proud about yourself. The satisfaction you derive during that moment is very high and worth the effort.(613)

> How about deriving great satisfaction from the fact that due to commitment to your domain you created so many avenues for creating new job opportunities for several young persons and the history of your domain's growth will be written studding it with diamonds of your particular contribution for so many years. (614)

> There is another incentive for engaged effort. An engaged worker achieves the capacity to take care of the needs of his relatives. He can lift them from poverty. This act is soul evolving and therefore the purpose of coming to this is well served.

> Couplet specifically says engaged effort is a protection for a person who will otherwise become a pauper (616).

> This is restated in a more powerful manner by bringing in two mythological beings one for misfortune named as *Maamugadi* and another for fortune named as *Thamaraiyinaal*. We should remember Thiruvalluvar was talking to a population to whom these mythological beings were familiar to convey his idea.

➢ For some of us whose potentials are not rich Thiruvalluvar says it is not a set back at all. What will be a setback is not putting additional effort to take care of the deficiency. One should chose his best bet and put in vigorous effort (618).

➢ The enemy for engaged effort is the mentality to seek pleasure always. This is an irrational desire for the simple reason that the world is not designed like that. Excepting for very few who are born with silver spoon in their mouth for others necessity to work is not escapable. You can do one thing about it. Break the work into small bits and take one bit at a time. You will find your resistance goes. Make it a point to work like that until such time work becomes your inner nature. I had some problem with my exercise regime. My plan was to make 30 pushups every day along with few other items. I was always failing to do it. Then one day I told myself I will have only one push up as my goal. When I did it I told again I will have only one push up as my aim. My god it worked wonders. Now it is several years very few days I miss my exercise. This example is not a great one. I myself do not like it. But it helps to understand the notion of breaking the work into small bits and imagining that was the only piece to be completed works very well.

➢ You may have inherited a non-productive karma or fate. Your fate or God says you cannot achieve. But think for a moment. Your karma is what was built in previous births. Why not rebuild it now. Engaged effort will gradually change your non-productive mentality and you will move towards productive mentality (619).

➢ Thiruvalluvar says one can turn the fate upside down through engaged vigorous effort (620).

63

Resilience

(Fortitude)

621. **W**hen adversity arrives, smile at it
The one that follows is often not as severe as the previous hit.

If you meet an adversity, smile at it. With this mentality you will find pain losing its intensity. (Smiling at the first painful event is possible by looking at it differently. Any pain gains strength when we demand that we should never get pain. Whereas holding pain as a natural occurrence and looking for a solution makes the pain to ease. A continuous practice leads to acceptance of the reality that life is not a bed of roses. This philosophical bent of mind gives the attitude to withstand painful events while doing what is possible to get relieved from them.)

622. **A**dversity, a ravaging flood, doesn't afflict
An intellect, who at his heart does reflect.

A pain may be as severe and large as a stream of flood. It doesn't afflict a wise man (as severely as in the case of an unwise)who reflects on the ways and means of alleviating it.

623. **H**e who refuses to get into a mood of pain
Cause pain to pain.

A man who refuses to be pained will make the pain to suffer pain. (Refusing to be pained is a response chosen by the person. Since a response at the level of one's mind cannot be forced upon him or her he or she is at liberty to choose a response of his choice.)

624. **At** every obstacle, he who increases his effort like a bull[150]
Has his visiting pain in trouble.

A bull which pulls a loaded cart exerts itself more intensely whenever the wheel of the cart gets obstructed. (In preindustrial days farmers would train their bulls systematically to take heavy loads of work. A bull thus trained will increase its effort whenever the wheels of the cart meet an obstacle). Similarly a man, who develops a self-efficacious confidence by systematically subjecting himself to difficulties and emerging victorious every time, will increase his effort and strategy whenever he meets a frustrating obstacle on his path. A frustrating obstacle meeting such an individual will be frustrated not him!

625. With the one who doesn't succumb to repeated woes
Pains that visit him get into blues.

A source of pain will be pained if it happens to confront a man of great resilience.

626. They don't gloat over their wealth and lock it
Hence they don't grieve when they lose it.

Those who do not rejoice their newly found wealth and keep it safe like a miser will not grieve when the same is lost.

---

[150] A bull is trained for hard work like ploughing by systematically training it starting with easy work and gradually pushing it to difficult work. By the time it is fully trained it would have mastered all the manoeuvres.

627. The body is open to pains. The wise know this
     They use this for their enduring process.

     Our body is open to risks. It is never designed to be pain-proof.
     Those who have this insight do not get into long grief. (Simple
     sadness and a temporary depression are natural in all painful events.
     But getting mired into deep worries is due to unhelpful thoughts we
     entertain in our mind says Thiruvalluvar.)

628. He doesn't crave joy; he holds pain as natural,
     He never suffers from pains several.

     He prefers but doesn't demand pleasure. He also holds suffering as
     normal. Such a person never gets into painful worry.

629. He doesn't crave for more pleasure when he is into it
     In the midst of sorrow he is not lost to it.

     An individual, who while in the fortunate moment of joy doesn't
     ask for more of it, doesn't suffer unduly in an unfortunate moment
     of pain.

630. If one holds pain as pleasure [151]
     His enemies praise him for his composure.

     He who chooses to hold pain as pleasure is able to maintain a
     composure which even his enemies appreciate. (Pain is not a painful
     one for those who look for the ways and means to convert it into
     prosperity. For achieving it they search what opportunity a painful
     situation opens for the individual.)

---

[151] Pain cannot be obviously held as pleasure. But the purpose of pain can be
searched for what meaning it offers for life in which case the person can benefit
from the experience of pain.

Skills to be learned:

➤ To be resilient at the face adversities.

Rationale:

➤ Resilience is an important skill for the human beings. One need not think of a colossal adverse situation when resilience is talked about. Slowly the population especially the middle class population is becoming adept to comforts of a life even a small inconvenience breaks them and sometimes they go to the extent of ending their lives.

➤ Therefore in today's world, the skill of resilience needs to be emphasized among the vulnerable population. The parents of rich, upper middle and middle class provide a comfortable life to their children. These are the proverbial children for whom comforts are presented on silver platter. But when they grow up and meet the challenges of life they miserably fail. Alcoholism, drugs, suicides and breakdown of marriages are the escape routes for people who are unable to squarely meet the adversities of life. Therefore it is imperative that the boys and girls are caught young and are taught resilience.

Coaching:

➤ "Simile at the adversity," says couplet number 621. This is not possible if you very weakly say something like: "Ok….. Let me try." Physically do it. Let us say you want to examine your adversity so that you can take an appropriate action to come out of it. For examining your adverse situation you must be able to look at it by remaining outside of it. What is meant by remaining outside? Being in a mood which is opposite of pain. Which is that mood? It is smile. Is it not? Therefore to have proper understanding of pain, invoke the opposite emotion in you: smile. Behavior, emotion, thinking and physiology are so connected a change in one will bring change in another. Therefore if you simile then your mind will be released to think. Thinking will show you the way to walk out of the problem (621).

> Couplet number 622 says, "A pain may be as severe and large as a stream of flood. But if you reflect on it you will find the severity reducing." Reflection can start from the first question: "What wrong did I do"? "What right I should do to come out of this"? "Has there been such situation in my life or in the life anyone I know or heard of or read"? "What did I do or what others did to overcome the adverse situation"? Such questions move you from the position of sufferer of an adversity to that of a solution giver for an adversity. You are no more part of the problem. You are part of the solution!

> Couplet number 624 says like a bull stepping up its efforts whenever its path is obstructed step up your efforts rather than giving it up as quickly as possible.

> Remember those who rejoice to the level of gloating over their wealth will suffer heavily when they lose it. Therefore never give great importance to wealth. (626)

> Develop the philosophy that human being however rich or powerful his back ground is, is liable to suffer at some point or the other. Accepting this will reduce the mental agitation in this regard freeing the brain to think of solutions. (627)

> When you are in the midst of a joyful experience never try to escalate it further through some added inputs. Do this as a policy. For example, let us say you have a house which is reasonably good in all aspects. Enjoy the house and continue to do so by refurbishing it as much as needed. But never wish for a new and bigger house. Live in the same house. Develop an attachment and feel contended with what you have. This will make you resilient if you are to meet a financial difficulty later.(629)

> Every experience has a lesson. An adverse situation is also useful in the sense that you do something and feel good about yourself and your enemies appreciate you for the effort you put in.(630)

64

Skills of a Minister (A Secretary of State)

(Executive excellence)

631. Strategizing, timing, execution, and fixing apt projects
     Being competent in these are a minister's objects.

     A minster (Secretary of State) should be skilled in strategizing, timing, process and choosing the projects which pass the test of priority.

632. Stubbornness, empathy, citizen's protection, inquisitiveness,
     Engaged dispensation – a great minister's five prerequisites.

     Ability to stick to the position he has taken after due process of data collection and deliberation, unmindful of consequences to oneself, empathic skill, holding the protection of citizens as a high priority subject, eagerness for continuous learning and fully engaged in his job are the five strengths of a great minister.

633. Expelling some, mentoring some, bringing back some
     A minister's competencies thus sum.[152]

     Expelling some incorrigibles, retaining some and improving them through mentoring and taking steps to bring back those who

---

[152] The words thus sum are added for the sake of rhyme. The list of competencies of a minister spreads along all the ten couplets.

are capable of making valuable contribution in improving the governance but have left due to some reason or the other are few other competencies needed for a minister.

634. **S**canning the quests, deliberating the best,
Clarity in directions, a minister's skills consist.

Posting oneself with all the shades of views and information (a total awareness, not a selected one) developing a highly deliberated perspective and giving clear cut instructions having no scope for different interpretations are the (other) competencies of a minister.

635. Well versed in *aram* and well informed opinion
Being tactful – in him a king has a good companion.

A minister (secretary of state) who is well versed in *aram* and has the habit of giving his opinion after posting himself with all the needed information and having tactful behavior to meet different situations as his personality trait is a best companion (co-professional) for the king (president).

636. Sharp intellect and learned scholarship if a minister possesses
For him what issue could be too comprehensive to process?

If a person is endowed with sharp intelligence and is an accomplished scholar can there be an issue which is very minute and complicated that he could not solve?

637. **H**e knows what is best to be done
Still let him have the world's mind factored in.

A minster (Secretary of State) may be very clear in his mind on what needs to be done in a situation. But still he would do well to take into account the nature of the beneficiaries before implementing a project meant for them. (Sometimes a mismatch between the culture or belief system of the beneficiaries and the input of the project may occur sabotaging the entire project.)

638. The king may kill his heed; may not knowledge earn,
Still a duty bound minister speaks what his mind contains.

A king (president) may happen to be a person who refuses to heed to what his minister (secretary of state) has to say on a matter and may also lack the ability to know it by himself even in such a situation a minister should stick to his point and say what he wants to say being unmindful of the net outcome. He is duty bound to do so. (This is very difficult especially for individuals who look for external approval (all the more from a boss) for what they say or do.)

639. With a minister, incapable of thinking smart, by his side
A king runs the risk of having millions of enemies' bide.

If a king has by his side a minister whose counsel is defective and or inadequate it is equivalent to having several millions of enemies.

640. They research and design but leave a task unfinished
Since in process skill they remain unfurnished[153].

Some people plan very nicely after doing elaborate research but when it comes to execution they may miserably fail. This is because they lack process skill.

Skills to be learnt:

> Each of the couplets except the last but one speak of skills stipulated for a minister's position. They are: strategizing, ability to take care of the issues in executing a project, being stubborn on one's view, empathic understanding, continuous learning, being engaged in the job, ability to manage the strategic human assets, scanning the data

[153] Unfurnished = not provided

and deliberate decision making skills, ability to give clear instruction, well accustomed with principles of *aram*, good diction and keen execution, sharp intellect, cultural sensitivity, being duty bound to advice a king even when he doesn't heed and process skill.

Rationale:

> These are also the skills needed for a CEO in today's MNCs as well as ministers/Secretaries of State and Administrative chiefs of governments, board members especially external directors who are not stake holders.

Coaching:

> Take care of the following when you are to screen someone for a high executive level post like Secretary of State or CEO of a big corporation:

> The candidate should have strategizing ability, a sense of time as an important input, methods and the ability to zero in on appropriate project. (631)

> He should have the ability to stick to a decision, have empathizing skill, give priority to safe guard the interest of the citizen (employees) and be involved in continuous learning. (632)

> He should be shrewd enough to expel some venomous and uncouth staff, foster friendships and accept the prodigals back into the fold after studying their motive thoroughly.(633)

> He should collect as much information as needed and develop a useful perspective. Applying that perspective he should be able to make clear decision and communicate the same in clear and unambiguous terms. No order should allow itself for different interpretations.(634)

> He should be calm and collected well versed in the principles of *aram* and versatile enough to meet different situations in a day. (635)

> He should have a high level of intellect obtained by practical as well academic knowledge. (636)

> He should act politically correct.(637)

> ➢ Sometimes his advice may not be heeded by the power that be. Doesn't matter he should not fail in delivering what he wants to say. (638)
> ➢ He should be free from any biases which may lead to faulty decisions. (639)
> ➢ He should be good in process skill. (640)

65

Powerful Speech (Powerful Words)

(Persuasiveness)

641. **P**owerful tongue is the best asset
It doesn't league with any of the rest.

Ability to speak convincing enough to derive home a point is the
best asset. It is a unique one and cannot be leagued with other assets.

642. **T**he zeal of a speaker makes the outcome good or bad
Hence let him stay away from sloth's shade.

The outcome of speech depends upon how far the speaker is able to
retain the attention of the audience. Therefore if the energy level of
the speaker is low it would catch up with the audience also and the
effort of the speaker would go as a waste.

643. A speech should get the listener spell bound
And motivate a 'haven't heard,' to come around.

A speech need to be so good that it makes the listeners to be with
the speaker all the time and through word of mouth attract future
listeners.

644. Speak to the level of the audience
That is the best *aram* and serves the purpose.

It is not necessary one should do justice to the depth of knowledge one has. Sufficient, if he speaks to the level of the proficiency of his audience. It is apt as far as *aram* and objective of the speech are concerned.

645. **U**se a word so precise
       Another word its meaning doesn't so comprise.

While using words choose words representing your thoughts faithfully. So also precise enough that any replacement will corrupt the meaning. (Some times for want of precise words we may use words in the same line but of a different shade taking the listener for a ride. We should avoid this. Alternatively we can explain the concept in so many different words as required and ask for a precise word or two which fully captures what we have said from the audience. It is likely that the audience may come forward to our rescue!)

646. **E**ntice your listeners and benefit from what they say,
       Spotlessly great speakers have this as their way.

Speak enticingly to your listeners and take care to listen to what they say. Find out what you can learn from what they say. This is the strategy of great blameless speakers.

647. **C**ourageous and eloquent, he has never ending zeal
       Winning him through divisive word always fail.

They are able speakers; their energy level is high; they are courageous enough to disagree. It is impossible to beat them in argument employing the technique of counter or disagreement. Countering argument can never detour them from their line of thinking and presentation.

648. **H**e speaks point after point in voice sweet
       To enjoy this skill the world rushes to the meet.

If a speaker uses sweet voice and describe point by point what he wants to say his audience from all directions will rush to his meeting to pick the professional skill from him as well as updating their knowledge.

649. It is certain they long to speak at length
But alas they are incapable of such strength

It is obvious that some want to give a long pithy discourse. But what a pity they would not prepare well even to deliver a small speech.

650. They can't deliver their knowledge to the listeners
Therefore they are like scentless flowers.

Some learned persons are like flowers which have no scents to send out. They cannot express what they have learned to the benefit of the listeners.

Skills to be learnt:

- ➢ Ability to speak persuasively
- ➢ Ability to avoid words out of context
- ➢ Ability to make the audience spell bound and make them as brand ambassadors for oneself
- ➢ Ability to speak to the level of the audience
- ➢ Ability to use words which are totally unambiguous
- ➢ Ability to listen and benefit from the audience
- ➢ Ability to withstand divisive argument
- ➢ Ability to speak point by point
- ➢ Ability to appreciate one's lack of caliber and avoid attempting to give a discourse
- ➢ Ability to accept the fact that with no ability to speak what one has learnt is of no use and do the needful to make good speeches in the future.

Rationale:

> A speaker speaks for the benefit of the audience. He should have skills which will help him to achieve this objective. In this respect there is no need to state that the above skills are essential.

Coaching:

> Persuasive speech comes from a persuasive tongue. A tongue becomes persuasive if its owner factors in the concerns of the audience in his speech making it most useful to them. The speaker may collect background information about the need of the audience beforehand and make his speech catering to that need.

> Words or concepts hurting the sentiments or belief system may be avoided. Every region has their own words/slangs which needs to be carefully handled. Otherwise the speaker may rub the audience on the wrong side.

> Audience become spell bound if the speaker creates a movie effect on the audience.

> The speaker should not speak using concepts and words alien to the audience making the speech going over the head of the audience.

> Simple words take care of ambiguity. Therefore use simple words. But always make them illustrative.

> Whenever you get an opportunity listen to the audiences and learn from them and acknowledge it immediately. The audience would become enamored by such a move.

> Someone in the audience may term you as belonging to a category and charge you on certain counts. Refuse to get into arguments with him.

> Speak point by point so that audience would be able to store them in different files in their brain. Otherwise if you ask them at the end they may not remember any thing.

> Do not go to a talk without proper preparation.

> Conducting a mock session will be a good idea for the beginners.

66

Pure Action

(Honest dealing)

651. **H**ealthy associates facilitate good outcomes
Healthy deeds get all one needs.

By the strength of healthy associates good outcomes are achieved.
By healthy action i.e., actions totally devoid of jealousy, greed, rage
and contempt all the needs can be realized.

652. Set aside acts which do not yield
Good and esteem inseparably held.

Your activities should bring esteem and good together. Therefore
set aside such activities which bring a good but no esteem from
discerning public. (The good which is not socially good is not a
pure good.)

653. **L**et them who aim for a rise in life
Shed activities spoiling their fame.

If someone is keen to grow and occupy high positions, let them avoid
from the very beginning of their career carrying out activities which
would show them in poor light. (It is common place, individuals
could not get important positions in Government or corporate
offices, at a later stage because of a background check showing

them in poor light in view of *aramic* mistakes they have committed early in their career.)

654. **D**espite distressed they wouldn't act mean
Because their vision doesn't suffer from illusion.[154]

People, who are crystal clear in their mind about what constitutes a mean act in a situation and what doesn't, never carry out mean acts.

655. **D**o not do a thing that haunts you to repent,
But having done, better don't repeat.

Never commit grave mistakes which haunt you again and again. In case you have already done, never repeat such mistakes again.

(In this couplet Thiruvalluvar may appear to go light on those who seriously fault on *aram*. In my opinion Thiruvalluvar wants to take care of a situation where individuals who fail to keep their resolution on *aram* under the pretext once a promise is not kept that is it! It is like a person who breaks his new year resolution finds it as a good excuse to give up his resolution once and for all,)

656. **H**e may witness his mother's hunger still let him not make
What *sandrones*[155] rebuke.

You may be in a situation of having to witness the hunger of your mother since you are left with no means to feed her. Even in such a situation never carry on an activity, which will be rebuked by *sandrones.*

---

[154] Illusion of mistaking this world and its material are real while only God and his abode is real.

[155] A sandrone is one whose character is firmly positioned on the five pillars of love, humility, benevolence, empathy and truthfulness. Recall the couplet no. 1047 which says a mother will look indifferently at a son whose poverty is not born out of acts of *aram.*

657. A *sandrone* considers poverty as superior,
To him wealth accrued through loads of sin is inferior.

A *sandrone* will consider a condition of poverty as superior than removing it through wealth earned by mounds and mounds of sin.

658. Those acts despised by men of *aram* shall never be done
Such acts rake in pain even after their time is gone.

An evil act to achieve something may appear to have served its purpose well and remain forgotten. But it will return with a full bang on a later date when it was totally unexpected. Therefore such acts should be always avoided.

659. What is amassed by other's tears is lost in tear
What is gathered through good even when lost brings good later.

If you earn at the cost of others, leaving them to weep, what you have earned will leave you, leaving you to weep in turn. Whereas what is earned through means of *aram* even if lost due to some unfortunate circumstances will bring good on a later date.

660. Making money through a plot
Akins storing water in a raw clay pot.

If someone thinks he or she can make money through a racket let that individual know that he or she is trying to store water in a mud pot yet to be kilned.

Skills to be learnt:

> The ability to keep off from ethically impure acts at any cost.

Rationale:

➤ Couplet 653 clearly says if you want to achieve great heights in life never do an impure acted attracting the deprecation of honest people. It is commonplace that many leaders and public personalities suffer and spoil their personal as well as professional life because they had act unethically earlier. Therefore honesty is the best policy is not a moral but the minimum thing to be carried out by anyone who wants their future to be safeguarded.

Coaching:

➤ Keep the following in your mind very clearly so that they will stop you from acting foul.

➤ Have a religious faith in the notion: pure (based on *aram*) action on your part will bring in all what you need in due course of time (651).

➤ Set aside an act if it wouldn't yield a socially useful product earning the thankful appreciation from the beneficiaries (652).

➤ If you want a bright future never carry on an unethical act (an act not based on *aram*) which will stand between you and your goal when you think the right time has arrived to realize your dream (653).

➤ Keep this very clear in your mind: acting mean should be avoided by all means. Your mind thus strengthened will stand by your side even if you are to undergo unbearable distress (654).

➤ Never make a mistake which will haunt you afterwards leaving you in self-pity. If you happen to commit one resolve not to repeat it and keep it up (655). (This is an ongoing soul evolving exercise therefore failing need not deter you.)

➤ There can never be a valid reason, mother's hunger included, to act foul (656).

➤ Beware a *sandrone* will hold poverty better if a rich life needs to be earned through foul means (657).

➤ Beware you may plan to get rid of the outcome of an evil act very well. But it will show itself at a later date and ruin you. (658)

> Beware what you have gained through right means will stick to you whereas what you have got through foul means will not (659).
> Beware your effort to build your fortune through deceit is equivalent to the effort of storing water in an unbaked mud pot (660)

67

Firmness in Action

(Not wavering in action)

661. Steadfast acts need a resolute mind
Other skills are not of the same kind.

Remaining steadfast in an *aramic* act is made possible by a resolute mind. The effort may benefit from a number of other skills in the possession of the actor but they are of different kind and cannot replace a resolute mind.

662. **P**lanning for nil hurdle and not caving in at its meet
Researchers say are the two needed for a feat.

Men of resolute mind take every precaution to avoid setbacks. However, in the event of meeting a setback they never give in. Researchers conclude they employ best practices for achieving this.

663. Hiding a deed until its fruition is good administration
Because revealing beforehand leads to pain.

The best management of a project is carrying it out in secrecy. Gullible transparency will bring pain due to the obstacles created by enemies.

664. **D**eclaring, "I shall make this happen," is easy for all
Rarely such pronouncements materialize at all.

It is easy for anybody to proclaim that they will achieve such and
such task. But it is rare such people keep their word. (Therefore take
a project which is not very difficult or very easy.)

665. The will of a person, greatly accomplished
Reaches the king and get eulogized.

The news about the great resoluteness of his mind proved by his
achievement will reach the king thorough folk lore and will be
appreciated by the king. (On a later date when an opportunity arises
the king may consider him for the same.)

666. When resoluteness is invested
What is aimed is harvested.

A man of determined action acts he achieves what he wants the way
he wants.

667. Don't go by the size of the body built
Puny plays the role a cater pin lent.

The work of a resolute mind doesn't depend upon the size of the body
of its possessor. The cater pin of a wheel is small. But its contribution
to the performance of the wheel is very big and pivotal. Like that, a
puny person can achieve great.

668. With clarity and no fear decide your target
Then don't dawdle, don't procrastinate.

One has to be very clear about what one wants to achieve. He should
clearly describe what are the specifications whose achieving makes
the project as having been achieved. Second, he should not waver in

the sense he should not think of other projects or other interests in between. Third he should not procrastinate.

669. An overwhelming suffering may visit
      Still act firmly and make great harvest.

At the face of adversaries in the midst of a project the option is: Firmly push ahead. Such an approach wins you the grace of victory and joy.

670. A man may possess several skills
      For want of firmness his skills hardly sells.

A man may possess several skills still the world may not show any interest in him if firmness is absent in his personality as evidenced in the history of his career.

Skills to be learnt:

➢ Learning to remain persistent to achieve a goal. In other words it is working unwaveringly towards achieving a goal. This is different from employee engagement in the sense that employee engagement involves expressing oneself in his job because his job or domain authors him.

➢ Here apart from deriving a sense of fulfilment a person may persist in a task because he has taken it as his duty or attached some value for it. For example, in India, during the struggle for freedom literally hundreds of well-paid lawyers, doctors, engineers and brilliant students from colleges from all most all the disciplines joined the movement of independence for the simple reason that they wanted to achieve freedom for their mother land.

Rationale:

➢ "Why should I be steadfast in my work?" Unless this question is satisfactorily answered steadfastness would not be attempted. The chapter offers three good reasons. If a person is steadfast is pursuing a task his reputation grows stronger and reaches those who are in the lookout for such people and would be too ready to offer a wonderful package. Second, a project which is carried out perseveringly yields lot of joy and other benefits at the end therefore steadfastness is laudable quality. Third, since the reference group to which one belongs would give good referrals only if someone has displayed steadfastness it goes without saying that steadfastness is a must possess skill.

Coaching:

➢ The advocacy offered by Thiruvalluvar regarding developing the skill of steadfastness is as follows:

➢ Apart from other skills one may need, the important one is being steadfast in your work (661).

➢ Plan taking enough care to rule out pitfalls. Despite of it if a hurdle greets you never buckle under its pressure. This mindset is what is called steadfastness is (662).

➢ Never reveal your plans to others until you complete your project successfully. This is needed if you have enemies who are bent upon to spoil you (663).

➢ Beware it is easy to take up a target. But very difficult to achieve the same. Therefore take care to take a project which is not too difficult or too easy to accomplish (664).

➢ Motivate yourself to remain steadfast by reminding yourself that your steadfastness makes your profile rich attracting good prospects through referral (655).

➢ Steadfastness also include not digressing to other projects even though you may return to your original project after completing those 'in-betweens', (666).

➢ Do not concern yourself with the unattractive features you may have. After all what is needed is perseverance on your part (667).

➢ Do not procrastinate or do things which do not form part of the project on hand (668).

> ➢ Any length of steadfastness is welcome because what you would get at the end is a joy yielding product (669).

> ➢ You may have other great qualities but the one who gives you a referral would not do so unless you have demonstrated your skill of steadfastness. Therefore it is simply necessary for you to pick up the skill of steadfastness and show it in your activities (660).

68

Issues at Work

(Strategizing)

671. Deliberation should lead to an action plan
     Cold storing would result in harm.

     Putting a plan of action, arrived after discussing every aspect thoroughly into cold storage is harmful.

672. Some action may require to be spread over a period
     Do so but not those whose time has arrived.

     Some work may have to be carried out in a phased manner. Do them accordingly. But in the case of works with a time frame stick to it. Never breach it.

673. Act in accordance with feasibility
     In case of a need look for a contingent possibility.

     Keep the final goal in mind and always work towards it. In case a particular strategy doesn't work in a particular situation choose a contingent strategy to reach the goal. (For example if your plan is to rehabilitate the landowners in a project site you may start with a proposal to build houses for them. In case they resist it and insist on getting jobs in your factory then think something like training them enough so that they become employable.)

674. Work and foe left unfinished
      Hurt like a fire not fully extinguished.

      Neither work nor foe should be left unfinished. If left the remains
      of the either will prove to be destructive like an unextinguished fire.

675. **R**esources, tools, opportunity, methods and place
      Clarify before launching phase.

      Availability of resources, tools, opportune time and plan and place
      of action needed to be clearly studied before taking a decision to
      start the task. What matters most is clarity. No aspect should be
      left unclear.

676. Break even, obstacles and benefit
      Study the feasibility and act if the effort worth's it.

      How much time it will take to break even, what are the possible
      obstacles and how much net benefit and what are the future prospects
      are the considerations to be pondered before taking a decision to start
      a project.

677. **T**o fix the task, personnel and procedure speak
      To an insider and information seek.

      To learn how to go about the task the best method is to get input
      from a person who has already carried out such a work and has
      practical knowledge about it.

678. **L**ike taming a wild elephant through a kumki[156]
      Through one work to another learn a new skill.

      As elephants are tamed using a tame elephant we can learn the art of
      carrying out a task by what is called transfer of learning i.e., taking

---

[156] Kumki elephant is an Indian term meaning trained elephant.

the skills learned in one work to another work where those skills are usable.

679. Like you rush to a help a friend in need
Act fast to gel the indifferent actor to the deed.

If you have someone in the team whose chemistry doesn't gel with the objective of the project, act fast to get him committed to it. This you should do fast enough as if you are rushing to help a good friend of yours who is in dire need.

680. Since the inexperienced(s) fear a fearful aftermath
They rush to the great for learning what is worth

People 'wanting in caliber' develop an overwhelming fear over getting stuck on a task and getting ridiculed by colleagues and others. Therefore as a precautionary measure they consult a person who is well accomplished and learn what they need to learn for successfully carrying out the task given to them.

Skills to be learnt:

- ➤ Thoroughly strategizing and arriving at an action plan
- ➤ Not procrastinating after an action plan is made
- ➤ Ability to make contingency plan
- ➤ Developing an attitude that clarity in every aspect is a must
- ➤ Ability to keep in sight the ultimate gain in every decision and acting
- ➤ Being thoroughly convinced that a man in the field should be consulted before launching a project
- ➤ Ability to use knowledge obtained in another field/project in the present project
- ➤ Ability to sync an alienated personnel to the project quickly.

Rationale:

> The strategies are practical and to the best of knowledge of the present translator enjoy research support in the discipline of project management. Therefore all of them are worthy of following by anyone involved in or planning for a project.

Coaching:

> Making a decision after elaborate thinking and discussion is a good strategy. But undermining the outcome of such a process by cold storing it is harmful. Therefore never do it. However, if you think a rethink is necessary in the light of difficulties faced while implementing the decision that is a different issue for which the solution will be reviewing the decisions made early not abandoning those (671).

> Planned postponement is fine. Differentiate the activities which can wait from others which should not and act accordingly (672).

> An action plan should be pushed as far as possible. If the plan could not be carried out due to unforeseen difficulties change the action plan and its aims so that the objective for which a project has been started can be realized. (See the example given in the explanation of the couplet) (673).

> Unfinished work and unreconciled enemy are like fire not fully extinguished. They are capable of fully powered backlash, difficult to contain at a later date. Keep this in mind always and act (674).

> Make sure you are adequately equipped on these: funds, tools (men and capital goods), suitable phase of time (economic opportunities), procedures of work, and place of work (in terms of availability of men and material at competitive rates) before launching a project (675).

> Study the feasibility of the project in terms of: 1) what you will be your net outcome, 2) what are the expected hurdles, 3) and long term increases or decreases in the net outcome etc., (676).

> Collect as much input as needed from a resource person working in a project which is similar to the one you are planning to know the

nitty-gritty of running the project. Never take it from an arm chair academic (677).

➢ Try to attract the best brains and arrange for training of your personnel (678).

➢ Work with anyone in the project whose goals or chemistry doesn't sync with that of the objectives of the project and get him gelled with the cause of the project. This should be done quickly (679).

➢ Visualize the degradation and ignominy you will suffer in case your project fails. This should motivate you enough to seek the advice of an accomplished wherever they are needed before starting the project and during the project (680)

69

Envoy

(Stipulations for the job of envoy)

681. **A**ffectionate disposition, lofty heritage, royal manners
Are envoy qualities to make them winners.

Kind disposition, having born and brought up in a family rich in
panbu and conditioned in royal etiquettes are the stipulations among
others for the job of an ambassador.

682. **D**evotion, intellect and informed eloquence,
These fulfills further eligibility.

Being committed to the king, being an intellectual and capable of
delivering powerful words born out of the strength of well researched
studies and discussion with scholars are the qualifications for an
envoy. (It seems Thiruvalluvar wants to give special importance for
these qualifications compared to others in the chapter. He uses the
word *indriamaiyatha* which means essential.)

683. **T**o win to his king from kings who are warriors
An envoy needs to be more read among the read.

In order to win concessions for his king an envoy needs to impress
the host King. This is possible if he unfolds as a credible person.
Such credibility is well achieved by his scholarship in various

subjects. Therefore an envoy should be the best scholar among other scholars.

684. Inborn wisdom, impressive looks, researched education,
The one rich in these shall assume an ambassador's position.

Inborn wisdom (because of an evolved soul), impressive looks and having acquired research and coaching based education are the three strengths needed for the position of ambassador. A person who is very rich in these shall aspire for the same.

685. Winning good for his king by brief, pithy and humorous talk,
Constitute an ambassadors' walk the talk.

An envoy's talk should be brief and pithy leaving aside trivia and house the same in humorous language (befitting the taste of the recipient king).

686. Well read, fearless of wrathful eyes and persuasive – an envoy
Updates himself with what the situation does convey.

An envoy should be a scholar, should show no fear in his eyes before the affront of a pair of wrathful eyes, be able to persuade the host king and shrewdly pick up from his audience and surrounding what is relevant for his king and his country.

687. Well aware of the purpose of a mission, an envoy
On an opportune moment rehearsed words conveys.

An envoy should be clear about the purpose of his mission and should wait for an opportune time and place to convey strategic information to derive maximum benefit from the host king to his king.

688. Genuinely pure, genuinely supportive, and genuinely daring
Vetting these in truth qualifies an envoy.

An envoy should be authentic in what he talks, he should also show a authentic support for the host king's position and if necessary should authentically differ with him. (Being authentic means not revealing everything an envoy knows. It only means whatever one talks is devoid of some component of a lie)

689. An envoy delivering king's message shall avoid discrepancy
     Shall be brave and shall display proficiency.

The envoy should avoid discrepancy. That is he should not miss or add something to his king's message. He should be brave otherwise he might drop or add something to what he has been instructed by his king.

690. Even if his life is in danger an envoy shall
     Endeavour to deliver his king's message in full.

It may be a risk to his life. Still an envoy should deliver the message of his king fully.

Skills to be learnt:

➤ The strengths stipulated by Thiruvalluvar for the position of an envoy are: affectionate disposition, qualities of the progeny of a great family[157], royal etiquettes, a disposition of kindness, intellect, and informed fluency, impressive looks, and research based scholarship.

Rationale:

➤ The strengths stipulated by Thiruvalluvar appear to be quite brilliant and concur with those prescribed for the present day ambassador.

---

[157] Chapter number 96 gives a list of great qualities of a highly family.

Coaching:

➢ Every couplet provides one or more stipulations for the position of ambassador. An ambassador in service or an aspiring one may be interested to check them and arrive at a list. If he or she is convinced of the list he or she may check about his or her standing on every stipulation and do the needful to avail suitable training where they lack.

There is one danger. Because of the atmosphere mainly orchestrated by unhealthy politicians and media usually skills other than these are learned by the candidates. One has to guard himself or herself against such attractions! Otherwise a job which yields day in and day out lot of opportunities for soul emancipation would lead one in the opposite direction.

70

Relationship with a Difference Conscious King[158]

(The dangers of a power center)

691. **A** shivering person sits by the fire neither near nor farther,
Around a difference conscious king courtiers shall similarly gather.

A person who tries to ward off shivering will not sit too close or too far away from a fire. Officials like ministers or other higher level officers who are in need to maintain relationship with difference (status or rank difference) conscious or position conscious king/ (president/ prime minister/CEO) should also follow the same policy.

692. **N**ot competing with the king on his interests:
Brings through the king many solid presents.

A minister should show no interest at all in areas where his king is also interested. (For example, a minster may be terribly interested in hunting but he should totally desist hunting if his king is also

---

158   The king referred in this chapter is a status or rank conscious person who would keep his personnel at arm's length including his ministers and other higher officials. There is only one word namely 'igal' which means division-consciousness in the first couplet. If this word is missed one will mistake this chapter as dealing with kings and higher officers in general.

interested.) Such sacrifices will be noticed by the king and suitably rewarded.

693. **G**ood practices are hard to practice: still carry out
Cooling an angered king for anyone is ruled out.

Carrying out good practices in trying situations or fighting powerful attractions of money, sex and power is very difficult indeed! But an executive should never fail. Because once the king scents it or a doubt is seeded in him to get rid of it is very difficult.

694. Hush-hush talk and winking smile, avoid,
In the court where great men are housed.

In the court of a king which houses great political pundits and great courtiers mainly the King, the highest in rank, do not exchange notes with someone else through whisper/wink and smile.

695. **P**retends not hearing or avoids a topic – a king maneuvers,
Beware you can afford to hear it only if and when he favors.

Sometimes a king may not be interested in a matter you want to tell him or he wants you not to talk on that. For either of the reason he may pretend he is not hearing what you say or he may try to change the topic. Understand that the king tries to manage it amicably and stop your effort. You can afford to discuss the topic with him only when he intends doing so.

696. **A**pt time, a mind to hear, avoiding his dislikes,
Speak in clamoring tone, synchronizing with his signs.

Read the mind of your king. Find apt time. Avoid a topic which he dislikes and speak those which he is eager to hear. For managing these read his body language and act.

697. **A**nswer his concerns and never talk on subjects needing no action
Even when King queries as he proceeds towards completion.

Bring the issues to him where you need a decision and answer his
concerns on that. Even if he asks for, 'any other agenda?' don't raise
an issue which doesn't need immediate attention.

698. A king may be younger to you and kin of a sort,
Still never undermine, treat him as per the position he has got.

The king may be younger to you and you may also belong to the
same royal clan as of him. Still never act in a 'taken for granted
manner' undermining his position. Conduct yourself in accordance
with his position not according to your 'special position'!

699. **E**mboldened by the acceptance from the king
An officer of upright perspective never does an unaccepted thing.

The king may have some soft corner for you. But never become blind
enough to do a thing which is not acceptable to him.

700. 'Being a veteran no etiquette for me, I shall do what pleases me,'
Acting on such a thought of entitlement leaves him gloomy.

You may be an old timer in his court. Because of this sometimes you
may feel that you are entitled to do what you want to do without
taking the permission of the king. This thought of entitlement and
action based on that will usher in painful moments for you.

Skills to be learnt:

> This chapter harbors sane guidance for anyone who must deal with
> another person with whom he has a big gap in power, knowledge and
> position especially when he is conscious of it and wants to keep you
> at his arm's length. It is a good idea to look at the guidance closely
> and adopt in our day to day life.

Rationale:

> The gap mentioned above may be due to the difference in possession of power, wealth, position, knowledge or skill and popularity etc. Added to it, if the person concerned also suffers from an attitude of intolerance towards any one not equal to him or her, maintaining a distance with him, apart from being a protocol requirement, is a wise decision to safeguard one's mental health.

Coaching:

> Keep a safe distance from your boss. (691)
> Do not compete with your boss under any pretext (692&693).
> When you are in front of your boss talking with another colleague or communicating something through wink sounding private should be totally avoided. (694)
> Sometimes your boss may not be forth coming to give you a hearing for what you want to say. Don't push. Keenly watch his disinterest and wait for a change. (695)
> If you are good in reading body language you can figure out an opportune moment on a later day (696).
> He may ask at the end of a meeting, "Any other issue?" Don't clutter his mind with issues which are not ripe enough needing his guidance. (Beware he suffers from checking every moment, "Am I or Am I not the boss here"?) It may not be the case with another boss who wants to know firsthand about anything that happens around. (697)
> You may be a veteran in a company. One weakness with veterans is that they take a boss, junior in age, for granted and do things which have all the symptoms of a parent delivering to a son or a daughter. No boss will accept such a dispensation. (698)
> Your boss may have a soft corner for you. Let that soft corner be not mistaken by you as an undeclared delegation of powers to you. Lest, you are likely to feel getting his permission as redundant. Beware by your act you are making your boss as redundant (699)!
> Whatever be your contribution never feel you are an entitled person. (700)

71

Body Language

(Reading the unrevealed mind)

701. He who reads what the other person has in mind,
Is the jewel of this earth, nondrying water bound.

For the land, surrounded by nondrying sea, a man who shows the extraordinary capability of sensing the mind of another man, who doesn't speaks it out, is a jewel on its crown.

702. Creating no suspicion he who reads another's mind
Is equivalent to God!

An additional reason for appreciating the person who is a sign reader is that he does so without eliciting suspicion in the mind of the person whose mind he reads.

703. Get him paying anything you could assign.
Who reads others intentions through their (body) sign

He who is capable of understanding others intention or feelings just by observing the body language of others is worth hiring parting with any of one's possessions.

704. The one reads signs and the one who can not
Only similar in limbs otherwise not.

One who is capable of reading the body language and get an inner sense of his subject is a class apart compared with another person who doesn't have such an ability.

705. If mind is incapable of capturing the body sign
     What better use their eyes retain?

Eyes play fundamental role in body language. But unless the individual trains his brain to make sense of the signals captured and passed by the eye the purpose of possessing a pair of eyes is not fully realized.

706. A marble reflects the object that is near
     A face shows what the heart has as dear.

The marble reflects an object lying before it. Similarly a face shows what the mind has. (For example if a person is sad his face is slightly darkened with no brightness in the eyes)

707. Is there any other organ where so much wisdom resides?
     Joy or rage face delivers leaving others[159] besides.

Of all the organs face is wiser. It communicates whether the mind is experiencing joy or anger much faster (for example, in comparison to mouth which can communicate the message of the mind) than other organs of the body.

708. You just stand in front of him looking at his face,
     For him who is capable of reading signs it is suffice.

It is sufficient for a person, who is capable of sign reading, that a person whose mind needs to be understood stands face to face with him.

---

[159] 'Others,' here refers other organs other than face.

709. Enmity and friendship communicate eyes,
     To someone well versed in reading differential cues.[160]

Eyes could clearly exhibit enmity and friendship. Those who are capable of sign reading can capture them.

710. They[161] claim, they measure others precisely,
     They look at eyes, not others[162], meticulously.

Those who are very skilled in understanding others intent are seen mainly relying on the eyes of others not other observables.

Skills to be learnt:

> Learning body-language.

Rationale:

> Communication is well understood, even without us being aware of it, through the observation of the signs exhibited by a communicator. In fact researches show a significant portion of communication is communicated through this medium. Therefore it is a good idea that we train ourselves in this art.

Coaching:

> The couplets of this chapter emphasize the usefulness of the skill of reading body language. It doesn't specifically give any lesson to learn this skill. This is fairly a large area in which one can train himself by registering himself at the universities where these courses are

---

[160] The existence of this capability which has a survival value has been proved by environmental psychologists.

[161] 'They' refer to a person skilled in reading body language.

[162] Other body parts of the other person.

offered. However to impress you about the usefulness of this skill few couplets are discussed here:

➤ A guy who is good in reading body language is an asset in an organization. In this respect he is like God.(701/02)

➤ You can pay him anything to get his service. (703)

➤ Two persons one good in reading body language and the other not so, may look similar as humans but in reality they are totally different class of people. (704)

➤ The best use for which eyes can be employed is reading the mind of others by looking at them.(705)

➤ Among body parts face is most expressive.(706)

➤ Face is the wisest since it flashes the heart much faster than other parts. For that reason for a person who is good at reading body language what is needed is a pose of the face of the person whose intentions are to be read. (707/08)

➤ Somebody hates you or not is expressed through his or her eyes. (709)

➤ If the face and eyes send different signs give more importance to the signs of the eyes since they are the best bet. (710)

72

Know Your Audience

(Speaking to the level of the audience)

711. Let the pure and learned speakers rich in diction speak
      To the level of audience which by research they pick.

Pure individuals who are capable of using words rich in fluency
and diction should query the level of their audiences on these
parameters before the session and choose words and depth of subject
comprehensible to their audience. (In other words they should not
be so motivated or snobbish enough to talk so high that what they
speak go above the head of the audience.)

712. Let the speaker understand the shades of words well
      And being benevolent shall apt words fill.

Let him vary the sophistication of his words suiting what is familiar
to the audience because after all he is a benevolent person and
therefore would like to do so.
(Some audience may understand just by hearing a word the underlying
concept. With them elaborate explanation would be gratuitous
whereas with others elaborate explanations may be needed. A good
speaker takes care of such aspects while speaking.
In our brain we have a number of 'cognitive networks' which are
something like our office files. Whenever we hear something we
store the information in the file which has similar information. If we
hear a word which cannot be fitted into any of the existing files we

have difficulty in comprehending. In such incidents the file has to be built bit by bit. This takes time and labor. Therefore, sometimes the speaker should use words which are part of the vocabulary of the audience and then slowly build upwards.)

713. Level of the audience some do not care to know,
Regarding deliverables they have nothing to show.

A person who doesn't appreciate the level of the comprehension of the audience will fail to pick up words which constitute the lore of his audience. As a result his audience will be left with no take away.

714. With intellectuals, go ahead of them
With less remain as clear as white lime.

In the presence of well-read and bright, go ahead of them in your content offering them the excitement of catching up with you. With others make it as simple as possible leaving no parts unclarified.

715. The best session practice before the seniors
Is, not a speech but a presentation.

Among the best practices in connection with scholarly sessions with senior scholars as audience one practice is the best: the speaker should feel humble enough to design his lecture as though it is a presentation not a scholarly lecture. (He should sound very modest in view of the void between him and the senior scholars in knowledge.)

716. A blunder before absorbing seniors.
Is a setback for one's career.

Widely read scholars have the culture of appreciating any contribution however small it may be. They do so in order to support the growth of youngsters. Utterly failing before them is a setback in one's career.

717. One's knowledge is on an acclaim pitch
     Before an audience who are diction-rich.

     The scholarship of widely read wins acclaim only from listeners who
     has a wealth of diction.

718. Speaking to persons capable of full grasp
     A flood irrigated crop's water usurp.

     Explaining concepts to audience having good grasp is similar to
     flood irrigating the rain fed plants. (The benefit to the graspers
     is very high like the dry land crop hugely benefitting from flood
     irrigation.)

719. If one has the skill to speak at a session of scholars
     Let him not speak at a session of knowledge-shallows.

     Individuals who have enough scholarship to engage a learned
     audience in a session either by oversight or for want of precaution
     should never speak among audience whose scholarship is very shallow
     but who suffer form a sense of arrogance which makes them to hold
     themselves as well read.

720. Talking to an audience dissimilar to one in scholarship
     Is like feeding the gutter with nectar, a foolish slip.

     Talking to an audience whose knowledge level is far low than the
     speaker is as wasteful as pouring nectar in the sewage.

Skills to be learnt:

➤   Ability to speak to the level of the comprehension of the audience
    and other issues.

Rationale:

➢ The chapter presents the various scenario of audiences before whom a speaker may be required to speak. Since the chapter vividly describe the variety of audiences and says a speaker should design his content and approach in accordance, the skill sets are worthy of learning and following.

Coaching:

➢ One idea which runs throughout the chapter is a speaker should view his speech as meant for his audience not for meeting any of his needs. Consumer is the king said Gandhi. Here the audience is the king. Therefore, you should try to do whatever it requires for enabling the audience to depart with a good take away.

➢ Querying about the level of comprehension of the audience ahead of the talk and designing the content and diction accordingly is a must (711).

➢ If it is needed you may pick up ideas and words from the folk lore of the audience and build your talk over it. For example, if you want to talk about genetics and your audience are formers, you can make use of the idea of good progeny of some of the varieties of the cows of the area and ask them how such qualities like good milk yield pass on from one generation to the next. The farmers will explain the phenomenon. Now you can introduce the concept of inheritance and genetics using the ideas given by them (712).

➢ Remember if you don't take enough precautions to reach your audience you would not be delivering much and your audience would not be taking away much (713).

➢ With people who are not well informed descend to their level and make things crystal clear to them (714).

➢ With bright and well-read don't waste their times by talking basics (714).

➢ If you happen to speak in the midst of senior scholars make your scholarly talk like a presentation. This modesty befits the occasion (715).

➢ Remember your behavior is against aram if you perform very badly before scholars taking them for a ride when they are prepared to appreciate a scholarship however small it may be (716).

➢ Never go to an audience without proper preparation. This is true even if you are giving the talk 100th time (717&718).

➢ Totally avoid audience who are shallow in their knowledge but arrogant or not level headed (719&720).

➢ Last but not least the notion that speaking to an audience is also an worship if one takes care to prepare enough and put all the energy in his command to push as much as possible for the benefit of the audience. Therefore if someone takes it casually or do not exert enough then it is like one has met with a failure in his soul evolving effort. (716)

73

Stage Freight[163]

(Speaking at a gathering without anxiety)

721. Using precise words with right shades of meaning
A pure person well prepared never dumbfounds in a meeting.

If a person is well prepared and is capable of choosing precise and
discerning words and if he is also pure i.e., he is free from jealousy,
greed, rage and a tendency to hurt others with foul words, he will
not suffer from the fear of a scholarly audience.
(Stage fear results from a mindset of feeling unequipped to the task.
If a person is well prepared as explained in the previous chapter and
in this couplet he will have no stage freight.)

722. Learned among learners is how he is held
When the house of learned accepted what he told.

Many persons may claim that they are learned. But only those whose
presentation is passed by a house of learned can claim that they are
learned. (The idea of *arangetram* where someone's scholarship is
examined through a presentation followed by question and answer

---

[163] Though the title will mean 'stage freight in general' the couplets of the chapter
show that the freight refers to fearing the stage of learned scholars. There is
an implicit understanding that the speaker should pass by giving an acceptable
speech in front of the scholar-audience which freight is inducing for all those
other than well prepared scholars.

session was in vogue in the days of Thiruvalluvar and the standard of someone need to be passed by the assembly of learned men in order to be accepted as learned is interesting.)

723. Men who dare death in a war are commonplace;
Men who do not fear an assembly are rare to notice.

It is rare to have scholars who are strong and confident enough that they do not fear the assembly of scholars. Compared to them it is easy to see many warriors who are not afraid of death in a war field.

724. **D**rive home your ideas among the learned
And learn from an audience whose knowledge is far ahead.

Make this as your strategy if you want to avoid stage fear: 'Let me drive home what I know very well and ask for the help from the audience when I am stuck.' (When you speak on something in which you are a master you would not experience fear. This is because you feel the situation is in your control. To put it differently you feel you are efficacious. Added to this if you are also confident that after all you can always take the help of someone from the audience if you are stuck then you will find your stage fear disappearing.)

725. **K**eep your knowledge up-to-date
Answer, fearlessly state.

Once knowledge of the subject should be current so that he will be able to field questions easily.

726. What use is a sword to a coward?
Or a book to him who fears a scholarly assembly?

What use a sword has for a man who is not strong and brutish? Similarly what use a book has for a man who suffers stage freight?

727. A dazzling sword with a coward in a battle field
Is equal to what a stage fearer's vast knowledge could yield.

The sword in the hands of a coward may be sharp and beaming but it will not serve any purpose in a battle field because the coward will be so overwhelmed by fear that he would not be able to use it. Similarly the knowledge possessed by a person due to his vast reading is of no use if he suffers from stage fear. (If the stage fear is a psychological malady the solutions offered elsewhere in the chapter may not be useful.)

728. A wide learning is of no use
If the learned doesn't make a well received discourse.

Reading wildly is of no use if he or she is not able to make a well received talk to an audience of learned scholars.

729. He who fears a learned house is far behind illiterates
In spite of his literary accomplishments.

A well learned person will be held far behind illiterates if he fears to appear before an audience and speak what he has learnt.

730. In spite of his scholarship a man is held as absent
Because stage freight makes him to go silent.

Some learned scholars may be present in a session of scholars. But they will be marked as absent if they do not contribute out of stage freight.

Skills to be learnt:

> Ability to overcome stage freight.

Rationale:

> This chapter gives few techniques which in their modern versions enjoy research support. Therefore they are worthy of giving a try.

Coaching:

> Remember the word 'pure' in the first couplet of this chapter and that of the previous chapter. Pure stands for the absence of ego. It means the speaker appears before the audience from his soul. A person shivers in front of an audience because his ego is very anxious to avoid a bad performance. If a speaker standing before the audience looks at the issue like this: 'Ok if my talk comes out nice it would be fine. In case if it doesn't hard luck . . . let me try next time,' then he would find his anxiety level dipping to a great extent.) Claim for thoroughness should be based on the fact that you do not have a single doubt ridden area in the subject (721).

> Take the help of peers and present your talk to them and answer their questions before the session. Peers would love to help you provided you have extended such help to them earlier (722).

> Always remember if there is a question from the audience beyond your knowledge, you should, in all fairness to the questioner, reply that you do not know the answer quickly following it up with a request to the audience seeking its help for an answer by anyone knowledgeable (724) (Equipping yourself with such a strategy will help you to overcome the fear: What if someone asks a question whose answer I do not know?)

> To overcome the stage fear you should create another fear worst than that. If you fail in your effort you will be held by people, who matter for you, as though you are good for nothing (730).

> If you keep the thoughts of stage fright and getting degraded together you will find the motive to avoid getting degraded will create enough pressure on you to prepare very well for the talk leading to a good performance at the stage (729&730).

74

Country (The Attributes of a Good Country)

(The attributes of a great country)

731. Sustained productivity, seasoned elite and great-minded rich,
    A land is a worthy country with these catch.

    A country is estimable if it has sustained productivity in agriculture
    and other fields, great people in all walks of life like sages, intellectuals,
    royals, business men and peasants and a band of rich people who can
    sustain philanthropy to the level needed in a country.

732. With huge wealth and afflictions[164] under
    Control a country is great.

    A country is worth the name if it has wealth in abundance making it
    an attraction for outsiders. It is more so because it also has methods
    in place to contain all the afflictions within reasonable limit thus
    sustaining its productivity.

---

[164] Tamil literature mentions a list of afflictions like excess rain or no rain, pest
attack, wild animals like elephants rampaging the crops, tribal insurgency big
tempest and similar events.

733. **B**urden after burden may press but to their King
His citizens offer what is his due with a song.[165]

A country is said to be a good one if the country's people, though
sometimes subjected to burden after burden, willingly pay what is
due to the king by way of tax and support him.

734. Famine, pestilence and fierce enemy
If these are rare it is a worthy country.

A country is a worthy land if it manages its governance in such a
way that famine, attack by the enemy and various afflictions are rare.
(It seems Thiruvalluvar admits that afflictions and other adversities
are not totally avoidable. Therefore strategizing to make them least
occurring is commended by him.)

735. **F**actions, internal strife and murderous king-harassing militancy
Absences of these make a good residency.

Cliques among royals, internal strife by way of regions and other
denominations, a cantankerous militancy are some among others
bothering a king. If a country is blessed enough that it doesn't have
any of these it is a worthy country.

736. A country which has these is best of all:
Either no afflictions or has matching wherewithal.

A country is a worthy one if it has no history of tormenting afflictions
or it had worst of them but had enough resources to sail through.

---

[165]   The idiom, 'with a song,' is used by me to bring in the sprit with which the citizens
pay their dues to the king. The Tamil Phrase used is: *irai orungu neervathu* which
means the paying of tax is done like an offering to God.

737. Springs, rains and perennial river from leafy terrains
     A secure fort – these are a good country's components.

     Perennial rivers fed by leafy terrains of mountains and surface water
     and fountains and an impregnable fort are the adorable assets of a
     country.

738. No diseases, good yields, wealth, joy and security
     These five are ornaments of a country.

     A country is decorated by five assets. They are: 1) absence of diseases,
     2) good yields, 3) wealth, 4) joy and 5) security.

739. A country is said to be resourceful, if with no import it is so
     It is not, if with imported resource it makes the go.

     If a country is self-sufficient with no need to import it is a good
     country. Another country even though it manages its needs through
     imports without any trouble cannot be ranked on par with the
     former.

740. (As pictured above) a country may be all set
     But it is of no use if a fitting king it doesn't get.

     A country may possess all the resources and assets (mentioned in
     many of the above nine couplets in this canto) but still they would
     not matter much if the country doesn't have a king who has all the
     attributes needed for a good and efficient king. (As enunciated in
     several couplets especially in cantos: Right Specter (55) and Crooked
     Specter (56)).

Skills to be learnt:

> This chapter gives a list of standards for evaluating a country. The
> ideas reflect the concerns of many great thinkers who write or speak
> about the wellbeing of the countries. Anyone in the business of

evaluation of the wellbeing of nations will find this chapter an interesting one.

Rationale:

➤   Though the standards presented are in very abstract form still they provide food for thought for the thinking of the professionals. For this reason the standards are given under the heading "Coaching" even though it may not be very appropriate to call them so the heading is retained to maintain uniformity.

Coaching:

Wellbeing indicators of a country:

➤   Sustained productivity (731).

➤   Excellent professionals in all walks of life (731).

➤   A good number of great philanthropists (731).

➤   Rich and therefore attractive for outsiders (732).

➤   Population which is capable of bearing adversities but amidst of them do not shun payment of taxes to the government (733).

➤   Hunger, afflictions of disease and enemies are under control (734).

➤   Cliques among ruling class, ministerial colleagues, internal strife by way of regions and other denominations, and a cantankerous militancy are absent (735).

➤   Never had a history of economic depression or was resilient enough to bounce back from an economic depression. (736).

➤   Presence of springs and rivers fed by leafy terrains and rain fed surface water and sea (737).

➤   Self-sufficient and doesn't subsist on imports (739).

➤   A wise king i.e., a person of great attributes. For these attributes please consult explanations for chapter numbers 55&65.

75

Fortification

741. Even for valiant an impregnable fort is an added strength
For the panicky and defendant it provides security in the same breadth.

A strong impregnable fort is an added strength for an army which is unbeatable. Even for those who are war phobic and are anxious to protect their assets the strong and impregnable fort offers a sense of security.

742. Deep water filled moat, vast land, mountain and thick forest:
These fortifications make the fort the best.

Deep and wide moat filled with crystal clear water, vast open land, mountains and thick forest track make a fort well secured.

743. Height, width, solidity and unique – these four
Ensure a robust fort says military lore.

The fort should be tall, wide and solid making it to be unnerving the enemy because of its unique strengths, say treatises on military lore.

744. An ideal fort has a small place to protect
But in between it is so vast the enemy's spirit plummet.

An ideal fort has a small place which needed to be captured in order to end the war. But the approach to reach it from the wall should be vast enough to make the enemy to lose his spirit.

745. **An** ideal fort is hard to conquer, it has ample food stored
And easy to stay garrisons provided.

A fort designed with enough storage space to store food and a number of garrisons for the army to stay is an ideal fort.

746. **An** ideal fort has all wares needed
It has critical actors wielded.

An ideal fort apart from being well equipped in terms of weaponry and other stores, for example having fail proof arrangements for continuous and critical replacement of men and material, should also have soldiers who are skilled at critical warfare.

747. **By** siege, by artillery attack or by deceit
An ideal fort is hard to capture, know it.[166]

Enemy may win by indefinite siege or by artillery attack or by bribing the commander to open the gate. An ideal fort is designed to meet all these contingencies successfully and stay impregnable.

748. **Stay** put inmates resist seizure's progress
Fully equipped fort it enables.

The inmates of the fort stay put sternly resisting the seizure indefinitely. An ideal fort is designed to achieve this.

---

[166] The words, 'know it,' are added for the sake of rhyme without altering the meaning.

749. Ideal fort lends to defeat the enemies
Later its invincible design[167] earns great fames.

An ideal fort lends to defeat the enemy because of which its fame travels across the land.

750. Whatever be the greatness of a fort
If there are no great fighters the fort is of no import.

Whatever is the design greatness of a fort it is of no use if it doesn't have warriors whose fighting skills are not varied and they lack excellence.

Skills to be learnt:

> The description of various forts resemble those described in Arthasastra the famous treatise written by Kautilya which is considered to be the world's first book on statecraft, economic policy and military strategy. A study of this chapter supported by drawings inculcating the description could be a useful exercise for those who are involved in industries like film and restoration.

Rationale:

> The chapter throw light on ancient forts and their design. May be it has some use for applying them or drawing inspiration from them to carry out restoration projects or for creating new sites for the tourism industry or usable in the cinema industry.

---

[167] The present translator is of the opinion that by an invincible design a fort can help the inmates to win the enemy. Of course this concept is only inferable here. Otherwise the couplet says when the enemies are won the fort earns fame.

Coaching:

➤ (With lot of hesitation I am writing this. I am not a scholar on this topic. Therefore I request caution on the part of the reader in handling this portion.)

➤ The present chapter refers to a particular book (743).

➤ But the name is not given by Thiruvalluvar. There is a school of thought which holds that Thiruvalluvar has read *smritis* and *Arthasastra*.

➤ *Arthasastra* has a detailed physical description of various types of forts.

➤ If *Arthasastra* has been the book referred by Thiruvalluvar then we can identify the descriptions in the couplets of the present chapter as covering specific structures of forts described in *Arthasastra*.

➤ In case, this thinking is validated this chapter should lead us to the original book and yield lessons for restoration projects, tourism development and historical film making.

➤ Several type of forts are explained in couplets from 742 to 749.

76

Method of Making Wealth

(The importance of wealth and the methods to earn it)

751. The one who is nobody becomes somebody
None other than wealth makes that body.

(Persons who lack wealth lacks respect too. No one cares to check what other worth he has. But the moment he acquires wealth the society accords him recognition and heeds to what he says on everything under the sun and pays attention to what he does.) Therefore there is nothing counting more than wealth on the earth. It simply elevates 'nobody' to 'somebody'.

752. Have-nots are pooh-poohed by all and sundry
The rich are praised by all, not alone sundry.

Poor people are slighted by all. Whereas rich are esteemed by everyone across the board.

753. Wherever into service you press
The unfailing light called wealth destroys the distress.

Wealth is the ready destroyer of distress. It can travel across countries and do the same.

369

754. **W**ealth earned through relevant skill and not by ill will
Promotes *aram* and joy to heart's fill.

If wealth is earned through the skills mentioned elsewhere with no
bad intention it helps a man to become *aram*-bent which in turn
brings in blissful joy.

755. **E**arning wealth devoid of love and compassion[168] shun
Drop it like a hot potato to win

If you plan to earn wealth disregarding the equity of the stake
holders and with no love for your associates drop that idea like a hot
potato because the wealth thus earned will not stick to you.

756. Wealth unclaimed, won from enemies and levy
Accrue to the king's treasury.

The king receive wealth from various sources: wealth unclaimed,
won from enemies and levy from peasants and other crafts and
trades men.

757. Compassion – the baby born out of love gets fed
By the midwife 'wealth's' feed.

Compassion is the baby of the mother Love. This baby is reared by
the midwife[169] namely wealth.

---

[168] The word compassion means an act of helping the deprived to enjoy their equity.
It is not sympathy based it is empathy based. Since I have introduced several
Tamil words in this book I thought I will make use the word compassion as an
equivalent of aruludaimai even though it is not exactly the same but more or less
same as for its implication is concerned.

[169] It seems in Thiruvalluvar days rich men's homes employed women to foster the
children. They were called in Tamil as *sevili* roughly translated into midwife or
foster mother.

758. Witnessing an elephant fight sitting on a hillock is easy
Making wealth employing one's own fund is as cozy.[170]

Sitting on a hillock makes it comfortable and risk-free to watch an elephant fight. Similarly a person on the mission of making wealth could do so comfortably if he has his own money to meet the day-to-day expenses.

759. Make wealth, nothing sharper than its cutting edge[171]
To clip the pride of the enemy leaving no hedge.

Earn wealth in large volumes. It acts like steel in cutting the arrogance of the enemies leaving no fallback.

760. Wealth amassed through rightful means does draw
The other two[172] in a row.

When wealth is made through the means of *aram* it makes the earner to release love and compassion in due course of time. The three, namely wealth earned through means of *aram*, love and compassion are close associates. This brings immense joy also. (Sometimes a crook may spend his money for philanthropic purposes. But it is to satisfy a stinging conscience which could not be satisfied at all leaving the person in perennial unrest. It is also possible he has the delusion that once he spends his ill gotten money on the welfare of others then he will be free from the sin. A third possibility is that it may be egoistic in the sense that it boosts his image.)

---

[170] The word, 'cozy,' is used in the sense of, 'warm and comfortable'.

[171] Poet uses the word steel meaning a knife and hence the translator has translated it as cutting edge.

[172] The other two refer to love and compassion. This is inferable from the meaning of couplet 757.

Skills to be learnt:

> Two skills are emphasized: One is making wealth through rightful means following the principles of *aram* and the second is keeping ready funds to meet day-to-day expenses of the enterprise.

Rationale:

> If you develop an interest in this chapter going by the title, "Methods of making Wealth' you may not find many tips right here. However, there are two strong time tested ideas which by themselves expand into all that you need to do for running your enterprise in a successful way.

> Couplet number 754 says earning wealth should be attempted after learning the relevant skills and employing them – never an amateur shall attempt it. Chapters 61,62,66,67 and 68 give these skills in a elaborate manner. Wealth earned following the principles and methods enunciated in those chapters award two benefits. One, it makes the effort and life worthy from the point of view that such a wealth maker lives a life of *aram* and therefore held as the apple of the eye by everybody including the authorities in governance. Second *aram* based life is blessed with blissful joy and a place in heaven in the afterlife.

> Couplet 758 gives a specific technique.

Coaching:

> Anyone who wants to start an enterprise may familiarize with the material found in the chapters mentioned above.

> You may recall they deal with the methodologies of running a project and managing the human resource. Mind you all the methodologies are vetted in *aram*.

> It is quite interesting all of them are catching up well with the notions our business schools teach us these days!

> Strictly following them automatically takes care of the requirement of ensuring *aram* in all our dealings. The life here on the earth is a

training period for evolving in aram as much as needed to land in heaven. This life is the preparatory for ushering us to live with God. Human being as such is not fit to be in the company of God. He has to undergo lot of metamorphosis. Wealth making (process of wealth making) gives yet another opportunity for undergoing that metamorphosis. This should be your guiding philosophy when you venture to make wealth.((754)

➢ Couplet 758 gives an input which has not been covered in the chapters mentioned above. An individual who wants to make wealth should have own capital. It makes it very comfortable to run the venture. It is as comfortable as witnessing a spectacle of an elephant fight sitting on the top of a nearby hillock! If you stand on the ground to watch the fight getting gored by the tusker cannot be ruled out (758).

➢ In today's understanding own capital should really mean ready money (working capital). It can be a loan from the bank or from investors. But one should have total freedom to use it as and when he wants it.

➢ This relieves the entrepreneur or CEO from botheration of hunting for money every day wasting most of his energy and time.

➢ This may look very simple. In reality it is not so.

➢ A proposal to start a business after duly approved by a bank and other lending institutions providing budget for every aspect of the business including working capital goes foul in no time not for other reasons but for the reason of diverting working capital for some other non-budgeted or even budgeted expenses.

➢ The working capital may be used to pay the loan installment or paying for machinery which has arrived as a result of an non budgeted afterthought, or may be spent to buy a car or a house, or buying a jewel to wife hoping that things could be managed in so many ways.

➢ Unfortunately none of them will behave as you expect and you will be in real trouble!

➢ Therefore the strong advice by Thiruvalluvar to keep ready money to meet the working capital requirement should be taken very seriously.

➢ One should accept this idea as a serious one and develop the financial skills needed to keep the working capital always ready.

➢   In addition to this sane advice for running a business the chapter has a piece of advice for some of us who are not interested in money for various reasons.

➢   Often the reason may be due to a controversial philosophy that real happiness lies not in money but elsewhere. This philosophy may itself result from self-defeating and debilitating thoughts the extreme of which is: making money is a sin!

➢   Thiruvalluvar smashes all such thoughts. Read a summary of what he has to say on the importance of making wealth:

1.   Wealth gets you respect in the community which you can use profitably to practice *aram* in your profession (751).

2.   Rich are esteemed across the board. This is also useful to further your vision (752).

3.   Wealth enables you to involve yourself in alleviating the distress of the sufferers even though they may live far away from you (753).

4.   If you employ foul free means to earn wealth you will find it yielding great joy and enabling you to live a life following the precincts of *aram* (754). (Remember this is the prescription to achieve the company of God in the afterlife.)

5.   Since wealth amassed through means lacking in *aram* and love doesn't serve the purpose of reaching the company of God in the afterlife such a plan should be dropped like a hot potato (755).

6.   Have a strong belief in this notion: love is the mother of compassion. Compassion means not sympathy. It is granting the equity to all around us and fighting for it where it is denied. This struggle is well supported and is made easy if you have wealth earned through rightful means (757).

7.   One important tip for making wealth: Always keep working capital readily available so that your project doesn't suffer for want of it (758).

One question arose in my mind when I was about to close this.

> If Thiruvalluvar lives now would he approve the present day capitalism which sees any regulation as anathema for a 'healthy' growth of a nation's economy?

> Will he be pleased by the philanthropy and CSR and other activities of our capitalists?

> I doubt very much. For him all the activities of the life including economic activities need to be based on compassion and love. Being compassionate in the case of corporations is taking care of the equity of all its stake holders. Whether CSRs in the present form are sufficient in this respect remains to be answered.

> In the present day corporate imperialism profits come from the excessive consumption by the middle class. Newer and newer needs are created by the corporate imperialists by creating goods which are capable of creating such new needs among the middle class. Middle class works round the clock to full fill its ever expanding needs. Corporations thrive on the manmade demands of the middle class. Poor people in the developed and developing countries are not considered as stakeholders at all. They languish in poverty conditions.

> In view of the excessive consumerism promoted and the poor not getting their equity make the present day capitalism far removed from Thiruvalluvar's model of economics for the following reason: Mother earth has kept her wealth in the form of land, water, metals, fossil fuels, and a number of other raw materials. These belong to every human and non-human creature of the present and future generations of the world. Looked from this angle the so called development model pursued by the countries are going against the wish of the mother. There is a vast gap between the haves and have-nots in utilizing the resources. Industries promote lopsided consumption by concentrating on the production of commodities meant for the rich and developed. The underdeveloped are ignored. They live several decades behind their counterparts in realizing their due share of resources of mother earth. In pre industrialization days

the gap was not this glare. Thiruvalluvar would not have approved this type of free economy which is selectively ethical.

➢ Sometimes the generous philanthropic activities also become suspect because the question arises whether the wealth has been earned using rightful means. If it is not do the philanthropists resort to philanthropy due to a sting by their conscience?

77

The Might of the Army

(The merits of an army)

761. A fortified army unafraid of enemy's attack
     Is a king's best stake.

     An army owned by a king with all divisions whose personnel are not
     afraid of getting wounded or fatally attacked by enemies, is the most
     valuable of all his assets.

762. Far away and tired still dares murderous attacks
     Such a power only a veteran battalion enacts.

     A force which is in the permanent roll of the king's army is hardened
     enough to withstand murderous attacks. Only such a force is not
     mentally afraid of fighting an enemy at a far of place.

763. Of what avail when an army of rats as big as sea roars
     If a cobra hisses they stop their breaths?

     An army of rats as big as a sea can roar like a sea. But as soon as a
     cobra hisses they will die out of fear. Like that an enemy's army may
     be large but if they are cowards they will also behave like rats before
     a powerful army like a cobra.

764. Un assailable, never to fall to deceitful game,
     Veteran men's valor is an army's fame.

     The permanent men in king's army will be valorous (due to so many
     reasons like loyalty to king, proper training and good nutritious food
     etc.,) and would never fall prey to chicanery at all. (Compare them
     to men drafted as and when the need arises.) A king's army attains
     its fame due to them.

765. God of Death comes face to face, be it
     United opposition makes an army's grit.

     An army should be bold enough to oppose even if God of death
     comes face to face. It should stand united and face the enemy with
     full conviction and strength.

766. **V**alor, pride, best practices, well selected officers:
     An army's four security assurers.

     An army's security is ensured by four aspects: valor of the army
     personnel, a strong sense of pride in them, time tested methods of
     conducting a war and commanders selected based on best practices.

767. **A**n army's onward march is guided by the one
     Versed in the art of resisting the enemy's frontline.

     A commander who is well versed in the art of resisting the front line
     of the enemy should only lead a battalion of an army.

768. No power of offence but has a military formation
     That army wins if it also has a decoration.

     An army may lack military prowess to resist or attack an enemy's
     army still it could achieve success by its column-strategies and by
     impressive turnout displaying military insignia in every possible ways.

769. Desertions, dissensions and malnourishment
If banished an army has its victorious accomplishment.

If a king take steps to avoid desertions so that the size of the army never diminishes, recruit in periodic intervals, nourish personnel with nutritious food and other requirements and attend to their grievances to remove disaffection, his army will be victorious.

770. An army has lot of veteran cadres
Still it fails for want of enough commanders.

An army may have enough veteran cadres. But if it doesn't have enough commanders then it cannot succeed.

Skills to be learnt:

➤ Combatant personality and attitude appropriate for a military personae.

Rationale:

➤ Well manned and fearless army consisting of permanently commissioned personae selected for qualities like being immune for treason, daredevilry, long history of valor, a strong sense of pride in their military prows will go a long way for the success of an army. Therefore an attempt is made to give a list of content drawn from this chapter meant for a syllabus on military education.

Coaching:

Military training syllabus may include the following:
➤ Training for fearlessness.
➤ Veteran qualities.
➤ Managing new territories and countries with murderous enemies: this involves a psychological readiness to go out of one's comfort zone.
➤ Loyalty to the country and to a noble cause.

> ➤ Good nutritious food habits managing the same with locally available goods and foods.
> ➤ Immunizing towards treason and desertion qualities.
> ➤ Daredevilry and presence of mind and creativity in war field.
> ➤ Strategies in pushing front line army.
> ➤ Uniform and insignia discipline.

Steps need to be taken by authorities:

> ➤ Personality tests to measure valor, sense of pride in being the custodian of the security of one's nation, and discipline to follow best practices may be carried out. Second corruption and favoritisms/nepotism free methods of selection need to be followed without fail (796).
> ➤ Desertions (an unnatural level of voluntary retirements) take place due to dissentions on several counts. Research based implementation of correctional measures may stop too many desertions or unnatural level of voluntary retirements.

78

Military Prowess

(Excellence of a military)

771. Do not stand before my Leader O! Foes
They who did so now stand as pillar stones.

A soldier says to his counterpart not to dare his king. He says there
were several instances in the past where those who stood before
his king latter became stone pillars of warriors. (Death is sure and
certain for those who dared his king in the battle field.)

772. Keeping an elephant- missed- lance as a toast
Pleasing than the arrow that killed a rabbit in a forest.

It is rather a matter of pride and joy to keep a lance which missed an
elephant than an arrow which killed a rabbit. (Read the interesting
interpretation made by Prof. Devaneya Pavanar below[173])

773. Manly valor is shown when bravery is the first operant
Next its steely power helps the distressed opponent.

A warrior's manly valor is well displayed in his attack on the enemy
force. But quickly, as warranted by the situation, he reverts to the

---

[173] He says this is a talk by a warrior who was really saying that it was better to miss
a commander or a king than a foot soldier. Elephant refers to a commander or
the King himself and the rabbit to a soldier.

compassionate act of taking care of a wounded soldier of the enemy army. (This is the supreme reach of his valor. MANly valor consists of protecting the rights of people. A wounded soldier is no more a soldier and therefore no enemy. He has a right to get cure. This is supported by persons whose hearts are compassionate enough to protect the rights of others.)

774. **W**ith his spear gone sticking with the elephant
He plucks with a smile one from the opponent.

A warrior loses his spear when the elephant fearing his attack disappears with the spear sticking on it. But he is quick to pluck one from the body of an opponent throwing a smile on him. (It appears this couplet and the one before presents a picture of war is being a field where there is no hatred but only an exhibition of muscle power for righting a wrong but still not hating an enemy.)

775. In his eyes if a hurled lance creates a wink,
"Is it not a blame for a warrior"? The world would think.

Even (by reflex action) if a warrior blinks his eyes for a minuscule of a second, witnessing a spear being aimed at him, it is a disgrace to his valor. The act is also out of place with the flush of valiance the warrior gushes.

776. Counting the days on which he was not wounded
A warrior accounts them as life not happened.

A warrior finds fulfillment only in taking wounds in the field of battle. Therefore any day which was spent not in the battle field thus not getting a wound will be accounted by him as a day not lived.

777. **A**iming stardom among the folk, he bothers not for life,
His anklet for that reason commands more hype.

The anklet worn by the warrior attains the status of 'a thing of beauty' since with the motive of winning the fame of 'talk of the town' for his martial spectacle in the battle field he fights unmindful of losing his life. (The anklet is a jewelry like any other jewelry commanding whatever admiration normally accorded by the society. But the one worn by the warrior because of its association with the warrior and his martial spectacle is able to share the appreciation along with its wearer. Therefore it attains a new beauty altogether.)

778. At the field of battle valiant men do not fear death,
King may reproach but they never cease.

The warriors are so conditioned that they jump to any opportunity for fighting in a battle field even if the king (for strategic reasons) scolds and seriously instructs them not to go on offence.

779. Can anyone reprimand him for not fulfilling his vow
When his life in that effort he gave?

A warrior may fail to keep up his vow. But can anyone use degrading words towards him if he has lost his life in the effort to fulfill his vow?

780. If a death occurred with the benefactor's tears shed
Begging such a death was deserved.

If a soldier could die causing tears in the eyes of his King, who all along has protected him and his family by taking care of all their needs, that death is a worthy one.

Skills to be learnt:

➢ An ability to look at the enemy as someone waiting to be crushed rather than someone to be feared (771).
➢ An aspiration to accomplish great and not settling down for easy targets (772).

➢ A clear vision of what real valor is. Valor is standing for just cause. It is not for giving vent for one's aggressive instinct. The awareness and acceptance that valor is exemplified in the ability to assume the duty of taking care of an enemy soldier the moment he becomes invalid due to wound or hurt (773&774).

➢ Total absence of fear while in war field (775&776).

➢ Eagerness to become a star among the folk for one's performance at the battle field (777).

➢ Fixing targets for each day in the battle and feel terribly committed to achieve the same (776&779).

➢ To aspire for a death causing tears in the eyes of one's king/ commander/leader (780).

Rationale:

➢ The combatant personality profile enunciated in the list appears to be quite relevant for modern day army. This is because they are not significantly different from what is needed for a modern army man who is day in and day out is struggling against so many odds to carry on in his career. The present scenarios in their physical manifestation may be totally different from the ones depicted in the couplets. But the psychological strengths needed are the same. (Am I correct?)

Coaching:

➢ Describe each quality in detail.

➢ Involve live models of ex-military personnel. Request them to narrate real life incidents from their life where they have shown the above characteristics, of course in totally different situations, followed by the type of reward and satisfaction they have got from such episodes. It should be made very clear and certain to the trainees that their valorous effort will not go as a waste.

➢ Another approach shapeable from the chapter is making the trainees to mentally put themselves in the scenarios and rate where they stand in comparison to the warrior described in several of the couplets. This can be done on a ten point scale. If they think they are as bold as the warrior in a couplet they can give 10/10 or less as the case may be.

➤ To achieve this trainees may be asked to narrate one incident from their real life having some similarity and compare his or her behavior at that time with the warrior in the couplet had he been in the trainee's place.

➤ In the second step the trainee may be asked to tell what actions and what attitude changes would be required if he wants to be like the warrior in question. At this point the participation of all fellow trainees may be encouraged to evaluate the proposals given by the trainee and one or two programs finalized to be followed by the trainee.

79

Friendship

(Friendship defined)

781. What is more difficult than cultivating a friendship?
What is more supportive for a task than it's 'stewardship?'

There is nothing more difficult than cultivating and maintaining a friendship.
(Choosing men of good *panbu*, intellect and sharing intimate information, and not hesitating to give money, time and labor when required are some of the activities needed to stabilize a genuine friendship. Therefore it is not an easy task.) But once you have an authentic and active friendship there is no better support for your life's activities and tasks.

782. Friendship of responsible men is like a waxing moon
Of fools a waning moon.

Friendship better be cultivated with men who are genuine and who are responsible too. It keeps on growing from strength to strength like a growing moon. The same is not true of friendship cultivated with fools. Their friendship reduces in strength day by day like a waning moon because the more one comes to know about a fool the more one loses interest in him.

783. Every time a good book is read a new beauty is relished;
Every time a man of *panbu*[174] is met new joy is experienced.

A good book is able to retain its freshness because for a discerning reader it offers new perspectives every time it is read. Similarly friendship with a man of *panbu* rejuvenates the hearts afresh every time when the friends interact and a new joy is experienced.

784. Friendship is not for pursuing smiling togetherness,
It is for indicting when good conduct the friend transgresses.

Friendship is not meant for time pass, cracking jokes and exchanging pleasantries. It is for accosting the friend and mentoring him when he does something significantly wrong causing hurt to himself or to the system or the society.

785. For making friendship, being together is not essential,
Self-disclosure gives a friendship its credential.

Authentic friends mutually disclose whatever happens in their personal and professional life. It is like friend 'A' knows most of the things verbatim his friend 'B' knows. They are similar in the content of matters involving feelings and other concerns. Of course extreme personal matters may not be shared. It doesn't matter as long as faking doesn't takes place regarding unshared materials.

786. Smile as large as the face is not what friendship is,
A heart warming up and sending it friendship has.

Smile as large as the face does not indicate friendship. It is becoming warm at the level of the heart to receive and entertain him or her

---

174 Please consult the legend for the full meaning of the word '*panbu*'. However, here it means compassion and equity.

which constitutes real friendship. The souls[175] of the individuals are involved in the exchanges. (Many people flash a broad smile when they meet someone. It is very hard to suspect them of authenticity. But very often they are not authentic. Perhaps Thiruvalluvar is refers to such persons.)

787.   Weans from ruin and guides into good
       Good friendship treads along distress.

If a friend is carrying on activities which are not appropriate for his wellbeing weaning him from those and putting him on the right path constitutes one of the responsibilities of friendship. In addition a friend should also put his might to bail him out from an adversity.

788.   When an attire slips [176] hand instantly grasps
       Difficulties of a friend his true friend similarly removes.

Friendship makes a friend to go to the help of his friend instantly like a hand which secures a garment slipping from the waist instantly.

789.   Possible helps without a let up makes the under grid
       On which sits friendship whose position never rid.

A friendship is said to be positioned on the firm under grid of helps offered in all possible ways by a friend to the best of his or her opportunities without a let up.

---

[175]   The phrase *"nenjaththu aga naga"* means the inside of heart smiles. The inside or the occupant of heart is soul, is it not?

[176]   In Tamil Nadu, India the ethnic attire wound around waist called *veisti* (Tiruvalluvar's time called it as *Udukkai*) sometimes slips off the waist. Hands go to its risk and hold the slipping attire instantly and get it back *to* its position on the waist.

790. This person in terms of this aspect is equal to me,
Though sanctifying spurious becomes the 'we'.

Friendship is not based on any financial and status considerations. Even comparisons like 'my friend is such and such person and in such and such ways we are equals,' spoils the sport.

Skills to be learnt:

> I have developed a working definition for friendship. I have assigned the same as the definition for love elsewhere: friendship is a togetherness involving the investment of money, time and labor as much as possible between two individuals. Couplets 786,787,788&789 put forth this idea in different ways.

> The specific skills to be learnt here are:

1. Ability to develop friendship with men of wisdom and character.
2. Ability to indict a friend when he acts inappropriate and get him back to normalcy without breaking the friendship.
3. Ability to disclose between the friends taking the friends to the same level of understanding on issues concerned with each other and personal life.
4. Ability to spend money, energy and time to ward off difficulties of the friend to the best of one's capacity but not undermining ones interest too much.

Rationale:

> Genuine friendship provides the platform for the expression of love and compassion. Therefore it is worthwhile to learn the skills of initiating a good friendship and maintaining it.

Coaching:

Developing friendship with men of character and intellect:

> ➤ The first couplet of this chapter and that of the next chapter say one thing: building friendship is very difficult (and once we get into a wrong friendship it is very difficult to walk out of it.) Therefore every step should be taken to ensure you land on good friends. How to achieve it? Keep yourself around a person whom you pass preliminarily for good *panbu*[177] for some time before deciding to propose friendship with him. Two important indicators would be of help: Is he a person who shows love and compassion which makes him to stand for the right of others? After a sufficient number of interactions and exchanges you can propose to him that you want to take him for a friend (781&791).

How to indict a friend when he does something inappropriate without breaching his privacy?

> ➤ Across the societies there is an unwritten law against breaching privacy. Individual right stands out so bold, anybody who harms it slightest is slighted for good. Whatever be the duration, whatever be the sacrifices made to build a relation the moment a little a trespass takes place the first thing to happen is cutting relationship, of course with heavy heart! So, how to indict a friend ever without trespassing his privacy? Shrink the space of privacy as much as possible so that you will have very little opportunity to breach (784). How to minimize the private space to the barest minimum? Read the next technique.

---

[177] '*Panbu*', is a Tamil word which doesn't have an equal word in English. It is quality which combines love and a number of other qualities like equity, a sense of shame, following best practices in any situation, truthfulness, humor, giving, using sweet words and not ridiculing others. In short we can say it means love coupled with equity.

How to achieve maximum disclosure?

> Couplet number 786 gives a definition of friendship. It says smiling at the level of lips is not friendship but at the level of heart is. Couplet number 785 says if both the friends have the same feelings that are enough for friendship. What is suggested by these two couplets is: sharing by self-disclosure. Both friends should find how much they can disclose about their private life including financial dealings. The more they disclose the less become the area of private space. The second step is entering into an implicit contract that each of the friends will enter into the privacy of the other if the situation warrants it. Each will have the right to indict the other, in case, after traversing into their private space, they find the need for corrective action (784). Practicing this approach for some time makes it easy to disclose and also to indict. But be careful. Do not disclose certain things which might turn against you in the event your friendship breaks.

Ability to spend money, time and energy for the friend.

> I have operationally defined friendship as sharing ones resources of money, time and energy for the sake of the friend as and when they become highly necessary. Giving time and energy is easy to come and also enjoyable between two good friends, but what about money? Couplet 789 by implication says to the extent possible financial help may be extended. There is always the possibility of saying no without feeling guilty. This is possible because of the trust that is built by applying previous techniques.

80

Choosing Friends

(Evaluating persons before making them as friends)

791. Cultivating a friendship without discrimination
    Is harmful as its nature prevents discontinuation.

    Entering into a friendship without screening a candidate is harmful
    because it is very difficult to end a friendship which later turns out
    to be a harmful. The difficulty arises on account of the indebtedness
    that develops meanwhile.

792. A friendship not studied well but held,
    Gives a pain as painful as death hold.

    Without studying his or her character, behavior and family
    background if a friendship is established it could lead to situations
    one after another which would land you into trouble lasting until
    you die. (Situations like earning fresh enmity of existing enemies,
    becoming collateral for devastating debts etc.)

793. Nature, lineage, history of blame,
    And his group: consider these and fix the game.

    The considerations to choose a friend are: his nature or qualities,
    what has been fostered by his family, whether he had a crime history
    and whether he keeps company with good persons.

794. Born of good lineage and ashamed of blame:
Friendship may be clinched if needed with a sacrifice.

A person born in a good family and afraid of committing a crime in view of the attendant shame is the apt person for cultivating friendship even by exerting oneself through some sacrifice.

795. By his story he drives you to tears or indicts you to know your mind
Look for such qualities and make him as your friend.

A friend should be good enough to know the issues bothering you. You may hesitate. But he should manage to get it by using techniques like self-disclosure or indict.

796. There is a benefit even in an adversity
It offers a critical measure of the friendship's quality.

Even an adverse situation has a use. It gives you an opportunity to know whether the friendship stays through an adverse period or not.

797. If you ask what is the best blessing
It is fool's friendship dropping.

A person can pat himself as a gainer if he drops the friendship of a fool.

798. Say no to incapacitating thoughts
Don't own a friend who cuts your strategies in times of stress.

Avoid the thought which debilitates your mind. Never have a person for a friend who discourages your plans while they are in the form of thoughts to the extent of making you to leave your efforts to come out of a difficult situation. (This person who cuts your enthusiasm to think of different options may himself suffer from debilitating thoughts.)

799. He who left us while we were in ruinous bout
      Remembering him even at the eve of death burns the heart

      The thought of a friend who left you when you were under a spell
      of misfortune will burn your heart if you remember him even
      during your last days. (Thiruvalluvar who advises us not to cultivate
      friendship with fools and persons who debilitates our thoughts refers
      to a third category here. We should cut our friendship with those
      who leave us when we are in the midst of a crises.)

800. Friendship of pure persons cultivate
      If you are to compensate an indifferent, do it.

      Cultivate the friendship of persons who do not have the four
      pollutants of mind namely, jealousy, greed, rage and hurting tongue.
      If these are absent the person will not be egoistic. Such a person
      will be a good one for making friendship. The friendship should
      be wound up in the case of a person whose philosophy of life and
      feelings do not match yours. If you are to compensate to wean him
      do not hesitate to do so.

Skills to be learnt:

> The first skill mentioned in the previous chapter is: ability to develop
  friendship with responsible people. The present chapter in its entirety
  deals with this issue of making right choices. Therefore the skills
  to be learnt here may be captioned as, 'Researching for Realizing a
  Good Friend.'

Rationale:

> The skills presented in the chapter while logically sound to be
  appropriate the practicality remains to be seen. However, in view of
  their logical soundness they may be given a fair try.

Coaching:

> Avoid friends who have this quality: Folly: principally confirmed by 1) actions lacking enquiry and research, 2) incapacitating thoughts and deserting a friend under adversities (793,797,798 &799).

> Make friendship with those: Who are born in great family[178] known for its great qualities after checking whether the prospective candidate is terribly averse to shame or not (794).

> Select a friend who: either by disclosing his story making you to shed tear so that you also open up or by reprimanding you for not revealing your story to get to know about the issue bothering you (795) and readily helps you.

---

178 For easy reference a list of qualities fostered by a great family is listed here. The list is extracted from the chapter 96: 1. Equity, 2.Modesty (showing humility) 3.Sense of shame, 4. Best practices, 5. Truthfulness, 6. Pleasant interaction during appointment, 7.Offering material help and speaking sweet words to the needy, 8. Never put down fellow human beings when they have to put down their behavior, 9. No meanness in what they do even if they are offered gold coins.

81

Old Friends

(Reviving old friendship)

801. What does an old friendship imply?
Suppressing inherent liberty it doesn't comply.

An old friendship is one wherein liberty taken by an old friend is always honored.

802. Taking liberty is the asset earned out of old friendship,
In the manner, 'salt in food,' *sandror*[179] support its ownership.

Old friendship keeps one asset open for the holders to exploit. That asset is nothing but the right to take liberty with the friend. Endorsing this, *sandror* lend support to it like salt adding taste to the food i.e. they cooperate with their friend so implicitly that the friend is not aware that he is taking liberty. (Salt in right proportion never attracts the attention of the eater but implicitly adds to its taste.)

803. Without accepting his right if an old friend is turned out
What other instruments in the friendship he could turn to?

---

[179] *Sandror* (plural of *sandrone*) means great men whose personality is strengthened with the five qualities of: Love, humility, benevolence/social obligation, empathy and truthfulness.

If a friend who takes liberty empowered by his old friendship is not accorded the due consideration then what remedy he could think of within the realm of friendship? (It is an unwritten law that old friends can exercise some right in using the resources of their friends. If someone fails that convention then the victim has no remedy. Therefore the one who breaks the unwritten law need to be very much sensitive to this aspect.)

804. Acceding to the liberty a friend gladly concedes
To the non-consented acts of old friends.

When old friends act without taking his consent he concedes to them holding it as their right.

805. Hold an old friend's act of hurt
Apart being a folly as his right.

An old friend's act of causing pain has two aspects. His foolishness and liberty issuing out of old friendship. Put up with his folly and relish his liberty.

806. Those who conform to the norms of an old friendship
Never sever a friendship which stood them through hardship.

Those who go by the conventions of old friendship do not severe the friendship of those who helped them through hardship in the past.

807. Love never severed even when hurt
A friendship nurtured through love manages it.

People, who are the products of a way of life wherein love guides life, will not severe a friendship even when an old friend hurts.

808. To him who never confronts his faults
If a friend does a harm that day is badly lived.

That man's day is badly lived as for as the evolution of his soul is concerned if he harms a friend who never questions his mistakes in view of the old friendship between them.

809. The world likes those who never shirk
      A long friendship that saw no break.

The world appreciates those who never shirk a longstanding friend under any harsh circumstances.

810. Even enemies appreciate the friend
      Who show regard to his old friend.

Some are kindly disposed towards their longstanding friends. Such people are liked even by their enemies.

Skills to be learnt:

> The ability to revive an old friendship and reap its fruits.

Rationale:

> Couplet number 802 says something like this: Friends, A and B were mutually giving and receiving support in the form of money, time and energy for several years. After thriving like this the friends get separated due to some reason or the other. Several years later they reunite. At this juncture can the friends take liberties with the resources of each other? The chapter says they can. It introduces a right called as *kezhu thakamai*, meaning a right born out of old friendship to take liberty with one's friend. This may be a convention recommended by Thiruvalluvar.

Coaching:

> This may be a convention but the way Thiruvalluvar has presented it is very appealing. Lend your ears to this appeal. Flow with the

thought. Don't resist even at the hearing stage itself. The chances are very high that you agree for the right called *kezhu thakamai*. Now read the following:

➢ A *sandrone* – person whose personality is firmly seated on the five pillars of 1) love, 2) humility, 3) benevolence, 4) empathy and 5) truthfulness – will concede that *kezhu thakamai* is an asset created by a friendship that was dormant for a number of years and presently in the process of revival. When a friend having been a party for creating that asset claims a stake from that asset a *sandrone* will accede to it readily. How will he do it? He will do it so naturally that even when a friend unawares stakes his claim by making a mistake, like trespassing one's privacy, a *sandrone* will cooperate with him naturally without ever showing an opinion of difference creating a guilty feeling in the trespasser. Salt added in right proportion will never be recognized because it is so harmoniously mingled in the dish. A *sandrone's* cooperation also will be alike!(202)

➢ If you read each of the couplets and their explanations you will end up as a votary for the convention so powerfully presented by Thiruvalluvar.

82

Hazardous Friendship

(Friends with ulterior intentions)

811. As if to merge you into him, he may pose
     Still a *panbu*[180] less man's friendship dispose.

     A friend poor in *panbu* may be very enticing. He behaves as if he
     wants you to seamlessly merge with him. Fine! Still never increase
     his friendship rather end it step by step.

812. **He** joins during prosperity and leaves on its recede
     Losing this indifferent leaves nothing to decide.

     He is around you as a friend harvesting benefits and leaves you when
     he finds being around you is no longer useful only to reach you on a
     later opportune time. What is there to ponder over to decide to leave
     his friendship who is so indifferent to your welfare?

---

[180] The word *panbu* doesn't have an equivalent word in English. It constitutes a
whole lot of items: best practices, sense of shame, respecting equity, humility,
truthfulness, sense of humour, speaking warmly, not degrading others, not
indulging in mean activities and even under poverty conditions not losing
sandranmai. Sandranmai, you may recall, consists of love, humility, benevolence
(*oppuravu*), empathy and truthfulness.

813. A friend who weighs the gains and she who minds the proceeds
Are on par with a thief who never on his job recedes.[181]

A friend who weighs his benefits to stay in the friendship and a prostitute who weighs what her customer gives, give good company to a thief.

814. Untrained military horse undoes its master's prowess
Better choose to be alone when a similar friend approaches.

A military horse not trained in the maneuvers it needs to manage while its master is involved in attacking the enemy is detrimental to the striking power of its master. It is better to stand on the ground and fight than mount such a horse to fight. Similarly a friend for want of good education and perspectives may do things hazardous to one's wellbeing. It is better to be alone rather keeping such persons as friends.

815. On a time of need he didn't offer you support
It is rather advantageous not to have this rapport.

If a friend fails to support you when you need his support most it is greatly disadvantageous. Therefore it is advantageous not to have such friends.

816. Wise man's enmity is million times better
Than a fool's intimate friendship offer.

It is better to have the enmity of a wise man rather than the friendship of a fool. The former is millions of times better. (Remember a fool is one who takes decisions not supported by evidence. In fact he is not versed in strategizing at all leave alone not collecting evidence for his action.)

---

[181] 'Never on his job is recedes' added for providing rhyme.

817. The enmity of foes are hundred millions times better
     Than the hurts by what 'time passing gossipers' muster.

     The hurts brought by friends who uses the friendship for time passing
     is millions of times worse than the hurts received from the enemies.

818. The friendship of them, gradually discord
     Who sabotage a task by what they accord.

     Wean the friendship, with those people who spoil a task which was
     on its way to success by doing something or the other gradually, so
     that they do not become aware of it. (This couplet is in the same
     direction of couplet number 816.)

819. Even in dreams their association is painful
     Whose behavior differs from what they speak, in full.

     The association of those whose activities are at variance with what
     they speak should be brought to an end because even in dreams their
     association is harmful.

820. At home they smile and pick hole in public
     At any cost with them avoid a closer link.

     There are some people who have the habit of speaking politely and
     very friendly in camera and blame in the presence of others. Leave
     them at any cost.

Skills to be learnt:

> Ability to spot hazardous friends and wean them.

Rationale:

> A list of good qualities of men of *panbu* is given in reference no.158.
> Imagine a person who is just the opposite. Lacking qualities like, not

being afraid of carrying out mean activities and lacking truthfulness make (a *panbu* less) person very hazardous. Therefore it goes without saying that such people should be weaned at any cost.

Coaching:

> Develop a clear vision over the concept of friendship by reading the chapters: 79,80,81,82 and 83.

> Firmly decide to have only two or three intimate friends. You can have as many acquaintances as possible which has its own use.

> Carry on research using the techniques given under chapter 80 and develop friendship. In this connection reviving an old friendship is a good idea. Read chapter 81.

> Once you develop a strong relationship with your new friends you may start weaning from old hazardous friends. Do not wean them totally. You can move them from friends to acquaintances. Occasional meeting with them and continuing professional exchanges, delivering the correct message to them that they no longer enjoy the confidence of yours will do.

83

Fake Friends

(Unfaithful friends)

821. **A**n anvil[182] helps to shape close and sharp,
     A 'disaffect' uses friendship for a similar morph.[183]

An ironsmith employs a molded structure called anvil to cut, shape and make implements. Similarly friends who do not have any affection for you may use your friendship with them to realize their objectives. In other words, there are people whom you consider as your friends do not consider you on similar lines but use your friendship for their purposes. Beware of them.

822. **T**hey pretend as though to you they belong,
     But they are like a woman whose mind falls along.[184]

---

[182] The Tamil word, '*pattadai*' is translated as anvil. Going by what is being used even today by a village ironsmith the device is used to cut and shape a hot soft iron into various implements. When the device is not under use it may not be recognized for its versatility. A pseudo friend (whose motive is never noticed) on getting a right opportunity behaves like the anvil.

[183] Morph means changing bit by bit. The crooked persons uses the so called friendship or the feigned 'belonging' for shaping the unsuspecting friend to their advantage.

[184] Take several positions.

Some people would behave as if they belong to you when in reality they are not. But beware they may change their mind like a woman whose heart changes without much fuss.

823. **The** mental health of low shows no improvement
In spite of their vast and quality learning input.

Mental health of persons who are low minded do not change in spite of vast learning of good material. (Perhaps their learning is mechanical and does not involve their souls.)

824. Fear a man who wields a friendly smile
But in fact is guile.

One has to keep off fearing a person who throws a friendly smile but in reality not only he doesn't possess warmth but also scheming at heart.

825. **Until** your heart gels with him clear him not for trust
In spite his jargons showing him as the best.

Do not pass a person for accepting him as your friend based on his words until such time you find your heart gelling with him. If there is some division in some corner of your heart act carefully.

826. **They** may, like friends, use friendly words to connect
But soon their words (deeds) will reveal their hearts' disconnect.

The words of people who are having a hidden agenda for their friendship may appear to be very affectionate but sooner or later deeds of disaffect can be noticed.

827. Do not heed to enemy' humble words as they are sham
Like a bow's bend is only meant to harm.

The bend in a bow is meant to make it's arrow as lethal as possible. People with treacherous scheme may also bend like the bow before you and use humble words. Therefore don't take the words from such people on their face value.

828. Within the palms that pray, a weapon might hide[185]
     Such an enemy's tears may hide his bide.[186]

A man may act as if he greets another fellow with palms pressing each other. (Like in the Indian custom) But he may hide a weapon in between the palms (as Gandhi's assassin did). Similarly the enemy's tears may hide his intention to strike by diverting your attention.

829. **P**raising you sky high if he despises himself
     Make him laugh and let go his friendship.

Men who downgrade themselves simultaneously throwing encomiums on you should be carefully dealt with. Their friendship should be severed in a phased manner engineered by friendly pep talk keeping them in good humor.

830. When a foe poses as a friend keep a friendly face
     But readily his friendship at heart deface.

If an enemy proposes friendship with you, you too show him a friendly face. But readily remove any attendant feelings of friendship from your heart.

Skills to be learnt:

➤   The ability to identify fake friends and enemies wearing the garb of friendship and avoiding them.

---

[185] Gandhi's assassin held his gun within the fold of his palms as he said his, *'Namaste,'* to Gandhi

[186] 'Bide' as in the idiom 'bide one's time'.

Rationale:

> You may recall the phenomenon of fake saints portrayed in chapter 28. A fake saint hoodwinks his followers and lives a princely life exploiting his followers into sustaining his Hi Fi life. Same thing applies to a fake friend. He makes you to believe that he is a genuine friend and exploits your love. Therefore take care to protect yourself from such friends. Similarly sometimes our enemies may pose as our friends and try to destroy us we should avoid them also needn't be mentioned.

Coaching:

> Four couplets in the chapter provide guidance to identify fake friends. They are: 822, 823, 825 and 826. Four other couplets talk of enemies who camouflage as friends. They are: 826, 827, 829 and 830.

> Since fake friends stay around you for ulterior reasons their interest in you will be on and off. Using this notion you can identify a fake friend. Here is an exercise: If you are disappointed with a friend of yours and if you suspect his authenticity analyze the interactions you had with him for the past one month. If he is a fake you will be surprised to see that in all the interactions either he got something done by you or at least he was after one from you which you denied. Whenever he was after you he would have also shown enormous interest in you by doing something you relish. On other occasions he would have shunned your company under some pretext. Thiruvalluvar says they may appear to possess two minds like women who are flexible with regard to the position they take on an issue (822).

> Their behavior will not concur with their level of learning. For example, a person may be a walking encyclopedia with regard to Bible[187] but will always have a ready excuse to back out from a

---

[187] The example of Bible is to make it at home with western readers in general. However, depending upon his religious affiliation the reader is requested to change the name of the book.

community action if the action's aftermath's has even a semblance of potential to hurt his interest (823).

➤ What they don't have at heart they will show in their words. They will swear they live for your sake. They will modulate their voice so much it will touch your heart and you feel very pleasant of course, only if you freely flow with what they say. They will shower encomiums when it is least warranted. Beware chances are they are singing your tune to milk you for something! (825).

➤ Earlier, I have translated the couplet 825 as: "Until your two hearts sync don't clear him for a trust // In spite his jargons show him as the best." I thought the Tamil word *amaiyathavar* would mean: 'if his heart doesn't sync with mine.' In that case we could hold Thiruvalluvar as saying, "If you have a fake friend before you, you will change your mind and your behavior will become artificial. Therefore, whenever you find yourself to be behaving before someone artificially know that person is not a genuine friend."

➤ Fake friends will not keep their promise. This happens because they are not for working/ sacrificing for your sake. You are a work horse for them. They will promise on the name of God but forget their words on the critical moment. Then once again it is same story of giving another fresh set of promises. By some indirect means if you check with them about what they have promised you will be surprised to find out they don't remember their promise fully (826)!

➤ Another angle from which you can spot a fake friend is: there will be a number of inconsistencies in their statements, tone, enthusiasm, suddenly diverting the topic etc.

➤ Beware enemies may also approach you as your friends. Don't take their words on their face value. Don't be carried away by the pleasing words they use. A bow also looks quite pleasing with its curvature and it is dangerous is it not? (827).

➤ Someone may weep for you but could have sinister motive inside. Be careful with them828).

➤ Be careful with persons who disregard themselves while regarding you very high (829).

➤ When your enemies try to cultivate friendship with you, you also act as if you are also friendly with them but carefully wean them (830)

84

Folly

(Cut the friendship of a fool)

831. What is folly? Charging oneself with ruin,
And discharging one's gain.

A folly is one who gathers all those which spell ruin (like, acts leading to poverty, disease, blemish acts, acting out of ignorance and earning enmity unnecessarily) whereas he lets go all those which will bring him good (like, wellbeing of body and mind, acts of *aram*, acts befitting appreciation of men who matters, gathering knowledge and gaining good friends).

832. The greatest of all folly is finding delight
In doing things not part of one's skill set.

The greatest fool is one who tries his hand on something in which he is neither skilled nor trainable.

833. Sense of shame, inquisitiveness, concern for others,
Cultivating an abiding interest: on these a fool never bothers.

Sense of shame, a researching mind, or showing concern to others or continuing in any activity for a reasonable period of time to avail the fruits of his or her labor are absent with a fool.

834. Learns and delivers but self-control he hasn't
      Can there be a better fool who he isn't?

      A foolish person learns by reading and teaching others. But the
      important quality of self-control which results from vast learning is
      absent in him. Therefore there is none other as foolish as him.

835. **T**he fool in one birth can commit such mistakes
      For seven the fool has enough miry stakes[188]

      A fool commits enough mistakes in one birth from whose hellish
      (miry) effect it would take seven reincarnations for him (for his soul)
      to come out.

836. Leave alone he would fail, would also be in chains,
      When a fool's untrained hand takes the reins.

      It is quite sure he will fail, apart from that he will also be arrested
      when he starts a job, being oblivious to the fact that he doesn't have
      the relevant skill, and commits grave mistakes.

837. His new fortune banishes stranger's hunger
      But he and his kin suffer stomach wringer.

      If a fool gets a fortune unconnected people will manage to enjoy
      while his kith and kin will remain hungry.

838. A fool and a fortune haul,
      Equals an arrogant man cheering in alcohol.

      If a fool gets a fortune he will behave like an arrogant man under
      the spell of booze..

---

[188] A fickle minded person would commit so many mistakes in one birth creating
       such a burden to clear the soul of its effects he will need seven births.

839. Friendship with a fool is worthy of keeping!
     Since later separation doesn't yield weeping!

There is one advantage in maintaining friendship with a fool. After all when he parts company one need not weep.

840. A fool intruding a session of great men,[189]
     Equals going to bed with feet unclean.

A fool getting into a hall where a great session of scholars is going on is like a person getting on the bed without washing his feet. (The Tamil word *kazhakkaal* literally translates as foot in clay. It is a euphemism for not washing the body while going to bed thus soiling the linen and somewhat like sleeping in dirt. It can also mean going to bed without performing prayer.)

Skills to be learnt:

➢   Getting rid of foolishness.

Rationale:

➢   Folly is the opposite of intellect or wisdom. A wise person or intellect is one who benefits from new data every time he gets them and turns his benefit into that of the society. A fool for want of inquisitiveness makes little use of data. Since he has no sense of shame the society has very little leverage on him. But he doesn't lack intelligence. Because he doesn't have constant abiding interest in anything his contribution becomes a question mark. Therefore it is useful idea to apply the insights from this chapter to help a folly to get rid of foolishness.

---

[189]   Here great men mean *sandrones*.

Coaching:

> Couplets 832 and 833 provide clue to an approach for working with a fool. The couplet says a fool who doesn't have any skill or knowledge for carrying out an activity involves in it out of interest. Whereas couplet 833 says he has no abiding involvement in any thing (Tamil phrase: *yathondrum penaamai*). Is it a case that lacking abiding interest is due to no opportunity to enjoy success in anything he does? Is it a case of no success because of no research and application of what one learns out of it? I think the answer for both the questions is yes.

Now what is the solution?

> If one suffers from foolishness the first thing he needs to do is check within himself and find out what interests him. It can be anything. Only condition is when he convert his interest into work it should not be against the law of land.

> Then let him start acquiring expertise in the area. Let him not get stuck with the notion of regular schooling if he is past that age. Let him pick up the knowledge through other modes. It can be any mode: on line, hands on experience in a work place, crash programs in a school or any other means.

> Let him make it a point that he will stay and work in an area of interest for a minimum of five years. This is for preventing him from falling into the vicious cycle of: doing something which interests him for which he has no skill → unhappy experience and lack of success → losing interest in it for want of success → a new interest.

> There is another issue with him: casualness! He lacks the seriousness needed for any human activity. In fact if he reflects a little he will realize that there is no room for casualness at all in this world. Not a minute can be spent casually. Even when one takes rest he should do it seriously. Let him not agitate his mind over some issue while resting. Religiosity or seriousness in whatever we do is a must for genuinely enjoying anything we do. Remedy for lack of seriousness

is remembering what is stated here and always keeping an eye on oneself. He should take things seriously tell this to himself every time he tends to become casual. Let him remember there is no casualness in the world anywhere excepting with human being!

85

Knowledge-meagre

(Poor knowledge acquisition)

841. Petty knowledge tops the list of poverty
     Wise do not consider others as of same variety

     Being poor in knowledge indicates that one seriously lacks something.
     Other shortcomings are not as detrimental as lack of knowledge
     according to wise men.

842. With full heart he delivers,
     Oh! It is tapas of the receivers!

     A person who is not aware of his superficial grasp of the subject
     whole heartedly lectures to others. It is only the great penance of the
     listener that he is bestowed to listen to him!

843. The hurt he brings himself on,
     Not even his enemies can.

     The harm a 'knowledge-Meagre' brings upon himself even his
     enemies cannot.

844. "I possess the best of knowledge,"
     Reveals his arrogance and ignorance.

A person with meager knowledge gloats over his 'superior' knowledge. Serious ignorance aspect of this is while he actually lacks knowledge he is not aware of it. Second, he declares his knowledge level as superior. That ignorance is ignorance of all ignorance.

845. He goes beyond what he knows
Doubt arises on what he really knows.

A person whose knowledge is meager has the tendency to talk much beyond what he really knows (perhaps using assumptions based presumptions). This makes others to suspect his credibility regarding even what he has learnt well.

846. Will he hide only his nakedness
When on exposing his wisdom he is shameless?

A person who clothes himself to hide his nakedness due to sense of shame doesn't have the same concern when it comes to his meagre knowledge. He shamelessly exposes it! What a pity!

847. On interpreting great treatise he makes mistakes
And receives lot of harm as takes.

A 'knowledge meager' wrongly interprets great treatises which have applications for real life. As a result he brings harm on himself by carrying on activities of life according to his false understanding. (I infer the treatises referred here are treatises on life skills (like Thirukkural) in view of the next couplet.)

848. He heeds no advise nor improves himself,
Until his end he is a disease to himself.

He neither learns from others nor learns by himself and acts according to what he knows. He is a disease on himself until he dies because of this nature. (He is also a burden to his care takers as though he is a disease on them.)

849. **T**he No-refresh shows, never refreshes, the New to refresh
Refreshes and sees like 'No-refresh.[190]

A person whose knowledge is meager has no idea that what he knows is insufficient or superficial or wrongly understood. While he never makes any attempt to learn new, insists showing to others what he knows without entertaining an iota of doubt. The unfortunate person who listens to him may also end in the same status of 'Knowledge-meagre'.

850. He negates the voice of world's wise,
The world considers him as demonic vice.

He has the habit of disagreeing with the wise sayings of the great people of the world.(This is like the tendency with some people who will raise a queer angle on any subject to create a sensation and win the hearts of people who are similar to them) He is treated as a demon by the knowledgeable.

Skills to be learnt:

> A Knowledge meagre should get rid of his arrogant pride. He should have clear awareness about what is the level of his knowledge and take steps to improve. He should stop assuming things and making

---

[190] Please note this is a second translation for the couplet 849. The first one I made goes like this: Since he wouldn't learn anew he ends Knowledge Meagre// The one who learns from him also has a similar go. The couplet is a delight to read it in Tamil. Therefore I have tried to bring out the 'delight' as much as possible in English as found in the text. But what has resulted is a poor imitation jewel! The Tamil couplet reads like this: *Kaanadhaan kaattuvaan thaankaanaan kaanaathaan // Kandanaam thaan kandavaaru*

presumptions based on his assumption. He should regard other learned person and benefit out of it.

Rationale:

> A 'Knowledge meagre' is a person who needs help because he is underutilizing himself and also harm others. As a human being, otherwise having no disorders or shortcomings, he is fully available for developing into a useful son of the nation.

Coaching:

> Surprisingly, Thiruvalluvar has not spelt any technique to help a Knowledge Shallow. However, I could do something. How about seeing the chapter as ten admonitions thrown by Thiruvalluvar at a Knowledge meagre? If you accept the idea then we have the therapy. Admonitions without condemning the person, showing the condition from different angles, using surprise presentations, disapprovals, humors and giving some predictions for the future in case the individual doesn't take corrective steps will work. Here are the admonitions:

> Hallo! My dear young man, "Do you know what a real lack is? It is the lack that you lack an awareness of where you stand vis-à-vis your level of knowledge."

> My dear young man, "People must have carried out great tapas to become your listeners!"

> My dear young man, "Do you know by not posting yourself with what is happening in your field you are hurting yourself more than what your enemies could do"?

> My dear young man, "With lot of difficulty and humbleness I say this. Your shallowness takes different shades. I am referring to your ignorance about your real standing in your discipline. It is really serious, otherwise how will you declare that you possess superior knowledge while in reality what you possess is very low"?

> My dear young man, "Do you know one thing, when you talk going beyond what you know for certain, assuming and presuming, your

audience will look at you as a sham. They will start suspecting your bona fides regarding what you know"?

➤ My dear young man, "Don't use your assumptions and presumptions to hide your shallowness. After all you can refresh your knowledge instead!"

➤ My dear young man, "You have wrongly understood the treatises teaching life skills and follow them as per that false understanding. Beware you are inflicting great harm to yourself!"

➤ My dear young man, "I hear people talking about you like this: "This fellow neither himself learns nor learns from others. He is a disease as long as he lives.""

➤ My dear young man, "When I thought about you few lines run in my mind: There are people who don't update their knowledge but dare to teach others. There are also those unfortunate people who go to such persons and end up as poor as their teachers."

➤ My dear young man, "You should know one thing. If you negate what the wise says you will be looked upon as a demon in human form,"

86

Non Acceptance[191]

(Showing no agreeableness)

851. The disease is called non-acceptance
A divisive *panbu*-less petulance.

Dividing humanity on the basis of some consideration or the other
and resorting to differentiated treatment is a mental disease. This is
a sore in the *panbu* (character or personality) of humanity.

852. Non-acceptance may make you to act indifferent.
Still your opponent you should never torment.

A person may differ from you. You may take a position of not
showing affection to him on account of it. It is alright. But never
convert your non-acceptance into a hatred and resort to tormenting
that person either physically or mentally or both.

---

[191] The Tamil word *igal* in my opinion means non-acceptance as in the case of
fanatic and fundamentalists who do not accept others who do not fall in line with
them (and go to destroy them). The words intolerance and tolerance denote a
difference in the position between the one tolerates and the one who is tolerated.
This proposition is against equity which is the central idea of Thirukkural.
Therefore I have translated the heading of this chapter as Non Acceptance rather
as Intolerance. All the couplets reflect this caption more faithfully than the other.

853. **G**et rid of the painful disease of non-acceptance
And receive spotless fame's radiance.

A body once cured of painful disease regains its original radiance.
Similarly if you get rid of the disease of non-acceptance and develop
a mind set of other-acceptance, then your fame will regain its lost
height.

(It seems Tiruvalluvar motivates people who have travelled a long
distance in the path of hate prompted by non-acceptance and lack
of secular acceptance and have become unpopular saying that such
people can regain their fame back if they start acting acceptingly.
Perhaps due to the coolness of the proposal it will get the attention
and close scrutiny of a larger population and status quo ante restored
easily.)

854. **J**oy Superior is what you get
If non-acceptance, the pain of all pains, gets cut.

Non-acceptance is the cause for the most painful of all the pains. If
secular acceptance is practiced you get the joy superior to all other
joys.

855. **I**f, 'falling apart of minds,' meets a decisive eschew
Who's capable of decelerating such a view?

Secular acceptance of others is a skill one has to pick up. If someone
skilled in that it is very difficult to push him or her more and more
into the path of non-acceptance.

856. **I**f non-acceptance is held dear
Without fail ruin of his life is near.

If someone accelerates the mind set of non-acceptance then he will
start doing grievous mistakes costing him the ruin of his life.

857. Those who escalate non-acceptance
Know not the truth of its aggressive advance.

Those who go more and more in the direction of non-acceptance may think they are motivated by a just cause. They really do not know that once they are in a non-acceptance mood and start acting they get a kick which keeps the flame unextinguished until the end.

858. Leaning opposite to non-acceptance yields prosperity
If it is accelerated it precipitates calamity.

Moving in the direction opposite to non-acceptance leads to strength and prosperity. If creativity is expended in upping non-acceptance then calamity results.

859. During prosperity he sees no subversion
Later he falls escalating division

When an individual starts making money he is totally devoid of non-acceptance as he is preoccupied in his efforts to make more and more money. Once he becomes rich he starts pushing non-acceptance far enough that he meets his end. (Perhaps 'other acceptance' in the beginning is a good business strategy to make use of every available space. But later when more than enough wealth is amassed exclusive group membership is handy in protecting one's wealth to start with. And soon an 'on and on' journey in that direction (fuelled by the new wealth fostered arrogance) brings in ruin.)

860. Non-acceptance nets ills
Laughing at division earns the proud tag "Highly cultured."

The hatred born out of non-acceptance is the root cause for all the undesirable and bad things the world suffers. Acceptance of others earns the pride of 'Oh! This person is cultured'.

Skills to be learnt:

➢ Developing the skill of other-acceptance and a secular outlook.

Rationale:

➢ Humanity, world over, suffers from the disease called non-acceptance of fellow human beings on some basis or the other. At the gross root level non-acceptance is simplistically practiced in the face of a real or imaginary provocation. But in most of the cases the provocateurs may be far away orchestrating the non-acceptance. The provocateurs are very strong money and authority vise. Since non-acceptance is their bread and butter it is nearly impossible to stop non-acceptance by operating on them. What is possible is working with the victims of non-acceptance. I mean victims at the hands of their own non-accepting mind.

Coaching:

The lead for this idea comes from couplet 855:

➢ How about accepting group formation as an insurmountable reality and converting the groups which are the breeding grounds of non-acceptance into patrons of other-acceptance?

➢ This is possible if we see the group as a channel to focus energy for any useful cause. The idea is: each group will do everything in its command to support the other group to maintain its identity, and exclusivity.

Advice the groups and individuals on the following grounds:

➢ Our group and every member of our group shall accept the fact that the other group is a reality and they are here to stay.

➢ Similarly our group (religion) is exclusive in several respects and very different in few aspects as compared to the other group. For our group and our members the differences are very important. We want to protect our identity at any cost.

> We realize the same holds good to the other group (religion) also with regard to their beliefs and therefore we accord the same importance we give to our beliefs to the beliefs of the members of the other group.

> To bring this notion into practice our group and every member of our group should support the other group and each member of the other group to maintain their identity and exclusivity.

> Similarly our group and each member of our group should demand the other group and its members to support our group and every member of our group to maintain our exclusivity and identity. This right we shall earn by supporting the other group and its members honestly.

> Let every member say to every member of the other group, "I shall do everything in my command to support you in upholding your identity and your exclusivities. I also expect you to support my exclusivity and my identity. I support your causes and you support mine."

> We know in India in several places in the remote villages Muslims and Hindus live side by side and they cooperate in every possible ways to run their lives retaining their Muslim-hood and Hindu-hood. Commerce in ethnic, religious and cultural products thrives. Invariably each neighborhood that includes individuals across all exclusivities give opportunities for both Muslims and Hindus and others to support each other for conducting great religious festivals, functions and marriages and their livelihood. This happens without compromising on the religious identity and exclusivity.

Therefore:

> As a human being I want to cooperate with you but I will do it without breaching anything that differentiates me from you. I will respect what you believe and your exclusivity provided you respect my beliefs regarding my exclusivity and support me in maintaining the same.

> Let this be our mantra hereafter: "I support you to be the 'who-you-are' and you support me to be the 'who-I am'."

> ➤ We are also aware of the menace of some cantankerous persons who are dead set against this mantra. They use racketeering methods to breach the exclusivity of vulnerable population for expanding their power base. I promise you by the name of Almighty that I will neither support them nor run the rockets for them. I also expect you to give me the same promise and abide by it.

> ➤ Read M.J. Akbar's delightful blog, "Hear it? Indian secularism is both enduring & audible."

87

What Ails Warring Might

(Estimating king's personality as an aspect of warring strength)

861. **Do** not beam your chest to the strong
Resist temptation on not so strong.

Do not take a tough stand with a king mightier than you. So also fighting a weakling to be avoided even though it is very tempting.[192]

862. With no tender heart and hence no allies, himself not strong,
How such a king could destroy the enemy's powerful throng?

If a king is not kind hearted then naturally he will not support his fraternity leaving them impoverished. In addition to that if he is also weak in terms of men and material then how he would be able to win his enemies?

863. A coward, ill-informed, unsocial and miserly,
His enemies could make him to surrender easily.

A king will easily find himself surrendering to his enemy if he is a coward, not well informed, not socializing and miserly.

---

[192] I have taken this view in view of Thiruvalluvar's opposition to, non-acceptance and war, as depicted in the couplet 871 and the entire chapter of 86. Moreover both the Tamil words *ombuga* and *omba* mean the same.)

864. Always angry, no self-control, anywhere to anyone
     He is an easy win.

     He is under constant devouring anger and has no self-control. It is
     easy for anyone to win him at any place.

865. **N**ever strategizes, fails an opportunity, cares no blame,
     And bereft of panbu, for enemies he is an easy game.

     A king, who never strategizes, never effectively uses opportunities,
     never ashamed of blame and has no character, will be easily won by
     his enemies.

866. **B**lind rage and inordinate lust,
     Not catering him his enemies have as must.

     An enemy king by policy utilize an opportunity to finish a fellow king
     if he come across one who gets into wild anger because he has not
     learnt to develop adept perspectives and spends lot of time on women.

867. He is a neighbor and his acts lack amity.
     It is a worthy act to earn his enmity.

     If a neighbor king is not amenable for harmonious relationship it is
     worthy to earn his enmity even spending for it.

868. Has no *panbu*, commits mistakes severally,
     He is a clan to his enemy surely!

     If a king lacks character and is in the habit of committing mistakes
     continuously his actions take care of the situation of his enemy not
     having a supporting clan!

869. With an ignorant and coward as an enemy
     Joy never deserts his company.

For a king who has a coward and ignorant as his enemy it is a never ending celebration.

870. Unlettered and on petty issues he does fume
With this temper never gets accolade.

A king who is not educated in political treatises and who has the habit of getting into rage over petty issues can never attain accolade.

Skills to be learnt:

> Estimating the military strength of a kingdom with special reference to the personality of the king.

Rationale:

> A king' personality is an important strength in the overall analysis of the strength of his military. It is surprising to note even today the personality of the head of the government – presidential, democratic or military – matters. In India for example, though we have democracy from the very first day of independence it was always the personality of the prime minister of the union government that brought eventful changes, be it mishandling China leading to war, be it war with Pakistan leading to its bifurcation.

Coaching:

While estimating the military might of a country the personality of the king (or president) need to be given special importance. The following personality related abilities are derived from the chapter:

> Ability to keep oneself off from the compulsive desire of waging even a winnable war, leave alone a war in which winning is not possible given the military might of the enemy country. (861)
> Ability to love one's country men and fellow kings. (862)
> Ability to give generously to military personnel. (863)

➤ Ability to know what and what not to fear. (863)

➤ Ability to avoid continuous angry mood.(864)

➤ Ability to strategize.(865)

➤ Ability to use the opportunities that crop up.(865)

➤ Ability to avoid doing things attracting blame.(865)

➤ Ability to cultivate *panbu*.(865)

➤ Ability to avoid perspectives leading to unnecessary anger. (865)

➤ Ability to keep off from seeking excessive sexual pleasures. (866)

➤ Ability to keep a neighbor king whose acts are not great at arm's length. (867)

➤ Ability to maintain more number of good qualities and less number of flaws. (868)

➤ Ability to be brave enough and well informed so that one doesn't become a 'support' to one's enemy (869),

➤ Ability to control oneself from getting into rage on petty issues. (870)

88

Strategy for Avoiding War

(Keeping oneself as invincible)

871. Enmity is a *panbu* less quality.
Even in humor do not theme enmity.

Enmity is opposite to the human quality of love, equity and compassion. Even one's jokes should be free from the themes of enmity. If jokes are built using enmity themes it suggests one is hyped over enmity. That will escape in some form or the other causing trouble and repercussions. Therefore even jokes punning on the issue of enmity should be avoided.

872. Afford an enemy who wields bow,
But not an enemy whose words are his bow.

You can at least afford to have enemies who wield bows. But never have enemies who use their words as weapons.

873. One who takes on several enemies alone,
More lunatic than an insane.

If a king moves on several enemies simultaneously with no friendly kings to support him with their armies it shows that he is utterly stupid. In that respect he is even worst than an insane person.

874. World remains under him due to his nature
Converting enemies as friends is his character.

Avoiding confrontations and converting enemy kings as friends and carrying on with them exhibits love, equity and compassion on the part of the king. Citizens are safe under such a king and therefore they rally around him.

875. You have two enemies but no support
Fight one, with another create rapport.

If confronted with two enemies a king should make one of them as a friend.

876. **W**hether tested or not throw him not
In the midst of a ruinous war being fought.

A king may have a person (minister or military officer or a friendly neighbor king) who's background and other credentials the king has not scrutinized while taking him in. He should not let him go in the midst of a ruinous war (when the king is suffering heavy losses in men and material).

877. Block your unknown miseries to friends
And your weakness to enemies.

Do not reveal your miseries to those who themselves did not notice. Take every step to keep off your enemies from knowing your weaknesses (in terms of men and material).

878. Make men, arsenals and king's security aright
Enemy's pride vanishes with no fight, right?

Taking into account, the various divisions of army and the materials and man power needs, plan well. Take every step to make the security of the kingdom fool proof. If you do this you will find that your enemy's belligerent warring pride and impetus dies without a war.

879. Nip the thorny tree in the bud
A fully grown gets a cutter's hands bled.

Nip the thorny bud when it is young. Once it is fully grown its thaws grievously. (The next couplet gives the full meaning of this couplet.)

880. He doesn't deserve to live
If he doesn't destroy enemy's overawe.

A king doesn't deserve to live if he doesn't destroy the arrogant pride of his enemy. (This he can do by bolstering the fighting might of his army and kingdom by following all the strategies presented in couplets 571 to 576. Later spying his army's and kingdoms military prowess the enemy will lose heart.)

Skills to be learnt:

> While avoiding war should be the main motto picking up few strategies to make the kingdom formidable need to be learnt.

Rationale:

> The country should totally free itself from the mentality to wage a war. Avoiding war with too many enemies at a time should be aimed. War can be avoided by keeping oneself in a formidable form. An attempt is made hereunder keeping India in mind.

Coaching:

> India had a humiliating defeat at the hands of China in the year 1962. The issues linger. As on date China is making heavy demands on India. Therefore unless one philosophizes a lot it is difficult for

any Indian to think of China as a friendly country. I have tried to find out what lessons Thirukkural offers to deal with China.[193]

> The first couplet (871) says we should take steps to wipe out enmity from our mind thoroughly, exampled by the absence of punning on China India enmity even for the sake of jest. In this context it may be noted that Indian media and the public are constantly taunting on this topic which is not at all liked by the authorities in China. Of course in a democratic country it is not possible to curtail it. But something can be done in the direction that confidence building also becomes a subject of interest to media and public. The earlier initiative of Aman ki Asha by Times group of India and The Jang Group of Pakistan are good examples in this regard.

> The second couplet (872) says never create enmity with writers (and activists who writes). Chinese as well as Pakistan writers are very quick to pick up what is stated by Indians. May be strategizing at the level of the government and suitable insights drawn for following a few guidelines will be a right step. More serious problem is the writers and activists in side India. India is an open society. As told earlier it is very difficult to handle press censorship. Keeping high values of national security and freedom of expression as the guiding forces a very patient cultivation of our activists to write and act without playing into the hands of our enemies need to be attempted. Presently we find some of our activists with good intention but inappropriate strategy write and speak playing into the hands of our enemies.

> The third couplet (873) without mincing words says, 'do not start a war against too many enemies (or at too many fronts). In the case of India this proposition can be modified as: do not escalate tension with both Pakistan and China at the same time.

---

[193] My knowledge on China-India tangles – territory - dams across rivers being built by China in which India has riparian rights – Tibetan issues   and others – is very little. But for my ingenious effort of connecting Thirukkural with China-India enmity tangle I am sure the real pages of contribution should be written by someone who is well versed in Thirukkural as well as India China tangle.

➢ The fourth couplet (874) says avoid confrontation with kings in the neighborhood. We have a number of neighbor countries other than Pakistan and China. With them also our relation is not in the pink of health. Dr.Subramaniam Swamy an acclaimed expert on issues of China and former Minister of commerce, government of India had this to say: "India needs to strengthen its military capability and forge closer ties with strategic neighbors to offset the growing influence of China in Asia. India, which has a history of squandering opportunities to cement ties with potential allies, has to win back its neighbours".

➢ He pointed out further, "At the moment almost all neighbours such as Nepal, Bangladesh, Burma, Pakistan and Sri Lanka shared closer ties with China than India. As a nation India is hesitant to seize the offer for friendship from Afghanistan, failed to see Indonesia as a natural ally, refused to undertake Sri Lanka's Hambantota port project (that went to China), India finds itself in a tight position where none of its neighbours would support it in a standoff with China."

➢ Dr. Swamy also wanted India to scale up defence expenditure to at least five per cent of the GDP for strengthening military capability and acquiring advanced weaponry. "Only an India that is stronger militarily and had more friends among neighbours could command respect from China," he said.

➢ We have to work on these perceptions and do the needful to change them to mutual advantage. Our Look east policy is a step in the right direction. With development of technology and globalization there is no need for geographical contiguity for establishing neighborhood. USA, Japan, South Korea and a number of European countries and EU itself could be our neighborhood countries in Thiruvalluvarian sense.

➢ The present Government under Mr. Narendra Modi is moving in the right direction. Mr. Narendra Modi with his mind boggling maneuvers at the national and international arena would be a chum for Thiruvalluvar had he been living today. His approach and active wooing of several countries is in line with the couplet 874. Keeping the contentious issues in the backburner he pushes business ties as much as possible. This strategy serves two purposes. While it is the need of the hour for an investment starved India the business ties when materialized fully creates enough stakes which would create a sobering effect on other issues and cause them to be amicably solved.

➤ The last couplet (880) gives the workable tips in the line explained above to handle China and Pakistan. Both China and Pakistan think that they can always keep us on tender hooks like at present. This courage comes to them, due to their belief that they are formidable for India, of course for different reasons country wise. We have to break this perception by building our military prowess as much as required. Thanks to our nuclear program we are able to deter them effectively but for their mischief. The mischief will disappear only when their perception is caused to change by our buildup of military prowess. We have to do everything to break their pride of "We are formidable." Remember, never a war, only the enemy's overawe needs to be crushed.

➤ We should also make our media and politicians to be more practical and not accept the reality in this part of the world. We should know what is achievable and what is not and stop agitating for each and every small skirmishes creating sensational news which may not be liked by Chinese.

89

Enemy Within

881. Water under shade could become hurtful,
Similarly hold relatives if they become spiteful.

Water under shade because of its chillness is a delight especially
during summer. But if it becomes harmful due to some reason
we have to discard it. The same logic holds good for members of
your kith and kin who become harmful because of their activities
of fomenting internal enmity. Like, you avoid harmful water, you
should avoid them also.

882. A visible enemy wielding a sword do not fear
Enemy in the garb of relative do fear.

You may have enemies as visible as a drawn sword. There is no need
to fear them provided you take enough precautions. But if you have
kith and kin around you who harbor enmity towards you but hide
it under the guise of relationship you should fear them.

883. Protect yourself from internal ill will
In times of decline it cuts like a potter's tool.

If there are internal squabbles and strife be careful and take steps
as a leader of the group for your protection. Otherwise when your
leadership undergoes trouble due to some other reason the internal
stripe will act like a potter's knife and cut you without fail. (Potter

knife is used to cut a 'to be kilned clay pot' to remove it from its base.)

884. If enmity is due to ill thoughts within
     Community suffers many unstoppable ruins.

If enmity within is, due to the poisonous and therefore wrongly guiding thoughts in the minds of community members, it will bring ruin, which the community will not be able to stop after it becomes too late.

885. If the strife is on account of management goof
     Deadly wipe could be in the pipe.

If intra-group and inter-group rivalry is due to the manner in which the leadership handles grievances, (mainly lacking dispensation of equity) rivalry towards the leadership will result. It will decimate the group. The leader needs to be careful in this regard.

886. It is a decimation rare to avoid,
     If minds of conglomerate[194] do not guild.

If the minds of groupers do not sync (due to the reasons mentioned in couplet 884 and 885) and discard arises, subsequent decline is very difficult to avoid.

887. A lid on its vial do not make it monolith
     A strife ridden group is similar with its blithe.

A vial with its lid in place gives a monolith appearance but in reality it is not so. Similarly group members suffering with internal strife may appear to be very harmonious but it is a false appearance.

---

[194] A conglomerate is a member of a conglomeration.

888. Like gold gets shred by a file
Inner squabbles corrodes group of its stabile.

Filing a block of gold scrapes it into powder. Similarly internal stripe in a family eats away the stability of the family.

889. The dissention may be as small as a sesame broken
Still it bears the chord for group's destruction.

Sesame itself is of very small size. Internal strife of the size of a broken sesame is enough to lead to the destruction of the group.

890. Agree or agree to disagree, if minds can not
It is a life with a snake in a hut.

If minds do not see eye to eye at least they should grant dissentions as acceptable. If this is not possible then living together is like living with a snake in a hut.

Skills to be learnt:

➢ The ability to manage intra and inter conglomerate rivalry as a leader of the community.

Rationale:

➢ Internal enmity arises out of three reasons according to Tiruvalluvar: due to poisonous thoughts amongst the members of a conglomerate (884); the way the community is managed (885) and division of minds (886) among members and inter conglomerate tensions.

Coaching:

➢ How to handle poisonous thoughts due to which members mentally alienate from each other? Poisonous thoughts develop due to the absence of rational thinking (354) and reality testing (355). The leader should train the members in the process of perspective taking. Raw data doesn't help. Only a perspective based on empathic understanding will help. Similarly, however reverent or big may be a source one should look for the truth in what one hears.

➢ Leader should train their members in the skill of perspective taking and reality testing. He should model it for them.

➢ For taking care of the divisions the leader should keep his eyes and ears open and see to that there is no much distance between him and the group members. Any dissention irrespective of its size has the potential to blow up. Therefore the moment a dissension is born the leader should sit with the person or groups and find out the root cause of dissention and identify which of the above two reasons caused it and do the needful by taking corrective steps.

➢ Regarding dissents that arise due to the management the leader should remember he derives his power only from the community or its conglomerates. He should realize that for his own long standing welfare he should totally avoid taking sides in the group. He should ensure that equity of any member of the community doesn't suffer (885).

90

Not Offending Great Men

891. Never slight the power of great men
Appreciators keep this at the top.

People who are capable of appreciation keep this motto at the top:
never discredit the strength of a person (boss) who is powerful
enough to create an impact on your welfare.

892. Showing irreverence to the powerful
Will net in troubles plentiful.

If one doesn't adapt to the powerful men and choose to slight them
then he is in for a crop of unsurmountable trouble.

893. If you desire ruin skip sane counseling
If you want total ruin offend a great man.

Taking the counsel of knowledgeable and experienced person is a
must for those who want to succeed in what they do. However, if
someone wants to sabotage his success he can undertake his work
without consultation. In the case of those who want to go one step
further and want to ruin themselves fully they can achieve it by
offending great man/men!

894. The incapable hurting the capable
Equals clapping to invite the god of death.

A powerless man hurting a very powerful person is equal to a mortal clapping to invite the god of death.

895. After incurring the wrath of a cruelly powerful king
     Wherever they flee they are on death's wing.

     If the wrath of a king, who discharges his power in a cruel manner, is earned the chance to survive even after fleeing to a foreign soil is nil.

896. Burnt by a fire one can survive sometimes
     Who offends powerful man sure into gallows.

     A person burnt by fire sometimes survives but not a person who offends a respectable and therefore a powerful man.

897. Multigreat life and great wealth would mean what?
     If a man of great standing is offended of his might.

     A person may possess great assets and celebrated life but they offer nil security if he earns the anger of a person whose power is born out of a principled life based on *aram* especially by following the principle of equity and acting compassionately on account of that principle.

898. If a man as statured as a hill is degraded
     The clannishly strong degrader (too) is doomed.

     An individual (even) fortified with a strong contingent of clan and kin will meet his end if he offends a powerful man as statured as a hill.

899. If men of great principles are angered
     Kingdom breaks and the king gets ruined.

     If a great man who lives following the principle of *aram* is angered by a king he will lose his kingdom.

900. If a well-disciplined sage is laid to peeve
Even men with limitless support cannot survive.[195]

Even with many strong supporters coming to their rescue men cannot survive the anger of great men after causing their anger.

Skills to be learnt:

➤ The ability to avoid disregarding powerful men under any circumstance. One can disagree but should not insult a powerful man whose power is derived out of his accomplishment through an *aram* based professional and personal life.

Rationale:

➤ Powerful men who are in a position to call the shots in your personal life or career need not be richer or physically more powerful than you. Please remember a powerful person is anyone who can impact your life. Especially, in a democracy anyone who stands for a just cause automatically gets the mass and media support. Public opinion develops in no time and your career gets doomed. Therefore it is very sane to pick up few skills from this chapter.

Coaching:

➤ Two types of powerful people can be discerned. People are powerful because they are strong in their *aram*. The second category is people who are in big position or rich who can command the service of the people in powerful position. A simple idea to find out who is powerful: ask the question whether someone can impact your life or

---

[195] Remember couplet number 204. People who get agitated over an injustice would collect together and act like a single man in punishing the person who did injustice. This would happen irrespective of the fact whether the person has a mass appeal or not. Therefore it is not surprising that in the case of a sage enjoying good will the population will be certainly act in fitting manner.

career if they wish. If the answer is yes then that person is powerful as far as you are concerned. The techniques to avoid confrontation with powerful people are given below:

➤ Do not degrade a person whose moral stature is impeccable and in that quality he is as tall as a mountain. He may be poor, he may have a very low position but soon a momentum will be created around him. Remember the *aram* sphere we have spoken in chapter four.

➤ Do not degrade a person who is rich and powerful than you. Remember it is suicidal to do it or at least very risky. Remember couplet number 759 which says, "Earn wealth in large volumes. It acts like steel in cutting the pride of enemies."

➤ Whether a clothe falls on a thorny bush or bush comes into contact with it the sufferer is clothe. This is true of anyone who rubs his boss on the wrong side

➤ Your career as a subordinate is wedded with your boss normally for a long time. Therefore you should not allow yourself to degrade him in any sense of the word

➤ How to achieve this? Couplet 891 says never degrade a powerful person. Ok! You may ask, "What can I do if my boss deserves it"?

➤ Read the answer:
A boss has his own strengths and weakness. He also prioritizes his work. You may have problems with his priorities and weakness but you may not have problem with his strengths. Make it a policy, "Let me work with my boss through his strengths always; never through his weaknesses or priorities." If you do it for a long time then you will earn the right for offering friendly criticisms also on his weaknesses and priorities in due course of time. This future possibility should assuage your feelings towards him in the present.

➤ Remember you are a great man for doing this.

91

Henpecked Husband

(Adapting to the Ways of Wife)

901. Wife-indulger doesn't accomplish great,
     Therefore, that ill, men of action shall negate.

     Wife centric husband doesn't accomplish great feats. Therefore if a person wants to achieve he should not hang around his wife most of the time.

902. He neglects his pursuit and dots his wife
     His professional outcomes invite a shameful miff.

     If a person busies himself doting his wife then what he accomplish professionally will be significantly nil. This brings great shame and ridicule on him.
     (Most importantly the offspring of the household may not develop into useful citizens. It is likely that daughters become the nagging wives and sons become the henpecked husbands!)

903. **If** a wife doesn't play a modest[196] role
     Midst of good men, a shameful Creole,[197]

   If a wife doesn't play a modest role supporting her husband in his
   efforts, her unusual exalted stature brings in lot of shame to husband
   among his decent friends.

904. **S**ince his acts never reach a powerful phase
     At heavenly abode a wife fearer has no place.

   A henpecked husband who fears to disagree with his wife on any
   matter, in spite of the fact that he wants to, will never be able to
   pursue his path of action dynamically. This lag robs him of his
   opportunity to reach heaven for want of completing soul evolving
   acts.

905. To do good to good people he prefers
     But fearing his wife he defers.

   A henpecked husband might want to help good people. But he would
   desist to do so because he is mortally afraid of his wife who would
   not approve his action.

906. **O**n martial arts he equals the immortals in the field
     But he shirks because he fears losing his wife's fold.

   A person may have a good profile in martial arts equaling the
   immortals in the field but still would not command much respect
   among his people if he is fixated in the fear of losing his wife's sexual
   company and dovetail his behavior to avoid such an eventuality.

---

[196] 'Modest' refers to humility which is needed for husband also.

[197] The word Creole is not used in Tirukkural. The shame that is brought on the
   husband who is overawed by his wife, who could do it because of her husband's
   weakness for her, creates a situation like a Creole language creates on the original
   language. I have tried to capture the meaning in the couplet by the example

907. A women with a sense of humility is a proud find
     Than a man who remains a women's errand.

     A modest woman with a sense of shame commands much respect
     than a husband who carries out the orders of a woman.

908. Neither attends grievances nor acts good
     He behaves as his wife says he should.

     A person who obeys his wife and carries out her whims and fancies
     will never be able to take care of the needs of his best friends or do
     any other good thing at all.

909. Acts of *aram*, high values, other activities in all
     Not found with men who are wives' beck and call.

     Henpecked husbands cannot carry out acts following the precincts of
     aram. They cannot follow great values to guide them in professional
     as well as social and personal life.

910. With a sense of scale and a determined heart,
     An incessant doting men depart.

     Men who have got a strong sense of measure and determination will
     not have the folly of indulging in incessant and excessive sex with
     their wives.

Skills to be learnt:

➢ An ability to neutralize the dominance of wife and establish an equal
   status with her.

Rationale:

➢ A henpecked husband spends most of his time, energy and money
   at his wife's service. Because of this he is not as effective as he can

in his personal and professional life. This is a disorder and therefore it cannot be gain said than it should be avoided at any cost with suitable counseling.

Coaching:

➢ Couplet number 904,906 and 910 can be put together to formulate a solution. Couplet 904 says that a henpecked husband i.e., one who allows his wife to dominate him has a fear for his wife. What fear is it? Couplet 906 gives the answer: fear of losing sex. The strategy suggested by Tiruvalluvar to overcome the dependency and fear is given in couplet 910: let the man regulate the frequency of sex. In other words he and his wife decide when to have sex independently and with mutual consent have it. Sex is not something like an offer which his wife can put on and put off. How to achieve this?

Look below:

➢ Husband should be given a good exposure to the subject of sexuality.
➢ Especially it should be made clear to him that sexual urge is common for both male and female.
➢ When she deprives him of sex unknowingly she also deprives herself: like pressure builds up in him it builds up in her too.
➢ Having a reasonable frequency like once in a week is fine. But feeling that one misses something if the frequency is reduced if a husband increases the frequency he becomes an addict to sex. The same thing happens with his wife also. But since it is she who needs to consent she can always make it conditional to him retaining her supremacy over her husband.
➢ To break this Thiruvalluvar tells the husband to use his sense of measure (910). That means a healthy reflection of how many times he needs sex. The questions he should ask is: Do I feel I miss some standards which I have set for myself regarding frequency of sex? Do I spend my time fancying on sex even when I am at work? Do I allow myself to be tinged throughout the day while at work and outside work with sexual thought which gets expressed in behavior

like flirting? In short how can I come out of the lusty atmosphere I create for myself?

➢ Thiruvalluvar says (derivable from 901 and 902): Concentrate on your work. Honestly engage yourself in work and start achieving success and taste the taste of success. This helps you to break your addiction for sex. Sexual energy can be sublimated through work.

➢ At home behave as if nothing has happened. Give some excuse when you decide to refuse a demand of her. Don't cut all her demands abruptly. Always attend and do the needful to meet her demands which are reasonable. By the by remember she is the gift of God to you and deserves all your love and affection. You are not manipulating her in any sense. You are only employing some strategy to mend her.

➢ Remember sex is a need for her also. Tell this to yourself as many times as possible and be very sure that days of mutually consented sex will come in your life instead of you beg for it and she puts it in your begging bowl reluctantly!

92

Wanton Women

(Sex worker)

911. She doesn't need love she needs money
      Her sweet words therefore breed ignominy.

      Since wanton women use sweet words not out of love but out of an
      eye on men's money the company of such women brings no joy but
      dishonor.

912. They measure the gain and release equal love,
      Therefore tossing them is what one should give.

      Wanton women use sweet words and display fitting etiquettes equal
      to gains. Therefore though they may appear very refined on account
      of their exhibits those exhibits should be considered as part of their
      trade and their company should be discarded like an undesirable
      substance.

913. The false embrace of a women in flesh trade fares
      Like a corpse in dark one chooses to caress.

      The women in flesh trade embraces without any attendant feelings.
      Therefore choosing to embrace her is as good as embracing a women's
      corpse in a dark mortuary.

914. He who researches and finds compassion values
     Never embraces woman for whom only money values.

Men who are in the habit of searching for a meaning in anything they
do from the point of view of compassion towards fellow humanity
and all living organisms will not chose to embrace a wanton woman.
Because in their opinion the women in sex trade have the right to
live a descent life like their counter parts in family life and therefore
it is an obligation for them to help such women to rehabilitate rather
than perpetuate them in the trade.

915. Great man of healthy intellect enjoy not at all
     The base pleasures the women keep for all.

Basically, speaking mentally healthy persons further accentuated
by great scholarship epitomizing into intellect would not enjoy the
embrace of wanton women because they know how much pain and
agony the women in sex trade undergo.
(Remember mental health flourishes with love, sense of shame,
oppuravu, empathy and truth. One may or may not have in them in
full measure as most people could be but an effort in that direction
is good enough for day to day activities which are challenging at the
least.)

916. He who fosters his wellbeing never embraces
     A woman who on her mean assets boasts.

A man who is interested in his wellbeing will never embrace a woman
who seeks to sell herself boasting about her mean assets (of flesh),
dance and show.

917. Man whose heart is not contended embraces
     Woman with her heart elsewhere reciprocates.

Those men who do not manage their sexual needs with their wives in
a mutually beneficial manner, which strengthens the family bondage,

end up as frustrated men. Only such men seek the services of sex workers who while serving them allow their mind and heart to foray about other upcoming customers.

918. For him who lacks a querying mind
      'Oh! She is a heavenly beauty' – is how a harlot is found.

Save those who are basically enquiry oriented for others the deceptive embrace of wanton woman is as great as by a heavenly woman. (The Tamil word *anangu* is used by Thiruvalluvar to denote a heavenly woman. But sometimes it also refers to a devil. This devilish woman is caricatured as attracting young men by her charm and killing them through her embrace. The fact that a wanton woman slowly but surely ruins her customers is brought out by this example.)

919. Senseless mean men lead themselves into hellish mire,
      The best decked harlot's soft shoulders they hire.

Men who have no sense gets deeply mired. The mire is the hell which is none other than the shoulders of a well decked wanton woman.

920. Men are removed from goddess Thiru[198]
      When they hire liquor, gamble and two minded wore.

Men who are prone to get destroyed of their wealth go to wanton women characterized by their fickle mindedness and in addition develop connections with liquor and gambling.

Skills to be learnt:

➢   Ability to keep away from a wanton woman (a sex worker).

---

[198] *Thiru* is another name of Goddess Lakshmi – the goddess of fortune in Hindu mythology. Thiruvalluvar has used mythological artifacts with specific connotation suitable for the context.

Rationale:

➤ Couplets 917 and 918 give reasons why married and single men seek sex workers. Both of them call for introspection on the part of men who seek sex outside marriage.

Coaching:

➤ Couplet 917 says men who are not contended within their heart about the sexual satisfaction in their married life go to sex workers. Couplet 918 says those who are not capable of researching and finding out the facts hold the sex worker as someone great. This implies they find attributes in a sex worker which they cannot find out from their wives. Some techniques to overcome this are as follows:

➤ Tell him this: "You may think the wanton woman speaks sweet words which you don't find with your wife (911). Remember you have to earn love and affection from your wife by showing it to her whenever she needs it. The same is true of her towards you. That means if the marriage suffers from lack of love and affection between you two, sit together and find out what is holding you both from showing it. If you or your wife think that you or she is more privileged than the other for any reason it is a mistake. Wife and husband are equal in the institution of family. Always remember this: your wife wants love from you whereas your woman in the brothel wants your money. Sexual incompatibility or having no satisfaction in sex may be due to a number of sexual disorders. Luckily all of them are treatable. Take treatment from a sexologist to overcome the difficulties utilizing the money you spend on the sex workers."

➤ Tell him this: "The wanton woman may look beautiful in her bangles. Her talk may be sweet. She may have nice manners and sophisticated etiquette. You may enjoy the moment of being with her. But know this: she is a fake. She is after your money. As soon as your money is exhausted she will not let you in into her chamber (912)."

➤ To strengthen the above thoughts in the client you can present an imagery. Tell him this: "Imagine you are with a wanton woman in a room. For some mysterious reason the room is not lit. But you don't mind it, and get nearer to her, and start embracing her. After sometime you realize the 'woman' is a corpse. Imagine how your experience will be. In reality your experience with a corpse and a wanton woman are not significantly different because neither the live or dead woman experience sex along with you.

➤ The wanton woman is like an apparatus. Do you think you can enjoy sex with such a non-participating woman? You are only deceiving yourself if you think you can (913)."

➤ Tell him this: "People who are research oriented will not go to wanton woman. I would like to request you to familiarize yourself about the pathetic life conditions of women who are forced into sex work by their circumstances. Try to decipher how they also aspired for a quality life but ended up in sex work. You must know how since this is a flourishing business touts and thugs forcefully push women when they are young into this, and once they are in even their own parents abandon them once and for all. This business which is the handy work of thugs flourishes only because of men like you who support this. If you are a compassionate person i.e., you will do your bit to support her equity you will not help to perpetuate this profession (914)."

➤ The next imagery can be developed around health. The individual may be requested to get imagery as vividly as possible about the life of having been infected with venereal diseases and AIDS or total economic breakdown to impress them about the consequences. Contrast this aftermath with the lures the wanton woman who offers boasting about her assets.

➤ Tell him this: "The apparent wellness displayed by her is not wellness at all. It is a diseased one. If you are ripe in wisdom about what constitutes well being you will not go to partake in it (915)."

➤ Tell him this: "If it is true that your wellness is a concern for you will never ever go after a woman who boasts of her feminine assets and attract men folk (915)".

➤ Tell him this: "You may imagine the wanton woman with whom you spend your time and money to be in superlative in all respects compared to your wife. This is utterly wrong. Compare your wife and her point by point and find out where each one of them stands.

If you are a gentle man who will honor the equity of your wife and that of the wanton woman you will always find your wife way ahead of the wanton woman for the single reason she is concerned about you whereas your women in trade doesn't.

➢ Tell him this: "You may consider the silky shoulders of the wanton woman as great. It is not really so. Her shoulders are the hellish mud you immerse yourself slowly (919)."

➢ Tell him this: "Another danger in going after wanton woman is it brings with it other evils namely alcohol and gambling as all the three are found together (920)."

93

Being a Teetotaler

(Drunkard)

921. Foes do not fear those who 'live' in booze,
Their glory amongst others too they lose.

Enemies get rid of their fear of men and women who madly love
intoxicating toddy (a variety prepared out of palm juice) and dedicate
their life to it. Apart from that they also lose whatever good name
and fame they had earlier.

922. In *Sandrones*[199] hearts drunkards are not held
Non aspirers with drink shall get geld.

Those who do not care to occupy a space at the hearts of *sandrone*s
shall take to
drinking liquor!

923. A drunkard creates distress even on the face of his mother
Then how the face of *sandrone* could be happier?

---

[199] A *Sandrone* is one whose character is built on these attributes: love, humility,
benevolence (social entrepreneurship), empathy and truthfulness

Even a mother shows distress on her face when she happens to see her drunkard son. Then is it a wonder that a *sandrone* never shows happiness at the sight of him?

924. **T**he good lady 'shame' turns her face away,
The disgusting vice of drunkenness moves her away.

Lady Sense of Shame who lives in sane men turns her back on the drunkard who is a defaulter on *aram* and therefore a serious offender.

925. It is foolishness born out of purposelessness
Paying and buying unconsciousness.

It is foolishness born out of purposelessness that a man pays and buys unconsciousness.

926. **B**oth *thunjinaar* and *seththar* mean dead,
Liquor and poison drinkers be similarly held.

Thunjinaar or *seththar* in Tamil mean dead. Similarly we can hold that drinker of poison and drinker of alcohol mean the same. Both commit suicide.

927. Psyching their stories the locals laugh
At them who sip palm wine and murmur.

A drunkard drinks and falls. From his murmurings the village comes to know his inside stories and laugh.

928. "I had no joy" don't drink saying so,[200]
     That hidden at the heart escapes during the go.

     To drink some people find reasons like, "I have not had any joy."
     This self-pity, Tiruvalluvar says, is not a justification because what
     you have hidden from others becomes known once you are under the
     influence of liquor which makes you a laughing stock and also brings
     new troubles which will offset the joy you had through drinking.

929. Searching a person under the water with a torch[201] is unwise
     Trying to make sense with an intoxicated is likewise.

     Once a person is under the heavy influence of liquor to make him
     understand anything or trying to reason with him is as foolish as
     trying to locate a person remaining under the water with a torch of
     fire. Burning fire can not be taken inside the water. So also reasoning
     with a drunkard.

930. When a sober witnesses an intoxicated
     In his heart will not his degradation get reflected?

     When a person observes another intoxicated person's plight (in the
     midst of his ridiculers and degraders) will he not reflect what would
     have been his position (in the presence of similar ridiculers)?

Skills to be learnt:

  ➤   To take the decision: "I will not drink here after."

---

[200] It seems self-pity justifies drinking. Tiruvalluvar says that the self pitying should
       be avoided because once a person drinks to come out this mood of self pity he ends
       up revealing his inner secrets earning the laughter of bystanders. As a result he loses
       his self esteem which is more pitiable than the pity of not being able to drink.
[201] A small handy burning bundle of twigs of bushy plants.

Rationale:

- ➢ Alcoholism is something that results from the initial decision to drink by the individual. (He may take the decision as a temporary measure to escape from some stress or just to test how it feels.) This idea emerges out of the chapter in an indirect but clear manner. All the ten couplets show it as a decision of the individual to take to heavy drinking. The couplets also say it is a great mistake on the part of the individual. If it is a decision of the individual then it is natural that the individual can also re decide to leave the habit.

Coaching:

- ➢ The addict can be counseled on the following lines (psycho education stage in a de addiction program):
- ➢ A drunkard is always slighted by all including kith and kin. A person delivers the greatest blow to his self-respect by taking to heavy drinking (921).
- ➢ If a person doesn't care about what impressions he leaves in the minds of *sandrones* then he is welcome to drink (922).
- ➢ Let him know even his mother who will forgive him for any of his mistakes will not do so for his wayward behaviors which he is likely to exhibit as a result of heavy drinking (923).
- ➢ People are scared to be the butt of ridicule at the hands of their well wishers and reference group. Sense of shame protects people from engaging themselves in undesirable behaviors earning the ridicule. In due course of time heavy drinkers lose their capacity to maintain the sense of shame which moves them into the trajectory of committing a number of crimes making their life heavily complicated (924).
- ➢ Indulging in heavy drinking indicates lack of a sense of what constitutes best for oneself (925).
- ➢ Drinking is suicidal. There is no difference between drinking alcohol and drinking poison. While poison instantly kills a person alcohol kills slowly (926).
- ➢ A drunkard becomes the entertainment for the people in the town (927).

➢ The sense of inhibition leaves a drunkard. He spills the beans about some of the never to reveal secrets of his life and suffer severe degradation of esteem in the minds of their reference group. Some times this will bring new troubles offsetting the so called joy he had under the spell of a drink. Therefore let him not resort to the excuse that he never had a joy in life and therefore he deserves one through drinking alcohol (928).

➢ Let the drunkards be aware that their friends and well wishers will not attempt to bail them out from their condition for the simple reason that they know such an effort is tantamount to searching a person under the water with a torch of burning fire (929).

➢ A drunkard when he is not in a drunken state may watch another person under it being ridiculed by others. He should know his case would not be any different. He should be therefore be ashamed of such a situation and avoid consuming alcohol. (930).

94

Gambling

931. Gamble not! You may win but the win is a bait
Like a wormy hook is out of fish's sight.

Gambling should be totally avoided. You should do so all the more
when you win. Because that winning is the bait – the worm wearing
hook – which a fish mistakes for food.
(Intermittent winning reinforces the gambling behavior so strongly
that the gambler goes on and on until he loses all his property.
Therefore never get conditioned!)

932. **W**ins once and loses hundred times but persists
Could there be a 'way-out' so that he escapes?

A gambler very rarely wins. Still he continues. Could there be a
way for him to break from this compulsive habit of gambling? (A
gambler becomes conditioned due to the intermittent win which is
very powerful than regular or predictable win.)

933. If he shouts the numbers at dice day in and day out
His means of sustenance will march out.

(Gamblers use a hexagonal nut with numbers marked on its faces.
They will roll the nut on a mat announcing a preferred number.)
If a person incessantly announces his preferred numbers (i.e.

continuously gambles) his wealth and well being will continuously roll out making him a pauper.

934. Gambling stymies the status of the player
None other so good in making him a pauper.

Pain in the form of degradation and loss of respect caused by gambling is colossal. Further none can beat it in awarding poverty!

935. Dice, chamber and in his skill he is prouder
Never leaving them he becomes a pauper.

A gambler who becomes cocky about his skills in gambling, about his so called insights of gambling skills and knowledge of the character of gambling houses needs to be bailed out as quickly as possible. Otherwise he will become a pauper in no time.

936. With empty stomach they are writhed
With dice, the misfortune they are closeted.

Gamblers do not eat properly and wreath in pain. This condition is because they are hoodwinked by the goddess of misfortune.

937. Ancestral wealth and nobility are lost
If in the morning itself the die is cost.

If a person makes gambling as a full time profession and enter the gambling house daily in the morning itself he will squander the comforts of life he is used to and his nobility.

938. It ruins wealth, inculcates lying, strips compassion
And unsurmountable sorrows are its last predication.

Gambling ruins wealth of the gambler. It inculcates in him the practice of lying. He loses the sense of justice. This foretells that unsurmountable sorrows are waiting for him.

939. Attire, wealth, food, recognition and education – these five
Gamblers never have.

The three things namely attire, wealth and food are not obtainable for a gambler because he may not have the means to buy them. He will also lose social esteem once the world around him comes to know of his condition.

940. Man hopes to live despite serious disease and pain
Gambler hopes against hope despite no gain.

In spite of excruciating pain and very dim prospects to recover from a deadly disease or from the repercussions of an advancing age human beings aspire and hope against hope to live for some more years. It is the same story with gamblers. They always nourish a hope that they will win one day win and recover all they have lost. This makes them to cling to their game.

Skills to be learnt:

➢   Ability to take the decision: "I will say good bye to gambling and abide by my decision."

Rationale:

➢   Like alcoholism gambling also starts from an initial decision. The addiction stage may have the touch of habit formation. But that comes only later (933). Like in the case of alcoholism a re decision regarding gambling need to be taken and adhered to in time before it becomes a habit or addiction. The contents of this chapter show how the life of a gambler deteriorates because of his gambling habit. This can be used to exhort him to revert his decision regarding gambling and strictly adhere to the changed decision.

Coaching:

Tell him the following:

> "You need not feel sorry or guilty about what I am going to say. It is bad luck you are into this. You can walk out of this provided you decide and stick to it. There is nothing special about you which make you to take to this. Please carefully listen to what I am about to say."

> "Beware you may win some times. But that win is the bait. Don't bite it and get destroyed like a fish which bits the hook considering it as a meal. It is time for you to escape from biting that hook (931)

> Despite losing again and again you continue to gamble. It only indicates that you have no idea of what a life of wellbeing constitutes and ways and means of attaining it. It is unfortunate you are ill equipped in life skills. Ask the following questions to yourself: A) Am I not putting my personal and social life in danger because of my habit? B) This can be a profession if and only if it has some fool proof methods. Can I without doubt claim there are fool proof methods? In the absence of any gambler whom I know always succeeds can I really think this is a profession at all? (932)

> If you keep on rolling the dice know it for sure you will become a pauper in no time (933).

> No other habit is as colossal as gambling in destroying the wellbeing of a human and destroying his life once and for all (934).

> If you think you are especially skilled in gambling ask the following questions and honestly answer them: A) Do you honestly believe that there is any thing called skill in gambling? B) Do you honestly believe that you have that skill in abundance compared to others? C) Is there anything like gambling place characteristics which one can master? E) Do you honestly believe that you know the characters of each gambling halls you frequent? If you answer these questions honestly you will find all your answers are negative. Especially one

point is very important: there is nothing like gambling skill which one can master (935).

> Beware the very fact that you don't eat properly, you wreath in pain shows you are already in the company of goddess of misfortune (936).

> Beware not only what you have personally earned your ancestral property also will disappear in no time if you continue to gamble (937).

> Beware you will soon descend to lies and scams earning the enmity of fellow gamblers and you will lose your sense of equity. The state of affairs soon will push you into multiple pains (938).

> Beware you condition will deplete day by day leaving you with no proper dress, wealth and food. You will lose your status in the society. Your education will take a beat (939).

> Beware of one thing. You continue to gamble due to one important reason. You, very secretly, nourish a thought like this: "I will win one day which will wipe all my loss." Poor man your hope is only similar to a seriously ill person who nourishes the hope that he would recover from the disease (940). His hope is futile. So too yours!"

95

Medicine

941. Either an increase or a decrease each causes disease
The learned thought they are three gases.

The three aspects that affect the body are air, phlegm and bile. The learned say an imbalance among these three cause disease.

942. Body needs no medicine if what is eaten is digested
Before new food is ingested.

There is no need to take medicine provided you take your next meal only when the previous meal is fully digested and you have a fully matured hunger.

943. Know your digesting ability
Eat only that quantity.

The quantum of meal is decided based on the digestive power and quantum of requirement (calories needed, and richness of the items in terms of calories). Longevity is assured if best practices in this regard are followed.

944. What foods are easily digested make note of,
Eat when in full hunger adoptive meals thereof.

Make a list of what food items are easily digestible to you and what food items you like and are acceptable to your body and age, and eat them only when your hunger is fully developed.

945. Eat appropriate foods; fill the stomach little less,
This is your option to leave the body painless.

Choosing the foods which are appropriate (in terms of one's calories requirement) and digesting ability and consuming leaving a little empty space in the stomach is the right procedure to avoid painful diseases.

946. Joy stays with an eater who knows how little to eat
Disease stays with one who thrills in eat.

People who have learnt it through observation that eating little less than what is needed to fill the stomach and strictly follow it live a joyful life. Similarly it is also a fact that people who eat for the sake of taste and strain the stomach by stuffing it more than what it could process, suffer from one disease or the other.

947. Eating limitless, disregarding one's digestive power
Leads to limitless diseases forever.

There are some who do not observe and learn how much quantity their stomach can digest with ease. They crave tasty foods and eat limitless making their bodies' home for several diseases.

948. Identify the disease, its cause and method of cure
With timed action, wellness ensure.[202]

---

[202] Prof. Devaneya Pavanar PhD., a renowned Tamil Scholar and well known Thirukkural commentator says the system identified in this couplet (and the chapter) is Siddha. Siddha system of medicine, one of the four approved systems of medicine by the Government of India is a system which originated among Tamils.

After identifying the disease, its critical cause, and deciding the method of cure, timed dispensation is needed to ensure cure.

949. [203]Patient's data, seriousness of the disease and the time – these facts
The learned takes into account and acts.

Patient's body type, age, strength of the body, resilience and the stage of the disease and the season are the parameters to be taken into consideration by the practitioner.

950. **P**atient, doctor, medicine and the process support – the four
Their excellence makes the core.

Each one of the aspects – patient, practitioner, medicine and the persons who administer the process (nurse, family members etc) – are equally important for the successful cure of a disease.

Skills to be learnt:

➢ Adopting a medically prudent food habit and the needed attitude to fight diseases.

Rationale:

➢ There is an internal mechanism in the body to take care of its health. Food habits provide the mechanics for it. Tiruvalluvar pays much attention to food habit as a means of maintaining health. Each couplet has a message in this regard. Also it appears very easy to follow. The central message of the chapter is: Food and your food habits are your medicine. No separate medicine is needed if you develop a healthy food habit.

---

[203] It appears Thiruvalluvar in this couplet covers the patient's age, body size and the seriousness of the disease to determine the dosage and the time of administration of medicine.

Coaching:

The technique is presented in the form of 10 recommendations one from each of the couplet:

- ➤ Air, phlegm and bile are the three substances which should be in balance in the body for maintaining health (941).
- ➤ There is no need for medicine if you eat after fully digesting the earlier eat.(942)
- ➤ Your requirement in terms of calories and the quantum digestible to you should decide the quantum of your intake (943).

Eat food easily digestible to you. Do not eat foods which your system doesn't easily digest. Follow a strict regimen in this.

- ➤ Eat only when you have full hunger (944).
- ➤ Never eat a food which your digestive system doesn't accept (945).
- ➤ Be assured if you take the precautions into consideration mentioned so far and eat no disease will visit (946).
- ➤ Beware you will end up making up your body a home for several diseases if you break the rule regarding digesting ability.(947)

In the unfortunate event of a client getting afflicted with a disease what a practitioner should do?

- ➤ Let him carefully diagnose the disease; find out the true cause; and work out the means of cure and administer the cure adjusting to the constraints of the patient and his situation.(948)
- ➤ Let him take into account patient's food and eating habits, body type, age, strength of the body, resilience and the stage of the disease and the season into consideration while deciding the treatment regimen.(949)
- ➤ Let him beware of that medicine has these four aspects to be taken care of: the condition of the diseased person, the skill sets of the practitioner, the medicine and the process support (nurse, family members etc.). The expertise of the doctor is very important. If

he is less competent the other three are vitiated. New and serious complications can arise. Patient also needs to have a proper appreciation of his symptoms keenly so that he can explain the same to the doctor. Moreover he is supposed to follow the instruction of the doctor which he would do only if he really believes in the system of medicine and attentive to what he is told. Therefore the doctor has to find out his attitude towards treatment and cure and educate him properly. In the modern days we have counselors for achieving this who serve as the interface between the doctor and the patient. The remedy or medicine need to be appropriate to the disease and the body condition of the patient. The process support means how the medicine is administered and whether the patient's discomfort is alleviated or not. The supporters like the nurse or patient's care takers/relatives should be compassionate (950).

96

Family Lineage

(The qualities fostered by a great family)

951. **N**ot for others but only for those of great family
Sense of shame and equity come naturally.

(In this couplet and others of the present chapter Tiruvalluvar
has highlighted the importance of family as a training ground for
inculcating several desirable strengths in human beings.)
Only individuals hailing from great families (families are held as
great if they have best policies and practices in place, not based on
any other criteria) exhibit the good qualities of equity and a sense
of shame.

952. **S**ense of humility, best practices and honesty
Men of great families, on these never show travesty.

Members hailing from great families' faithfully adhere to the
good human qualities of humility, following best practices and
truthfulness.

953. Pleasing smile, giving, kind words and not despising
Are the attributes of a truthful family's sailing.

Receiving fellow human beings with a pleasing smile, offering them
material help and speaking sweet words and never putting them

down are the qualities found with individuals hailing from truthful families.

954. Even for the consideration of multiples of a million
To mean acts, men of great family refuse to be driven.

Individuals hailing from great families will never take to meanness in their activities even if they are to get millions of gold coins. (Gold coins are used only to indicate some currency).

955. The resources of great families for gifting may reduce
Still on *panbu*[204] these families never compromise.

The volume of what they gift may dip due to economic downturn met by the family but still men from great families do not dip in their *panbu*.

956. In spite deceit they never act unethically
Since they are committed to the creed of their family.

Individuals hailing from families where great panbu runs as a heritage would not stoop to unethical ways even when provoked by deceitful hurts by their enemies.

957. As the black spots on the moon are conspicuous
The blame of a family, as lofty as the sky, gets the focus.

The blames of persons born in a family held as high as sky by others stand highlighted like the black spots in the moon are always spotted.

---

[204] The word *panbu* represents qualities which are listed in the first three couplets: equity, sense of shame, best practices, truth, humility, pleasing nature, and philanthropy, displaying sweet and kind words, and not degrading any one. The present translator is of the opinion that the word character which comes very close to the word *panbu* may not be as comprehensive as the word *panbu*. Therefore he chooses to use the word *panbu*.

958. **A**mong the good qualities if unkindness is spotted
The quality of his family stands suspected.

A person may have several of the good qualities bequeathed in a high family lineage. But if he shows unkindness in the midst of kindness it is a good enough reason to suspect his claim that his family is a great one.

(Some families may be held as great by the community. It reality they may not deserve that accolade. This aspect is highlighted in this couplet. Tiruvalluvar has used the Tamil term *narinmai* to denote lack of love. In the same canto couplet number 953 says pleasing smile, compassionate helping, using kind words and not using words degrading a visitor are found among the high born. All these acts are operational parts of love. Therefore if someone shows the absence of any of these that may indicate his family is bogus vis-à-vis good qualities.)

959. Growth of plant shows whether the soil is good or bad
Member's word shows the families they had[205].

The growth of the plant shows the nutritional status of the soil. Likewise a man's words show the nature of the family in which he grew. If the elders in the family do not nurture the great qualities in the children they would have no opportunity to learn them. The job has all the seriousness of a penance. Recall couplet number seventy: The return gift a son owes his dad: //'What a hard work his dad has made,' heard.)

960. **I**f wellness is desired a sense of shame be practiced
If a family brand is desired let humility across the board be adopted.

With a strong sense of shame and acting at its call our wellness is assured. Similarly if we desire our family to enjoy a brand name for nobility then we should be humble with everyone.

---

[205] Past tense is used to translate the idea of 'how they were brought up.'

Skills to be learnt:

➤ Ability to practice *panbu*.

Rationale:

➤ *Panbu* is a generic term that stands for several qualities:

   ➤ Equity
   ➤ Sense of shame
   ➤ Humility
   ➤ Truthfulness,
   ➤ Following best practices in carrying out an activity
   ➤ Giving pleasant audience to any one in interaction
   ➤ Charitable
   ➤ Using sweet words and never despising

➤ Tiruvalluvar is very firm in stating that *panbu* is learned at home (958&959). An individual is taught the quality of *panbu* through modeling by the family members who are seniors like father and mother and other relatives.

➤ It goes without saying that all these qualities are desirable strengths for a person. A married couple who plan to run a household and members like parents would do well if they take steps to learn these skills and take every step to instill them in their offspring. By doing so, they will be immensely contributing to the nation. A country needs such feed stock for building valuable human resource.

Coaching:

➤ Every member of the family may familiarize himself/herself with the eight qualities that constitute the generic quality *panbu*. A little reflection will show that the qualities of equity and sense of shame essentially call for the presence of all the remaining six qualities. (958&959)

- ➢ Sense of equity can be strengthened in a child by allowing her to enjoy it first. The child is the future adult. Whenever a decision is made regarding him asking for his opinion and accommodating it wherever it is possible and firmly saying no where it is not possible explaining the reason moral as well as practical to him and sticking to that decision is the first step.

- ➢ A person who earns his equity the right way will give it to others also in the right way.

- ➢ Regarding developing sense of shame parents can make it as a positive thing.

- ➢ The notion of sense of shame can be profitably employed if we can take the ridicule of others as a feedback given in a hoarse language. In this way the child will learn to show the necessary importance for feed back in a ridicule and act accordingly.

- ➢ The persons in a family who are parents or in parental position should not fail on any of the qualities. If they happen to fail they should apologize readily and make amends before the children and other members. The message that while everyone should take at most care to avoid any mistake it is ok if someone does make a mistake provided he apologizes and decides that he would never do it again and stick to it.

- ➢ Nobody should take the moral high ground and ridicule others. (Hardly anybody can keep himself or herself totally pure with regard to these qualities. This will be established in due course of time.)

- ➢ A system of friendly confrontation may be installed in the family which empowers any member irrespective of age or status to question the other who faults on any of these qualities. An alert family can install these qualities in all its members.

- ➢ Every time a mistake takes place immediately it should be analyzed in terms of the qualities namely, lacking in equity, shameful act, a bad practice, falsehood, lack of humbleness, lack of humor, lack of benevolence, lack of speaking sweetly and ridicule.

> ➤ After fixing it with reference to one or more of the qualities responsibility should be fixed and amends be demanded from the person concerned. If this is done regularly throughout the day by everyone with every other person in a friendly way all the members will learn these qualities.

97

Self-respect

(Dignity)

961. Indispensably significant benefits they may yield
Leave them aside if your self-respect you cannot field.

By pursuing an act you may get important benefits which you
may consider indispensable. Still drop the plan if the act involves a
degradation of your dignity.

962. Desiring esteem they never do an unappreciable act
Since they need accolades only through Manly act.

It is true men want appreciation. But even under threat self-respecting
men will never do an act compromising on the principle of equity.
They would rather insist appreciation for their acts which they carry
out without compromising on self-respect because carrying out an act
compromising on the principle of equity is against their self-respect.

963. When prosperity arrives humility is wanted
With shrinking prosperity self-respect be hoisted.

Showing disrespect to fellow human beings is an attack on their
dignity and therefore should be avoided. In the case of rich men
since there is a scope for this to occur the person concerned should be
cautious enough to be humble to avoid this. In the case of poor men
since they are vulnerable for disrespect by rich people they should be

careful enough to assert their dignity with them. (They can achieve this by their accomplishments in fields other than economics and reap pride which will discourage the rich to degrade them.)

964. A fallen hair reaches a trash
A man whose self-respect is lost meets similar crash.

A hair which enjoys so much of care is trashed once it falls from the head. Similarly a person who loses his dignity due to his inglorious acts is held on par with a fallen hair.

965. Hill-like man he is but miniaturizes in status
When he makes a mistake as small as the berry called abrus.

A man because of his dignified acts may have attained a status as high as a hill. But when he does an undignified act he reduces himself to the size of a small berry called abrus.

966. Not estimable and on account of it *puthezhir ulagam* is inaccessible
Then why you go behind your despisers? Horrible!

Esteem earned from the beneficiaries of one's altruistic act is soul evolving and therefore ridden with the prospect of attaining heavenly abode. Whereas the act of waiting upon those who despise is of no use whatsoever. They may appreciate the service rendered but that appreciation doesn't equal the earlier one. Therefore one should not stoop to forgo one's self-respect.

967. It is better, 'he is dead', is heard
Rather than a, 'a despiser's sustenance he has availed'.

It is preferable to be referred to as, 'someone who is dead' rather than as, 'someone who stoops to the level of availing a life support from a person who despised him.'

968. Can this body-thriven-life be a solution
To redeem the self-respect lost for providing it the nutrition?

Resources spent on a medicine can be reduced by resuming work
after regaining health. Whereas if a person loses his self-respect in
order to sustain his lively hood the self-respect lost can never be
redeemed by the life thus saved. (Since living a life upholding self-
respect under any condition is a soul evolving endeavor one has to
uphold his self-respect at any cost. It should not be lost even for the
sake of sustaining one's life.)

969. Removal of hair causes the death to a yak
Men of similar flair die when their honor should muck.

A yak will die instantly when it loses its hair. Similarly a man, who
holds his honor as his essence, dies when he loses his dignity.

970. Men end their life when shame visits them
The world adorns in worship their esteem.

The world reveres those who choose to end their life when they fall
into disrepute on account of trading off their self-respect for some
consideration. Since they give their life as a price for their mistake
the world praise and salutes them.

Skills to be learnt:

➤ Up holding your self-respect.

Rationale:

➤ Self-respect is a commodity which as God's children all of us are
equally gifted. A sane humanity respects the self-respect of all its
members. Wealth, health, education and status in offices or any
other consideration with regard to a person should not be used to
undermine the self-respect of a fellow individual. The soul of a man

who makes every effort to uphold his self-respect matures and a fully matured soul reaches god.

Coaching:

➤ The couplet 961 provides the technique to protect ones self-respect and couplet 962 gives the policy

➤ Discard any thing that comes with a tag of undermining your self-respect (961).

➤ Make this as your policy: 'I want appreciation and positive feedback from my fellow humans. But let them not expect from me an inestimable act as a price (962).'

➤ If you are rich and/or in a high position you are likely to be dismissive of others who are not equal to you. Therefore be careful to practice humility always. If you don't, people will ignore you making you to feel that your self-respect is undermined by them. As a result you will become more indifferent to them and it becomes a vicious cycle (963)!

➤ Whereas if you are a poor man or in a lower position you are likely to be ill-treated by others who are above you. Therefore be very firm to resist such a tendency. What could empower in that situation are your accomplishments. You can have a reasonable pride in your accomplishments which you can make use of to stand them (963). If that is not possible don't have any interaction with people who are rich and are likely to be indifferent to you. Do not go to such places at any cost (963).

➤ Always remember you will lose the appreciation of others the moment you descend from the moral high ground. Remember a fallen hair is trashed without any remorse (964)!

➤ You may have built reputation as tall as a hill. But it will be demolished in no time if you do the small mistake of undermining the self-respect of others or acting against the common wellbeing of the society (965).

➤ Remember if your acts do not have altruism as the principal component they would not win public-esteem. For the same reason they would not usher you into heaven. Therefore why do you go behind a person who despises you, undermining your self-respect? (956).

➢ Never cringe before a person who does not respect you. Rather than do without it even it is to cost you, your life (967).

➢ Remember you are a mortal. Acting undermining your self-respect is not a solution to win death. Then why you behave losing your self-respect? (968).

➢ The world has full of stories of great self-respecting persons who gave away their life when they committed mistake bringing disrepute to themselves. But the beauty is after their death the world worshiped them for the supreme cost they paid in repentance of the mistake they have done (970).

98

Esteem

(Self-Esteem)[206]

971. Esteem rests with a willful and vigorous mind
It is degrading when one decides to live leaving it behind.

Willful and vigorous effort is the real means by which a man wins esteem. If somebody abandons such a mindset and lives, it is equivalent to demeaning himself.
(The Tamil word used by Tiruvalluvar to denote fully energized or charged effort is *verukkai* chapter number 60 deals with it.)

972. Men are born similar but later statuses[207] are not similar,
Differential excellence in work makes them dissimilar.

Status is decided by the esteem people enjoy in the minds of fellow human beings on account of the excellence they show in their work

---

[206] There is a difference between this chapter and the chapter under the title "Fame". While fame refers to the appreciation by the public at large especially by the beneficiaries of the fame winning altruistic acts, esteem refers to the appreciation on account of one's performance or excellence in performance at his work. This esteem can take two shapes – the one developing within the individual about himself or it can be the appreciation by the colleagues/peers/organization over the excellent performance of the individual.

[207] Status is the esteem offered by fellow humans.

not by their birth. At the time of birth all are similar in the statuses/ esteem they enjoy because no achievement is possible at that age[208].

973. **O**ccupying a high position[209] never confers a high esteem
Nor low position confers a low esteem.

The high position occupied by a person will not earn him esteem if he doesn't make great achievements. Similarly if a person occupying a low position accomplishes he will be esteemed high.

974. **O**nly by her hardened determination a woman remains chaste
Esteem, only by a regimen of hard work men hoist.

A woman by her hardened determination maintains fidelity. Similarly humans only through their determined effort could achieve high esteem.

975. **M**en who esteem themselves carry out significant acts
Acts are so because they are rare feats.

Men with self-esteem carry out act which are so difficult making them rare.

976. **M**en with nothing to their credit has no mind
To adapt to a mentor and a way find.

Men with no achievements to their credit do not develop the helpful strategy of learning what is to be learnt in their domain – education and skill etc., from those who are rich in all those capacities and act, finally earning high self and other esteem.

---

[208] The meaning of this couplet is given a twist showing Thiruvalluvar as a non-votary of cast system prevalent in India. There is absolutely no basis to dispute it but this couplet doesn't say that. We can even say that Thiruvalluvar says as having born as human beings men should endeavour to bring the best in them into full use.

[209] High position may be due to wealth or office.

977. Laurels to a non-achiever is a death kneel
      Knocking the achieving climate of its even keel.

      According laurels to a non-achiever is colossally harmful because
      it would kill the motivation of the real achievers by vitiating the
      atmosphere of its accomplishing potential.

978. High achievers are always humble.
      Low achievers indulge in self-awe.

      Men of high achievement remain humble. Whereas men of mean
      achievement eulogize themselves for whatever small achievements
      they manage to achieve.

979. Esteem marks lack of proud
      Meanness 'let me proud abide.'

      Absence of pride marks men highly esteemed for their accomplishments.
      Meanness is a state of mind whose predominant ingredient is pride.

980. High esteem hides others' faults,
      Low esteem speaks only such sorts.

      Great mind (a mind which enjoys genuine esteem due its achievements)
      hides other's mistakes. But mean mind (a mind in the absence of
      useful and whole hearted effort and therefore nothing genuine to
      esteem) will concentrate only on the shortcomings of others.

Skills to be learnt:

  ➢   Ability to feel pure proud at one's contribution in his field and always
      aspiring for it.
  ➢   Never finding satisfaction in one's position or status either in the
      work place or in the society's so called ranking in preference to the
      esteem one wins because of his good work and achievement.

Rationale:

> This is an important ability in the sense an individual who feels proud or satisfied about himself because of his contribution is motivated positively to reach new heights. Such individuals are assets for a society because by their work they take care of the need of the society. Whereas an individual who develops pride over anything other than his contribution reaches a pseudo satisfaction that he has achieved whatever needs to be achieved and starts manipulating others to retain his supremacy. Such individuals are hazardous to themselves and to the achieving society. Therefore the skills to feel pride not proud needs to be developed.

Coaching:

> Couplet 974 says a person is eligible to feel esteemed only when he out performs earlier standards achieved in the field including the one created by him. He can work on the following lines.

> He should make it a goal to excel in what he does in comparison to others (972).

> In order to enjoy pride or self-esteem an individual should sharpen his axe every time when it is needed. This he can achieve by approaching great resources in his domain (974).

> He should not lose sight in mistaking high ranks or positions as reasons for feeling proud about him unless they are merit based (977).

> He should keep his head above self-eulogizing (978).

> He should check within himself every now and then whether he feels pride (self-esteem) or proud (self-eulogizing) (979).

> He can practice a policy of according appreciation to others on account of even small achievements they make. Let him also make another policy that he would never speak of other's shortcomings, however big or small they may be to third parties, unless for official or court purposes they are called for (980).

99

Sandranmai [210]

981. **F**or a *sandrone*[211] who is proactively dutiful
Any societal good is his duty to fulfill.

For a *sandrone* (whose nature is made up of love, humility, *oppuravu*[212], empathy and truthfulness) any good that needs to be carried out (in the best interest of humanity) becomes his duty.

982. **H**ealthy qualities are only of those of a *sandrone*
Don't call any other for one.

---

[210] *Sandranmai* has no equal word in English language. It means a character solidified by the presence of love, humility, *oppuravu*, empathy and truthfulness. The couplet no. 983 gives this definition for *sandranmai*. Since it was difficult to find a near equivalent word or coin one covering all the five qualities I have decided to use the Tamil word.

[211] Sandrone is one who has characteristics of sandranmai.

[212] *Oppuravu* means a venture to help the needy and eligible to establish in life or simply, 'a growth enabling venture.' May be its modern version is what is called as: social engineering/philanthropy/social entrepreneurship /social responsibility. Since these days discussion is going on about the difference between charity and philanthropy (corporate social responsibility) in which clarity is yet to arrive I thought the Tamil word found in the title of this chapter namely *oppuravu* can be the right word to mean social cooperation/social engineering/ philanthropy/ social entrepreneurship/social responsibility etc.

If psychologically healthy attributes are to be enlisted the list starts and ends with what a sandrone possess. Other aspects like wealth, position or even education cannot be categorized under the same list.

983. **L**ove, humility, *oppuravu*, empathy and truthfulness,
     Sandranmai is the pillar bearing these qualities' usefulness.

     Love, humility, *oppuravu*, empathy and truthfulness are the five qualities which make the personality of a *sandrone*. They form the pillar (bedrock) which bears the personality of *sandranmai*.

984. **P**enance has non-killing as its good
     Hiding other's faults is *Sandranmai's* good.

     Not slandering is the good a *sandrone* offers. Similarly a penance's good is not allowing animal sacrifice.

985. The strength of a man of action, is humility
     It is sandrone's arsenal to win enmity.

     The power of a *sandrone* is his humility. Employing it he changes his enemies' mind in favor of the cause for which he stands for.

986. An evidence for the presence of *sandranmai*[213] is
     Accepting defeat from an unequal with ease.

     A test for the existence of *sandranmai* is demonstrated in the act of accepting defeat by a *sandrone* at the hands of persons who are not equal to him. This they achieve because of sense of shame, empathy and truth present in them.

987. **R**eturning good in return to bad if he can't
     What better use has *sandrone's* wont?

---

[213] *Sandranmai* means *sandrone* personified by his five qualities

Sandrone is one from whom no harm to others shall come. That being the case if a *sandrone* doesn't return good to a person who hurts him what better use his *sandranmai* has?

988. **P**overty is not demeaning
If one is hardened in *Sandranmai's* meaning.

Being poor is not degrading. If a person's personality is hardened by the five attributes of *sandranmai*.

989. **S**eas may whelm but a *sandrone* doesn't succumb
Since his character is as deep as the seas themselves.

Since a *sandrone* commits himself to live the five attributes and his commitment to them is as deep as an ocean he never buckles even under pressure created by the whelming seas.

990. **I**f *sandranmai* go down in a society
This great earth will be unable to bear the polity.

If the qualities of *sandranmai* reduce in a society due to the reduction of the population of *sandrones* from whom the society picks them up then the burden of the society will increase because of the destructive behavior of ill informed people. The universe will not be able to bear it.

Skills to be learnt:

> The ability to employ the five qualities namely love, humility, *oppuravu*, empathy and truthfulness in personal, professional and social life.
> A sample of behaviors of a *sandrone* given by Tiruvalluvar are:

1. He would always be proactive in carrying out what is good (needed for the community) holding it as his duty (981),

2. He would not reveal mistakes of others affecting them adversely(984),

3. He would use humility as a device to win the heart of his enemies(935),

4. He would accept defeat even at the hands of a person who is not equal to him(986),

5. He would return good to a person who has done bad unto him(987),

6. He would never give up on moral behavior under as grave a circumstance as whelming seas (989).

Rationale:

➢ Couplet 990 says if the qualities of *sandranmai* go down in a society due to the fact less and less number of people live that way the burden of mother earth will reach a level unmanageable to her leading to big chaos and destruction. Therefore it is a necessity the society continuously creates any number of *sandrones*.

Coaching:

➢ You may roughly check within yourself how do you fare on the five qualities of *sandranmai*: 1.Unlimited love towards fellow human beings and other living organisms of the universe, 2. A keen sense of humility, 3.*Oppuravu* towards others to help them solve their livelihood problems, 4. Ability to assume the position of others and get a sense of what he or she subjectively feels or thinks on an issue (empathy) and 5. Always speaking and acting truthfully.

➢ To show love means sharing our resources of time labor and money with willingness for the sake of others. You may note it is not always money that is needed to help others.

➢ To act humble means not acting meekly. It is a nonviolent way of persisting on one's stand without posing a threat to the position or welfare of the opponent. This posture makes the other person to come out of the fear induced aggressive mind set and start looking at the reality of an issue.

- ➤ To show *oppuravu* (philanthropy/social responsibility/social engineering/social entrepreneurship), an individual can rise to an opportunity to participate in any endeavor to help the members of the society to grow. It need not be always donating big money. Sky is the only limit to help society to grow. Even if you chose to live a life of reasonable consumption in terms of energy because of you green concerns you are showing *oppuravu*. While that may be a passive act an active act can be going to a community center and teach children a particular subject for as many hours as needed to make them to come out of their laggard position and thus mainstreaming them.

- ➤ To show empathy an individual should sharpen his listening skills. Any message passes through two stages: understanding stage and acting stage. Understanding stage should give importance to the subjective sense of the individual and acting stage involves delivering equity. Empathy is not sympathy. Empathy can and should lead to punishment if need arises.

- ➤ Sticking to truth is a second nature for a *sandrone*. In this connection an individual may use some discretion as to what to reveal and what not to reveal in the service of common good in view. But whatever he speaks out should be totally free from any falsehood.

100

Panbu in Action

991. Easy, courteous access offered,
Is how *Panbu* is lived.

An aspect of *panbu* is providing warm access to anyone.

992. Love and a great family lineage
Are the hall marks of *panbu*.

This couplet gives a definition of *panbu*. Canto number 96 gives the
list of qualities which a good family instills in its offspring and canto
number 8 gives the definition of love. *Panbu* is a behavior where
those qualities and an additional quality of love are actively present.
The qualities a good family instills in its offspring are: (1) equity, (2)
humility, (3) best practices, (4) truth, (5) sense of shame, (6) pleasant
smile, (7) charity, (8) using sweet words, (9) not despising fellow
humans while entertaining them and giving leave to them. *Panbu* is
an amalgamation of all these qualities

993. Limbs and legs themselves do not make a man
Manners rooted in *panbu* make it happen.

People with *panbu* and without *panbu* may look similar because they
are human beings. But the real comparison is about *panbu* in action.
Therefore men with *panbu* and without *panbu* cannot be held as
equal in humanness.

994. Good wrapped in courtesy, *panbu* offers
Praise for that quality world showers.

Men of panbu are benefactors. They offer goodness in a refined manner too. The world showers accolades on them.

995. Even in humour ridicule is painful
Within enmity *panbu* refuses spiteful.

Even while cracking a joke ridicule should not be used as a theme or mode. Because it is hurtful to the individual referred to in the joke. People inclined to show *panbu* are courteous even to their enemies.

996. World is sustained by men of *panbu*
In their absence it would collapse.

The activities of the world go on because of the critical interventions by people who are embodiments of *panbu*. Otherwise the world will suffer from the persons lacking the quality of *panbu*. (Recall 571and 990 echoing similar notions with reference to empathy and *sandranmai*.)

997. Someone can be as sharp as a steel file
Still is a tree if he lacks *panbu* in his profile.

A person by his intellectual capability may be as sharp as a razor. But his intelligence is of no use if he lacks *panbu* in his dealings with fellow human beings. 'He will be as insensitive as a tree. Another way of looking at the couplet could be: a file made out of steel serves the purpose of shredding/polishing another metal. In case it is made of wood it ill serves its purpose. Like that a man made of some other substance like intelligence (only) but bereft of panbu will be of no use to a suffering humanity.

998. Incapable of friendship and uncourteous
Being uncourteous even to him is discourteous.

Some people are incapable of building and maintaining a genuine friendship. As a result their behavior remains unrefined. Still paying them in their own coin is an act of meanness.

999. For them the day being dark is inescapable
Since throwing smiles on others they are not capable.

We have people on whose lips friendly smile always lives. For others who are incapable of throwing a smile as and when warranted the day is as good as night. During night in the absence of light normally people do not interact with each other. So also people who do not smile at the look of others effectively close the door for interaction making the day time similar to night.

1000.The huge wealth of an unrefined man is futile
Like the milk in an unclean vessel is a cocktail.

Wealth lying with a man lacking *panbu* is equivalent to milk stored in an unclean vessel. As the milk goes waste the wealth of a *panbu* less person is also liable to be wasted because he fails an opportunity to put his wealth to a better use.

Skills to be learnt:

➢ Ability to act with *panbu*.

Rationale:

➢ There is no equal word for *panbu* in English. The concept has four additional qualities to that of a *sandrone*. But it appears there is a short cut. Two generic qualities namely equity and sense of shame and love will cover all of them. Practicing a fine sense of equity and totally avoiding shameful acts is all about acting with *panbu* (951).

Coaching:

> ➢ Techniques for practicing a keen sense of shame and equity are given under chapters 12 and 102 respectively. Chapter 96 also elaborately deals the topic.

101

Wealth Not Creating Good[214]

1001. His house is full of wealth. He doesn't enjoy
He is as good as dead since he had no joy.[215]

He gathers wealth enough to fill his entire house. But never enjoys it nor put it to the proper use of helping the needy. Looked from this angle he is as good as dead because what needs to happen by his wealth doesn't happen.

1002. His life is trivial, you know why?
He mistakes wealth as all and refuse to give, that is why.

His life slips into insignificance because he is not employing his money for the best purpose it is meant for. This scrooge behavior is due to his misunderstanding that wealth alone is the summum bonum of life and therefore his life is well lived.

1003. He fails to give and esteem he doesn't require
His existence is a burden for the biosphere.

He who is not interested to achieve public esteem by investing his wealth/time /labor for enabling growth at the level of individuals and society is a burden for mother earth. (He is also burdensome in the

---

214 This chapter is a continuation of the chapter 22. Wealth is a resource in a fiduciary sense. Thiruvalluvar is of the opinion that wealth needs to be properly deployed in order to alleviate the suffering of humanity.

215 Joy includes his and the joy of others who would benefit from it and grow.

sense he doesn't use his life on the earth to evolve at the level of his
soul. After all the purpose of life on the earth is to win social esteem
out of altruistic action which is a soul evolving exercise.)

1004. Of his life what outcome he could think of
After all no one esteems him thereof.

Having failed to put his wealth to the right use what aspect of his
life he would hold as commendable when he takes stock of his life
during his last days? Is he not concerned that he would have to feel
dejection for having lived a futile life?

1005. He who neither gives nor enjoys
In spite millions in poverty he lives.

In spite of huge wealth gathering dust a person remains poor if he
chooses not to enjoy it himself and enjoy giving it others.

1006. 'Neither enjoy nor give,' this is his whim
Wealth remains diseased with him.

The wealth is a diseased one because it is nonperforming.

1007. The wealth not spent on a needy,
Likens a healthy women going singly.

The wealth of someone who is scrooge enough to deny giving it
to any one is wasted like a mentally and physically healthy and
resourceful lady choosing spinsterhood. (Perhaps Thiruvalluvar
posits that a woman who is well equipped to mother a child and
grow her as a useful human resource should not choose to remain
as a spinster.)

1008. A person's wealth who is liked by none
Likens a poisonous tree whose fruits people shun.

A tree with poisonous fruits may stand at central place of the town thus being accessible to everyone. But nobody likes its fruits. Same with the wealth of a scrooge.

1009. Wealth made forgoing love, *aram* and comfort
Others shall misappropriate.

A scrooge disregarding personal comforts, love to fellow humans and ethical issues may earn huge wealth. But nemeses would have it squandered by others.

1010. The short lived poverty of the glorious[216] rich
Is like the cloud presenting a dry patch.

Sometimes a glorious philanthropist may undergo a resource crunch. But it is like during some months in a year clouds going dry. As they revive as quickly as possible the rich man also revives and continues his charitable activities.

Skills to be learnt:

> To relinquish the hoarding mentality.

Rationale:

> According to Thiruvalluvar wealth lying with someone who does not put it to proper use i.e., using it for growth enabling endeavor is a total waste. He encourages those who possesses wealth to put it to proper use. A wealth which is hoarded is like a poison in the society. The chapter admonishes anyone who hoards wealth without putting it to good use.

---

[216] Glory comes to them from those who are helped by him.

Coaching:

The following observations of Thiruvalluvar may be used by the coach to wean a hoarder from hoarding after taking his permission.

➤ "You hoarder, you are as good as a dead corpse if you do not make happen what should happen through your money."(1001)

➤ "You think a great life is lived if you hoard money! What an ignorant person you are!"(1002)

➤ "You are a burden for mother earth because you shun social esteem which you can earn from your beneficiaries by employing your money for their growth. Your soul would evolve out of such altruistic acts and ultimately would usher you into God's company. Since soul evolution is the only purpose of the life of a human being you are wasting your life by not pressing your money into social good" (1003).

➤ "What the hell you think you will leave behind you when you die? Don't you think any person lives a worthy life only when he leaves a benefit to the society and thus live in the memory of his beneficiaries?"(1004)

➤ "You know one thing? You are as good as a pauper if you chose not to give and not to enjoy in a descent manner what you have."(1005)

➤ "Your money is a diseased one and you are a burden for the society if you choose to hoard it."(1006)

➤ "Your wealth is wasted like the youth of a woman who chose to remain as a spinster."(1007)

➤ "Your wealth is like poisonous fruits borne by a poisonous tree standing at the center of the town."(1008)

➤ "Beware the money you have earned through your hard labor will be squandered by someone before your very eyes."(1009)

To a philanthropist whose resources goes dry:

➤ "Oh my dear philanthropist do not feel panicky. Your resource scrunch is only like the brief famine in between monsoons."

102

Sense of Shame

1011. Shame and women's shrink show variety
Good people's shame relates to their probity.

Modest women are ashamed of immoral behavior. They instantly shrink when confronted by someone with bad intension. In the case of people who are mortally afraid of getting ashamed the same thing happens. They drop a wrong idea or action like a hot potato.
(A women in whom chastity is ingrained as her nature shrinks instantly when someone approaches her with evil intention. A man of probity also instantly reacts against an immoral act.)

1012. Eating, dressing and procreating are common
With their sense of shame great men show distinction.

Eating, dressing and procreating is common for all human beings. But few distinguish themselves by the presence of acute sense of shame.

1013. Life's dependence on a body is very acute
Sandranmai's on sense of shame is on similar foot.

The need of a body for life and the need of sense of shame for sandranmai are similar in nature and operation. If body is fatally wounded life departs. Similarly if a *sandrone* experiences extreme level of shame because he has done something terribly wrong he dies instantly or suffers from death pangs. The urge to preserve life and the urge to preserve one's honor are the same for them.

1014. Is it not a *sandrone's* sense of shame a jewel?
Is it not the proud strides of a shameless a disease?

A *sandrone's* humility is a decoration on him. Therefore his natural strides themselves are majestic. Whereas even the proud strides of a man in whom sense of shame is absent appears diseased.

(This happens because without a sense of shame their strides will become brazen in order to conceal their shame.)

1015. Of their blames and of other's they feel ashamed
"They are the embodiment of that sense," says the world.

Great men feel ashamed of not only when they commit immoral acts but also feel the same shock when others with whom they are in some way connected commit mistakes.
(Like when you are in a foreign soil you are ashamed when another Indian commits a grave error. You would say, 'I am ashamed of saying that I am an Indian after this behavior of my fellow Indian.')

1016. Unfenced by sense of shame
Great men never attempt to thrive.

Sense of shame is like a fence which great men erect around themselves so that they do not find themselves doing shameful acts. They never remain unfenced by the sense of shame.

1017. For the sake of shame they give up their life
But never gives up shame for life's sake.

Men with a sense of shame will shed their life in the face of an acute shame they incur by their mistake. But they will not commit a shameful act for even rescuing their life.

1018. If one is not ashamed of what others are ashamed of
His act makes *aram* ashamed of.

If a person is not ashamed of what others are ashamed of either to witness or to hear Aram will be ashamed of him.

(You may remember *aram* as an abstract noun refers to an entity enlivened by a civil society. The moment the entity comes to know that one of its members has indulged in a shameful act it will feel ashamed and start acting to remove the shame off its back.)

1019. A mistake in the policy for the family scorches its standing
For its wellness a shameful act does similar lending.

If a mistake takes place in evolving an appropriate policy to run a family the family is liable to lose its standing. Similarly the family's wellness suffers if its members involve in shameful acts.

1020. With no sense of shame in heart men's maneuvers
Akins string-led puppet's fares.

People who have no sense of shame may act as if they have. This sham behavior is like the acts of puppet orchestrated by a string. The movements of the puppets fake human behavior so also the maneuvers of a human being fake sense of shame.

The skills to be learnt:

➢   Installing a strong sense of shame in one's personality and living by it.

Rationale:

> Thiruvalluvar enlists a number of values i.e., standards any society should follow in order to live a prosperous and healthy life. In this chapter the value of sense of shame or avoiding shameful act under any circumstance is emphasized. Sense of shame weans a person from faulting on the values which he holds very dear to him. Sense of shame also protects man from committing mistakes which undermine his well being and those of others connected with him.

Coaching:

> Sense of shame is activated by two aspects namely the internal standards one has regarding human activities and norms put forth by his reference group. Therefore a two pronged approach may be attempted to install this skill in a person.

> For installing a sense of shame the client may be admonished on the following lines after taking his consent for the approach.

> "Look all organisms are comparable with regard to what they eat, what they do to protect themselves from harms and their act of procreation. But humanity distinguishes itself by its sense of shame. Therefore I urge you to develop a deep sense of shame to qualify yourself to be called as a great and worthy human. "(1012)

> "Food is essential for the body. Sense of shame is essential for wellbeing. Will you not be interested in your wellbeing?"(1013)

> "Sense of shame is a sanitizer of any ill will in you. If you have a strong sense of shame that will put the necessary inhibitions in you which will prevent you from doing wrong things preventing from getting ruined. That is the reason why *sandrones* have a very keen sense of shame. A sense of shame strongly installed in you will keep you away from evil things by severely cautioning you. In fact a deeply ingrained sense of shame will shell shock you when you attempt to do something not proper and leave you numb. With such a sense of shame on your side and a life free from evil doing and evil thinking your gaits will become splendid. Otherwise your aping the strides of a *sandrone* will look ugly."(1014)

➤ "For persons whose sense of shame is very deep the objects related to shameful acts automatically become objects of aversion. The aversion is so high they are even ashamed to talk about it. When they hear about someone close to them or someone whom they hold in high esteem committing a shameful act they feel so much ashamed of it that they don't even discuss it with them. Don't we hear sometimes people telling us something like, "I was so ashamed of his action I could not even open it with him"? (1015).

➤ A fence of sense of shame which you erect around you will protect you from the attractions in the environment which will tempt you to carry on evil acts (1016).

➤ "Persons with a deep sense of shame will rather kill themselves instead of relinquishing their sense of shame, you know that"? (1017).

➤ "You are aware that a family will get ruined if it doesn't follow well thought out policy based best practices." Similarly, "Take it from me; if members of your family do not have a strong sense of shame the wellbeing of your family is in great danger." (1019).

For creating the connection with reference group and sense of shame of the individual you may say the following to your client:

➤ "You should build a group of people drawn from among peers, relatives especially your wife/husband, children and parents, colleagues, peers and friends and mentors to act as your reference group whose opinion you hold as very important to you. If you keep your life open to these people by disclosing to them about your activities as much as possible then you will find it is very difficult to do things which will show you in poor light to them. This is the fence which will protect you from pitfalls which from time to time any human being is likely to meet." (1016)

One word of caution:

Do not act as though you have a sense of shame when you don't have one. People who watch a puppet show know that the puppet gets its 'life' from the string. But they would rather be interested in the story. Similarly if you act as though you have a sense of shame and do things shameful, people will rather enjoy your story than taking it up with you!"(1020)

➢ Their silence regarding your activities may give you a false notion that everything is under control when you are already on a slippery ground (1020)!

103

Family[217] Management

1021. "**I** shall not back out from my duty to my family," – proclaimed
No accomplishment of better pride could be claimed.

An individual who proclaims, 'On any account I shall not back out
from doing what is needed to run my family and push its programs
as it deem fit,' and diligently shows it in action is an asset for the
family and the nation. There is no better accomplishment for a
human being to aspire.

1022. If engaged effort and wide knowledge are sustained together,
The family is conserved forever.

A family's welfare and missions go on and on if engaged efforts and
wide knowledge are pressed into service continuously by the leader
and members of the family.

1023. '**My** family! I shall take it ahead,' if someone vows so,
With sleeves up, fate[218] goes ahead of him to help the go.

---

[217] The family may be an extended one in which several parents and children live.

[218] Karma or fate is pliable. One could do good karma so that bad karma becomes
dysfunctional for want of practice. In the present example the head of the
family presses it with such vigour the evolution of the fate is instantaneous
in the direction of its owner. Please remember nowhere in Thirukkural God's
intervention is made a mention of.

If a man declares and plunges into action to do everything to take his family on its onward march, fate or karma evolves instantaneously and leads him or soul instantly raises to the occasion and leads him.

1024. If engaged effort is pressed into the service of the family
Plans and strategies line up themselves.

A person need not plan and strategize beforehand to take his family forward. Once he sets his action on a strong footing and engage himself through his mind body and soul the plans and strategies will reveal themselves.

1025. Through faultless means if a person sustains his family
The world, around him, seeks to belong to him as his family.

With a mind free from anxiety, if a person does every appropriate thing to sustain his family, the world around him will make note of it and seek to join him to do their bit to support him.

1026. Best calibre consists of taking the lead
On the family's need when one is called.

The best of management caliber is exhibited if a person sensing the need of the family for a new leadership (as vouchsafed by failures under the present leader) assumes the responsibility of running the family.

1027. The burden of war is on the militant most
The burden of the family is on the one who acts robust.

Strongly willed and muscled, hard core warriors bear the brunt of a war while others play a supportive role. So also in a family the responsibilities of the family are shouldered by the one who engages himself most in managing the family among other members of the family.

1028. For a family man there is nothing like specified time
Loafing and holding to dignity ruins the aim.

An individual who wants to grow his family can not have the luxury of fixed number of hours of work. Loafing and keeping oneself agitated over maintaining one's pride, if a person choose not to act appropriately every second in the family, then the ruin of the family is around the corner.

(For example, if a person hesitates to approach an agency for help for his son's education because such an act undermines his self-respect it will affect the family. He cannot think of self-respect at that time. After all he is seeking the help only for his son. "If I get it, it is ok. If I don't get it, it is hard luck," should be his attitude.)

1029. He who protects his family from inadequacy
Is his body a container of pain because of his efficacy?

The best among the members of the family should come forward to take the management of the family. Once he takes over every member would offload their worries on him. He should not shirk. He should rather consider himself as a natural receptacle to receive those worries and work towards solving them.

1030. When adversity strikes at the root a family falls
With no man of valour to fall back it fails.

A family succumbs to an adverse situation if it lacks a person to support it. This is a direct translation which does not bring out what Thiruvalluvar really means. Tiruvalluvar has used the phrases *kaal kondrida* which translates into, 'when the trunk is destroyed,' suggesting he refers to a tree. Next he uses the phrase *aduththuundrum* meaning something which rises to support. It seems he gives the example of banyan tree that puts out aerial shoots that grow down into the soil forming additional trunks supporting the tree and suggests a family also needs persons who will rise to the occasion when the main actor perishes causing an adverse situation. In the absence of such persons the family will get ruined.

Skills to be learnt:

> The ability to take this pledge and carry it out under any circumstance: "I shall do whatever it takes to take my family to the objective of success in its missions. Under any circumstance I will not back out from this endeavor."

Rationale:

> Family is the basic institution of the society. If the head of the family who is like the CEO of the institution is not fully engaged in running the activities of the family then the family will perish in due course of time. Therefore important management inputs need to be put in place. The chapter mentions four inputs of family management in this regard. Please familiarize with the concepts found in the first five couplets of the chapter before reading further.

Coaching:

> Accept this: There is nothing about which one can be more proud of than taking the pledge, "I shall not back out from taking care of my family." (1021)
> Do you know the caveat, "Engaged effort and intellect are the two aspects that sustain a family in perpetuity?"(1022)
> Take this from me, "If you make efforts in right earnest to run your family and take the bull by its horn your soul will instantly evolve or would become active and march ahead of you thus leading you or making you to actualize all the power present in you." (1023)
> Do you know "If you are a person who will toil for your family, fruitful results will be achieved without great difficulty?"(1024)
> Do you know people around you will voluntarily come forward to belong to you if they notice that you are a person who sincerely tries to run the show of your family?(1025)

➢ If you claim you have great caliber in managing organizations and you are proactive in this regard then it is proved only if you step in if the present leader of your family is not up to the mark. (1026)

➢ The above is evidenced in a battle field where the critical roles are played by those who are capable not by others because of their positions. (1027)

➢ It is hard. But it is a fact. For those who are vested with the responsibility of running the family there is nothing like convenient time, procrastination and sense of honor etc., (1028)

➢ It is a pity. But it is a fact. Running the family entails enormous difficulties as though his or her body who manages the family is a container to off load difficulties by every member of the family. Accept the responsibility graciously. (1029)

➢ Take care to groom a successor even when you are strong and going. This is important because in the event of you disappearing the family should not suffer for want of a new leader. (1030)

104

Agriculture

1031. World lives in multiple theatres but agriculture alone caters
Farmers toil no doubt but they are the leaders.

World has spin out of the original profession of agriculture and has established in several modern professions. Still everyone looks for agriculture for their meal. Therefore in spite hard work let farmers stay in farming.

1032. Farmers are pivotal for the world,
They sustain men in other professions behold.

Farmers' role is pivotal to the world. Their products alone sustain people in other walks of life who were agriculturists earlier.

1033. Those who till and live really live.
Others salute and go behind them for a living.

Farmers alone produce what they eat. So their life is great. Others need to depend on them and eat what they give after thanking them.

1034. Land under several forest shades
Farmers bring under the shade of their rice blooms.

It is to the credit of farmers that through the hard work of deforestation they bring new lands under paddy cultivation.

1035. They don't beg, they give to the one who does require
They do not shirk labour and that is their inner fire.

Farmers don't beg others. They give to those who need. They don't shirk labor. That is in their blood.

1036. If farmers stop work even for those who renounce
Should renounce their 'renounce'!

Even for those who renounced everything the service of farmers is needed. Otherwise they have to renounce their renounced life.

1037. If soil is tilled and dried one to four[219]
Even a fistful of fertilizer is not needed.

If soil is tilled enough to make it into a fine dry powder there is no need to add even a handful of compost.

1038. Applying fertilizer is better than tilling followed by irrigation
And more important is crop's protection.

Applying compost is better than tilling. After fertilizing irrigating the land is important. Still important is the protection of the crop.

(It appears Thiruvalluvar says all the operations of agriculture namely tilling for pulverizing the soil fully, fertilizing, irrigating and protecting the crop are important. In order to drive home the point that all are important he mentions each one of them in turn belittling the next.

It is also possible to look at it as making use of one operation as a substitute to another. Let us say, for some reason applying compost to the extent needed is not possible. In that situation pulverizing the

---

[219] In a dry and pulverized soil (ploughed enough to make four times soil weight to one time) crop can send roots easily to a large area ensuring enough nutrient.

soil minutely will help easy penetration of roots to deeper level of soil from where the plant can get nutrients.)

1039. If a husband chooses not to attend his wife sulks
If a farmer chooses not to work farm also hulks.[220]

If a wife is not attended by her husband she sulks and spoils the mood at home. Similarly if a farmer chooses to remain at home without working at his farm daily the farm will go baron. (Continuous and watchful management and hard work is highlighted.)

1040. 'I have nothing, 'saying so if a person idly remains,
Mother earth looks at him and smiles.

If a person says he is in a pitiable condition since he doesn't have the means to live mother earth will smile at him.

(Probably Thiruvalluvar points out that humanity should never feel poor because mother earth has the resources waiting to be exploited by the mankind. An individual, who is lazy and not properly skilled and unable to change his or her preferences to make the best use of opportunities the universe has for everyone, will suffer. Since the suffering is due to him mother earth similes!)

Skills to be learnt:

> Ability to appreciate the pivotal importance of the avocation of agriculture. The modern trend in India is to look down at agriculture. It is not a stable profession for a number of reasons people hold. While there is lot of truth in it, it doesn't represent full truth. This mind set should change. New entrepreneurs equipped with the knowledge and skills sets incorporating latest technology should once again usher in a golden period for agriculture.

---

[220] Hulks means becoming unwieldy like an abandoned ship or machinery.

Rationale:

- ➤ Anyone who gets an opportunity to do agriculture or look at it as an option can motivate himself or herself by looking at the nobility of the profession. Moreover with modern day advancement in technology and demand for agricultural produces going sky high agriculture will become a money spinner at the earliest. The agronomic practices suggested by Tiruvalluvar can be practiced in places like green house farms.

Coaching:

- ➤ To appreciate the greatness of agriculture, six couplets starting from the first may be taken into account. Please read the couplets along with the explanation and imbibe the sprit.
- ➤ The agronomic practice relating to plowing of the land: plough the land as many times as needed the objective being the soil should be very finely pulverized.
- ➤ Fertilizing is very important compared to tilling. But remember a short supply of fertilizer can be taken care of by fine tilling which facilitates the easy and far and wide reach of root system facilitating access to nutrients.
- ➤ Irrigating on time and right quantity and hoeing are very much needed.(Interestingly in green house farming the pith like material in which the plants grow and the computerized application of fertilizer and water appear something like an upgraded version of what Tiruvalluvar has prescribed!)
- ➤ Management of the farm activities under able supervision and participation of the owner of the land is very important.
- ➤ If a wife's demands are not met or slighted upon she will sulk. Similarly a land which is not cultivated well day in and day out will not yield!
- ➤ If a farmer says, "What a pity my farm has given me nothing mother earth will respond with a smile." This means those who work in the field will have no poverty. The secret lies in hard work, new technology, new skill and optimism.

> ➤ India is a country of opportunities. The proof comes from a simple fact that some days direct foreign investments are pouring like anything creating head ache to reserve bank governor and finance minister of central Government. If foreign investors do not perceive India as a promising destination will they invest in such a large scale? Many of MOUs signed are by corporates

> ➤ They must be throwing plenty of opportunities for franchisees to start high technology oriented lab supported agricultural enterprises. Therefore if some of us do not grab an opportunity which we scout and find let us not blame mother earth later at least!

105

Poverty

1041. What is more painful than poverty?
It is lack of poverty alleviating strategy.[221]

If you ask what is a real poverty the answer is poverty is a condition where the person is poor in the sense that he lacks strategic initiatives to remove his poverty condition. (Poverty is a vexatious problem, no doubt about it. But what is more vexatious is lacking no plans to tackle that condition.)

1042. The rogue poverty robs a (contributing) life here
(And therefore the prospects for) a life there.

Life in this earth is barren because the person who suffers from poverty is not able to carry on a socially useful life enabling his soul to grow in maturity corresponding with the present birth. Therefore this birth is a wasted opportunity vis-à-vis achieving heavenly abode.

1043. Ancestral pride and goodwill (fame) get hit
Importunate seeking, in one go earns it.

---

[221] Line to line translation of this couplet is: What else is more painful than poverty? // It is lack of absence of poverty. Most of the interpreters hold this view. I have taken the position shown above because if I don't do so then this chapter remains as the only one having no lesson for alleviating the condition it deals with.

A poor person having no means of his own is likely to pester others for help. Naturally people who are not able to put up with his pestering lose their sense and forget for a moment the glorious past of the person and ridicule him. This costs him the pride of his family and the good will of his friends.

1044. Poverty loosens self-guard and he speaks foul
In spite his birth being noble.

Even though born in a highly cultured family dire poverty makes a man to lose alertness of mind on account of which he ends up speaking foul.

1045. Poverty is a basic pain
With it several hardships join.

To start with poverty is a symptom of pain. Soon it matures itself into a syndrome.

1046. Worthy topic, well informed words, he does speak
Still the speech of a poor man doesn't make.

A poor person owing to his scholarship in his field may speak very well on a subject showing a good understanding. But his exposition will fail to earn the appreciation it deserves (because his unimpressive looks due to his poor dress and ill-nourished body would psychologically repel the audience in the initial stage of the presentation itself!). As a result he will not be able to monetize your talent.

1047. If poverty visits a person due to a *aram* related blunder
His mother intentionally takes him for a stranger.

Even a mother willfully becomes indifferent towards her son who deviates from the basic precincts of *aram* and becomes poor on account of it. (After all she always wants him to be a *sandrone* (69).)

1048.Will today also be the same?
Yesterday I had poverty's killing game.

Yesterday I suffered almost death due to my poverty. Will the condition change today or should I suffer the same plight today also? This is the blighting thought that greets the man in poverty as soon as he wakes up.

1049. Sleeping in the midst of fire is possible
With penury sleeping is impossible.

It is possible to sleep in the midst of fire. But with poverty sleeping is impossible. (Body especially skin can adapt to heat to some extent. Since poverty will bring in newer and newer issues every day haunting the mind fresh it is not possible for the mind to adapt like body adapting to fire. Recall couplet 1045 which says poverty which starts as a symptom soon becomes a syndrome. Adapting to a syndrome is very rare to happen.)

1050. The poor are not able to abstain amply
They borrow salt and vinegar making it silly.

Poor people do not come to terms with poverty squarely. They linger with some of their old habits which unnecessarily make them borrowing things like salt and vinegar from their neighbors. (If they accept the reality they will readjust their food habits strictly according to what is available with them. In that case salt and vinegar which are only optional additives will not be sought. In some parts of the world people eat cooked rice without salt even today. This is what 'coming to terms with the conditions of life squarely' means.)

Skills to be learnt:

> The first couplet of the chapter speaks about poverty from a trouble shooting angle. It says the real poverty is the lack of strategic initiative. This interpretation results from coupling the last couplet

of the previous chapter and the first couplet of this chapter. The last couplet of this chapter says one should come to terms with poverty and start acting on it. Coming to terms with poverty may involve downsizing ones requirement to the bare minimum. In between these two couplets the remaining eight couplets describe the severe condition of poverty. From this angle this chapter may have been written with two objectives: motivating people to do the needful to avoid poverty by showing them how treacherous poverty conditions are. Second, if some one happens to fall in poverty they should come to terms with poverty and accept it and adjust with it in a graceful manner.

Rationale:

➢ Thiruvalluvar's cognitive approach to motivate people to take steps to avoid poverty is based on the principle of: "Accost the client with the consequences of what he does or doesn't do."

Coaching:

➢ "My dear man, the severest poverty is lacking the initiative and effort to wipe out poverty. (1041)

➢ My dear man beware if you don't act to stem out poverty you will be afflicted permanently. Don't think poverty which has come now will go later on its own. (1042)

➢ Pride of your longstanding family and fame will be wiped out by your importunate seeking from others what you need. (1043)

➢ You will loose your best practice of never badmouthing about others in their absence or in their presence. (1044).

➢ To start with your poverty may be only a symptom. In due course of time it will become a syndrome because of so many additional afflictions. (1045)

➢ You may research and deliver a good piece of talk. But since people will slight you on account of your poverty your good talk will have no receivers and your chances to eke a living out of it would not succeed. (1046)

- ➤ Your mother will hate you because by this time you would be indulging in acts failing the test of *aram* due to the pressure of your poverty. (1047)
- ➤ Every day without fail poverty will torture you. (1048)
- ➤ Oh! My dear man one can sleep in the midst of fire but not with empty stomach. (1049)
- ➤ But with all this let me tell one thing: you should come to terms with your poverty and accept it as a reality while doing everything to alleviate yourself from it. If you do this, two things will happen. You will not pester people around you for small help like a helping of salt and vinegar (this means you are effectively avoiding yourself from becoming a parasite on others) rather you will explore the opportunities around you to get out of poverty (1050).

106

Begging

1051. Beg a man who can afford. Mind you,
   If he hides blame lies with him not with you.

   Find out someone who has the means and request him to help you.
   In spite of having the means if he turns down your request he is to
   be blamed not you.

1052. Begging is a pleasure if what is begged
   Comes with no painful pleading needed.

   Begging becomes a pleasant work if the people from whom you seek
   help readily come forward and help you. After all, begging severally
   pressurizing a person to give is not a pleasant job you see.

1053. Never hiding heart and dutiful mind is ideal
   Standing before him and begging is beautiful

   If a person doesn't hide and wants to help you out of a sense of duty
   then standing before him and begging makes a beautiful scene.

1054. Begging, is tantamount to providing
   From him who doesn't even dream hiding.

   Begging a person who even in his dream would not consider hiding
   what he has is as happy an exercise of giving.

1055. With the authentic givers world is truly powered.
      Since to stand before them and beg beggars feel empowered.

Since the presence of genuine (who will not hide what he has) givers
is a fait accompli people boldly stand before the givers and beg.

1056. If men who do not inflict pain by hiding is sighted
      The distress of poverty instantly gets exited

If a man in need happens to meet a person who doesn't inflict pain
by denying, his pain of want disappears instantly. Therefore let him
encourage himself to ask for help.

1057. If a giver who doesn't condemn and reproach is sighted
      With Joy from its bottom heart gets delighted.

If an alms seeker comes across a person who gifts without contempt
or ridicule his heart gets delighted bottom up. Therefore let the world
be kind enough to help those who are in need.

1058. If requesters are absent, the mighty and cool universe
      Remains as a land of lifeless puppets.

Let the world be aware an universe will be as lifeless as puppet if the
events of several people without any inhibition coming forward to
request and several people whole heartedly obliging requesters are
not happening.

1059. People eager enough to give have no action left
      If persons needing to request cease to exist.

The most important purpose of life on this earth is to make use of
the opportunities and evolve at the level of one's soul. One activity
which is a soul evolver is giving to the destitute and the needy food,

labor and time. Therefore those who need patronage from others need not shy of seeking it.

1060. When denied, a beggar not to get anger
For poverty being across the board is evidenced by his hunger.

A beggar should not get anger at a person who denies giving him. Perhaps he doesn't have enough to give. The evidence for such a possibility is borne by the fact that the beggar himself is seeking alms only because he doesn't have.

Skills to be learnt:

➤ One should come out of the script of: I shall not ask for help from anyone under any circumstance.

Rationale:

➤ Society according to Thiruvalluvar is a big family in which anyone who has the means to help others should come forward to do so. Such people experience no difficulty to give because they consider helping others as their duty. They also choose it as a way to evolve at the level of their souls. They know only way to reach God is achieving an evolved soul. That being the case anyone in dire poverty condition should avail help from such persons without any hesitation.

➤ An attitude of, 'don't hesitate to ask for a help and don't hesitate to give a help,' need to be developed in an individual to instill the above skill. Most of us may not have this attitude because we have a strong belief that we should be independent and under no circumstances ask for help from others. This is a good objective in terms of chapter 107. But this should not be pursued to the extent that we create a taboo in our mind regarding receiving help.

➤ Perhaps there are three thoughts in most of us which discourages us to give help or receive help. We may feel asking for help is an onslaught on our ability to look after ourselves. Second, we may think if we receive help from someone we would love to follow it and return the help to the one who helped us at an appropriate time which is bothersome and therefore should be avoided at any cost. Lastly, what if we ask for help and are denied in the event of which is it not a great insult for our self respect?

➤ Asking for help is not an onslaught because if a person has an enlightened ability to give love to others he or she will readily come forward to help you. It is a natural functioning of the society. Everyone gets opportunity to help others. Hardly there is anyone who has not taken any help from others in their entire life.

➤ Of course remembering the help received and returning it at the time the helper wants and in the form he wants is bothersome. While we can take enough effort to meet this contingency we can easily tell the person while receiving help from him to approach us when he or she wants a help. Alternatively we can also tell him or her that we will remember the help and return it to some other needy person and dedicate it to him or her.

➤ The idea that you lose self-respect in the event of your request for help getting turned down is countered by Tiruvalluvar through the couplet:

> Beg a man who can afford. Mind you,
> If he hides blame lies with him not with you.   1051

Coaching:

➤ The technique adopted by Thiruvalluvar to encourage people to seek help in case they need it is: Remove the stigma attached to begging. The following culled out from the chapter presents such an exercise:

➤ "If a person has the means he should give. Go ahead and request him. If he denies he is at blame. Not you."(1051)

➤ You may think begging is very pain full. My dear man it is not really so. You will find it as a pleasure and an act of grace if you have a chance to beg a person who would never hide what he has and feel duty bound to help the needy. (1052)

➤ In fact begging is on par with gifting because with a person who would never hide what he has it is an exercise of mutual joy: One finds joy in giving and another finds the same in receiving! (1053)

➤ I will even go one step further: begging is equivalent to gifting. You know for a person who even in his dream would not think of hiding what he has, you are gifting an opportunity to him to feel good by receiving from him. (1054)

➤ How do you think this habit of people who are depleted seeking help from the one who has and doesn't hide has come about? It is because such a phenomenon has been a reality for over a long period here. (1055)

➤ Even before you receive your pain is gone if you are lucky to meet someone who is too ready to give and will never ridicule you. (1056/57)

➤ Remember you give the zing thing to the world by your act of begging. (1058)

➤ How donors could pass their litmus test for a charitable heart unless you give them an opportunity to show it? (1059)

➤ Sometimes you may come across someone whom you know has but hides. Perhaps he also suffers from poverty like you!" (1060)

107

Fear of Begging

1061. Hides not; whole heatedly gives; apple of your eyes
Even with him not begging worth millions.

It is worth billions in bringing good to you if you decide not to beg
even from those who readily and whole heartedly and joyfully give
to you because they are capable of empathizing with you regarding
your plight.

1062. If humans are but ordained to beg to make a living
Let the creator of the world go pillar to post begging.

If it is true that God who has created this universe ordained that
some should take to begging I curse him to go begging like the ones
he has ordained.

(If you recall the couplets 1040 and 1041 you will agree that
Thiruvalluvar would not hold God responsible for the poverty of
someone. Then why is he cursing god in this couplet? Perhaps he is
trying to wean human beings from begging by using a technique.
When something absurd is pushed to its logical end its absurdity will
be revealed. Therefore when Tiruvalluvar curses God they will be
startled to realize their folly after all God can never be responsible for
the misery of human being. Still some of us have the habit of finding
fault with our fate or lack of blessing from God or excepting a dire
condition as god given etc., Thiruvalluvar attacks this mind set in

this couplet. It will shake the persons concerned out of the mindset to beg. I believe this is the technique used by Thiruvalluvar.)

1063. 'Poverty is painful; let me beg and get rid of it,'
      On you, your decision is crueler than the cruelest.

The decision that, 'I shall beg and take care of myself,' is the worst cruelty you can perpetuate on yourself because it crushes the immense potentials present in you! You will soul will be terribly upset with your decision.

1064. He ill affords still his great nature prevents him from begging
      His worth is more than the universe's purveying.

If somebody in spite of being under a trying predicament which makes him ill afford avoiding begging decides not to beg his worth cannot be contained within what the world could hold.

1065. A gruel as lite as water
      Is tastiest if earned by one's labor.

A gruel which is as lite as water is the tastiest if it is earned out of one's own labor. (The soup is lite because the individual cannot afford nutritious ingredients.)

1066. 'Water for cow,' may be a welcome request,
      But it demeans the tongue because of its begging context.

Even begging for water to feed a cow is demeaning to the tongue which makes the request because the act still is begging.

1067. I would like to beg those decided to beg
      Don't beg from those who conceals what you beg.

I would like to beg those who decide to beg from someone who doesn't conceal what he could offer to beggars.

1068. Begging is an unprotected boat
It gets destroyed when a rock – 'the hider' is met.

Begging is like a small weakly built boat not safe on waters with hidden rocks. The dream of making it through begging gets smashed once you meet a person who conceals and declares that he has nothing to offer.

1069. Thinking the plight of beggars any heart softens
With the thought of hiding, denier's heart further hardens.

Humans in general find their hearts softening at the plight of a beggar. But the hider quickly thinks of concealing what he has as a result of which his heart hardens fully.

1070. Life crumbles hearing a beggar's plight
Where on earth the denier hides his heart?

If we sight a beggar our heart crumbles. Where on earth the one who conceals his heart hides his heart to escape crumbling?

The skills to be learnt:

➤ Ability to dissuade oneself from begging.

Rationale:

➤ Thirukkural is a treatise which concentrates out and out on human capacity building. The previous chapter concentrates to remove the stigma about begging because begging, like a first aide, has a very urgent role in the endeavor of capacity building. But should be a lost resort and one should come out of it as quickly as possible.

> ➢ Therefore it is befitting it has the present chapter which urges people in unequivocal terms not to beg providing a counter weight.

Coaching:

> ➢ The technique adopted by Tiruvalluvar resembles a technique of Adler: "Spit in the cup of tea." If somebody is about to enjoy his cup of tea if you take the cup from him and spit into it and return it saying, "Now drink," how will he feel? Of course you getting slapped by him not being ruled out he would lose his interest totally. Is it not? This is what Thiruvalluvar has done in this chapter after commending begging so much (as a first aide) in the previous chapter here he says just the opposite. For that reason a decision by a person to beg (who doesn't need to beg) will get shattered. That is what in my opinion Thiruvalluvar wants to achieve.

He says to the person who thinks he can somehow manage through begging thus:

> ➢ You may find a person who never conceals. But if you decide not to seek help even from him your act is splendid. (1061)
> ➢ Don't say God has ordained you to beg. If it is really so I curse him to take to begging. (1062)
> ➢ No other hurt you can release on yourself as brutal as your thought: "Let me take care of my poverty condition through begging. (1063)
> ➢ The noble quality of deciding not to beg even under trying conditions worth's the whole universe. (1064)
> ➢ Even if what you could manage was a lite soup only it should be the tastiest because your labor has got it for you!(1065)
> ➢ Remember even begging water for feeding a cow should be avoided because it is also an act of begging. (1066)
> ➢ I beg all those set on the intention to beg to look for a donor who would not hide what he has. (1067)
> ➢ Begging cannot be permanent strategy because it is like a weakly built boat which will be smashed if it collides against hidden rock

under the water. Beware you may land on a situation you hardly find a donor. (1068)

➢ It is a fact if someone begs us our heart melts but it is not the case with those who wants to hide. Their hearts rather harden when they hear a request for help. (1069)

➢ I have seen them and have wondered where they would have hidden their hearts after all our heart melts even when we hear the voice of help seekers? (1070) Therefore do not think you have a permanent solution in begging.

108

Unscrupulous (Meanness)

1071. Unscrupulous looks human like
Nowhere have I seen such a look alike

Unscrupulous persons also look like normal people. I have not seen such similarity anywhere.

1072. Unscrupulous are gifted than the good-conscious
Since such scruples are out of their conscious.

Unscrupulous people are fortunate compared to people who are conscious of what is good and make efforts to adhere to it. You know how? Because their hearts do not suffer on such issues! (Scrupulous people always fight within themselves to up hold *aram*.)

1073. Like heavenly beings unscrupulous are free
On what they do they are also on a wish-spree.

Heavenly beings are free to carry out what they want to. Unscrupulous men also do not abide by any dos and don'ts. (You may see the surreptitious put down of mean minded people by the poet after all even though divine beings can do anything they wish they will always adhere to *aram* whereas the mean minded would not.)

1074. Sighting their likes they over power them
And take pride in their thuggish claim.

If unscrupulous men happen to come across people who are similar to them they will suppress them and take pride in it. ((They follow the pecking order principle and stabilize their position. That means in case they find a thug who is superior they will fall in line.)

1075. Creating terror is their modus operandi first
Next they may also exploit a small virtue list.

Creating a terror in the minds of the victims and make them carry out what they desire is their strategy. Sometimes they may follow a virtuous path if the same can bring the results of their choice.

1076. Unscrupulous are drummers [222]
Since the secret they hear they drum.

Mean minded people proclaim any secret they come to know of someone across the town like a drummer. They are least bothered about the repercussions their announcement have for the victims.

1077. Until on his jaw a smashing fist lands
Even a gravel an unscrupulous never throws

They wouldn't spare even those few grains of food sticking to their fingers after eating to a needy person on their own accord. But they would do so once they see that by doing that they can save their jaws from crushing by the powerful blow delivered by the mighty ones.

1078. On request great men readily release benefit
When crushed like a cane' unscrupulous does it.

Physical torture, like crushing a cane for extracting its juice is needed to extract a benefit from unscrupulous persons. Whereas a *sandrone*

---

[222] In the past drummers were used to proclaim state subjects to the people. They would do so after getting the attention of the people by beating a drum.

comes forward to help the moment he hears a narrative regarding some need.

1079. Of the good dress and food another enjoy
Unscrupulous attributes foul means and find joy.

Unscrupulous are unable to bear the sight of prosperity of others. Probably they have a sense of entitlement: a variety of it, wherein they feel they should have and they can enjoy what they have only when others do not have them on equal measure. Because of this they call it foul when they see others also have a good life in terms of material benefit like them.

1080. What does an unscrupulous possess?
He sells himself at calamitous.

An unscrupulous person lacks self-respect. He will quickly sell himself to wriggle out of a calamitous situation.

Skills to be learnt:

> Looking for any trait of unscrupulousness in one's personality and getting rid of it.
> Skills to safeguard oneself from unscrupulous persons.

Rationale:

> Unscrupulous behavior leads to all sorts of trouble. Perhaps it is a good idea to check within ourselves for the presence of any of the traits discussed above and get rid of it or them.
> Second picking up some skills to safeguard oneself from the unscrupulous persons is also a worthy idea.

Coaching:

> If you are a casual person not taking charge of your life change yourself. Creating time management charts and sticking to them will help. Second if you tell lies it is easy to stop it if you take a conscious decision and stick to it. Initially you may fail. Don't make it as an excuse to abandon the decision. It is ok to fail as long you restart your effort with new vigor. It will dawn on you one day. You will become a changed person from then onwards. A care free attitude is another aspect of personality which one has to fight (1071).

> Are you a person who generally do not break his head over issues of right and wrong? If yes please understand that it is an unscrupulous trait. Always look for good in any act you do. Avoid activities which do not deliver good (1072).

> If you have a tendency to ill-treat persons below your rank or social class drop it (1074).

> Never use aggression or positional or muscular power to subordinate any one (1075).

> Never carry the stories of others around the town (1076).

> Don't be stingy (1977).

> Never reel out pooh-poohing stories about others achievements or assets (1079).

> Never belittle yourself and readily compromise on a matter (1080).

Skills regarding safeguarding from unscrupulous persons:

> Couplet 1074 indicates a rowdy or unscrupulous person has a natural tendency to subdue anyone who crosses his path. Therefore the best policy it to keep away from such an individual. In case confronting an individual is absolutely necessary enough force should be mobilized to tackle him. Many whistle blowers in India who crossed sword with mafias lost their lives because they kept themselves vulnerable after blowing the whistle (1074).

> Sometimes an unscrupulous person may become soft all of a sudden as though he had a change of heart. Be careful. Check several times

through several independent channels to establish that change of heart is real (1075).

➢   Beware any nonviolent approach or HR technique or Gandhian approach will not work with an unscrupulous person. Gandhi himself would not have succeeded but for the fact British was his opponent. What you should do if you somehow get entangled with an unscrupulous person? You should immediately move away and wait for time to do its work. (1077)

Book on Love[223]

Section on Secret Love

---

[223] In this book instead of a prose commentary I provide the prose of the poem. Of course in few places commentary is given in brackets.

109

Stunned at the Sight of an Angel like Woman

(He excels in reading her body language and finds a complying message in it.)

He speaks to himself

1081. A divine damsel? A rare peahen? Rich ear ring is her plus
Is she a woman? Will she be amenable for my love? My heart
nonpluses.

Is this a woman from heaven? Is she a beautiful peahen created by a
tasteful God? Her rich ear ring perhaps shows her as a woman and
also as available for marriage. Will she agree to my offer of love? My
heart staggers!

1082. Angel's look in turn is a sweeping power
Because an attack of an army her eyes configure.

Her returning looks unnerves me as though I am attacked by an
army.

1083. I know not devouring power of death earlier,
With this fittest[224] damsel's warring looks it is hear.

---

[224] Thiruvalluvar has used the word *penthakhai*. *Thakhai* means standard. The
beauty of the woman is a standard is what the poet wants to say. I have translated
it as 'fittest,' which unfortunately doesn't get us close to the original sense. I
would have happily used 'standardest' if only English allows it!

I have no idea earlier how overwhelming the power of the God of death would be but I realize right now I am under that power thanks to the fittest women's darting looks.

1084. This fittest damsel is bestowed with devouring eyes,
Innocent she may be but the onlooker will be left in shivers.

This fittest woman's looks devours its target in spite of the fact that she is innocent.

1085. Life sapping eyes? Scanning eyes? Arresting eyes?
This young women's eyes combine all these.

Her eyes saps my life; scans my heart; keeps me spellbound. My God! She arrests me!

1086. Out of fear my heart will not palpitate
If stern looks her brow doesn't precipitate.

If she doesn't crook her brows her looks will lose their sternness. Then my heart has no reason to palpitate.

1087. Bra on the full-swell straight virgin breasts of her
Resembles the forehead shield of a rutted tusker.

Her well-built breasts protrude straight. On them the bra sits. The picture compares very well with that of a tusker wearing a bronze shield on the forehead (the two halves of the shield mimic her breasts and bra the shield!).

1088. My might which my enemies fear at wars
Before her lustrous forehead disappears.

My daredevil-might which my enemies fear crumples before her lustrous forehead.

1089. Who the unthoughtful gave her those alien ornaments?
When doe eyes and modesty are her possessions.

Who gave her those jewels which look alien on her? Moreover what additional beauty those ornaments could bring to her who is spectacular with her deer like fear mixed young looks, and modesty?

1090. Arrack needs to be consumed to get the kick
Whereas her lusty look alone does the trick.

Arrack of fermented palm juice or fruit juice gives kick only on consumption of it. Whereas this woman gives kick to me simply by looking at me.

Skills to be learnt:

> Ability to appreciate the beauty of women in whom a person develops an interest.

Rationale:

> 'Beauty is in the eyes of the beholder,' goes the saying. This chapter describes where the beauty of the lady lays. Of course cultures vary in their emphasis. The heroine and the hero should be reading from the same page. Otherwise what is given importance by the man may be ignored by the woman which could pose serious problem for the relationship!

Coaching:

> To start with the hero is stunned by the looks of the frame of the heroine.(1081)
> Later he is stunned at the beauty of her eyes, fore head, eyelashes. (1082)
> Probably after little time(?) he sees her straight breasts.(1087)
> Above all what he appreciates is her blush and vine like body.

> ➤ The above description tells one thing: while the hero is trying to eat her with his eyes she is also at home with what he does. That means there is a cultural tally between the tastes of both of them with regard to what constitutes feminine and masculine beauty.

> ➤ It is a good strategy to find out what makes a man or woman attractive to his or her partner and do the needful to increase the attractiveness. Find out the cultural expectations of your partner in this regard and meet him or her after equipping yourself suitably.

> ➤ One should not think this as trivial because the sensitivities and mental imagery of both men and women have been very keenly cultivated in this regard and any man or woman should take it seriously to avoid issues over it. Many a love goes not blossomed due to lack of cultural compatibility regarding what constitute good looks in a given culture!

110

Reading the Signs

(He excels in reading her body language and finds a complying message in it.)

He speaks

1091. Two looks exist in her dyed eyes for sure
    One instills sickness another its cure.

Her eyes through their looks do two things. They instill sickness and cure it as well. (Perhaps the woman throws an indifferent look or look away only to play a prank on him. He panics. Later she throws a concerned look and relives him of his panic. God saved mother land. She is amenable for him! This conformation scenes continues up to couplet no.1095.)

1092. Her small but stealing look
    Provides more than half of the lust.

The pleasure offered by a look which shifts before it is reciprocated is more than half of what an intercourse could offer.

1093. She looked at me and looked servile
    This act of hers sent my head into cool.

She looked at me and (perhaps an intimate thought of love made her blush) she bent her head and looked down. This excessively pleasing act of hers piped ice into my head.

1094. If I look at her she would look down
      If I do not she would look at me and smile.

      When I look at her she looks down and when I don't look at her she
      looks at me and throws a small smile.

1095. She wouldn't look at me straight
      Only through the end of her eyes right?

      She would pretended as if she was not looking at me. But she would
      send her eyes sideways to extreme end and look at me. Not only has
      that she would also smile at me.

      (Perhaps her friends chide her and in response she speaks loudly what
      is meant for him which the poet has not covered. What is contained
      in the next couplet is observation made by him.)

1096. Tone of voice could show as if it chides a stranger
      But words devoid of anger would show the owner nearer.

      Though the tone of voice might indicate chiding the words chosen
      would show it is not the case! (This is the observation by him on
      what is spoken by her. Perhaps she speaks simultaneously to two
      constituencies – her friends and him! For them, harsh looks and tone
      of voice and for him not harsh words.)

1097. Words indicating no anger but looks bearing anger,
      A pretending woman's signs of emotional languor.[225]

      Her words are not harsh but her looks are. This shows this guy is
      soft and all her signs are but the handiwork of womanhood which
      will not make it known daringly but make it after making one to
      wear.

---

[225] Languor means a soft or tender mood or effect.

1098. Her sensibility is her strength and beauty
When I persist she responded with a small smile.

To my persistent look her answer is a small smile. This shows her
sensibility which is her strength as well as beauty.

Her friend
1099. Gazing at the open like a stranger
Looks, present only with a lover.

An aimless look at the horizon ignoring the lover as though he was
a stranger is present only with a lover.

1100. What one look reveals if the other matches
There is no use for speeches.

When pairs of eyes look at the same page there is no need for words.

Skills to be learnt:

> The skill involved here is known as reading the body language.
A man who is very good at this skill will have no difficulties in
following the mind of his lady love. Of course this was written some
2000 years ago. There is lot of change in the present scenario at least
in cities. May be the innocence, panic and tension are still undergone
by lovers in the rural areas? Reading body language has lot of role in
love. It is a worthy skill to learn.

Rationale:

> Couplet number 1092 gives an idea about the usefulness of body
language. It says the coming together of eyes secretly but surely
communicating yes for an answer serves like foreplay in sex. It goes
to the extent of saying that the pleasure is more than half of what
one gets in intercourse! Learning the body language to maximize the
sexual pleasure is suggested indirectly in this chapter.

Coaching:

For men

➤ A woman is likely to communicate her interest more through her eyes. Learn to catch it (1091).

➤ When she looks at you, to derive the maximum pleasure what you have to do is completely letting your inhibitions go. If you flow with her leaving aside any other consideration you will find the experience very enjoyable. In sex you should behave as though you are a child i.e., total absence of inhibition (1092).

➤ When she looks at you, if you allow a full depth for your emotions you will find your head becoming cool (1093).

➤ A woman however modern she is will blush when she meets her man for the first time (1094). This is a process. Allow it to go as long as it goes.

➤ A woman will show her positive feelings in so many different ways using her eyes, words, body postures and gestures. Unless you develop the skill to catch them you may disappoint her (1095, 1096, 1097, 1098 and 1099).

➤ Poet emphatically says if only lovers develop the skill of reading body language you don't need spoken communication at all (1100).

111

Enjoying Embrace

They taste it for the first time and he explains it with joy

1101. In this bangled beauty reside the feast
Sight, sound, touch, taste and smell Oh! Vast.

In her glorious beauty there lies a suave which caters to all my five senses.

1102. An affliction's medicine is not from itself
But for the pain she creates she is the cure herself.

In general an affliction can be cured by a medicine whose source is different from the disease. But for the disease created by her she herself is the cure. (Perhaps next days also he had sex with her. The craving induced by the previous day's intercourse could be catered to only by another intercourse is the message one should get from this statement of his.)

1103. Is lotus-eyed God's[226] world a sweeter den
Than sleeping on the shoulders of a woman who wills in?

---

[226] Refers to god Lord Narayan whose eyes are eulogized as beautiful as lotus.

You[227] say the world of lotus-eyed God is sweet and blessed. But is it better than the shoulders of your lady love that willingly lets you sleep on them? (Perhaps a friend of his who tried to dissuade him got a fitting reply!)

1104. Wherefrom she got this magical fire? Tell me
It burns a separated me and cools a united we.

She is like a magical fire. If I am closer to her it cools me. If I separate a little it burns. Wherefrom she got this magical fire?

1105. Desires dip and raise catering pleasures anew
This flower decked haired woman's shoulder needs no renew.

Desires satiate only to spring afresh later for harvesting a new joy. The pleasure offered by this flower decked lady with copious hair has no such ups and downs. It is always up.

1106. Since each embrace of this young girl help life rejuvenate
Her shoulders are made of nectar must be a caveat.

Whenever I embrace her shoulders I feel very fresh and fine. Because of this the proposition that her shoulders are made of nectar must be valid!

1107. The joy obtained by embracing this dame
Equals sharing self-earned food with stake holders in own home

The joy (satisfaction) of embracing her is similar to owning a self-earned house with enough self-earned food and being able to share it with dear and near who have a right over what the householder has earned.

---

227 Perhaps disputing with a friend who said to him that instead of seeking the permanent bliss at the world of Lord Narayan one should not indulge in such transient and ephemeral pleasures.

(He brings in social obligation in the context of sexual pleasure! Social obligation by investing what one has earned through one's sweat is an example to the pure joy of sex.)

1108. Air cannot travel through that tight embrace
With this a willing couple pleasure brace.

When a couple willingly embraces air cannot pass between embrace. The couple reaps real pleasure through such an embrace.

1109. Lover's sulk, give in and proceed to intercourse
Lust due to this is on the mode of increase.

The lady sulks and yields. This process brings great relief for the man doubling his sexual feelings leading to enhanced performance. The enhanced feelings and performance are the fruits of the measured sulk.

1110. Every new learning exposes an old ignorance
Every embrace of this beautifully bangled is a new experience.

Every time a concept is perceived anew new an earlier ignorance is realized and a new learning takes place. Similarly every embrace of her is a new leaf of experience.

Skills to be learnt:

> Sexual experience is enhanced if and when the male concentrates on the women rather than concentrate on his orgasm. This concept is revealed very well in this chapter. This is a skill which requires conscious cultivation to master it.

Rationale:

> Woman's body is like a sex facility with several centers through which a woman offers and receive sexual satisfaction. Therefore it is

natural that man should pay attention to all those centers adequately to get the pleasure as well offer them to her. Perhaps to avoid a tag of porno getting attached to his master piece Tiruvalluvar has avoided few centers here which are not difficult to identify.

Coaching:

> According a very high importance to sex is emphasized in couplet number 1103. Hero becomes enigmatic regarding the claim that after life in heaven is more enjoyable than the life in this universe. "How life on this universe which involves sleeping on the shoulders of a woman who willingly offer sex can be less pleasurable," asks he. Some of us, especially due to some difficulties/restrictions in carrying out sexual performance, may undermine the need for sex in the life of human. That is wrong, tells the couplet.

> Body warmth is enjoyable and is a facility for enhancing sexual joy. Care should be taken by the man to give it to her fully and also enjoy himself receiving it from her in equal measure. (1104)

> Lady's shoulders are like mines wherein ingenious men can unearth several pleasures fresh every time. (1105)

> Embracing the shoulders are like mines wherein ingenious men can unearth several pleasures fresh every time. (1105)

> Embracing the shoulders intensely at the same time gently yields a rejuvenating joy. Take care to harvest it by doing the needful (1106)

> A person derives joy in dining with others who have a stake over his earnings. There is enormous belongingness involved here which provide the reason for the joy. Same thing holds well in the case of sexual joy, provided the women feels she belongs to him and he reciprocates that sense of belongingness. Achieve this in your relationship. (1107)

> Couplet 1109 says women should use her act of sulking intelligently. If she extends it too long it will become counterproductive. Very nominal sulking will not get him motivated enough. Therefore study the situation and master the art of sulking (1109)

> How much seriously a man should approach the art of sex like a student who approaches learning. Every time a student approaches his subject he learns something new. A man in sex also can reap new skills in the art of sex.(1110)

112

Praising Her Beauty

He evaluates her beauty

1111. "Hail to thee delegate *anicham*[228] my love
      Is slenderer than you to whom 'me' I give

      My dear delicate *anicham* long life to you! But my beloved is more
      delegate than you.

1112. Oh! My heart how confused you must be
      To hold my love's eyes as common as these flowers.

      Flowers seen everywhere by everyone are commonplace. O! My heart
      you misperceived my beloved's eyes as similar to those flowers.

1113. Tender shoot body, pearly teeth, she is aroma wound
      Dart- eyes, tender bamboo-shoulders too found.

      Her body shines like a tender shoot, her teeth are like pearls. She has
      a sweet aroma around her. Her eyes are like darts due to the picture
      painted around them and her shoulders are tender bamboos.

---

[228] *Anicham* is a plant whose flowers are very tender. In couplet number 90 Valluvar
makes use of its delicateness to describe how delicate guests are. He says *anicham*
needs a puff of breath to wither. Whereas guests do not need even that. An
indifferent look is enough to dishearten them.

1114. *Kuvalai*[229] bends its head in shame
For it holds its flower and her eyes by looks are not the same.

On seeing her eyes water lily bends her head in shame. This is because the lily which usually is proud of the beauty of its flower now finds her flowers are not as beautiful as my beloved's eyes.

1115. She wore *anicham* flowers with their stalks
Oh! 'They would break her waist!' bet the drums.

The drum of distress announces that she wore *anicham* without removing their stalks and her waist would break not being able to take the load.

1116. Moon and her face the stars could not differentiate
Their lost position in relation to moon they could not reinstate.

My beloved's face is strikingly similar to the moon. Stars which sometimes think, 'her face is the moon' sometimes think, 'moon is her face'. They are confused indeed!

1117. Moon is not constant in size and has spots black
Does my girl?

(It appears this couplet and the previous one need to be read together to get the mind of the poet.) Hero questions the wisdom of stars which mistake his beloved's face for moon. He asks, 'How come stars mistake my beloved's face for moon? After all moon waxes and wanes. More over my beloved doesn't has black spots on her face.'

1118. If your face shines like that of my woman
I bless you a love life O! Moon.

---

229 The water-lily

If you strive to become spotless and shine like my woman my blessings are for you to be successful in getting a lover.[230] Let another great chapter on love begin.

1119. If your face looks like that of my woman with lotus - eyes
Don't appear before several eyes.

If you gain a face like my woman then don't show it to all. (Reserve it only for your lover.) (It appears the hero is carried on further in his thought that the moon deserves a good love life. In order to achieve that she should avoid appearing in the presence of many which could give an opportunity for a scandal.[231])

1120. *Anicham* and swan's flowers are nettles
When on them her sole settles.

Anicham and swans feathers hurt like thorns on the tender sole of my woman. (Probably hero is reflecting over the contingency of taking his woman to the far of place where he has to go for the purpose of business. Since the path is a baron stretch of land with lot of thorny plants and his woman's soles are so tender that even swan's feathers and flowers of anicham plant would prove thorny he concludes that it was impossible to take her along with him.)

Skills to be learnt:

> The wellbeing of the woman in terms of the stature of her body is highlighted in this couplet. For intimate sex a sound body with proper shape is very helpful. Therefore men and women should pay attention to improve the shape of their bodies.

---

[230] This couplet and the next are interpreted showing the hero not aversive to polygamy which is not acceptable to me.

[231] Scandal results with many competing for her love and fighting among them and stories in the grape vine taking unhelpful themes or giving twists or too much of publicity complicating the matter.

Rationale:

➢ Body shape plays a very important role in a satisfied sexual experience and also ensures a continuous wonderment to the woman's man. May be woman should carry on appropriate exercises to get a proper shape. A body exercised well will become more attractive than before. Therefore it is worth trying at least for the sake of enjoying a quality sex. But too much of exercise, will reduce sexual urge and your performance will suffer.

Coaching:

➢ Couplet 1111 speaks about tender body which can be achieved by aerobics and swimming.

➢ Couplet 1112 says that her eyes look like a flower. The eyes may look like a flower provided the skin around the eye socket is kept healthy. If the skin looks aged the eyes will lose luster. Skin moisturizers specifically meant for eyes may be used for making them to look shiny. The pit below the eye ball may be very deep by making the eyes look like as though they are inside a well. Simple sculpting technique (allowed by insurance) is available for this defect.

➢ Most of the other defects including squint eye are correctable and most of them are supported by insurance. Therefore it is a wise decision to rectify simple correctable defects.

➢ Couplet 1113 says the skin of the body of his woman shines like a new shoot. The wisdom which our elders pass on to us in this regard is: 'eat lot of greens and vegetables, drink two liters of water every day and consume little ghee regularly.'

➢ The same couplet (1113) also mentions about kiss, seductive smile and perfume having important roles in sex. A problem which is so common and on which hangs business worth of several hundred billions is the oral odor. Odor due to dental cavities, bad gum and bad stomach condition are distressingly common. Many of us do not take it seriously and take steps to avoid it. Oral and body odor can be real killers of sexual pleasure.

➢   Some of the basic and simple substances like baking soda or a mixture of 50% hydrogen peroxide and 50% water help to maintain good oral health.

➢   The role of perfume of the right choice and seductive smile can never be taken as casually.

➢   Couplet 1115 speaks about thin hips. Thinning of hips is achievable along with slender body through swimming and aerobics.

➢   A well exercised body also helps to overcome depression.

113

Praise of the Beloved

(In separation they muse on the great qualities of each other.)

HE

1121. Her cool words and clean teeth's dew
Are honey mixed with milk.

She is a woman of cool words. Her clean teeth's due together with her cool words is honey mixed with milk.

1122. The bond between me and my dame
Is same as that of body and life.

The bond between me and she is as intimate and intricate as the bond between body and life.

1123. O pupil of my eye! vacate the place
She who falls for me has no other space

Pupil of my eye please vacate making room for my woman who willingly yields to me.

1124. The 'jeweled' is for me like life to soul
When she is away it is death.

To me the jewel adorned woman is like a living body to soul. When she is away it is like soul lives no more in a dead body.

1125. Only forgotten qualities are recalled
     I don't need to, on the warring bright eyed.

Bright and warring eyes are her supreme qualities which I never recall after all one recalls only what is forgotten!
SHE

1126. He lives in my eyes and would never leave
     So well integrated my winking doesn't hurt him I believe.

My man has become part and parcel of my eyes. Even if my eyes wish he would never leave. For the same reason when I wink it doesn't hurt him.

1127. I don't paint my eyes where my lover lives
     Since I know during painting his image I miss.

I don't want to miss his image in my eyes even for a second. Therefore I have done away with painting of my eyes because I know while painting I miss him.

1128. My lover lives in my heart. I don't eat hot
     Since I fear if I do so he would feel the heat.

Since my lover lives in my heart I don't eat hot as he is likely to be affected by the heat of the food if I eat hot!

1129. I fear losing his image therefore I keep awake
     Villagers ridicule him as a deserter for giving me the wake.

I have noticed that when I close my eyes he disappears. Therefore I keep awake. Villagers mistake it as distress and ridicule him for causing it.

1130. He resides in my heart gladly forever
Since he is away village holds him for a deserter.

My lover lives happily in my heart. Since he physically lives elsewhere the villagers assume that he has no love for me, he is a deserter etc., and blame him.

Skills to be learnt:

> When lovers are separated for some reason they should develop the ability to create vivid mental images of their earlier life and relive the same at the level of their mind. This is a strength which will keep the flame of love glowing and help to overcome the separation.

Rationale:

> Human mind doesn't differentiate much between imagining something and actually experiencing something. Therefore mentally reliving the past life/living a resolution is a good strategy to keep the love and concern for an intimate person, who is at present is not around, intact and beating.

Coaching:

> All the couplets revolve around a healthy vivid reliving of earlier life which the man and the woman enjoyed together. This is a process which is necessary to tide over the difficulty of not having the husband/wife around. Some of the techniques adapted by him and her are:

HE

> He recalls his experience of kissing her. He says juice of her lips is a mixture of milk and honey.

- ➢ He says his union with her is like that between life and body. Creating an emotion reflecting this sentiment is important not a poetic or intellectual statement at the level of lips (1122).
- ➢ He takes it seriously and flows with the feelings is demonstrated quite surprisingly when he orders the pupil of his eyes to get out making room for his woman. The absurdity demonstrates how authentic he is in dwelling in his feelings. This is what is needed (1123).
- ➢ His mental life becomes quite rich when he compares his relationship with her to that of soul and a living body.
- ➢ His resolve makes it appearance once more. He says since he forgets her not even for a second the question of remembering her doesn't arise (1225).

SHE

- ➢ She and he are not two entities. This is mentally re-experienced by her. She says to an imagined doubting Thomas that he lives integrated in her eyes! (1126).
- ➢ The seriousness with which she believes what she has said earlier is brought out by her next statement. She says she has stopped dying her eyes for the reason it might hurt him (1127)!
- ➢ Now she feels he is merged into her. Look what she says. "Since my lover lives in my heart I don't eat hot as he is likely to be affected by the heat of the food if I eat hot." (1128)
- ➢ There is no end to this inclusivity. She takes it to a different front. She says, "Since my lover's image would disappear if I close my eyes I keep them open permanently. This village with no idea on why I keep awake ridicules my lover assuming that because of the distress he has created I have gone sleepless. What a pity!" (1129/30)

114

Relinquishing Shame

(He loses patience as well as his sense of shame. He decides to sit
on a palmyra horse — a nonviolent demonstration — to impress
upon her parents his ardent love for their daughter and get their
consent to his marriage with their daughter!)

HE

1131. For a love sufferer there is only one recourse
That is powerful 'palmyra horse.'[232]

For a deep sufferer due to a stalled love there is no further push other
than the Palmyra horse.

1132. Setting aside shame my suffering body
And soul proceed to embark *madal.* [233]

---

[232] Palm horse or *'madal'* in Tamil means a horse like structure made out of the
hands of palm leaves. The lover sits on this thorny horse and the horse is pulled
by persons interested in his welfare singing songs of pathos. Since the thorns in
a Palmira horse are like the teeth of a saw he receives several cuts and bleeds. In
this bleeding condition he also sits at the town square. By subjecting himself to
such hardships and physical hurt and shame he proves his resolve to the parents
of the heroine. The girl's parents impressed by the seriousness of the wooer might
agree to give the hand of their daughter in marriage to him.

[233] *Madal* another word to mean a palmyra horse

Body would find it extremely difficult to withstand the pain. Soul would find losing the honor as painful as death but still both of them (soul and heart) are determined to mount the Palmyra horse unmindful of pain and losing honor.

1133. Sense of shame and manly valor were my possessions early
Today lovers' Palmyra riding is my mission barely.

I had strong sense of shame and physical prows earlier but today I have only Palmyra horse riding.

1134. Love, the stormy flood, washes away the raft,
Of manly resolve and sense of shame built.

Love behaves like a powerful stormy current of flood. It can wash away the raft built with manly resolve and sense of shame.

1135. She who wears bracelets of flowers gave the innings
Of Palmyra riding and sorrow of the evenings.

On account of my lady, wearing small bangles of flowers, I have this Palmyra riding and separation-pain woven evenings.

1136. My eyes on account of she never go to sleep
Even during the midnight my thought on *madal* riding I keep.

I am incapable of sleeping on account of her. Even during midnight I keep awake and contemplate about Palmyra horse.

1137. She is drowned in love but still riding palmyra resists
Nothing more admirable than this. [234]

---

[234] It appears riding a palmyra horse is common for both the sexes.

My woman has not resorted to palmyra horse riding despite of her painful separation and bite of love. Nothing more admirable than she.

She

1138. No social etiquette neither pity on me
To such people my lust exposes me.

People around me do not have any social etiquette. They will poke their nose into what is happening with me. They don't have any consideration on account of my pitiable situation. It is a pity to such indifferent people my lust exposes me!

1139. My heart says, not everyone knows
To make it known with anxiety it roams.

My heart thinks that everyone do not know my love situation. It wants to make it known as widely as possible. But alas it is anxious about the outcome.

1140. When they sight me they laugh, idiots
They have not walked our steps.

When some of them who have some idea of what is happening around me smile in silence I get irritated. Idiots they don't know how it feels. They have not walked my steps after all!

Skills to be learnt:

> Lovers may meet opposition for their marriage from the parents or other powerful sources like the so called custodians of culture! In such situations they need to come out of the feelings of embarrassment thoroughly. Other considerations also may have to be dropped. They should start working to realize their marriage

Rationale:

> The chapter portrays a picture that existed among ancient Tamils. The lovers who secretly meet each other fall in love and may have sex. When they want to marry later they may want to take their parents along with their decision. If parental support is not readily coming they resort to the method of subjecting themselves to torture to prevail over their parents. Parents, who otherwise may not oppose the concept of love marriage do so for some time for other reasons and ultimately will come around and give their consent. In today's India which is divided by so many denominations love marriages are opposed by parents and communities for reasons (principally economic and caste) other than compatibility between the man and woman. But among the educated and well employed middle class inter caste or inter religious marriages do not meet such stiff opposition.

Coaching:

> Difficulties may appear in the form of parental pressures who would oppose a marriage for other considerations other than compatibility and consensus between the man and woman who propose to marry. Parental acquiescence no doubt is very important and every effort should be taken to obtain it. But at the same time the man and woman should not suffer out of any so called obligation to parents or for that matter for anyone because life with a person whom you love is more important than anything else.

> Nonviolent and persistent effort to obtain the permission is laudable. Declaring that you and your lover will marry only when your parents' consent for that is a good idea. The suffering you undergo may be similar to the one illustrated in the chapter (114). You may also wait for that consent for few months or one or two years giving time to your parents to overcome some real difficulties but once you reach a situation where no more valid reasons exists you should decide to marry. Women in India suffer from sentiments of not offending parents or they are under permanent obligation to their parents. Such

sentiments are misplaced. No child is obligated to her or his parent to the extent of foregoing his or her choice in marriage.

> In several parts of the world particularly in India parents want to prevent their daughters and sons from freely choosing their partners. For example, in Haryana, an Indian state, parents come together under the banner of *khap panchayat*, a sort of village court, obviously not allowed under the law of the land, to prevent 'unauthorized' marriages. The *khap panchayats* give from time to time diktats to kill both the boy and the girl who through their marriages defy some obscure norms upheld by the *khap panchayats* regarding who can marry who. Recently an Indian court has decreed death sentence to 7 jury members of one of the *khap panchayats* for awarding death to a couple. In such situations Tiruvalluvar time method of mounting a palmyra horse will not work. It will be foolish to try to convince the parents who obviously have other hidden agenda for their action. Prof. Jagmati Sangwan, Director, women's Study Centre, Maharishi Dayanand University, Rohtak[235] has this to say regarding *khap panchayat*: "As couples are selectively targeted, it is clear the real motive is to control women's sexuality to ensure that property remains within the patriarchal caste domain."

> Men and women who suffer such prospect should make arrangements to migrate to totally different part of the country before marrying. Lot of careful planning, like one would do to get rid wild animals or pests, should be carried out.

> As the stories, time and again appearing in the newspapers in India suggest young couples thinking they should be brave enough to go back and live in the same place where they face grave danger do so only to be hacked to death by parents and their accomplices. Gandhian sprit of *satyagraha* roughly translated a willingness to suffer for the sake of living what one thinks right and just will work with people like British not with brutes. Therefore young couple should be shrewd enough to avoid such adventures.

---

[235] The reader is requested to consult the open source to find out the reference.

➢   Any posture of valor or resilience will not work with brutes that do
not have hearts. What is to be feared should be feared without fail
(428). (It should also be remembered such atrocities which are by
and large rare confining to few pockets are slowly disappearing in
India. (They will die sooner than now provided the politicians due
to vote bank politics do not support such attitudes in the society.)

115

Spread of Rumor

(Rumor in the village)

He
1141. Rumor sustains my life. It is good luck
Many are yet to know that I and she are stuck.

Rumor is good for me since it keeps the issue of my love alive thereby
sustaining my life. The life is sustainable because of the hope as
newer and newer areas are added more pressure will be built making
her parents succumb. It is good luck many are still to know about
the affair keeping the steam intact.

1142. She the lotus-eyed is a rare birth
Village ignorantly gifts me that worth.

With her lotus like eyes she is a rare birth. Village not knowing her
worth inadvertently gifts her to me through the rumor they create.

1143. Will not the rumor attain a full coverage?
My mind already projects it having reached full range.

Will not the rumor catch the entire village? Right now it is negligible
confining itself to few corners. But my mind day dreams that rumor
has covered the entire village!

1144. Love bloats on being talked about. Without rumor
     It loses its warmer

Love bloats feeding on rumor. Without rumor it loses its heat.

1145. Every time one drinks every time he rejoices
     The more rumor spreads the more one's joy is.

Every time one drinks alcohol every time he rejoices. Similarly the spread of rumor as and when it wins new fronts my joy reaches new bounds.

She

1146. In fact we met only once. But the rumor is so replete
     As the serpent's swallow[236] of moon is complete.

In fact we met only once. But the spread of rumor is as complete as complete can be. It is like the serpent *Ragu* swallowing the moon fully.

1147. Rumor manures and mother's words waters
     My love, a chronic disease grows.

Rumor amongst villagers provide the nutrition and my mother's words provide the water. With these two, my disease of love – the plant grows on and on.

---

[236] It is a culturally well engrained mythological story that a celestial serpent called Ragu swallows the moon creating an eclipse. Tiruvalluvar uses mythology stories in very few places relating to Hindu religion to drive home apoint. Otherwise his idea about God is well pictured by him in chapter one, which is a secular one. It will be gratuitous to find his reference to mythological events as indicating his orientation to any religion'

1148. 'Let us Dissuade love through scandal,'
Tantamount to, 'let us put out the fire using oil.'

If the plotters presume that they can kill my love through rumor and reprimand, they imagine that by pouring oil they can douse a fire.

1149. "Will you be shy of scandals? Don't fear them,"
He says so, after I have ignored several of them!

I have dissociated myself from bothering about rumor long back. What a surprise now he says, "Will you be shy of scandals? Don't fear them!"

1150. The village readily raises the rumor I desire
On my proposal consent will come from my Sire.[237]

The village is doing a great service to me. It raises a great scandal over our affair. He will feel justified enough to embrace me if I so desire.

Skills to be learnt:

> The ability shown by the man and woman here is what is termed as, 'converting the problem into prosperity.' Both the man and woman look at the incriminating gossip by the villagers as good enough to bring immense pressure on their parents to agree to their marriage.

Rationale:

> Human beings, especially parents who are democratic and live their life following the precincts of *aram* are highly susceptible to the concerns of the reference group. In the present case the entire village may play the role of a reference group to them. Therefore the scandalous gossip in the town related to their wards is something which they will immediately address and do the needful. Therefore

---

237 The word 'sire' is used in the meaning of an important person or 'Lord for me.'

the technique of keeping the rumor alive instead of seeing it as problem is a right strategy.

Coaching:

> Using the village which provides the reference group for any one in a village/small town or community to bring pressure on the parents is a good strategy provided the village (few villagers constituting the reference group) buys your plan to marry your lover. In case the idea is against the norm, espoused by the reference group namely, only marriages arranged by the parents on both side are acceptable, then your strategy will back fire. Therefore the mindset of the villagers/reference group need to be studied and if the mindset of the villagers/reference group in general is against the notion of love marriage care should be taken to avoid publicity about your love affair lest the pressure from the villagers on your parents will become negative. In the case your reference group is against your marriage then you should try to build a new one by exploiting the existing connections who can be of help to you.

> May be contacting the community leaders who are the gate keepers of the community in the village and winning their support is a good strategy. Couplet 1147 says the talk of the town and mothers support grows the plant of love. It can be the mother or any one who is genuinely interested in you. Catch hold of him or her and take steps to connect her with the gate keepers of the community. They can stand as a support for your effort. Remember rumor can be converted into a useful pressure on your parents provided the rumor is converted into valid information. This can be achieved by the help of the community leaders and your mother.

> Rumor also has another benefit. The bondage between the lady love and the lover becomes more bonded due to the rumor (1150).

Section: Wedded Love

116

Suffering from Separation[238]

(Now they are married but he is on a business trip and she suffers separation.)

She to her friend
1151. Tell me if he is not taking leave,
'Soon return' to those until could live.

If he is not leaving me tell it to me. Otherwise on his plans on when he will return better inform those who would live until such time.

1152. Earlier mere expectation gave pleasure
With his intention to depart even intercourse leaves displeasure.

Earlier even a slight expectation created by him was enough reason for pleasure. But now with his intension to leave even his act of intercourse is a cause for pain.

1153. If wise men who promised not to leave did leave
Faith in him is difficult to have.

We know even wise men broke their promise and left in search of fortune. Therefore it was difficult for me to believe him when he told that he would not leave me.

---

[238] Excepting the first couplet the remaining ones comprise a conversation with her helpmate.

1154. "Don't be afraid," were his compassionate words
Can you blame me for believing him If he deserts?

If he who assuaged my feelings promising me not to afraid over the fear that he would leave now decides to leave can fault be found with me?

1155. If you intend saving my life stop my fiancé
If he leaves meeting again has no chance.

If you are serious about saving my life stop my lover. If he goes away he would never return. I would never have the joy of union.

1156. If he is hard enough to say good bye
Hardly he would return and say hi.

If he has made a stone of his heart to say good bye to me hardly he would return and greet me again.

1157. Will not the town ridicule him[239] for abandoning me
My slipping bangles announcing it before me?

Even If I do not inform the village about his desertion of me my bangles loosening out of my wrist will announce it to them.

1158. Hard to live with no associates around
Harder still with lover not found.

It is harder to live without friends who show a keen understanding of a situation and do the needful. It is hardest to live without one's husband.

---

[239] I have used the word 'him' in place of the Tamil word *thuraivan* used by Tiruvalluvar to refer to the hero. It means the owner of a cool port. The translator has done so to avoid a long line.

1159. Flame could burn only when contacted
Do you know it cannot burn like lust when separated?

Flame burns only when contacted. But lust burns when not in contact. Do you know that?

1160. By digressing into hard projects many are alive
Thus they take on their separation and survive.

By taking the mind off and thrusting it on some project many are able to come to terms with their separation and survive it.

Skills to be learnt:

> The ability to live through separation and emerge out successfully from self-pity.

Rationale:

> From the days of Tiruvalluvar people migrating in search of livelihood has been common place. Wife under such circumstances need to keep herself from being shattered. Especially for the new wed wife this is a time having the potentials to dip her into depression. Depression may be caused because of self-pity. Couplet 1160 gives a method for beating self-pity. Take your mind off from the loss and concentrate on a new project which absorbs your time and energy. This makes you to ease your sufferings to a manageable level.

Coaching:

> Couplet 1160 says women beat their loneliness by engaging themselves on a project which has got great value for them.
> The project selected should be absorbing for the woman. It should be something which has been waiting in her for an opportune moment to come out. A fulfilling project is a good substitute to tide over the difficulty of separation (1160)

➤ Maximum effort needed to be put into it so that a different psyche is created in the person.

➤ The project is like a process which makes the woman to gather herself fully to meet the challenge which makes her to forget her husband for several hours in a day. She could also keep her husband informed about her project and receive constructive suggestions for undertaking it. This provides the active interaction that is needed to fight loneliness.

➤ Otherwise few exchanges of pleasantries will become boring as a result of which the motivation to get in touch with your beloved will dwindle but a mute gloominess will set in.

➤ With modern facilities of video conferencing the experience of discussing your project with your beloved will be more wholesome.

➤ In this context the episode of Nehru writing letters to his daughter Indira Gandhi in the summer of 1926 from Jail (though the separation is different from the one we are discussing) gives a good idea how a project which is absorbing can kill loneliness and simultaneously be helpful for maintaining a relationship in a healthy state of condition. He wrote on several topics ranging from how the earth came into existence to Ramayana and Mahabharata.

➤ Its usefulness in eliminating the loneliness for his daughter is brought out by her comment: "These letters deal with the beginnings of the earth and of man's awareness of himself. They were not merely letters to be read and put away. They bought a fresh outlook and aroused a feeling of concern for people and interest in the world around. They taught one to treat nature as a book. I spent absorbing hours studying stones and plants the life's of insects and at night, the stars."

117

Pinning[240]

(She pines and languishes)

She
1161. I try to conceal this affliction
But it wells up like a spring.

The deeper the sand is dug the more voluminous the spring. The more I try to hide my condition the more apparent it becomes.

1162. I am unable to hide this affliction
Also I am ashamed of informing him.

I am not able to conceal this condition of mine from the neighbors. To seek a remedy I could have sent a message to him seeking his help. But I am ashamed of doing so because neighbors would find it unacceptable. After all he has left only recently and that too on a mission of earning livelihood for both of us.

1163. My wearied life is a shoulder-pole[241]
With lust and shame on its ends it is unbearable.

---

[240] Mental and physical decline.

[241] A bamboo pole held on right or left shoulder of a man with load hung on both the ends of the pole. In addition to the mechanical advantage a springy walk by the man carrying the load makes the work little easier.

Life in my wearied body due to our separation is like a pole resting on my shoulder. Lust and shame hang from its two ends.

1164. The pangs of lust I suffer is as massive as sea
But I don't have a raft to cross it (as you are of no use).

The separation is deeply distressing. It is as deep and vast as an ocean. I have no means to come out of it.

1165. If even while in friendship one brings pain
What would when friendship is shunned?

I wonder what he would do if we fall out because even while in friendship he is not doing anything to alleviate my suffering.

1166. Pleasure of love is as vast as sea
When it is frustrated its pain is much greater you see.

The joy of love is as vast as an ocean. When it is frustrated its pain is vaster than sea.

1167. My erotic feeling is a vast pool
I am alone and could not swim to the other shore

It is mid night. I determined to overcome the feelings of lust. But could not. The pool of lust is not crossable by determination. The condition rather calls for the company of my lover. But I am alone. What can I do?

1168. Night has put the world to sleep
Other than me it has no company to keep.

In the night everyone is sleeping. Therefore the night has no company but for me.

1169. His cruelest act of deserting me is not as cruel
As this prolonged night in real.

Since he has left me I hold him as the cruelest of all. This night which is unusually long (because of the separation she feels so) becomes more cruel than himself.

1170. My heart goes to him as and when it wishes
If similarly capable my eyes don't need to swim in their gushes.

My heart can hold him together as and when it wishes instantly. If my eyes also have such capacity and see him as they please then there is no need for them to swim in the pool of tears they send out. It is a pity they do not have that capacity.

Skills to be learnt:

➤ Ability to come out of the sense of powerlessness.

Rationale:

➤ In the chapters from 117 to 127 Tiruvalluvar explains the various psychosomatic conditions a woman undergoes. They are like processes, emerging successfully out of which, make the woman stronger and psychologically healthier.

➤ Each chapter represents one process which the woman has to undergo without resistance. It appears these processes do not follow any hierarchy. They may occur exclusively or two or three of them may occur together. A new insight will be born in the mind after undergoing each one of these processes which is nothing but the needed strength to not only withstand the present trouble but also be prepared to meet future troubles in life.

Coaching:

> ➤ Suffering from erotic feelings and feelings of helplessness on the part of a woman because of the absence of her husband is natural and she should suffer it fully in order for a way to show itself up (1161/64/67/69).

> ➤ Her feelings of helplessness and being ashamed of it are normal. Let she accepts it. (1162/63).

> ➤ She may develop doubts about her future. This is also normal (1165).

> ➤ She may develop some new insight which is quite normal (1166).

> ➤ She may find no body's company giving her any relief (1168).

> ➤ After all this she will gain confidence. She will find herself to be calm and hopeful at the bottom of her heart.

118

Frustrated Eyes

(She is in frustration but says her eyes are responsible)

She

1171. Ever since my eyes showed him I fell into this disease,
Now how come so much tear they release?

When my eyes showed him I fell into this ever increasing disease.
Now while I am pained by the disease how come they pester me to
show him? After all they are the ones who showed him to me earlier
and should they not be doing the same now instead of weeping?

1172. My non inquisitive eyes caused me this pain
Instead of pitying me, themselves, why they strain?

My eyes before choosing to look at him did not study him studiously.
They looked at him just like that and I fell in love. Now he is gone
and I am in pain. Instead of empathizing (and showing love to) me
why they keep themselves under pain?

1173. Instantly my eyes went after him that day
It is funny they weep today.

That day my eyes went after him instantly. All the trouble started
thereafter. It is laughable that they weep today. After all they are not
victims of somebody else's decision.

1174. Having given me inescapable chronic disease
Even to grieve along me they have no tears!

My eyes have caused me incurable chronic disease and have exhausted all their tears. Poor beings even if they want few tears to grieve for me they have none.

1175. A woe of love bigger than a sea they made me to gain
Now my eyes endure unendurable pain.

I am distressed by a woe of love bigger than a sea. My eyes that got this to me also undergo the unbearable pain like me.

1176. It is very pleasing, my eyes who caused this to me
Also got struck in this like me.

I am pleased to note my eyes which are responsible for my suffering also struck with the same disease.

1177. Dancing to his tune and by craving my eyes got him near
I curse them to suffer pain after pain and empty their tear.

My eyes went after him. They craved for him that they adapted themselves indiscreetly to him, sought and had a sight of him. Having him gone now I curse my eyes. They shall suffer pain after pain until they exhaust all their tears.

1178. He didn't nourish relationship but feigned it best
Still without seeing him my eyes could not rest.

He never had the intention to nourish our relationship. He put up a façade as though he was in deep relationship with me. Still my eyes could not come to terms and they insist to meet him. What a pity!

1179. When he is not here eyes do not sleep
When he is here (in fear) either, an unbearable grief.

Occupied with thoughts of him my eyes miss sleep when he is not here. When he is here due to the fear that he would leave any time they do not sleep. In either way they are undergoing unbearable pain.

1180. It is not difficult for the village to make it out
With eyes like mine who drum it.

The condition of my eyes is clearly revealing my predicament to this village. They are as good as a drum in this regard. Therefore without much difficulty the village makes out what otherwise I wouldn't like the village to know.

Skills to be learnt:

> Ability to recognize the feeling of anger one has towards herself and working to come out of it.

Rationale:

> Like self-pity anger towards oneself is another psychological condition. Though the woman is shown as having anger towards her eyes in reality she feels anger at her is it not? This process of feeling angry towards oneself is a process which takes her towards the stage of accepting the reality.

Coaching:

> Let her be aware that she may feel like condemning herself for not bestowing enough thought before falling in love with him (1172).
> Let her be aware that she may feel like laughing at her foolishness (1173).
> Sometimes she may feel that her eyes have lost the capacity to shed tears (1174).

- ➢ On some days she may find herself going sleepless (1175).
- ➢ Sometimes she may feel a strange satisfaction over what has happened to her (1176).
- ➢ Sometimes she may find herself cursing herself for all that have happened (1177).
- ➢ All these conditions described above are normal and the woman should undergo these emotions (anger camouflaging as a quarrel with eyes) as and when they come without resisting them.
- ➢ When she undergoes these frustrating thoughts and exhausts them all she has a space to develop hope for the future. At the end of her frustrating thoughts (presented by the poet as if it is an issue between she and her eyes) she becomes confident of his coming back and even indicate how she would be spending a sleepless night with him (1179).
- ➢ You will agree with me that What I have inferred as correct if you see the next and last couplet which says, "It is not difficult for the village to make it out
- ➢ With persons like me whose eyes drum it."

119

Pain of Palling

(She suffers psychosomatically)

She grieves over her pallid condition

1181. To whom I can tell my tale?
I failed to refuse, he left leaving me in pale

When he pleaded to permit him to go I failed not to disagree. With his leaving this pallor has spread on my body. To whom I could express my condition when I am responsible to what has happened to me?

1182. My pale is rightfully here since he has caused it,
On my body, its spread is rampant!

This pallor is proud because it has the permission from him to spread on me. Deriving a right out of that pride it spreads quickly all over my body!

1183. He took away my dignity and finish,[242]
In gratitude he gave sickness and pallor for me to furnish.

He took away my honor and comely appearance and as an act of gratitude gave me sickness and pallor making it as an exhibit to everyone. (Perhaps this is a response to her friend who might have

---

[242] The comely appearance

impressed upon her that she should take care of her dignity and beauty.)

1184. I muse, "After all, I talk about him all the day
May be the pale is pseudo by the way."

I am living with him virtually as I am thinking and talking about him throughout the day. Since it is told that pallor comes only on account of separation from one's lover the one I have may not be real pallor!

1185. There would go my lover,
Here would on my body spread pallor.

No sooner my lover leaves pallor spreads on my body.

1186. On the light to go darkness waits,
For my husband to call it a day pallor waits.

The darkness waits upon the light to go to spread its tentacles. On a night when my husband finally says enough was enough quickly pallor spread on me.

1187. Me in his embrace remained, moved a little,
What instantly embraced me was pale.

I was in his embrace. Rolled on the side a little. As though in a single swoop it should make it, pale appeared everywhere on my body!

1188. My pallor is the talk of the town
No one blame him for desertion!

People spend time concocting about my pallor and my role in it. But no one talk about his role who deserted me causing the same to me.

1189. If he who made me to agree to him is well

Let pale make my body as its citadel.

If he who made me to yield to him bodily is keeping well very strictly at a far off place I will feel greatly relieved. Therefore as a proof of that let my pallor be in full bloom.

1190. Called as pallid is fine as long as he is not guilty
With the village as lacking civility.

If the village can be made to hold him as not guilty it is ok for me to be known as a person earning the pale on account of lack of self-control. (I am only at fault madly longing for him and suffering when he is not around giving an opportunity to pallor to spread on me.)

Skills to be learnt:

> An ability to develop a therapeutic perspective over the illness of paleness of the skin.

Rationale:

> This psychosomatic condition of skin taking a yellow tinge and body becoming weak is due to a perception of holding the separation of the man as an indication that he would permanently move out of her life. Until the woman develops a helpful perspective over her fear pallor would continue. Of course developing a perspective takes a long route like what is illustrated in the couplets of the chapter.

Coaching:

> Paleness is due to the anxiety that the separation may become permanent. This is pessimism. The helpful perspective is to think optimistically.

> After worrying so much as revealed in the couplets 1180 to 1188 in couplet 1189 she develops an optimistic perception that her husband

could be ardently faithful to her. With this perception her anxiety comes to an end. We learn it from her 'green signal' to pale ("As a proof let pale make my body as its citadel," 1189).

➤ The removal of anxiety is further evidenced in the couplet 1190 wherein she takes kindly on pale by saying, "It is ok to be known as a pallor as long as he is not guilty //As per the village, of no kind quality."

120

Anguish of Loneliness

(She suffers the anguish of loneliness)

Perhaps she feels hers is an one sided love

1191. You fall for him and he reciprocates,
It is a seedless love fruit by the way it tastes.

If someone for whom you fall also finds you interesting enough to invest his soul in you that love is as sweet as a seedless fruit. (Reciprocal love is as sweet as a seedless fruit.)

1192. Rain is benign to life on earth
A man who reciprocates offers similar worth.

For those who look at the clouds for rain in order to sustain themselves if the clouds yield it is great. Similarly if a person who is sought turn to become her beloved she has enough reasons to be happy. (The simile goes beyond what the eyes see. Cloud is depicted in the second chapter by the poet as a large hearted one which gifts it wealth to the world without expecting anything in return. Similarly a man who indulges in sex may do so keeping the joy of his partner in focus which may yield more joy to the women.)

1193. The wish to belong is belonged all along
To them the pride "We live great" does belong.

If the person to whom she falls becomes her beloved the couple make a life they can feel proud of.

1194. The one who is longed is not belonged
This is just a matter of luck

It is hard luck sometimes a lady who is longed by many is not loved by another whom she wants to belong. (Perhaps for a woman who was wooed by many not finding the person whom she woos wooing her is a pathetic situation leading to self-pity. Some interpreters say this is a condition resulting from a pap from the previous birth. Thiruvalluvar has not accepted the Hindu notions of pap and punya.)

1195. If the one whom I love doesn't reciprocate
What other use he has to me, appropriate?

If the one whom I love chose not to reciprocate in equal measure what other benefit he could offer to me?

1196. Intense intensity one side and more on the other
Like unequal load on a *kavadi*[243] should happen never

Love, like equal load on a *kavadi,* should be of same intensity with both the parties.

1197. Cupid darts at me only
Is he not aware I grieve and pain wastefully?

Cupid sends his dart on me only. Is he not sensitive enough to note my pain and grief and cast his spell on him also?

---

[243] A *kavadi* is a pole of a length of less than two meters held on the shoulder on whose ends loads of material are hung. The loads are equal in weight. It appears with equal loads on either side and with a springy walk material can be transported relatively easily.

1198. None more hardened in the world than he
My words, the offer of love, seeks not you see.

I fall for him. But he doesn't care to spend time with me rejoicing my words of love. There could be none in the world harder than him. (She means if he loves to spend time hearing her sweet words he must have come back. Since he doesn't do so she concludes he is a hard hearted person.)

1199. He has no love for me, I know it
Still praise on him is sweet.

He has ho liking for me. Still words of praise about him are sweet on my ears.

1200. To the insensitive you plan to communicate your stead
Long live my sweet heart! Fill the sea instead.

Oh! My sweet heart you are planning to communicate your condition to him who is not moved at your plight. Long live the! Better fill up the sea!

Skills to be learnt:

> Ability to overcome the anguish of loneliness through catharsis.

Rationale:

> Loneliness creates more anguish if the heroine attributes his not returning on time to his lack of love for her. She emphasizes severally about the reciprocity needed in love. She suspects he has no love for her. This beginning thought starts a catharsis. Ultimately she attains a piece of mind. This is discernable from the couplets 1198 and1199. Catharsis can be profitably employed for overcoming anguish due to loneliness and also suspicion about lover's intent in not showing up.

Coaching:

Helping her to catharsis is good strategy.

➤ She wears a hallo and hence speaks thus: "love is as sweet as seedless fruit if whom you love chooses to become your beloved."(1191)

➤ She has a poetic and apt and an example for it: "timely rain is great for those who look for it. So also for a person who falls in the faller."(1192)

➤ She opines: "Only the life of a 'falls in' and a 'faller' deserves accolades. (1193)

➤ She hypothesizes: If a person doesn't reciprocate the offer of love then he will have no opportunity to do it later. (1194)

➤ She questions: "Other than reciprocating what other use love has"? (1995)

➤ Once again she gives another hypothesis: love like a porter's pole should be equally reciprocated. (1996)

➤ She curses the cupid for his impartiality. (1997)

➤ She finds her heart to be hardest on the earth for it manages a life even when not hearing from him at all.(1998)

➤ From the vexatious thoughts she gets some relief when she hears some good news about him through someone who has recently seen him.(1999)

121

Sad Memories

(A journey in memory)

He to a messenger sent to him
1201. Thoughts of love is enough to intoxicate
Hence love is better than toddy in taste.

Palm sap needs to be consumed to get the kick. No such effort is
needed vis-à-vis love. Recalling a mental image of love (involving
an earlier embrace) is sufficient to tap the yield of inexhaustible joy.
Therefore love ranks better than palm sap.

1202. The thought of one in whom I fall brings joy
Nothing is as sweet as it O! Boy[244]

The very thought of your lover to whom you proposed first brings
joy. There is no other thing, a thought on which brings joy.

She
1203. Perhaps his thoughts about me he quickly terminates
In me a sneeze[245] develops as if to mature but aborts!

---

[244] The Tamil word *kaan* means calling some one's attention in order to tell him
something. I have used the English expression O! Boy as equivalent to it.

[245] It is a traditional belief in India that a sneeze occurs in a person when another
intensely thinks of him.

(She suspects that her lover is not love locked with her as she is.) Perhaps a thought about me that develops in him is quickly set aside by him. That explains why a sneeze which starts in my nostrils calm down without appearing.

1204.Do I too have a space in him?
      In me it is an exclusive and constant him.

I wonder whether among other things I too have a place in him. But poor me it is only him and him only in me and my world doesn't have anything else.

1205.Restricting my access into his heart curtly
      Will he not be ashamed to come in me incessantly?

He has restricted thoughts about me arising in him. (Perhaps they are hindering his work too much.)Then how he takes it freely to come into my heart? Is he not ashamed?

1206.How do you think I survive?
      I muse my past with him to thrive.

How do I survive you may ask me so. I survive by vividly reliving the life we lived when he was with me. With my vivid musing for the whole day I live my present life.

1207. If I am to forget him what would happen of me?
      I never forgot; the very thought scorches me.

(Since my life is what his vivid memory brings in) what would happen to me if I forget? Therefore at any point of time I shall never forget him. The very thought of forgetting him burns me.

1208.Any number of time I may think of him he never gets angry
      Oh! What an honour my lover bestows on me!

I can think of him any number of times (which he could figure out because of his continuous sneezes) but he wouldn't get angry. What a great gift my lover offers me!

1209. "Let my life be finished if you and I are to separate,"
While saying so he will think of committing an unkind act. [246]

He will swear on his life, "Let my life be finished if I leave you." But even while swearing so he would think of his inconsiderate plans of leaving me (to go on his business trip).

1210. Leaving him in me, on farewell, he has left,
Give me company O! Moon until our eyes meet.

He has not left my heart but physically so. "Long live my dear moon! I want to wait on him. Give me company until then."

Skills to be learnt:

> The ability to keep the flame of memory intact in you by reliving it so that it nurtures and soothes your painful feelings due to the temporary separation from your lover and also keep your relations as strong as it was early.

Rationale:

> Human beings, sparing the unfortunate, will have someone from whom they have enjoyed love and nurturing. Those moments of comfortable life may be absent at present. But the comfort harvested then is still available in them to bank upon. They can draw from that bank to get relief from the present suffering. Since the earlier comfort is absent only temporarily and is likely to revive in due course of time

---

[246] Though this allegation is serious and casts aspersions on the fiancé it is only meant to tease the person in order to get him.

their reliving those moments cannot be discredited as day dream and therefore a good strategy to beat their loneliness.

Coaching:

A patient hearing to what she says will help her to empty her mind and give her relief while strengthening it to bear the separation.

➢ She hypothesizes: Love is capable of rendering great joy compared to palm wine because palm wine needs to be consumed whereas love gives it even by a thought of an earlier experience of love making (1201)

➢ She loudly thinks: love (embrace) unlike other objects brings joy the moment you tread upon it by thinking of your lover. Therefore no other object is equal to it in bringing joy and pleasure (1202).

➢ She keeps herself fully engaged by actively remembering him. She tries to figure out what he might be doing at a given moment of time. She draws few conclusions based on her failed sneeze (1203).

➢ She allows a doubt to develop in her: "Do I exist in his memory? But in my memory he alone lives" (1204).

➢ She is in a questioning mood: "The fellow who has restricted my entry into his thought has no business to intrude into me. But he does so. Is he not ashamed of his behavior"(1205)?

➢ She knows she can utilize the memory of the memorable time she had with him to escape her present predicament: She recalls them again and again and benefit from their elixir power (1206).

➢ Any voice that arises in her suggesting that she leave his memory is startling to her. She pleads with a voice which suggests better she forgets him for some time: "Since my life is what his vivid memory brings in what would happen to me if I forget him? Therefore at any point of time I shall never forget him. The very thought of forgetting him burns me. Please do not insist" (1207).

➢ This above idea regarding his permission makes her to give a sarcastic comment reflecting her irritation and disgust (1208).

➢ This takes her memory to an earlier incident of how he has failed his promise of not to leave her (1209).

> Her mild irritation and distress soon gives way and she returns to her earlier sweet musings. She assumes that she has moon for her company and discusses his arrival with her. This brings to the surface a fact that he is on a leave of fare well (1210).

122

Speaking of Dreams

(She speaks of her dreams)

1211. What great feast I could organize in its honor?
To the dream that brought the message of my lover.

What feast I could organize to honor the dream which brought the message of my lover?

1212. If, my dyed fish-eyes go to sleep and dream revives,
To him, who had me, I will narrate how I survive.

I request my eyes to go to sleep. If that happens then I get an opportunity (in dream) to explain to him, who had me early, how I manage to survive without perishing in his absence.

1213. I see him in dreams who doesn't show up when I am awake
That is how my survival I make!

(My answer rather will be that) I survive because in my dreams I get all the comforts of love which he otherwise denied me during the waking hours.

1214. In dreams I enjoy love
From the one who denies in awake.

I enjoy love with him in dreams. I am thankful to the dreams for they bring him who otherwise refuse to come when I am awake.

1215. Then my love in awake was great
In dream too it is sweet.

(Life without love is a curse. Therefore) whether real or dreamt love is sweet and great.

1216. If there is nothing like 'waking part'
My lover in my dream would not depart.

If only life's scheme of things do not require waking hours I can keep sleeping always and enjoy the company of my lover.

1217. This cruel being doesn't grace me during awake
But should he distress me in dreams too?

It is very cruel of him not being with me and offering the joy of embrace. Adding to that how come he distresses me by what he does in the dream?

1218. In dream he sleeps on my shoulder and quickly depart
Poor me I wake up to find him only in my heart.

(You know what he does in dreams?) He sleeps on my shoulders and quickly leaves. Poor me I wake and alarm not finding him around.

1219. He who doesn't grace during wake is found fault
By those who miss their lover in dream as a default.

Only who are not fortunate enough to get dreams where they meet their lovers will find fault with their lovers who do not meet them during day time.

1220. They don't see him while awake, they say he is left,
      Perhaps they don't dream their lover while slept!

Since he is not around they think he has left me. Perhaps they do
not get their lovers in their dreams.

Skills to be learnt:

> An ability tinged with creativity to keep oneself mentally healthy
  using imagination as a means.

Rationale:

> When the husband is away the woman subjects herself to a series of
  mental processes which helps her to keep herself collected and be
  able to maintain a healthy mental status. The present process is built
  around dreams. The strength fortified here is: if you don't get what
  you enjoy most enjoy something lesser of the same genre.

Coaching:

She manages herself very well. Perhaps similar she may be encouraged to
construct similar scenes.

> This strength in action is fully captured in the couplets thus:
> The woman goes in the direction of her dream several steps. She asks
  within herself what type of feast she could arrange for the dream
  which brought the presence of her lover (1211).
> (She tells to herself) if my eyes heed to my request and go to sleep I
  will explain to him in my dream about how I manage my life without
  him; I will tell him since I see him in dream I could manage to live
  (1222/23).
> She hypothesizes: dream is a best platform to yield the joy of deprived
  embrace and actual embrace and the dreamed one yields joy in same
  measure (1214/15).

➤ (Her satisfaction with her dreams was so high) that she wishes for a lack of wakefulness facilitating the continuous show of dream (1216).

➤ (Alas! Real life scenario takes over dreams also?) She is vexed with him for 'misbehaving.' She pours: "How come the cruel person who denied physical company does so in the dreams also? His face which was dipped onto my shoulders disappeared leading me to a startling wake" (1217/18).

➤ (She regains her composure and philosophizes :) people who are incapable of dreaming perhaps finds fault with their men (1219).

➤ (She perceives this incapability to be spread across the village population :) this villagers who charge my man as a deserter perhaps have no experience of having met their men in their dreams (1220).

➤ The last couplet shows she has got benefitted from the process.

123

Grief during the Evening

(Living through the Tide of the Time)

1221. Bless you, Evening! "Are you simply day's end?"
Or a spear to promote a married women's end

My greeting to you evening! Are you simply penultimate day? You are not. You are a bride killing spear.

1222. Long live! My suffering evening!
Is your fiancé cruel like mine?

My greetings to you evening. I find you distressed and in fear. Is your fiancé like mine a cruel person and has left you alone?

1223. Progressing chillness becomes painful in the night
Pain of love quietly makes a follow suit.

Chillness develops and becomes painful along darkening while a disgust (because of his behavior) grows into anguish.

1224. When my lover is not around
Like a deadly enemy evening does surround.

When my lover is not near me the evenings like deadly enemies in a battle field are marching on me.

1225. What thankful deed I did to the morning?
What harm I did to the evening?

My mornings are relatively free from distress whereas evenings are embodiments of pain and sadness. What good I did to the morning which I did not to the evening?

1226. Evenings could hurt, I did not find
Until my man was not around.

Evening for sure hurts. I did not know it until my man left me.

1227. My distress buds in the morning
Opens through the day and blossoms in the evening.

My distress starts budding in the morning, flowers throughout the day and attains full blossom in the evening.

1228. Shepherd's flute sounds like a deadly weapon
Since it delivers that evening is just to happen.

Sheppard's flute acts on the behest of deadly evening by announcing its arrival.

1229. In the evening my mind gets blurred
The village looks distressed

The village and mind panic and immerses in distress during evening.

1230. It is evening: I think of him he thinks of money
I panic and my life is on death's journey.

My mind goes after him. He has gone in search of money. Evenings panics me and I suffer a slow death.

Skills to be learnt:

> The ability to allow oneself to feel distressed during the tide of time and getting useful insights out of it.

Rationale:

> To get a cure from a disease a doctor has to understand the manifestation of the disease. Similarly to tide over the difficulties caused by something like a circadian cycle in a day with various mood inducing shifts one has to live through them and arrive at a useful insight.

Coaching:

The 'living through the tide of time in a day' is achieved by the woman thus:

> She attributes criminal intentions to Evening. She says, "Oh, Evening you are not just a tide of time. You are a spear. You kill married but lonely woman." (1221).
> Later she changes her perception of Evening totally. She says, "Oh, Evening I see you dazed. Are you also a victim like me? Is you love is also a hard hearted like mine?"(1222).
> She falls in line with the rhythm of time. She laments, "Chillness starts as small as a twitter only to build into a monster late in the night. The worst thing is while it does so it takes along my disgust regarding his behavior to the level of anguish." (1223).
> She perceives Evening to be like a marching army bent up on destroying her (1224).
> She becomes enigmatic about the difference between morning and evening in inflicting gloom over her (1225).
> She thinks it was unfortunate that she didn't know earlier that with an absentee husband tide of evening was very difficult to navigate (1226).

➢ She observes the distress caused by loneliness starts as a bud in morning, opens slowly to reach the stage of full blossom in the evening (1227).

➢ For a distressed person that she is, the flute of the shepherd prompting the return of the cows in the evening sounds like a bugle of a war (1228).

➢ The distress in her makes her to project her distress on the village. She sees the whole village as suffering similarly (1229).

➢ After suffering so much, an insight – a fruit of such a grieving process occurs. She says, "After all he has gone to make money meant for both of us. But this evening tide of time brings me so much anguish I miss the cause for separation and feel the pangs of death like anguish unnecessarily."

124

Wasting Away Limbs

(She becomes thin due to separation)

Her friend to her

1231. To remove our wants he went afar
Your eyes shy before flower.

He has gone to earn for your sake. Your eyes due to continuous weeping have lost their shine. They are ashamed of showing before flowers which earlier were ashamed of them. (Her friend mentions 'our' instead of 'your'. This shows her empathy!)

1232. He loved you then but not now
Pallid eyes pouring tears show.

You solemnly love your man. Your eyes lost their sheen and pour tears! Their behavior appears as if they want to announce that they do not believe him that he will reciprocate your fondness.

1233. Shoulders that on nuptial day swelled
As if to expose your separation thinned.

Your shoulders which beamed on the nuptial day remain thinned as if to expose your separation.

1234. Thinned shoulders, bangle-slipped wrists,
With your lover's separation earlier charm too dips.

Your shoulders have thinned. Your earlier beauty and that you got after your marriage are gone. Same thing with your wrists as evidenced by the slipping bangles.

1235. Hanging bangles reveal his cruelty
And drooping shoulders show lost beauty.

Drooping shoulders and hanging bangles hold your lover is cruel and by that they reveal his cruelty to the town!

She speaks to her friend
1236. 'Loose bangles and supple shoulders,' my heart aches
"He is cruel," when it hears.

I am not pained to witness my supple shoulders and loosened bangles. I have consoled myself and remain calm. In spite of that they have become like that. Therefore my heart pains to hear you and the town accusing him as cruel for creating this to me! More over mark it my shoulders and limbs have thinned because of the pain I undergo hearing the accusations hurled at my husband.

She speaks to her heart
1237. My Heart, to my cruel lover will you not proclaim?
'The slurs my shoulders create' and claim an acclaim?

Oh! My heart will you not win the acclaim of my song sung in your honor by going to him and proclaiming my condition and the slur my shoulders create? (This couplet is a prelude to the next chapter.)

He speaks to himself while returning remembering what happened before

1238. My embrace I loosened a bit,
My gold 'bangled' innocent's brow lost its gilt.

(One day) when I moved a little away from her embrace I found her forehead losing its glow.

1239. Through the embrace a cool breeze traversed
Eyes of the innocent lost their shine and rained!

(Another day) when a breath of breeze passed through our embrace the innocent girl's eyes lost their glow and started shedding tears of rainy proportion!

1240. The brow's sheen is lost. Eyes this message got
In pain they lost their shining dart.

Do you know what has really happened? When I loosened my embrace a bit it was my fore head to be affected first. It lost its shine. On seeing my forehead reacting first my eyes have become pained for not having been able to make it first. Because of this they have become ashamed of and lost their shinning ray like dart. (Eyes are the tools for empathizing. Perhaps they weep because in spite being in an advantageous position they lost the competition.)

Skills to be learnt:

> To become sensitive to your physical condition and to come to terms with your status of being temporarily separated from your beloved.

Rationale:

> Becoming sensitive to ones bodily condition is psychologically helpful because sensitization is a process which helps to kill the time of separation effectively.

Coaching:

Instead of turning a blind eye to a problem becoming sensitive to it is helpful.

➢ The woman under temporary separation demonstrates a high caliber of sensitivity. Every time she becomes sensitive about a wasted organ of hers she relates it to him without fail. What she states is true is confirmed by her man in couplets 1238&1239 and by the poet in 1240.

➢ She forgets to appreciate the flowers for some time. She suddenly remembers it and attributes it to the reluctance on the part of her eyes. And eyes are reluctant because they feel guilty over enjoying life in the absence of her man who has gone to a far off place to earn for providing her. Look at the powerful association made with her lover through her poetic sensitization (1231).

➢ The stimulus yielded by her lack luster eyes and their tears leads her process of sensitization. This results in her saying that her eyes complain about the unkind act of her lover (1232).

➢ After this sensitization several of them follow relating to her shoulders (1233/34/35).

➢ Then comes the master stroke in sensitization. She is rather worried about the bad name her shoulders earn for her lover in the eyes of the folk of the village (1236).

➢ Did I talk about master stroke early? I am sorry it comes only now: she sends her heart as a emissary to her lover to keep him informed about the confusion created by her shoulders and how it casts him in disrepute (1237)!

➢ Her man's sensitization is quite deep than hers. He sensitizes about a whip of cool breeze that found its way in between two tightly embracing bodies of him and her as creating a pale on her forehead (1238/39).

➢ Observing this the poet is completely last in what he saw and his sensitization leads to a memorable understanding about her eyes. He says her eyes starts shedding fresh tears because they found themselves to be trailing behind the forehead in its reflexive reaction to the hero's unkind act of loosening his embrace (1240)!

➢   This is a narration of how sensitization process can keep a women temporarily separated from her husband fully engaged and thereby retain her mental health.

125
Soliloquy

(She dialogues with her heart)

Heroine speaks to her heart:

1241. My heart can't you suggest a medicine
To ward off this distressing disease?

O! My heart will you not apply your mind and suggest a medicine
to cure our distressing disease?

1242. Long live my heart! He has no love for us
It is stupidity you grieve and fuss.

Long live my heart! He has no love (as evidenced by his act of not
returning on the appointed date or not sending a messenger to know
about our health) for you and me. In spite of that you grieve and
undergo pain. Don't you see it is foolishness?

1243. My heart, the pain giver has no empathic verve
What purpose your kind brood over him does serve?

Oh! My heart you are sitting here and brood over him again and
again out of love. But what purpose it serves when he has not put
himself in your place to make a sense of how you feel and act on
that?

1244. O! My heart! take these eyes to him when you visit
On the wish to look at him through pest they insist.

Take with you these eyes of mine, O! My heart when you go to meet him. They want to see him. I am pestered by them day in day out.

1245. Our love no doubt he doesn't reciprocate
But, for that reason will anyone hate?

When we want him he doesn't respond positively. But can we hold that he dislikes us and decide that we should stop our effort? Does anybody do like that?

1246. When you meet the one capable of joyful embrace
Oh! My heart, do not rush but feign for joy to increase.

He is capable of awarding great joy through thorough integration with my body. When you meet him do not rush. Feign a little to get the best of him. (Feigning is a taste maker too much of it spoils the dish!)

1247. Either leave aside you blush or desire
Sporting both I cannot bear.

My dear heart either you leave your desire for embrace or leave your blush. I cannot bear you keeping both. (Since there was a long gap newness and attendant blush must have been felt by her. She responds to that.)

1248. He would not empathize and offer
This thought makes you to go after.

My heart you hold that by himself he would not come forward to embrace you. Therefore you plan to go stand before him. How uninformed you are! (She feels he has no empathy and that is root cause for the long separation.)

1249. O! my heart when my lover is inside me
Outside behind who go after thee?

When our lover live in us oh! Heart outside behind whom you go?
(Ruminating on a different plane must be giving her solace.)

1250. Totally our company he has detached
Our charm will dither if we remain attached.

He has detached himself fully from me. With my heart continuing to hold him I will lose my charm more and more.

Skills to be learnt:

➢ Ability to hope against hope.

Rationale:

➢ The days are moving. No sign of his return. She becomes like what the medical condition would indicate using the term emaciation. But she doesn't lose hope. Through a proper grieving process if a person is able to view all the eventualities the person attains what is called resilience has a proof in her case.

Coaching:

This is a two chair technique of Gestalt. Encouraging her to repeat with another two like body and mind would also work very well.

➢ The chapter comprises of a dialogue between the heart and the head. Heroine asks her heart for a way out from her distress caused by the separation (1241).

➢ To the heart which breaks down for having no answer to her question she becomes a counselor and says, "After all that guy has no love for us. Why the hell you in his thought distress"? (1242)

- ➤ She continues, "You live in the thought of him day in and day out. But what use? He doesn't put himself in your place and understand your distress."(1243)
- ➤ Since you are so fond of him you go after him in spite of the fact he has no love. What can I say about you, your poor fellow? (1248)
- ➤ Then she switches tact. She says, "Ok if you have decided to go after him take these eyes along with you. They pester me for seeing him."(1244)
- ➤ She assuages her heart further, "Does any one would leave her lover for the reason that he doesn't reciprocate"?(1245)
- ➤ She remembers she has something to say to her heart in the event her heart meets him: "When you meet him don't fall quickly for him. Sulk for some time."(1246)
- ➤ This advice makes her heart to be cast into de capacitating blush. She becomes irritated about this and admonishes her heart: "Either forget your love for him or set aside your blush. I can't bear both of them."(1247)
- ➤ At this juncture a new realization dawns on her. She calmly addresses her heart: "After all our man is within us. If you attempt to make a travel to reach him whom will you reach"?(1249)
- ➤ After this she calmly accepts the fact it was her decision to keep him in her mind and it is natural to lose her beauty due to that. (1250)

126

Self-Restraint Beaten

(She breaks self-restraint and speaks about her lust)

She to her friend who perhaps advised her to hide or suppress her feeling

1251. Axe of love breaks the door
Called restraint, bolted by the sense of honor.

Love is like a strong axe. It breaks open the door of self-restraint bolted by the sense of honor.

1252. Lust is one, has empathy none
Midnight even, on my heart its job is to porn.

Lust never understands my position. It doesn't leave me at all. It does the job of stimulating erotic feelings in my heart even at midnight.

1253. Lust I suppress
But like sneeze with no sign it arrives.

I suppress feelings of lust. But like a sneeze which comes without any preceding sign it arrives.

1254. I say I am a woman of self-restraint
But openly comes out my lust breaking that constraint.

I want to restraint myself from acting on my lust in order to save my honor. But my feeling of lust breaks that constraint and expresses itself openly. (I go after him.)

1255. Not going behind a hater is a matter of dignity
Lust afflicted is incapable of such civility.

It is not possible for lust afflicted individual to uphold the dignity of not seeking someone who rejects her.

1256. My grief wanted me to obtain the unconcerned
What a distress to be handled!

A grief in me pushed me madly to seek him who is least interested in me. The resulting distress is too much for me to handle.

1257. In regard to lust I know no shame
When my lover acts out his intended game.

When it comes to the question of pursuing feelings of lust I do not have any sense of shame restraining me. I yield to my lover.

1258. The stooping words of the man of ruse
Is, the arsenal that breaks my womanly poise.[247]

My stability of mind upholding womanly virtues gives away when it meets the fellow who is severally tricky enough to use words of subordination.

1259. I went thinking I will remain away whatever come may
But when my heart longed to couple I embraced him right away.

---

[247] Women's stability

I went to him thinking on any account I would neither allow him nor allow myself to embrace. But in his presence my heart developed a deep longing which broke my resolve. I straight away embraced him.

1260. Can a meat like heart that in the midst of fire melts
Bare resilience when its lover it meets?

Meet cannot resist being cooked when in fire. My heart is at the behest of my lover becomes like a meat. It cannot resist for long when it meets its lover.

Skills to be learnt:

➤ The ability to fully immerse in the feelings of love and feel free to enjoy the embrace.

Rationale:

➤ From the last couplet of the previous chapter we come to know that she could not erase him from her mind at all. A new manifestation other than the psycho-somatic distress we have seen so far takes over her now. She reaches a stage of highly activated feelings of lust which she could not help explaining to her self/friend openly. This is also a process which will help her in fighting her psycho-somatic distress

Coaching:

Encourage her to go in the direction further until she decides to act.

➤ She says lust acts like an axe which breaks the natural restraint a woman has.(1251)

➤ She admits that lust occupies her so much and will not allow her to sleep even after midnight.(1252)

➤ However hard she tries to suppress it, her lust, she says, will appear taking her unawares.(1253)

➤ She says, "I will hold myself as a woman of restraint. But before I finish saying so my lust will appear daringly." (1254)

- ➢ She confesses: "The pride of not going behind a person who doesn't like you is not possible for a woman who suffers from lust."(1255)
- ➢ She wonders, "Perhaps he wants me to go after him. This lust must be his gift. What a suffering I am made to undergo."(1256)
- ➢ She admits, "I forget blush when he who has doted me does something he wants with me."(1257)
- ➢ She thinks his ruse in using subordinate words does the trick of breaking her restraint.(1258).
- ➢ She recalls an earlier occasion when her resolve not to embrace having failed. (1259)
- ➢ She finally concludes: for persons like her whose heart are not stubborn enough it is never possible to sulk successfully.(1260)

127

Each Longing to See the Other

(He also feels the same)

She to her
1261. My eyes lost lustre and focus
Marking his absence my fingers thinned.

Since I have set my eyes for so long on the direction from which he was supposed to arrive my eyes have not only become fuzzy but also lost their focus. Marking and counting the dots I put on the wall accounting his days of leave my fingers have become thin.

1262. Oh! My shining beauty if I forget him today
Thinned shoulders and lose bangles will greet the day.

Oh! My jeweled beauty if I forget my lover I am sure to become much thinner, my shoulders paler and my bracelets looser. (This seems to be a reply to her friend who might have suggested that she could divert her thought from him for some time in order to get some relief from the worry.)

1263. With my heart as his companion he is on his mission
Myself to be alive to receive him, I grant permission.

He likes victory out of his muscular power. He has gone with my heart as his companion to achieve his mission. I would like to receive him on his return. For that purpose only I am alive.

1264. Like a seasonal tree rupturing into branches
On the arrival of king of lust my heart burgeons

On the thought that my man who embraced me earlier (and exhausted his great lust) comes back with full of new vigor my heart branches in all directions in joy.

1265. When I see him as deep as my eyes please
Discolor of my shoulder is sure to cease.

When he returns and I am chanced to look at him as long and as deep as my eyes wish paleness of my shoulders should vanish.

1266. My husband certainly will come some day
I will indulge as long as my separation pain stays

My husband will come someday. On that day I will indulge all my five senses on his pleasant body as long as my pain of separation ceases to exist.

1267. When he as dear as my eyes returns
Will it be sulking, hugging and yielding in turns?

When he, dearer to me like my eyes, returns will I sulk or will I embrace? May be on the thought that he has heartlessly deserted me I may sulk and because of my vulnerability I may embrace or I may be sometimes be angry with him and sulk and sometimes mad on him and embrace deeply.

Hero speaks to himself

1268. With his martial strike let our king win
To her I will throw a party with what I get.

Let my king by his martial prows win the war. With what he gives as my share I shall return and on that night will throw a feast to my wife.

1269. A day is as long as seven for those who languish
Waiting for the return of their men in anguish.

I know a day is as long as seven days to those (my wife) who are in aguish due to their long separation.

1270. If by a broken heart my woman did demise
Whether I get the reward or not what use?

What use it has whether I get my share of the bounty or not if my wife due to long separation has lost hope and with a broken heart has died?

Skills to be learnt:

➢ Ability to allow the mind to freely indulge in thoughts of reunion tinged with eroticism.

Rationale:

➢ This is a process which prepares her to be mentally well prepared to receive her husband with any possible resistance having been overcome.

Coaching:

➢ Her attitude towards her husband is totally free from any reservation or resistance is borne by what she says:
➢ She allows herself to be fully miserable. (1261)

- ➢ She refuses the suggestion that she better diverts her thoughts about him as a strategy to overcome her despair. She would rather say it was the thoughts of hope that she would receive him one day keep her alive. (1262/63)
- ➢ She beautifully portrays her mind: the thought of his home coming who embraced her early is burgeoning like a seasonal activity of a tree sending its new branches and shoots on and on in every direction. (1264)
- ➢ She is quite sure that her bodily conditions will regain normalcy once she is able to give a sumptuous feast of his body to her eyes. (1265/66)
- ➢ She takes her exercise very seriously is borne by the couplet 1267.
- ➢ Her man's condition is not any thing different:
- ➢ He says once the war is over and he gets his share of what has been won from the enemy he would arrange for a feast to his lady. (1268)
- ➢ He empathizes with her and concurs those days and nights do lengthen themselves for woman who suffers loneliness. As a sequel to this another alarming thought comes to him: "what use of my amassed wealth got out of the victory if out of her inability to withstand my separation her heart has broken and she has succumbed to it." (1269/70)

128

Empathic Understanding through Body Language

(When they meet again he reads what she wouldn't reveal)

He to her

1271. Your efforts to conceal, your dyed eyes don't oblige
For their message they have a compelling liege[248]

Your eyes are not cooperating with your indifference you show to me. Through their message they reveal your love to me without fail. (Perhaps the hero has delayed because of situations beyond his control and the heroine is putting up a false indifference expressing her vexed feelings.)

He to her friend

1272. This bamboo shouldered girl's beauty fills my eyes
Her aura of innocence is her great bliss.

The looks of my woman are capable of catering fully to the scope of my eyes' capabilities to enjoy. Her shoulders are like bamboo. She has a fortune of innocence ridden women hood.

1273. Hidden thread gives the gem-necklace a poise,
Similar, in my woman, gives her guise.

---

[248] liege   means loyal or faithful

The curves that the thread assumes make the threaded gem necklace poised on her chest. Something similar running in her body gives all the curvatures she has.

1274. In a closed bud its fragrance lives,
In her budding smile her intentions hives.

The fragrance of a flower is dormant in its bud. Similarly in her simile which is about to happen but never happens lye an intention (her interest in me).

1275. Secret sign the bangle decked kept
A potion by which my pain swept.

For the cruel pain of separation she has a potion in her secret smile (showing a condemnation not rejection for delaying my homecoming inordinately)

She to Her Bosom Friend
1276. Abandonment then powerful embrace now
Harbors the note for a loveless future.

His extraordinary interest in me and his over considerate and powerful embrace tells me perhaps he is again planning to leave. My future is destined to be the same loneliness.

1277. Now, on his will my cool beloved is cold
That my coral bracelet, before me, told.

He gives up coolly his resolve to stay with me. My bracelets know it in advance. They have become loose. (In reality from what she says in the previous couplet we can infer that she has read his intention through his body language. Whereas she projects it on her bracelets.)

1278. My beloved left yesterday
Today pallor is as rich as of seventh day.

My beloved took leave only yesterday. Already my body has developed yellowish tinge as deep as what would happen in a week's time.

Her Bosom Friend to him
1279. Her bracelets, her soft shoulders, her feet
She saw later in silence she kept

She saw her hanging bracelets, supple shoulders and her feet and did nothing else. (Perhaps her friend leaves the main message that she is forlorn to his inferring ability.)

1280. Expresses love-pangs through her eyes
Seeking relief thus shows her feminine grace.

She showed her pain of sexual deprivation through her eyes which demonstrated her feminine charm.

Skills to be learnt:

> The ability to read the body language of your lover.

Rationale:

> Reading the body language of a spouse involved in sexual relationship is like a fore play before the sex. It entails erotic thoughts and facilitating a satisfying sexual experience.

Coaching:

Reading body language is very useful for successful sexual relations. A man and women who are good at it will be able to strike the iron when it is hot. This skill may be learnt.

➤ The hero seems to be very good at the art of reading the body language or signs of his lady love. He reads:

➤ "You may hide but your eyes reveal the message of your interest in me."(1271)

➤ "The feminine blush adds to the beauty for my lady with bamboo like shoulders." (1272)

➤ He becomes poetic: "The threaded gem necklace on her presents curvatures synchronizing with the curvatures of her body. But there is something in her body which makes these curvatures in the first place!"(1273)

➤ His enigma doesn't subside that easy. He says further, "The scent hidden in the bud is not known unless the flower blossoms. In her tight lipped lips a smile meant for me similarly hides."(1274)

➤ He has a real benefit from his skill of reading signs now. He says in her budding simile he could see the reception for not rejection of him.(1275)

➤ From couplet number 1276 to 78 her ability in reading body language is pictured by the poet:

➤ She confers to her friend: "He might leave me again on another trip. I get an inclination of this by the way he embraces me. (Perhaps he takes enormous care to make her fully satisfied – an obligatory embrace on the eve of leaving?) (1276)

➤ She says further: "My bracelets knew it even before me."(1277)

➤ She has further proof: "He was here with me until yesterday. But today itself my body's yellowish tinge is seven days old."(1278)

➤ Her friend reads the body language of the heroine and tell the following message to her lover:

➤ She conveys the distress undergone by the heroine picturesquely to the hero. (1279)

➤ She says further, "I could read from her eyes two things she is terribly distressed. She longs to embrace you again."

129

Desire for Reunion

(Both desire to embrace again)

She
1281. Thoughts leading to joy and sight leading to pleasure
Not wine's but love's treasure.

Love is capable of netting in joy by mere thought or seeing. This is not possible for palm wine[249] which gives pleasure only when consumed.

1282. When thoughts of lust are as big as palm
Even a millet size sulk has no room.

I should not entertain thoughts of sulk when thoughts of lust are present because thoughts of lust as big as a palm tree will be affected by thoughts of sulk as small as a minor millet.

1283. He doesn't care me and he is on his mission
My eyes see no calm until they see him in person

My man didn't care to take care of me. He is gone on his mission. But still my eyes will not take rest until they see him back.

---

249   Sap of the palm flower head obtained by the ooze from the new cut surface of the head made every day by the toddy tapper and allowed to ferment.)

1284. On the track to sulk, my friend, my heart forgets it's tact
      It goes to embrace him intact.

      My friend, I went with a resolve to sulk. But my determination caved
      in. Straight I went and embraced him!

1285. While writing eyes see the letters not the pen
      When my husband is back I would see him not his sin.

      The eyes do not notice the writing instrument while writing.
      Similarly when my husband is back I forget the hurts he hurled on
      me by parting company with me.

1286. When I am with him I see in him no fault,
      When he is away none other than fault.

      I am unable to take note of his mistakes when he is with me. But when
      he is away I am unable to think anything other than his mistakes.

1287. The youth know where the stream is safe and jump
      But sulk has no safe bet then why to keep?

      Those youngsters who jump into the stream know where it is safe
      to do so. Therefore they qualify to take the risk of swimming in the
      stream. But I do not know how to stay put in my sulk long enough
      to create frustration in him. Then why should I try it?

1288. Palm-wine harms and wrecks still reveler persists
      O! Dear thief! Your chest is wine when on mine it rests.

      Palm sap harms and wrecks people. Still revelers persist in enjoying
      it because of the addicting power of the sap. You are also creating
      such an addiction in me. Your chest is the palm-sap I revel when it
      rests on mine.

      He

1289. Love is more tender than flower
Some enjoy knowing when it is tender.

Easy distractions turn out to be love's destroyers. One loses heart over it and loses interest in love. Therefore one (especially male) should manage time and other nuances. (Other nuances may range from interest of the partner, supporting tools, condition of the body and well established best practices.)

1290. A sign of sulk appeared in her eyes but soon she melted
Later her embrace tighter than mine resulted.

I observed a small sulk with her which quickly disappeared and she has given herself more than me and her embrace was better than mine.

Skills to be learnt:

➢ Ability to get rid of reservations/resistance while looking for an embrace and rushing towards it in order to achieve best embrace.

Rationale:

➢ Sulk as a fore play in sex needs to be very carefully employed. Otherwise it has the dangerous potential of turning into a spoil sport.

Coaching:

➢ Any obstacle like using contraceptive or other issues need to be taken care of and
a full relaxed mind is necessary to enjoy sex.
➢ Allow your thoughts to go uncensored. Thoughts of embrace itself yield lot of pleasure unlike wine which brings pleasure only when consumed. (1281)

- ➤ If you want a bounty of sexual joy do not sulk at all because even a small measure of it in an inappropriate time will kill the pleasure. (1282)

- ➤ Allow your system to overtake you. (1283)

- ➤ She brings the above clearly when she says to her friend, "I went with a resolution that I will sulk like anything. But the moment I saw him I ran to embrace him."(1284)

- ➤ Do not pick holes with your lover for sundries. Look what our heroine says, "Like we don't see the pen when we write I do not see his blames when I am with him." (1285)

- ➤ "When I am with him I do not see his mistakes otherwise only his mistakes," says she further. (1286)

- ➤ Regarding sulking she is not prepared to try it at all due to another reason: She is incapable of sticking to it! (1287)

- ➤ Once again she thrills herself thinking about his intoxicating chest. (1288)

  HE

- ➤ He reminds himself about how to go about the process: love is as tender as a flower: therefore needs to be handled as softly and catering to its nuance. (1289)

- ➤ He makes the observation: "In her a trace of resistance arose and disappeared quickly. The embrace followed was better than mine." (1290)

130

Chiding the Heart

(The delay is killing)

1291. His heart confirms to his wishes
    But with me why my heart you are rebellious?

   His heart confirms to his wishes and with its cooperation he can ditch me and go. But when I want to be indifferent to him, my heart, you are not cooperating with me. With him you are going!

1292. He has no love for you, you have seen it
    Still hoping against hope you pursue it!

   Oh! My heart you are going behind someone who is not interested in you in the fond hope that such an act will be reason enough for him to become cool with us. What can I say?

1293. 'Don't be on the side of a fallen.' My heart
    On that, behind him you go, is it not?

   It seems my dear heart, you have a strategy that anyone who has fallen from the crest should be deserted and another should be sought. Otherwise how come you go with him who has deserted me successfully and proves himself great in that act?

1294. Who will discuss it with you? my heart
      You refuse to sulk to get the best yet.

      Hereafter who is going to talk with you on this matter? You are not
      on the line of thinking that by sulking one can increase the pleasure
      of love (by the by you can also make him stay with us for long).

1295. Fear of not gaining then fear of not retaining
      Over him, chronically my heart is paining.

      First you were anxious of getting him and having got him you
      become anxious about your ability to retain him. You are paining
      me in either way, my dear heart.

1296. Musing alone on this I recognize a pain
      My heart eats me in vain.

      When I am alone and reflect on my life and on him I feel a pain in
      me. It is my heart trying to eat me.

1297. I am stuck with my useless foolish mind
      Hence I forget shame and continue with my find.

      I am irrevocably caught with my 'foolish and also exist type of mind'
      which doesn't forget him at all. Due to that I forget dignity and
      continue to hang on him.

1298. To poo-poo him is mean since he is my man
      Holding so, my heart speaks the virtues of that MAN!

      After all he is our lover, ridiculing him is not fair, holds my dearest
      heart and it eulogizes his manliness instead.

1299. In grief who could provide support
      If my heart doesn't sport?

Let me accept my heart's position. After all if I do not accept my heart who else could support me in my distress?

1300.Of support, strangers cannot be of use
When our own heart refuse.

Strangers support is of no use in this regard. It is the heart which should try and understand the situation and remain in peace.

Skills to be learnt:

> An ability to introspect on a subject matter like the unavoidable event of husband going on a mission and coming to terms with the temporary separation.

Rationale:

> This is a dialogue between she and her heart. This format is best for introspection is proved by the fact that at the end she accepts the reality that she should search for that calmness within herself.

Coaching:

This gestalt two chair technique is quite useful to sort out any issue including sexual issues.

> She asks her heart why the hell her heart goes after him when his interest is in the least. (1291)
> She wants to find out from her heart whether her heart is under the assumption that it could get his love by going behind him even when he is estranged. (1292)
> She wonders whether her heart has decided to desert her holding she being a negated guy is no good bet. (1293)
> She is fed up with her heart for not accepting her suggestion that they sulk first and keep love next – a best strategy to enhance sexual joy. (1294)

- ➢ She is also vexed with her heart for developing cold feet when he is around fearing a possible separation and becoming anxious when he is not around. (1295).
- ➢ She announces that she has forgotten modesty because of the influence of her heart over her. (1297)
- ➢ Her heart according to her says having accepted him as their MAN it is mean to degrade him.(1298)
- ➢ This statement of her heart shows a change in her. She accepts her heart as her only help and accept its decision that having accepted him as her hero she has no reason good enough to ditch him.(1299/1300)

131

Coyness in Sex

(Her friend suggests her to sulk)

Her Friend
1301. Keep off and let sulk prevail
Let us watch his stress for a while.

Her friend suggests that the lady could sulk a little (by not entering the chamber) so that they could watch the stress of the hero for a while.

She to her friend
1302. Sulk should be of useful level
Like salt in excess sulk too spells ill.

Sulking is like salt. Added in excess salt will spoil the taste. Similarly sulking in excess will spoil the sexual joy.

She to him
1303. Not embracing the one who has sulked.
Is like inflicting fresh pain to the distressed,

If you chooses not to embrace me since I am sulked, it will be like inflicting new distress to the one who is already distressed.

1304. Not empathizing a sulking heart is equal to
Cutting a withering vine at its foot.

Your act of ignoring a sulking woman is equal to cutting a withering creeper at its foot.

He to himself
1305. Good qualities shine splendid on good men
Sulk on a soft and tender woman.

The presence of all that are good present in a person adds to his charm. Similarly for my woman, in whom flower like softness resides, her sulking is another beauty.

1306. If in embrace reticence and sulk are absent
It is like what an unripe or over ripe fruit lent.

If reticence and sulk are absent the embrace is less in tasty like a overripe fruit or a raw one.

1307. In long sulking an anxious concern does rest
It is: shortened intercourse may spoil the crest.

If a woman sulks and sulks there is a sad possibility for a shortened period of intercourse.

She to herself
1308. What for, any one should grieve
If the man by empathy your grief cannot arrive.

What is use of feeling bad about the situation? After all he has no empathy to understand my feelings!

1309. Water under shade is sweet
Sulk before its appreciator is great.

Water lying under the shade is sweet and cool. Sulking is also sweet only in the presence of he who falls for the woman.

1310. He lets my sulk to loose it's steam
It is crazy my heart for him still does beam.

He lets my sulk to go hard. But still my heart due its undying desire wants to embrace him!

Skills to be learnt:

➢   The ability to use sulking as a fore play efficiently.

Rationale:

➢   Sulking, as a fore play in sex, serves the good purpose of increasing the romantic mood. Increased romantic mood keeps the brain fully immersed in sexual imagery which releases hormones in enough quantity to get good and longer erection. Since foreplay is part of intercourse an elongated foreplay due to sulk by the woman may result in quick orgasm. Therefore the prescription by Tiruvalluvar through his hero to employ sulk in right level is very apt. His example of the ripe fruit instead of an unripe or over ripe gives the message.

Coaching:

Sometimes a woman may think sulking is a good strategy to make her man to come to terms with her. This may not always work.
➢   A thorough understanding of the nature of sulk is obtained by the example of the role played by the salt in the taste of food. To much or too little salt will spoil the taste. Similarly too much of sulking or no sulking as a sexual foreplay will spoil the sexual pleasure. (1302)
➢   The joy of sex is more satisfying if the need of the partner is considered along with one's need. This message is delivered in couplets: 1303/04.
➢   Hero also acknowledges the usefulness of little sulking. (1305/06)

> ➤ He is also aware of the fact that too much of sulking is risky.(1307)
> ➤ Another lesson about sulking is given by the woman. She says sulking works well only with him who falls for the woman. In case you have to motivate him for sex sulking will be counterproductive. (1308/09/10)

132

Art of Fine Sulking

(She says sulking is an art)

She

1311. Every woman let her eyes on your chest to feast
    On my bosom I shall not allow your whore chest to rest.

    I know many women let their eyes to feast on your chest. Therefore I shall not allow your whore chest to rest on mine.

1312. I feigned indifference he sneezed rather a peeve
    Expecting me to break in and say, "Long live."

    I feigned indifference (sulked) he sneezed loudly. I know he did it in the hope I would come forward to say, "Long live."

HE

1313. When I wear floral garland[250] she would on me bounce
    "For which woman?" with scorn she would pronounce.

    When I wear a garland made of flowers from a tree she would make a negative note of it and take serious exception to it. She would charge me that I wore it to present myself to another woman.

---

250 The garland is made of a flower known as *kottuppoo* meaning flower of a particular tree.

1314. "I love you above anyone" I said
      "Above whom, above whom?" sulking – she pitched.

      (Then I tried another strategy) I said I loved her above any one. She
      could still pick a hole and query above whom?

1315. "In this life no separation for us" I said
      ("What about next?" on such a thought perhaps)[251] she tears shed.

      (Then I said) in this birth there was no separation. She started
      shedding tears because of a thought about the next generation.

1316. "I thought of you" I said. "That means you forget me before?"
      Saying so she de-clasped from me and created a furor.

      When I said I thought of you she created uproar by shouting which
      meant I forgot her earlier.

1317. I sneezed when with her words she caressed
      "Who thought of you?"[252] Querying so tears she shed.

      She caressed me with her words. An unexpected sneeze escaped me.
      She started a fresh quarrel (It is a cultural belief that if someone close
      to us think of us we would sneeze.)

1318. Next time when I resisted a sneeze she wept
      That someone thought of me, I away from her kept.

      (Fearing further rebuttal when) I tried to suppress another sneeze on
      its track. She noticed it and said someone was thinking of me which
      I tried to conceal from her.

---

[251]   What is mentioned within bracket is inferable from the couplet.

[252]   It is a folk belief that when someone dear to us think of us we sneeze.

1319. A self-explanation from me, another shrill from her
That I did the same elsewhere causing her sore.[253]

When I tried to explain to her that I was a clean person and she should not suspect me she shot back, "Did you say the same thing to others also?"

1320. When I looked at her lost in thought
'Whom you just now thought?' saying so she fought.

This made me to get lost in thought. She asked me about whom I was thinking!

Skills to be learnt:

> The fine art of feigning anger at the same time expressing one's love.

Rationale:

> Sulking is not an exercise meant for showing one's hatred. It is a different way of expressing love for the purpose of enhancing sexual joy. A woman who is good at it will be able to offer better sexual experience to her lover and to her self.

Coaching:

> Create a very mild perturbation in your man and up the ante gently. Don't push too hard. You should always leave some room for him to make him to believe that he could manage the situation and come out successfully. (See how she does it by going through all the couplets of the chapter.) The rest is left to your imagination. One thing I can add is that sexual fore play need not be confined only to the bed room. It can be a very decent undercurrent throughout the day!

---

[253] The words, 'causing her sore', are added for the sake of providing rhyme which also augments the meaning.

133

Sulking Pleasure

(She shares her experience with her friend)

She to Her Friend

1321. He is blameless still I allow sulk to pass
I do it because it makes him in his art to surpass.

(Perhaps when the woman confided in her friend that she was enacting a sort of pseudo sulking with her husband by teasing him over a nonexistent extra marital affair she perhaps asked her why the woman did it for which she replied) he has no fault still I feigned sulking because that makes him more obligatory and motivated to give the best of him in intercourse.

1322. Small rift in the form of sulk is a good gift
After the initial damp it takes sex to a worthy height.

Sulk is a like a good foreplay. After that it takes sex to a greater height!

1323. Is there a joy in heaven as coy?
Hearts Like water and soil mix and enjoy.

In intercourse two hearts lose in each other like water and soil put together. This is possible only due to the sulking preceding intercourse. Can we find better joy than earthly sulking in heaven?

1324. In a prolonged sulk arises a weapon
That breaks my minds' solemn.

Something inbuilt in sulking behavior makes it to give away sulking after sometime!

1325. My beloved is faultless but his weaning
From my tender shoulders has a special meaning.[254]

I know my lover is faultless. But his weakening clasp of my shoulder informs me of some preoccupation of him. (Perhaps she suspects him of thinking about the next business/war trip.

He to himself
1326. Completed digestion is joyous than tasting the meal
Foreplay surpasses what an intercourse does reveal.

The pleasure and satisfaction derived after the digestion of the same is greater than the pleasure born out of the taste of the food. Similarly the foreplay like feigned sulking gives more pleasure than intercourse!

1327. Failing to cure sulking in fact is winning
Since in intercourse the looser is found shinning.

The man who fails to get her out of sulking but wait for her to break is the gainer in the pleasure of intercourse!

1328. Will I get the taste of her eye brows' salt?
Feigned anger followed by Intercourse brought.

Will I get the opportunity to taste her foreheads sweat by a sulk-escalated intercourse?

---

[254] It appears when the clasp of her man is weakened she reads a message of impending separation in it.

1329. Let she, my golden ray, sulk continue
On my prayer let long night shall be my retinue.

Let my sweet heart continue to sulk and break it with intercourse.
Like that let the night prolong!

1330. Sulking is embrace's sweetener
Its taste is found on the tight embrace's tenor.

Prior sulking enhances the pleasure of the following embrace.

Skills to be learnt:

> Managing sulking

Rationale:

> Man in sex should totally come out from the thinking that sulk by his woman is a hindrance. Flowing with the expectation underlying in sulking behavior and trying seriously to assuage her sulking by trying some 'gymnastics' is suggested in the chapter

Coaching:

> Sulking is a planed one. True grievances and acts thereupon do not qualify to be known as sulking. It is a mood enhancer with the aim of bringing the best out of both the couple.(1321/22)
> The joy of intercourse which is total like rain water and soil mixing together results from the sulking. Therefore is their a better joy in haven? This question asked by her reveals a deep lesson for you. Don't have any reservation about enjoying sex. Don't have any reservation about sulking. Both are fine and are divine. (1323)
> "I will maintain sulk at any cost": this should never be your position. When you find your sulking being overtaken by the desire to have sex gracefully yield to it. (1324)